PERIPATETIC PHIL(

200 BC TO AD 20

D1197414

This book provides a collection of sources, many of them fragmentary and previously scattered and hard to access, for the development of Peripatetic philosophy in the later Hellenistic period and the early Roman Empire. It also supplies the background against which the first commentator on Aristotle from whom extensive material survives, Alexander of Aphrodisias (*fl. c.* AD 200), developed his interpretations, which continue to be influential even today. Many of the passages are here translated into English for the first time, including the whole of the summary of Peripatetic ethics attributed to 'Arius Didymus'.

ROBERT W. SHARPLES was Emeritus Professor of Classics at University College London. He published extensively on the Peripatetic tradition in antiquity, notably in the context of the Theophrastus Project and of the Ancient Commentators on Aristotle series. He also published a successful textbook, *Stoics, Epicureans and Sceptics* (1996), and a number of editions of ancient texts. Professor Sharples died in the summer of 2010 shortly before the publication of this book.

PERIPATETIC PHILOSOPHY

200 BC TO AD 200

An Introduction and Collection of
Sources in Translation

ROBERT W. SHARPLES

with indexes prepared by

MYRTO HATZIMICHALI

CAMBRIDGE
UNIVERSITY PRESS

CAMBRIDGE UNIVERSITY PRESS
Cambridge, New York, Melbourne, Madrid, Cape Town, Singapore,
São Paulo, Delhi, Dubai, Tokyo, Mexico City

Cambridge University Press
The Edinburgh Building, Cambridge CB2 8RU, UK

Published in the United States of America by Cambridge University Press, New York

www.cambridge.org
Information on this title: www.cambridge.org/9780521711852

First published 2010

Printed in the United Kingdom at the University Press, Cambridge

A catalogue record for this publication is available from the British Library

Library of Congress Cataloguing in Publication data
Peripatetic philosophy, 200 BC to AD 200 : an introduction and collection
of sources in translation / [edited by] Robert W. Sharples.
p. cm.
Includes bibliographical references and indexes.
ISBN 978-0-521-88480-8
1. Philosophy, Ancient. 2. Peripatetics.
I. Sharples, R. W.
B111.P47 2010
185–dc22
2010031687

ISBN 978-0-521-88480-8 Hardback
ISBN 978-0-521-71185-2 Paperback

Contents

DISCARD

Preface

The period of ancient Greek and Roman philosophical thought that falls between the Hellenistic philosophers of the third and second centuries BC, on the one hand, and the Platonism of late antiquity on the other, is at present the least known in the English-speaking world. During the second half of the twentieth century much scholarship was devoted to showing that the thought of those two periods was of general philosophical interest and deserved a place in standard syllabuses. For the Hellenistic period, in particular, one problem was the difficulty of finding, and making reference to, much of the textual evidence, scattered as it was in a wide range of mostly later ancient authors. This problem was solved, and the philosophical interest of the material highlighted, by the publication in 1987 of A. A. Long and D. N. Sedley's sourcebook *The Hellenistic Philosophers*. For late antiquity a similar role has been played by Richard Sorabji's sourcebook *The Philosophy of the Commentators, 200–600 AD*, published in 2004. That had its origins in a conference held at the Institute of Classical Studies in London in 1997, with the express intention of introducing the period and the main personalities and issues within it to those who might be familiar with some aspects of ancient philosophy, but not with that period, and might be encouraged to work on it.

It was with a similar intention that a conference on the philosophy of the period from 100 BC to AD 200 was held at the Institute in 2004. The proceedings of that conference have been published in Sorabji and Sharples 2007; but it was also intended that it should give rise to a series of sourcebooks, of which this is one, containing a selection of material relevant to the study of the Peripatetic tradition between 200 BC and AD 200. Some explanation, both of the use of the term 'Peripatetic' and of the chronological limits, is called for.

Aristotle's views and writings were discussed in this period both by those who identified themselves as belonging to the Aristotelian tradition in philosophy and by members of other schools, the former indeed often replying to attacks by the latter. During the period, interest in Aristotle shifted from discussion of his doctrines, often mediated through second- or third-hand witnesses, to detailed study of the text of his unpublished or 'esoteric' works, those which we still possess today; but the two approaches were not mutually exclusive, and one advantage of the arrangement by themes which I have adopted is that it highlights the way in which certain philosophical issues remained central throughout. I have used the term 'Peripatetic' rather than 'Aristotelian' simply because of the ambiguity of the latter, which could be taken to imply that the views in question were those held by the historical Aristotle himself. Those who discussed his philosophy in our period did not indeed hesitate to describe the views they set out as 'Aristotelian', for they regarded themselves as simply spelling out the implications of what Aristotle himself had said, even, as we shall see, on questions which he had not himself considered and which only entered the philosophical arena later. To follow them in this would, however, run the risk of misleading the reader.

Michael Frede showed (Frede 1999) that there was a decisive shift in ancient philosophy at the start of the first century BC. It was at this point that philosophers started to look back to the great figures of the classical past and to treat their writings as in some sense canonical. This was indeed, as he argued, part of a general shift in ancient Greek culture; it affected philosophy later than some other areas, for example literature.[1] The new interest in Aristotle's texts in the first century BC shows that the Peripatetic tradition was no exception to this – it may indeed be seen as a paradigm case. (See further below, on 2A.) The interpretation of Aristotle's works has continued to be a focus of, and an inspiration to, philosophical activity from the first century BC until the present day; so the present collection will be of interest to many not least because it traces the earliest stages of that story – in so far as the available evidence enables us to reconstruct them.

Aristotle's colleagues and immediate successors in the late fourth and third centuries BC, such as Theophrastus of Eresus (head of the school from 322 until his death in 288/7 or 287/6 BC) and Strato of Lampascus (head from Theophrastus' death to *c.* 269 BC) continued his work by conducting enquiries in the areas in which he had worked, and by developing doctrines which

---

[1] Why this should have been so is a question to which simple answers are not going to be adequate, but *one* relevant factor seems to be that the centre for philosophy in the third and second centuries BC remained Athens rather than Alexandria, and that it was with the latter that antiquarian study of earlier Greek culture was particularly associated – even though, ironically enough, the model for that study was itself Aristotelian. See Glucker 1998, especially 312–14. Alexandrian scholars were interested in Plato's dialogues, but above all as *literary* and stylistic models. (I owe this point to Herwig Maehler.)

recognisably form part of the same intellectual agenda, even though they were ready to disagree with him and even though they emphasised some of the areas in which he had worked more than others. What they did not for the most part do, as far as we can see, was to regard Aristotle's writings as containing a body of doctrine which it was their task to interpret. This, the invention of Aristotelia*nism*, was to come later, its foundations being laid in our period. Much of the work of Aristotle's immediate successors was in what we would now regard as natural science rather than philosophy; the questions with which they were concerned were not, in general, the ones which were dominant in the Peripatetic tradition in our period, and to attempt to survey their work in the present sourcebook would both increase its length massively and reduce its coherence. The issue of the boundary between philosophy and natural science – once, significantly, known as 'natural philosophy' – is one to which we will need to return.

In the second century BC there was a change. After Strato the Peripatetic school had gone into decline; the reasons for this have been much debated, but a central one seems to have been that already under Aristotle himself the Lyceum was not so much a school of philosophy, in the way that term was understood in fourth- and third-century Athens, but an organisation conducting research in a wide variety of fields, and that in this area it could not compete with the state-sponsored activities in Alexandria. The exception to the decline, however, was Critolaus. As far as we can tell from our evidence, he was interested in Aristotelian doctrines rather than in Aristotelian texts; but to a large extent he seems to have defined those doctrines in conscious opposition to Stoicism, a trend that was to continue in subsequent centuries, and some of the issues on which he took positions are those which were central to subsequent debate as well. Consequently Critolaus is part of our story in a way in which Theophrastus and Strato are not.

At the other end of our period, the decision has been made to exclude Alexander of Aphrodisias, the commentator on Aristotle who flourished in about AD 200, for two reasons. The massive scale of his surviving writings – about two thousand pages of Greek text survive, even though much has been lost or survives only in quotations by later witnesses or in Arabic translation – means that a selection would either be hopelessly inadequate or else would unbalance the entire collection. And, secondly, Alexander has already been covered in Richard Sorabji's sourcebook (Sorabji 2004). Passages from Alexander have therefore been included here only either when they are evidence for the earlier thinkers with whom the present collection is concerned, or when they continue and elucidate the debates characteristic of our period.

As already indicated, the material here is arranged thematically. After an initial chapter comprising material relating to the identification and activities of the Peripatetics of this period, subsequent topics are arranged approximately in the order of themes familiar from the standard arrangement of Aristotle's own works in the Bekker edition, with certain modifications. Material on metaphysics, in the sense of general ontology, has been placed after that on the categories, not after that on physics in the broad ancient sense of that term. Especially for this period, when discussion of ontology and discussion of the categories were closely linked, this seems more appropriate than placing metaphysics after psychology and biology. Material on theology, including providence and the ordering of the world as a system, has been placed within physics, for this again suits the nature of the discussions in this period;[2] and within physics it has been placed between discussion of the heavens and that of soul, for it relates closely to the former. The standard order with which modern readers are familiar in the case of Aristotle's own works is logic–physics–ethics; but in late antiquity the standard order of Aristotle's works was logic–ethics–physics. This may or may not be the ordering introduced by Andronicus (cf. Barnes 1997, 32–3), but it seems likely that the ancient order developed during our period, and it therefore seems appropriate to follow it.

Two extended texts have been included as units in their entirety, rather than being divided up thematically: the account of Aristotle's doctrines in Diogenes Laertius 5 (Chapter 3) and the account of Peripatetic ethics in Stobaeus commonly attributed to Arius Didymus (15). The former is available in English translation in the Loeb series; the latter has not, as far as I am aware, previously been available in English in its entirety. In both cases it seemed appropriate to include the whole of these texts, since numerous parts of them are relevant to other, thematic sections and are cross-referred to from them. While there are other texts too for which a case for inclusion of the whole could be made, such as the pseudo-Aristotle treatise *On the World* (*De mundo*), in these cases it seemed more appropriate to include, in the thematic sections, only those passages which are particularly important for specific themes; *De mundo* is available in English translation in Furley 1955, and much of it is concerned with natural science, such as its chapter 4 on meteorological phenomena. Although some

---

[2] Runia 2002 has shown that there was a major change in theology from Philo of Alexandria onwards; it ceased to be studied, in the Hellenistic manner, as part of physics, and the divine came rather to be regarded as a subject of study *sui generis*. In my own 2002a I have attempted to show that this shift applied especially to the Platonic tradition, broadly defined; it did not apply, or did not to the same extent apply, to the Peripatetic tradition.

information on Nicolaus of Damascus has been included and his compendium *On the Philosophy of Aristotle* has been mentioned occasionally, excerpts from it do not play a large part in this collection, for reasons explained in the Introduction below; the same applies to the Peripatetic material in pseudo-Andronicus, *On the Passions.*

Study of the thought of this period, and not only of that in the Peripatetic tradition, encounters the difficulty that some background knowledge is required not only of Aristotle's own thought and writings, but also of the differences between Aristotle and Plato on the one hand and of the Stoic tradition on the other. All philosophers have, however, to varying degrees reacted, and continue to react, to the thought of their predecessors, and the fact that Descartes was influenced by his predecessors (cf. Menn 1998 and 2003) has not led to arguments that no one should study Descartes unless they have first studied later ancient and medieval philosophy. The thought of most of the period with which the present book is concerned is however intrinsically backward-looking to an extent to which not every period of philosophy has been, and I have therefore attempted, in the discussions which follow the selection of passages in each chapter, to provide some essential background. I have assumed that most readers will at least have some familiarity with the general chronology of ancient Greek and Roman history and of the major philosophical figures and movements within this. Beyond that, there is a question how much background knowledge should be assumed, and how much incidental information given; I hope it will at least be clear to readers where they should look for information if it is not given here.

A more intractable difficulty in coming to grips with the period of thought examined in the present sourcebook, at least for beginners, is that what is at issue is not a developed system of thought, but rather the earlier stages of the process by which such a system – Aristotelian*ism* – eventually came to be constructed on the basis of Aristotle's works. As it has increasingly come to be realised that many doctrines which have for nearly two millennia been regarded by students *and critics* of Aristotle as central to his philosophy are in fact interpretations by Alexander of Aphrodisias, and only questionably held by Aristotle himself,[3] there is a particular interest in examining the stage in that process which preceded Alexander himself.

---

[3] For example: that Aristotle identifies form with the essence of the species (see Rashed 2007, especially 30–1, 151–2); that Aristotle's theology is to be found in *Metaphysics* Λ (Bodéüs 1992, 67 n. 34); that the movement of the heavens is caused by a desire to *imitate* the Unmoved Mover(s) (Berti 1997, 64; 2000, 201; cf. Broadie 1993, 379; Laks 2000, 221 n. 37).

Three further lines of demarcation have also had to be drawn, though, as in all such cases, their precise location has inevitably been to a certain extent arbitrary. First, the materials collected here are intended to elucidate the history and development in our period of the Peripatetic tradition – what might loosely be called the Peripatetic school, though not in our period a school in the sense of a formal institution. They are not intended to shed light on the whole history of the reception of Aristotle in the period. (After all, it is not usual to regard 'Platonism' as including every discussion of Plato.) Consequently, although interpretations of Aristotle by members of other philosophical schools are included to some extent, the emphasis is necessarily on the views, observations and agendas of those who defined themselves, or were regarded by others, primarily as followers of the Aristotelian tradition. There is, after all, some danger in assuming that, because a non-Peripatetic author makes an observation about Aristotle, their doing so must necessarily reflect discussion among Peripatetics at the time. Few, one hopes, would still suppose that, whenever Cicero mentions Plato, what he says necessarily and always reflects current inter-pretations of Plato to the exclusion of acquaintance with the actual text.[4] True, while Cicero demonstrably could and did read Plato for himself, it is less obvious that 'outsiders' were reading, or would have wanted to read, Aristotle's complex and obscure unpublished writings for themselves. That Cicero in *On the Nature of the Gods* 2.95 makes his Stoic spokesman Balbus cite the adaptation of Plato's cave analogy in Aristotle's *published On Philosophy* (Aristotle, fr. 12 in Rose 1886) may not tell us anything about Peripatetics *in the time of Cicero*. If Cicero could read Plato for himself (as we know he did, for he translated several passages), he could also read Aristotle's published or 'exoteric' works. The sort of source-criticism which rested on the assumption that Cicero read a text or entertained a philosophical thought only if someone else in his own period or just before it was already doing so is now rightly discredited. Cicero's – or his Stoic source's – use of Aristotle in *On the Nature of the Gods* 2.95 is part of the history of the reception of Aristotle, but that is not the same thing as the history of Peripatetic philosophy. Seneca's account of the four Aristotelian 'causes' (**12C**) is included, because there are features of it which may suggest that it could tell us something about contemporary Aristotelian exegesis, presumably by Peripatetics (see, however, the commentary on this passage). However, Seneca's references to Aristotle in the *Natural Questions* are

---

[4] Cf. also, on the question of Seneca's direct use of Plato, Inwood 2007a, 108–9; 2007b, 150.

almost all taken from the *Meteorology* itself, and so do not seem to tell us much about Peripatetic philosophy in his day.[5] See also **18T**.

A particular problem is created here by the approach of Antiochus of Ascalon, known to us chiefly through the writings of Cicero. Antiochus claimed that Plato, his immediate followers in the Old Academy, Aristotle and his early followers, and the Stoics, grouped together as 'the old philosophers', all shared a common set of doctrines, though with individual variations. Antiochus' interpretation of Peripatetic ethics, and the contrast he drew between Peripatetics and Stoics in this regard, can legitimately be regarded as part of the history of the topic, because it connects both with Aristotle's own statements and with points made in our period by those who were Peripatetics in a more straightforward sense than Antiochus was. Even Cicero's criticisms of Theophrastus for weakening the original doctrine and allowing fortune to count for too much are in a sense part of our subject, just because, by contrasting Aristotle and Theophrastus, Cicero or Antiochus is advancing a particular interpretation of Aristotle. However, when Antiochus states the Stoic doctrine of two physical principles as that of the Old Academy and the Peripatetics (Cicero, *Academica* 1.24), even if there may be some historical truth in this where the *Academy* is concerned (see Sedley 2002), the sense in which it can be regarded as a contribution to the interpretation of *Aristotle* seems at best tenuous; or at least, if this aspect of Antiochus' views belongs in the history of Aristotelianism, it does so no more, and possibly less, than it does in the history of Platonism.

Secondly, this collection is structured around the philosophical themes and topics which seem to characterise Peripatetic thought in our period. This is necessary if the contents of the collection are to be manageable and easily understood. In general, no attempt has been made at comprehensiveness in including contributions which were made by one thinker but do not seem to have preoccupied others. For some of the authors included here, indeed, there at present exists no complete collection of fragments and testimonia; the present selection has been designed specifically as a sourcebook, that is to say a convenient collection of material for those who wish to become familiar with the main issues relating to its subject matter, and no

---

[5] The exceptions are *Natural Questions* 7.5.4, which reports Aristotle, *Meteorology* 1.6, but appears to add detail not in the text of Aristotle (so Corcoran 1971–2 ad loc., vol. II 237 n. 2), and 7.30.1 = Aristotle, fr. 14 Rose 1886. But the former is probably due to misunderstanding; what Aristotle says is that the light of the comet in question extended *spatially* as far as Orion's belt and was dispersed there, but Seneca interprets this as a process *in time*. The latter apparently derives from Aristotle's lost dialogue *On Philosophy*, and there is no reason to suppose that Seneca's referring to it is significant for Peripatetic discussion *in his own time*.

attempt has therefore been made at the completeness which is needed in the definitive collection of all the evidence relating to a particular thinker, which in these cases is something we still have to await. The fact that certain themes were of particular interest and were topics of discussion is itself significant for the way in which Peripatetic philosophy in our period operated within a larger philosophical and cultural context;[6] the key influence here is that of Stoicism, which explains the prominence of concern with substance (Chapter 12), with the place of sense perception in achieving knowledge (14),[7] with the emotions (16), with the ethical development of the individual (18), with the eternity of the world (20), with providence (22) and with fate (23) – for in all these areas Peripatetic thought was reacting to, and to a greater or lesser extent disagreeing with, Stoicism. The aspect of Aristotle's legacy that is strikingly *absent* is above all his work on biology; this is to be attributed to the way in which systematic investigations in this area had come to be replaced by the collection and transmission of information in reference works of various sorts;[8] other omissions are political theory (for the context of political activity had changed beyond recognition from the autonomous city-states which Aristotle himself studied; see, however, below, 15A(47)–(52)), and rhetoric and literary criticism (for here Aristotle's contributions had been absorbed into traditions that had separate lives of their own apart from philosophy). One puzzle which has not yet I think been adequately solved is why there was such interest – and not only among Peripatetics – in Aristotle's work *Categories*; this *may* in part be just an impression created by the place of this text in later philosophical teaching and the perhaps disproportionate amount of information on it that we possess, above all through Simplicius' commentary (approximately 171,000 words of commentary on 10,500 words of text),[9] but I do not think that that can be the whole story. (I have advanced some further suggestions in Sharples 2008b.)

Thirdly, the emphasis is on discussion of *philosophical* issues. Aristotle was, after all, a polymath, and it is not easy to separate his contributions to philosophy from his contributions to what we would regard as the natural sciences. In so far as it is possible, however, the focus here is on the former rather than the latter. Aristotle's work in natural science was not, in general, being developed in our period by those who identified themselves as

---

[6] I am grateful to one of the anonymous referees for Cambridge University Press for emphasising this.
[7] The way in which sense perception *operates*, however, has been placed under physics, linked as it is in Aristotle himself with the topic of the soul.
[8] See Lennox 1994; Sharples 1995, 32–7, 126.
[9] Word counts taken from the on-line *Thesaurus Linguae Graecae*.

specialists in Aristotle (the exception being astronomy – see **21** below; but even here we are concerned with attempts to interpret Aristotle's *texts*, or to reinterpret them in the light of advances that had been made in the subject). Topics such as Seneca's disagreements with Aristotle's views on the causes of meteorological phenomena (for which see, e.g., Kidd 1992) do not therefore belong here.[10] A special case concerns the use and criticism of Aristotelian theories by Galen; passages in which there is reason to suppose that Galen is reacting to Peripatetics of his own period rather than directly to Aristotle or to Theophrastus (**25B**, **26AE**) have been included, but Galen's attitude to Aristotle's own writings is not part of the history of *Peripatetic* philosophy in our period.[11] Moreover, it is hoped that a further volume in the present series will consider the relation of Galen to *all* the philosophical traditions of his day, and it is in this context that his attitude to Aristotle in particular will best be considered.

The present book follows the principles and layout of the first volume of Long and Sedley 1987 (LS). Selected passages on each topic, in translation, are followed by a discussion setting them in context. An attempt has been made to provide information necessary for immediate understanding of the passages in the footnotes to the passages themselves, but the discussion at the end of the chapter should also be consulted. Within each chapter passages in the same chapter are referred to by capital letter only; those in other chapters by chapter number plus letter. Where reference is made to a passage in another chapter, the discussion of that passage in the commentary on that chapter should also be consulted. Longer passages are subdivided into numbered sections for ease of reference; these divisions are made purely for the purpose of this book and do not reflect standard editorial divisions of the passages involved. For Aristotle's *Nicomachean Ethics* book numbers and Bekker column-and-line references are given, but not chapter numbers, because of the risk of confusion where there are two systems in use and some texts have both. Difficulty may also be caused if 'source for B' is

---

[10] It seems possible that the first book, and the first part of the second book, of the *Supplementary Problems* variously attributed to Aristotle and to Alexander, but not in fact by either (1 and 2.1–38 in Kapetanaki and Sharples 2006 = Aristoteles, *Problemata inedita* 1 and 2.1–38 in Bussemaker = Alexander, *Problemata* 3 and 4.1–38 in Usener 1859), were compiled in the second century AD, and so in our period (see Sharples 2005, 54–6, and Kapetanaki and Sharples 2006, 9–10); but these texts tell us little of any systematic developments in Peripatetic thought (cf. Kapetanaki and Sharples 2006, 22–7). The pseudo-Aristotelian *Problems* in Bekker's edition seem to date, in the main, from the third century BC; there are scattered references to Aristotle's *Problems* by Aristotle himself and others that correspond to nothing in either collection (cf. Flashar 1991, 303–16), but the texts referred to are impossible to date precisely and again do not connect with central themes of Peripatetic philosophy.

[11] It is, however, usefully discussed by Moraux 1984, 687–808, and Gottschalk 1987, 1166–71.

used to refer both to an earlier writer (A) from whom a writer B drew material, and to a later writer (C) who is *our* evidence for lost works of (B); to avoid ambiguity, I have confined the use of 'source' to the former case, and in the latter have spoken either of 'evidence' or of 'witnesses'.

A particular note of explanation is needed in connection with references to 'Aëtius', the doxographical writer or compiler of a catalogue of the opinions (*doxai*) of various philosophers whose work was 'reconstructed' by Diels in his *Doxographi Graeci* (= *Dox.*: see the list of abbreviations below). Diels' reconstruction is, as has been shown above all by Mansfeld and Runia 1996–, open to question in many of its details: he treated as sections of the original work material preserved in only one of the witnesses for it, rearranged the material in one of those witnesses (Stobaeus) to fit the sequence in the other (pseudo-Plutarch), and, inevitably, sometimes made questionable judgements as to what material in Stobaeus came from Aëtius and what from elsewhere. I have therefore given references to 'Aëtius' only in cases where a passage occurs in both witnesses; where it is found only in one I have given the reference to that witness first and then added the reference to 'Aëtius'. Nevertheless, it seems clear that Aëtius did produce his catalogue of opinions in about AD 100; what he says in his preface (5E below) about the scope and organisation of Peripatetic philosophy is surely evidence for one way in which this was seen during our period, and I have therefore included not only the preface but also other passages in which Aëtius, as reconstructed, refers to Aristotle or (in particular) to 'the Peripatetics', as these too *may* be evidence for Peripatetic activity in our period, though such reports may also be repetitions of earlier material whose time of origin cannot easily be determined.

The compilation of a sourcebook such as this naturally involves drawing on information from many sources, both published work and informal discussions. Among the former I should especially record my indebtedness to Moraux 1973 and 1984, to Gottschalk 1987, and to those in addition to myself who gave papers on aspects of Peripatetic philosophy in this period in the conference on philosophy between 100 BC and AD 200 held in London in 2004 and published in Sorabji and Sharples 2007; Tobias Reinhardt, Jonathan Barnes and Richard Sorabji; among the latter, to the participants in a colloquium on Boethus held in Paris in 2007, especially Maddalena Bonelli, Jean-Baptiste Gourinat and Philippe Hoffman; also to Victor Caston, Riccardo Chiaradonna, John Dudley, Philip van der Eijk, Erik Eliasson, Andrea Falcon, Bill Fortenbaugh, Pamela Huby, Thomas Johansen, George Karamanolis, Inna Kupreeva, Tony Long, Herwig Maehler, Vivian Nutton, Jan Opsomer, Marwan Rashed, Malcolm

Schofield, and to the anonymous readers for Cambridge University Press. I owe a particular debt to Bill Fortenbaugh, not least because, by asking me to participate in the Theophrastus Project and to write a paper (Sharples 1983b) on 'Arius Didymus Doxography C' he first introduced me to the complexities of the Peripatetic tradition after Aristotle and before Alexander. Some of the material contained here has been used in teaching an undergraduate course on Philosophy under the Roman Empire, in 2005–6 and in 2007–8, and I am grateful to the students involved for their comments and questions, and also for misunderstandings which showed me where clarification might be particularly needed. I should also record my gratitude for the library facilities and intellectual environment provided over many years by the Institute of Classical Studies and the Warburg Institute, and to the Department of Greek and Latin, University College London, for the way in which it encouraged staff to pursue their own research interests and to develop informal contacts with scholars with similar interests from other institutions and indeed from other countries. Translations are my own except where otherwise specified. I am grateful to the following for permission to reuse translations by myself previously published elsewhere (full details are given at the end of each passage). Akadémiai Kiadó: from Sharples 2008b, **8ABC**; E. J. Brill: from Sharples 2002b, **22O**, **24L**; Gerald Duckworth and Co. Ltd: from Sharples 1983a, **1Ab**, **23HSTU**; from Sharples 1992, **22T**; from Sharples 2004, **12JK**, **17CDEF**, **22F**, **23V**, **26C**, **27BIJK**, and material in the commentaries on **12** and on **17**; Walter de Gruyter and Co. Ltd: from Sharples 1999, **18Ab(4)**; Institute of Classical Studies, University of London: from Sharples 2003b, **22V**; from Sharples 2007a, part of **6A**; from Sharples 2007b, **22D(1)H**, **23ABOPQ**, and material in the commentary on **23**; from Sharples 2007c, **18HIUVW,Ab** (1)–(3),**Ac**; from Sharples 2007d, **24GKPRSTUW,Aa**; Oxbow Books: from Sharples 1991, **23R**. I am also grateful to Liverpool University Press and to Philip van der Eijk for permission to take, from Sharples and van der Eijk 2008, **23N**; and to Tobias Reinhardt and the Institute of Classical Studies, University of London, for permission to take **9B** from Reinhardt 2007.

Abbreviations

Abbreviations of journal titles correspond to those used in *L' Année philo-logique* and abbreviations of ancient sources correspond to those used in the *Oxford Classical Dictionary*, with the following additions and variations:

ANRW	Temporini, H. and Haase, W., eds. 1972–. *Aufstieg und Niedergang der römischen Welt*. Berlin.
BT	Bibliotheca Teubneriana. Leipzig and Stuttgart.
CAG	various eds. 1882–1907. *Commentaria in Aristotelem Graeca*. Berlin.
CB	Collection Budé. Paris.
CMG	various eds. 1907–. *Corpus Medicorum Graecorum*. Lepzig and Berlin.
Dox.	Diels, H. 1879. *Doxographi Graeci*. Berlin.
DPA	Goulet, R., ed. 1989–. *Dictionnaire des philosophes antiques*. Paris.
EK	Edelstein, L. and Kidd, I. G. 1972–99. *Posidonius*, vol. i: *Fragments*; vol. ii: *Commentary*; vol. iii: *Translation of the Fragments*. Cambridge.
FHS&G	Fortenbaugh, W. W., Huby, P. M., Sharples, R. W. (Greek and Latin) and Gutas, D. (Arabic), with five others (eds.). 1992. *Theophrastus of Eresus. Sources for his Life, Writings, Thought and Influence*. Leiden.
FrGrHist	Jacoby, F. 1923–. *Die Fragmente der griechischen Historiker*. Berlin.
GCS	*Die griechischen christlichen Schriftsteller*. Leipzig.
KRS	Kirk, G. S., Raven, J. E., and Schofield, M. 1983. *The Presocratic Philosophers*, 2nd edn. Cambridge.
LS	Long, A. A. and Sedley, D. N. 1987. *The Hellenistic Philosophers*. Cambridge.
PG	Migne, J.-P. 1857–66. *Patrologia graeca*. Paris.
PL	Migne, J.-P. 1844–65. *Patrologia latina*. Paris.

RE	Pauly, A. F. von and Wissowa, G., eds. 1894–1978. *Real-Encyclopädie der klassischen Altertumswissenschaft.* Stuttgart.
RUSCH	*Rutgers University Studies in Classical Humanities.* New Brunswick, NJ.
SA	various eds. 1885–1903. *Supplementum Aristotelicum.* Berlin.
SVF	von Arnim, H., ed. 1903–24. *Stoicorum Veterum Fragmenta.* Leipzig.

Introduction

This Introduction and the chronological table that follows it are intended to give readers who may not be familiar with this period of Peripatetic philosophy a guide to the major trends and developments, and to introduce some of the philosophers who will be considered in the following pages. The actual ancient evidence relating to some of the identifications and dates will be found below in Chapter 1, 'People'.

Aristotle's school, the Lyceum, has been regarded both in antiquity and by modern scholars as entering a period of decline after its third head, Strato. This impression may in part be the result of tendentious representation in the ancient evidence,[1] but in so far as it is accurate, the fundamental reason for the decline seems to be, not that Aristotle's works were no longer available (below, 2), but that the Lyceum had never had an agenda that was philosophical in the narrow sense of that term predominant in antiquity, as promoting a way of life and an attitude towards its events. From Aristotle himself onwards, the concern of the school had largely been with the collecting and analysis of information on a wide range of topics, and it thus suffered from the double disadvantage that, on the one hand, it did not have such a clear evangelical message to propound as did the Epicureans or the Stoics (for the message of *Nicomachean Ethics* 10, that the highest human activity is theoretical study for its own sake, was probably of no wider appeal in antiquity than it is now), and, on the other, that such research was being carried on elsewhere, above all in Ptolemaic Alexandria.[2] The notion of Aristotelianism as a distinctive philosophical system, in a sense closer to modern understandings of 'philosophical', is in no small part the result of a process that had its beginnings in the period considered in the present book.

Critolaus of Phaselis in the second century BC (below, 1A) was the most distinguished head of the Peripatetic school between Strato and the

---

[1] See White 2004; Sharples 2006, 323; Hahm 2007.   [2] See Glucker 1998.

apparent end of the school as an institution with Sulla's sack of Athens in 86 BC.[3] Critolaus' philosophical positions are in many respects, though not all, marked by an apparent desire to distance Aristotelianism from Stoicism (see below, 16T, 18EHIM, 20AB, 22KLO). Hahm has argued (2007, 76–81, 95–6) that Critolaus' subsequent reputation suffered doubly, first from the way in which Antiochus of Ascalon (1B) deliberately emphasised Critolaus' divergence from Aristotle while suppressing how similar Critolaus' views were to Antiochus' own, and then from the shift from philosophical debate to text-based exegesis; see further below, on 2A and 18M.

Antiochus of Ascalon (*c*. 130–69/8 BC) regarded himself as an Academic, and indeed as restoring the true tradition of the Academy after the sceptical interlude of the Middle Academy of Arcesilaus (316/15–242/1 BC), and the New Academy of Carneades (214/13–129/8 BC) and his followers. Antiochus taught that the views of Plato, his immediate successors in the Old Academy, Aristotle and the Stoics were essentially similar – a view which has a degree of philosophical plausibility, especially if one contrasts these three schools with the Epicureans and the various sceptical traditions. Unfortunately Antiochus was too ready to attribute apparently Stoic theories on specific topics to the Platonists and the Peripatetics, though it has recently been argued (Sedley 2002) that in the case of the former at least there may be more historical accuracy in this than has often been supposed.

After Antiochus' death his school was taken over by his brother Aristus. Ariston of Alexandria and Cratippus of Pergamum left Antiochus' school and declared themselves Peripatetics. Cicero shows great admiration for Cratippus (1JKLM, 27EF). Subsequent historians of philosophy have not endorsed Cicero's view, but Cicero may be judging Cratippus as a teacher (and debater; see Hahm 2007, 94) rather than for acumen in the more technical aspects of philosophy. The significance of Cicero's praise of Cratippus in modern discussion has chiefly been as an argument from silence, suggesting either that Andronicus of Rhodes was not active until after Cicero's death (1KLM being written in November 44) or that Cicero was not interested in the unpublished writings of Aristotle that preoccupied Andronicus. Cratippus taught Cicero's son in Athens; but in the first century BC and thereafter, although Athens continued to be a centre where the sons of the Roman elite went to study, philosophers were active in the major centres of the Roman Empire, including Rome itself, and it is not always possible to be certain where a particular individual studied and taught.[4]

---

[3] See Lynch 1972, 192–8.   [4] See Barnes 1997, 23–4 on Andronicus and Boethus.

Andronicus is best known for his alleged part in editing, and thus making available again, the unpublished works of Aristotle, though the extent of his contribution to the editorial tradition has recently been called into question.[5] What is clear is that he was among the first to engage in the activity of writing commentaries on these Aristotelian texts, which remained the centre of Peripatetic activity until, and even after, the Peripatetic tradition largely ceased to exist as a separate one by being absorbed into Platonism in the third century AD.[6] In producing commentaries Andronicus was followed by his pupil Boethus.[7]

Also in the mid to late first century BC, Xenarchus of Seleucia (on whom see **17C, 21D–I, 24K, 27A**) is best known for his criticisms of Aristotle's view that the heavens are composed of a fifth element different from those which constitute the sublunary region. This raises questions as to how far Aristotelian orthodoxy was and should now be a criterion for regarding someone as a Peripatetic, and how far it was simply a matter of a predominant interest in the views and writings of Aristotle rather than in those of any other philosopher or school; see Falcon 2008 on this, and on Xenarchus' relation both to Hellenistic critics of Aristotle such as Strato and to the later commentary tradition. Xenarchus criticises Aristotle's views by using arguments drawn from Aristotle's own works, unlike a Platonist critic of Aristotle such as Atticus, and unlike Strato, who developed his own theories rather than arguing on the basis of Aristotle's. There is, however, a danger of reading back into the first century BC, as Moraux arguably did, Alexander's concern in the second to third centuries AD to establish a consistent and orthodox Aristotelian doctrine; the shift from the Hellenistic continuation of Aristotle's work to the focus in the late Republic and early Empire on Aristotle's *works*, that is the texts, did not necessarily bring with it an immediate concern for orthodoxy.[8]

Possibly from the latter part of the first century BC we have two summaries of Aristotelian doctrine, of rather different types but similar in the problems relating to their origin. One, conventionally attributed to 'Arius Didymus' a courtier of the emperor Augustus, is a summary of Peripatetic ethics (**15** below), which draws to some extent on Aristotle's esoteric works but also shows the influence of Hellenistic philosophical

---

[5] Barnes 1997, 28–44. See below on **2BFG, 6A, 7C, 8A**.

[6] Largely; but Themistius, who wrote paraphrases of Aristotle in the fourth century AD, is one exception, and Nicolaus of Damascus may be another (see further below).

[7] Not to be confused with the *Stoic* Boethus of Sidon (second century BC), or with the sixth-century AD Roman Neoplatonist Boethius.

[8] For these points I am indebted to Andrea Falcon.

preoccupations both in its content and in its structure. We also have some
much shorter reports of Aristotelian physics customarily attributed to the
same writer; but the identification of the author of all these texts is a highly
complex matter, discussed in the commentary to 1 below. The other
summary, by Nicolaus of Damascus, is, or rather was, a condensed paraphrase of some of Aristotle's esoteric works; it survives only in a Syriac
version which has itself been drastically and arbitrarily summarised by an
epitomator and which has then suffered further damage owing to the loss
of parts of the sole MS. Here the problem of attribution relates to whether
the Nicolaus in question is the associate of Herod the Great and Augustus,
or a later writer of the same name. See the commentary on 1PQ below.
The compendium occasionally supplements what Aristotle actually says
by questionable interpretation of its own (Drossaart-Lulofs 1965, 156;
however, see below, 21 n. 29),[9] but in general it reproduces Aristotle's
thought and has rather little contact with the issues and debates which
preoccupied Peripatetics in our period, and still less with the thought of
other philosophical schools – facts which led Drossaart-Lulofs 1965, 20–1
to suggest that 'it seems doubtful whether Nicolaus', who worked in
various literary genres and above all in history (his *Histories*, alluded to
in 1P, occupied 144 books), 'had any connexion with the schoolmen of his
time, and was not rather a kind of freelance'. Nicolaus seems to have
disregarded the *Categories*, the *Organon* and the ethical[10] and political
works altogether, concentrating on physics and biology, and paid considerable attention to Aristotle's *Metaphysics*.[11] Although he followed
Aristotle's texts as his source, he rearranged material in the interests of
clarity, expressing dissatisfaction with the way in which in the *Metaphysics*
all the problems for discussion are collected together into a single
book, *Metaphysics* B, whereas in the *Physics* they appear at the start of

---

[9] Cf. also Drossaart-Lulofs 1965, 8–9, 17–19, but the points here (on the Presocratics Xenophanes and
     Diogenes of Apollonia; Simplicius, *In Phys.* 23.14, 25.8, 149.18, 151.21) relate to Nicolaus' *On Gods*,
     which Drossaart-Lulofs suggests was an early work on physical doxography, rather than to the
     compendium *On the Philosophy of Aristotle*. A paraphrase *can* indeed be a form of commentary or
     interpretation (cf. the comments of the Arabic authors cited by Fazzo 2008, 111) but, to judge from the
     extant remains of the work, there is rather little of this in the compendium.

[10] In the compendium. But see Drossaart-Lulofs 1965, 7 and 16 (T2) for another work *On What Is Noble
     in Actions*, and 1965, 13–14 (T13) for an *Introduction to Ethics*, judged spurious by Drossaart-Lulofs
     because it refers to Plotinus, but cf. Fazzo 2005, 289 n. 52; 2008, 114–16 and references there.

[11] Both the interest in the *Metaphysics* and that in the biological works are remarkable if the work is first
     century BC in date; Fazzo 2008, 118–19. It is true, as Jan Opsomer reminds me, that others such as
     Eudorus the Platonist took an interest in passages in the *Metaphysics* in this period (see Dillon 1996,
     128 n. 1), but that is rather different from dealing with the work as a whole.

the relevant sections,[12] and placing material from the philosophical lexicon in *Metaphysics* Δ in the sections to which it seemed relevant.[13]

Also probably from the latter part of the first century BC or the first half of the first century AD are: the surviving pseudo-Aristotelian treatise *On the World* (*De mundo*), which goes beyond Aristotle's explicit statements in giving an account of the world as a whole as a system governed by a divine ruler, who does not, however (unlike the Stoic god), himself become involved in the details; the work *On Philosophy* by Aristocles of Messene, surviving only in fragments, which seems to have been a general history of philosophy inspired by Aristotle's exoteric work of the same name (see Chiesara 2001, xxxv–xxxviii), though making use also of the esoteric works (Chiesara 2001, xiii), and engaging in controversy as well as in narrative (below, **14**); and the treatise *On Emotions* falsely attributed to Andronicus, which is a combination of Stoic and Peripatetic material, the latter chiefly on virtues and vices and indeed largely dependent on the pseudo-Aristotelian treatise of that title, which may itself be from the same period.[14]

After this there appears to have been a decline until the second century AD in distinctively Peripatetic activity known to us (which does not mean that Peripatetic views were not discussed by members of other schools, notably the Stoic Seneca); the exception is Alexander of Aegae, teacher of the emperor Nero (AD 37–68; **1S**), who produced a commentary on Aristotle's *Categories* and discussed an argument in *On the Heaven* (*De caelo*) (Moraux 1984, 222–5; see **1Y**). Aspasius, much of whose commentary on the *Ethics*[15] is still extant and is the earliest commentary on Aristotle to survive substantially rather than in the form of second-hand reports,[16] also commented on a wide range of Aristotle's works (Moraux 1984, 226–93); he is to be placed in the first half of the second century AD (see **1T**).[17] So too is Adrastus (see

---

[12] Averroes, *In Metaph.* 168.5 Bouyges 1952= Nicolaus T7.4 in Drossaart-Lulofs 1965, 12.

[13] Averroes, *In Metaph.* 476.3 Bouyges 1952 = Nicolaus T7.5 in Drossaart-Lulofs 1965, 12, 32–4; for example, a rearranged version of *Metaph.* Δ.1, on principles, along with material on these from elsewhere in the *Metaphysics*, introduced his summary of the *Physics*, Drossaart-Lulofs 1965, 99, and a version of *Metaph.* Δ.8 incorporating material from Z introduced the summary of Metaph. Λ, Drossaart-Lulofs 1965, 144–5.

[14] See Moraux 1973, 138–41; Gottschalk 1987, 1129–31.

[15] I deliberately put the matter this way, for, while Aspasius includes the 'common books' (*Nicomachean Ethics* 5–7 = *Eudemian Ethics* 4–6) in his commentary on the former, it is not clear that he regarded them as actually belonging to the *Nicomachean Ethics*, and in fact there are indications that he did not do so. See Barnes 1999, 21, and below on **2I**.

[16] At a time when books could only be preserved through laborious copying by hand, later commentaries tended to supersede earlier ones; why bother to copy out a superseded commentary, especially when later ones often include quite extensive parts of their predecessors (explicitly attributed or not)?

[17] Donini has argued (1974, 98–125; 1982, 217–19) that Aspasius shows markedly Platonising tendencies (and see below on **16Ad**); however Barnes 1999, 5–6 (cf. 30) rightly maintains that Aspasius is using

1UV), who produced a work on the *Ethics* which seems to have been a discussion of specific passages, explaining allusions in Aristotle's text, rather than a general commentary (1W). Adrastus also updated Aristotle's theory of the heavenly spheres to take account of developments in astronomical theories since Aristotle's time (21MN) and apparently did so in a commentary on Plato's *Timaeus* (see the commentary on 1V; Moraux 1984, 296–300) – which is significant for readiness to cross boundaries between schools in our period; on this see also the commentary on 23LMN. Adrastus' work on the *Ethics* was apparently utilised, though we have no explicit evidence of this, by the anonymous commentator on *Nicomachean Ethics* 2–5, who may have written in the latter part of the second century AD (see below on 1X).

In AD 176 the emperor Marcus Aurelius established publicly funded posts at Athens for teachers of Platonism, Aristotelianism, Stoicism and Epicureanism.[18] It is doubtful whether there was any institutional continuity with the Hellenistic schools, which had probably ceased to exist as such centuries earlier.[19] Alexander of Aphrodisias was appointed to the post of teacher of Aristotelianism between AD 198 and 209 (1Ab,Ac).[20] Alexander was taught by Sosigenes (for whom see 8G, 13F(2)G(1), 21KL, 26D), Herminus (1Y, 21J) and perhaps Aristoteles of Mytilene (1Z, Aa).[21] Although we do not know at what stage in Alexander's career he was appointed to the post in Athens, it seems likely that Sosigenes, Herminus and Aristoteles of Mytilene, as Alexander's teachers, are to be dated rather later in the second century than Aspasius and Adrastus.

SOME NOTABLE PERIPATETICS (AND OTHERS) AND THEIR DATES

For the period before 200 BC no attempt has been made to list all known Peripatetics, or even all significant members of the school; the listing is confined to those whom there has been occasion to mention in this sourcebook, and it is provided for the convenience of the reader. For the same reason some individuals who were not primarily identified as members of the Peripatetic school have also been included. Where dates can only be given in terms of a century or part thereof, the reference is to the time when

---

philosophical ideas which had become common property, and that he not only does not subscribe to the most distinctive Platonic doctrines, but never actually disagrees with or criticises Aristotle. See also below, 16Ad and commentary.

[18] Philostratus, *Lives of the Sophists* p. 566.   [19] See Sharples 2005, 52–3 and references there.

[20] For Alexander of Damascus, who may have held the post at some point before Alexander of Aphrodisias, see 14KL and the commentary there.

[21] See Accattino 1985; Moraux 1985; and also below on 27K.

the person seems to have been philosophically active. For the historical evidence behind the identifications and dates see below, Chapter 1.

Aristotle of Stagira	384–322 BC
Theophrastus of Eresos	372/1 or 371/0 – 288/7 or 287/6 BC
Eudemus of Rhodes	latter part of fourth century BC
Strato of Lampsacus	head of Peripatetic school from death of Theophrastus until *c.* 269 BC
Ariston of Ceos	later third/early second century BC
Critolaus of Phaselis	early to middle second century BC
Staseas of Naples	born before 120 BC
Apellicon of Teos	first quarter of first century BC
Antiochus of Ascalon (Academic)	*c.* 130 – *c.* 69/8 BC
Cicero (Academic)	106–43 BC
Cratippus of Pergamum	middle of first century BC
Andronicus of Rhodes	mid to late first century BC?
Xenarchus of Seleucia	mid to late first century BC
Boethus of Sidon	second half of first century BC
Athenodorus of Tarsus (Stoic)	second half of first century BC
Arius Didymus (?) (Stoic)	late first century BC (?)
Nicolaus of Damascus (?)	second half of first century BC (?)
Aristocles of Messene	late first century BC/early first century AD
Alexander of Aegae	early to mid first century AD
Seneca (the Younger) (Stoic)	*c.* 4 BC/AD 1 – AD 65
Cornutus (Stoic)	first century AD
Aspasius	first half of second century AD
Adrastus	first half of second century AD
Sosigenes	second half of second century AD
Herminus	second half of second century AD
Aristoteles of Mytilene	second half of second century AD
Alexander of Aphrodisias	*fl. c.* AD 200

Individuals

CHAPTER I

People

A. Cicero, *On the Orator* 2.155

[Scipio the younger, Laelius and Furius] said that the Athenians did something most welcome both to them and to many of the leading citizens, in that, when they sent envoys to the senate about their most important concerns [in 156/5 BC], they sent the three most distinguished philosophers of that age, Carneades and Critolaus and Diogenes [of Babylon]; and so these, while they were at Rome, were frequently listened to both by themselves and by others.

B. Cicero, *On Ends* 5.14

Critolaus wished to imitate the early [Peripatetics], and indeed he is closest [to them] in seriousness, and his style is free-flowing; but not even he holds to the principles of his ancestors. Diodorus, his pupil, adds to moral virtue [*honestas*] freedom from pain. He too has a position of his own; and since he disagrees about the supreme good he cannot truly be called a Peripatetic. It seems to me that our Antiochus follows the opinion of the ancients most carefully; he teaches that it was the same for Aristotle and for Polemo.[1]

C. Eusebius, *Preparation for the Gospel* 15.2.13

Concerning Hermeias and Aristotle's friendship with him many others have written, and in particular Apellicon; whoever reads his works will cease from blasphemy against [Hermeias and Aristotle].

D. Cicero, *On Ends* 5.8

'You know that I agree with you on [the importance of Aristotle and the early Peripatetics], Piso,' I said, 'but your mention of [the Old Academy] is

---

[1] The fourth head of Plato's Academy.

timely; for my [cousin, Lucius] Cicero is eager to hear what is the opinion concerning the moral end of that Old Academy which you mention, and of the Peripatetics. We think that you will be able to explain it very easily, because you have had Staseas from Naples in your household for many years, and we are aware that for many months you questioned Antiochus at Athens about these same things.'

E.   Philodemus, *Index of Academic [Philosophers]* 35.2–17

[Antiochus'] school was taken over by his brother and student Aristus; although he was busy he had several students including my friends Ariston and Dio of Alexandria and Cratippus of Pergamum, of whom Ariston and Cratippus, <since they had heard Xenarchus and were enthusiastic [about him]>,[2] became Peripatetics, leaving the Academy.

F.   Plutarch, *Life of Brutus* 2.3

[Brutus, the killer of Julius Caesar,] did not greatly approve the New and the so-called Middle Academies, but attached himself to the Old, and was a constant admirer of Antiochus of Ascalon and made [Antiochus'] brother Aristus his friend and associate, a man who was inferior to many philosophers in argument, but a rival of the foremost in his self-discipline and his mildness.

G.   Strabo, *Geography* 14.2.19

[Strabo is listing famous people from Cos] . . . and in our time Nicias who was also the tyrant of Cos, and Ariston the pupil and successor of the Peripatetic. Also famous was Theomnestus the harp-player, the political opponent of Nicias.

H.   Strabo, *Geography* 17.1.5

But I will pass over these things [the causes of the annual flooding of the Nile] which have been discussed by many people, of whom it will be sufficient to mention just two, those who have composed a book about the Nile in our own time, Eudorus and the Peripatetic Ariston. For except

---

[2] Puglia's supplement, following Buecheler; only the letters -na- are readable. See Karamanolis 2006, 81 and n. 110.

for the arrangement, the rest is the same both in expression and in argument in both. At any rate I, when I did not have copies to compare, compared one with the other;[3] but which of them passed the other's work off as his own would need the oracle of Ammon to decide. Eudorus blamed Ariston; but the expression is more Ariston's.

I.   Strabo, *Geography* 14.5.4

Xenarchus, whose pupil I was, did not spend much time in his house, but, choosing the life of a teacher in Alexandria and Athens and finally in Rome, and being a friend of Arius and subsequently of Caesar Augustus, he continued to be honoured until his old age.

J.   Cicero's translation of the *Timaeus*, 1–2

I have written many things against the natural philosophers in my *Academica* and have often debated them with Publius Nigidius [Figulus, the Neopythagorean] in the manner and style of Carneades [the Academic Sceptic]. [Nigidius] was a man distinguished in the activities which are worthy of a free man, but in particular a keen and careful investigator of those things which are seen to be intricately fashioned by nature; indeed I judge that, after those noble Pythagoreans whose learning became in a way extinct, when it had flourished in Italy and Sicily for several centuries, he was the man to renew it. When I was setting out for Cilicia he waited for me at Ephesus, himself returning to Rome from an embassy. At the same time there came to Mytilene, in order to greet and see me, Cratippus, in my judgement easily the chief of all the Peripatetics I myself have heard. I was very glad both to see Nigidius and to make the acquaintance of Cratippus. We occupied the first occasion of greeting in inquiry . . .

K.   Cicero, *On Duties* 1.1–2

Marcus, my son, you have now been a pupil of Cratippus for a year, and in Athens; [so] you should possess an abundance of philosophical precepts and

---

[3] This, on the face of it, seems self-contradictory. H. L. Jones 1932, 20–1 nn. 1 and 2 suggests that Strabo did not himself have copies of the two works to compare (Jones says, the relevant passages; but it would appear that the *whole* was relevant) and therefore compared them in the Alexandrian library. The wording perhaps suggests that the point is just that Strabo did not have multiple copies of *each* work to compare (in order to establish a text?) and so could only compare the two works with one another (cf. the translation in Radt 2002, vol. IV 421). But either way, the point of the remark is hard to detect.

principles, on account of the very great authority both of your teacher and of the city; the former can provide you with knowledge, the latter with examples ... So you will learn from the leader of the philosophers in the present time, and you will do so for as long as you wish ...

L.   Cicero, *On Duties* 2.8

Although you, my [son] Cicero, are a student of that most ancient and noble [tradition in] philosophy, with Cratippus as your teacher, he who is most like those who originated those distinguished [doctrines], nevertheless I did not want you to be ignorant of these [doctrines] of ours which are very similar to yours.

M.   Cicero, *On Duties* 3.5

Although the whole of philosophy, my [son] Cicero, bears a rich harvest and no part of it is wild and uncultivated, nevertheless there is no more fertile or richer region in it than that which is concerned with appropriate actions,[4] from which the precepts of a consistent and honourable life are derived. So, although I am confident that you are diligently hearing and receiving these from my Cratippus, the leader of the philosophers of the present time, I think it beneficial to fill your ears with such utterances from every side, and that, if possible, they should hear nothing else.

N.   Strabo, *Geography* 16.2.24

In my own time there have been distinguished philosophers from Sidon, Boethus, with whom I studied the philosophy of Aristotle, and Diodotus his brother.

O.   Seneca, *Consolation to Marcia* 4.2

I do not doubt that the example of Julia Augusta [Livia], whose close acquaintance you were, will please you more; she summons you to take her advice. In the first raging [of her grief at the death of Drusus], when wretchedness is hardest to deal with and fiercest, she sought consolation from Areus, her husband's philosopher, and testified that this had greatly benefited her, more than the Roman people, whom she did not want to make

---

[4] *officia*, 'duties', rendering the Greek *kathēkonta*.

sad by her own grief, more than Augustus, who was wavering through the removal of one of his supports and did not need to be brought down by the grief of his family, and more than her son Tiberius, whose loyalty brought it about that she did not feel that, through that bitter death lamented by all the nations, anything was lacking to her except the number [of her sons].

P.   Nicolaus of Damascus, *Autobiography*, *FrGrHist* 90F135 Jacoby (Drossaart-Lulofs 1965, 3)

Herod dropped his passion for philosophy again, which is what tends to happen to those in positions of supremacy because of the multitude of good things which divert them; he became keen on rhetoric again and compelled Nicolaus to declaim with him, and they declaimed together. Now a passion for history seized him when Nicolaus praised it and said that it was very much connected with politics and was also useful for a king, in order to enquire into the deeds and achievements of those before [him]. Eagerly setting about this, he encouraged Nicolaus too to practise history. He set about the matter to an even greater extent, collecting the whole of history and undertaking great labour, such as no one else [had done]. Working hard for a long time he completed it and said that if Eurystheus had set such a labour for Hercules, it would have completely crushed him. After this Herod sailed to Caesar in Rome and took Nicolaus with him on the same ship, and they philosophised together.

Q.   Sophronios, *Encomium of Saints Cyrus and John* (*PG* LXXXVII/ 3.3622D; Drossaart-Lulofs 1965, 5)

From Damascus was also, among those distinguished and in power, Dionysius, who had sprung from a family which had continuously been illustrious, its origin and root being the philosopher Nicolaus, the teacher of Herod and instructor of the children of Antony and Cleopatra. [Starting] from him twelve Nicolauses flourished in succession, priding themselves on their philosophy; they made the family distinguished and brought it to a high degree of reputation and distinction.

R.   Note in some MSS at the end of Theophrastus, *Metaphysics* 12a4–b4

This book was not known to Andronicus and Hermippus, nor is there any mention at all of it in the list of Theophrastus' books; but Nicolaus, in his *Study of Aristotle's Metaphysics*, mentions it, saying that it is by Theophrastus.

S.   *Suda*, s. v. Alexander of Aegae (A 1128)

A Peripatetic philosopher, teacher of Nero the king along with the philosopher Chaeremon. He had a son named Caelinus. He called Nero 'clay mixed with blood'. In my view the teachers of bad pupils are even worse themselves. For excellence is teachable, and wickedness comes through practice.

T.   Galen, *On the Diagnosis and Cure of the Passions of the Soul* 8, vol. v.41.10–42.5 Kühn

Well, this is what my education by my father was like. When I reached the age of 14 [AD 143/4] I was the pupil of philosophers in my city, chiefly a Stoic, a pupil of Philopator, and also of a Platonist, a pupil of Gaius, for a short time, since he did not have leisure, being dragged into political business by the citizens, as he seemed to them the only person who was just and able to rise above financial concerns, approachable and mild. At this time another fellow-citizen of ours returned from a long stay abroad, a pupil of Aspasius the Peripatetic, and after him another from Athens, an Epicurean. For my sake my father examined the way of life and doctrines of them all, going to them with me.

U.   Theon of Smyrna, *Exposition of Mathematics Useful for Reading Plato* 49.6–10

The Peripatetic Adrastus, giving a clearer account of harmony and concord, says: 'As of written speech and of speech in general the first and largest parts are verbs and nouns, and of these syllables, and syllables are formed of letters . . . '

V.   Porphyry, *On Ptolemy's* Harmonics 96.1–6

Adrastus the Peripatetic in his *On the* Timaeus says the following: 'sounds are concordant with one another when, if the first is struck on some stringed instrument, the other too sounds with it according to some affinity and sympathy. In the same way when both are struck a smooth and pleasing sound is heard from their mixture.'

W.   Athenaeus, *The Sophists at Dinner* 15.15.673ef

[Hephaestion] behaved like this also concerning our noble Adrastus. For the latter published five books *On Historical and Linguistic Questions concerning What Theophrastus [Says] in his* On Ethical Characters,[5] and a sixth *Concerning What Aristotle [Says] in the* Nicomachean Ethics, and added a wealth of ideas on Plexippus in the tragedian Antiphon, and said a great amount about Antiphon himself. [Hephaestion] appropriated this too and wrote a book *On Antiphon in the* Memorabilia *of Xenophon*, making no additional discoveries of his own.

X.   Anonymous, *On Aristotle's* Nicomachean Ethics 248.21–9

Gaining an unjust advantage is not a matter of assigning too much of just anything to oneself, but of some good. For this reason those who say that such things are indifferent as far as human beings are concerned, and what is more do not grant them any value but say they are on a level with their opposites – previously Aristonymus,[6] and now certain people who claim to be Platonists but have cloaked themselves in this doctrine, of whom Atticus seems to be one – well, these declare that justice is altogether useless; for it does not distribute or rectify the goods that relate to the virtues, and to seek things like these that are completely indifferent is useless.

Y.   Alexander of Aphrodisias, reported by Simplicius, *On Aristotle's* On the Heaven 430.27–36

[Alexander of Aphrodisias] says that what [Aristotle] says is rather unclear because he did not place the division first.[7] And it seems that Alexander of Aphrodisias was himself the first to interpret the demonstration thus in terms of the division. At any rate, he gives the interpretation mentioned previously, that the slowing down must necessarily be infinite because there is nothing to restore the power of the Prime Mover and rectify its loss of power, as [being] that of Alexander of Aegae. 'And I heard Herminus', [Alexander of Aphrodisias] says, '[saying], as was also current in the

---

[5] *Peri ēthōn*; to be distinguished from the surviving work of Theophrastus, the *Characters* (*[Ēthikoi] kharaktēres*).

[6] Heylbut, the *CAG* editor, refers this to Aristonymus, the father of Cleitophon (Plato, *Republic* 328b). But there seems to be no evidence connecting him with the particular view in question. Perhaps the reference is rather to the collector of sayings (*gnōmai*), excerpts from whom appear in Stobaeus.

[7] The point at issue is the structure of Aristotle's argument in *On the Heaven* 2.6 that the speed of rotation of the heavens must be constant.

[writings] of Aspasius, that if there is a slowing down of the heavenly body, there was previously a speeding up . . . '

Z.   Galen, *On Habits* 11.4–12 Müller

Aristoteles of Mytilene, a man in the forefront of Peripatetic study, became ill but could be benefited by a cold drink; because he had never taken such a drink, he stopped those who were advising him to drink it, saying that he knew well that he would suffer a spasm if he tasted cold [water]. For he said that he had seen this in the case of someone else who had a bodily condition and temperament similar to his own and [who had] the custom of drinking warm drinks.

Aa.   Alexander of Aphrodisias, *On Aristotle's* Metaphysics 166.18–167.3

[Aristotle] himself showed that there cannot be an infinite number of causes by reasoning methodically in this way [sc. in *Metaphysics* α.2.994b27–31]. *Our Aristoteles* himself too showed this by dialectical argument.[8] Since there are causes of the things that there are, either these [causes] are several in number or there is just one. But there cannot be just one cause of the things that are and come to be, as has been shown elsewhere: for there is need of some substrate for what comes to be, and for an efficient [cause]. And it is shown that something that comes to be does so according to a form. So there is not just one cause. So there are several. But if there are several, either they are all infinite or some are or one is. But it is impossible for all or some to be infinite; for there cannot be a plurality of infinities. But neither can one say that one is infinite and the others finite; for the infinite, being everywhere, grants no admittance to anything else, either infinite or finite. Nor, even if there were just one cause, could this be infinite; for it would not be the cause of anything. For there will be no room for that of which it is the cause, since the cause is everywhere. For it is clear that, being infinite, it will be of a certain quantity in this very respect, whether it is everywhere in respect of quantity or of time. – The argument seems rather dialectical and abstract, and not appropriate in a similar way to those stated previously.

---

[8] That *epikheirōn* refers specifically to dialectical argument is noted by Dooley 1992, 56 n. 151 on this passage.

Ab.   Alexander of Aphrodisias, *On Fate* 1.164.3–15

It was my desire, great emperors Severus and Antoninus, that I might myself come into your presence and see you and speak to you, and give expression to my thanks for the benefits I have received from you on many occasions, always obtaining everything I requested, together with a testimonial that I deserved to receive such things when I asked for them. But even if we cannot sacrifice to the gods by being present at their sacred rites, [we are] commanded to sacrifice to them everywhere and from every place, and to send votive offerings which we cannot bring ourselves; [and so] I have ventured to follow in your case the example of what is allowed in the case of the divine, so as to send to you, as a votive offering, some offering of my first-fruits, the most appropriate for you of all offerings.

For what could be a more appropriate offering to those who genuinely honour and promote philosophy than a book that undertakes philosophical speculation? The book contains the opinion concerning fate and responsibility held by Aristotle, of whose philosophical teaching I am the principal exponent, having been publicly declared teacher of it by your testimonial. (Sharples 1983a, 41)

Ac.   Inscription from statue-base from Aphrodisias in Asia Minor, published in Chaniotis 2004

By a vote of the council and the people, Titus Aurelius Alexander, philosopher, [one] of the successors [to philosophical headships] at Athens, [set up this statue of] his father, Titus Aurelius Alexander, philosopher.

This chapter includes a selection of texts relevant to the identity and chronology of some Peripatetics in our period. Discussion in the present chapter is limited to details that will assist in identifying them and clarifying the biographical relationships between them; their specific contributions to philosophical discussion will be considered below in the appropriate chapters, and the reader should consult the Index of personal names for references to these.

Critolaus' visit to Rome in 155 BC along with Diogenes of Babylon (the Stoic) and Carneades (the Academic Sceptic) is recorded in **A** and provides the only fixed point for his chronology. **B** reflects Antiochus' view of Critolaus which, as explained in the Introduction, may not have been entirely disinterested. Diodorus, Critolaus' pupil, in making the goal of life freedom from pain (**B**) was reviving the view of the third-century BC

Peripatetic Hieronymus of Rhodes, though combining this with moral virtue (White 2002, 90). Staseas of Naples, born probably before 120 BC, is the first Peripatetic known to have spent considerable time at Rome (**D**: Moraux 1973, 217. For Staseas see also below, **18S**).

If the supplement in **E** is correct, the defection of Aristo of Alexandria and Cratippus from Antiochus' school was due to the influence of Xenarchus (on whom see also **I**, and below, **17C, 21D–I, 24K, 27A**), in which case we have evidence for Xenarchus being active relatively early in the first century, but the limitations of Aristus recorded in **F** may also have played a part.[9]

The odd reference in **G** to 'the Peripatetic' with no further details is most naturally understood as referring to 'the Peripatetic Ariston',[10] though it is unclear why the one succeeded is referred to as a Peripatetic while the successor is not. **G** has usually been interpreted (e.g. Goulet 1989–, vol. 1, p. 404, no. 399; Sharples 1996) as indicating that the Ariston in question was a successor of Ariston of Ceos, who was active in the later third/early second centuries BC. This may be thought to strain 'in our time'[11] and would mean that the Ariston referred to in **G** must be different from the one referred to in **H**, as Eudorus was active in the first century BC; Goulet 1989–, vol. 1, p. 404 indeed distinguishes the two as nos. 398 and 399 respectively. Another possibility is that the Ariston in **G** was the successor of the one referred to in **E**, but that would imply that some sort of Peripatetic institution continued to exist in the middle part of the first century BC, which seems doubtful. There is also a question whether the Ariston referred to in **H** is identical with the one referred to in **E** or indeed with the one referred to in **9G**; see Moraux 1973, 182, and also **13A**.

N is unfortunately ambiguous, for it could indicate either that Strabo (born *c.* 64 BC) was a pupil of Boethus or that they were both fellow-students of Andronicus. The latter implies a later date than the former for Boethus and so also for Andronicus his teacher. That Boethus was Andronicus' pupil is indicated by Philoponus in **5A**; but Tarán 1981, 731–4 questions how good Philoponus' information was, six centuries later. Moraux 1973, 45–58 argued for the earlier dating for Andronicus;

---

[9] See further Dillon 1996, 124 n. 2.

[10] Hahm 2006, 305 suggests that 'if ... the entry about Aristo ... was excerpted from an entirely different context ... such as a succession of Peripatetic leaders, it can reasonably be taken to refer to Critolaus, who is known to have had a student named Aristo' (see **4BC**). But it would seem careless, to say the least, on Strabo's part, if the source was a list of Peripatetics, to refer just to 'the Peripatetic' without giving Critolaus' name.

[11] Strabo was born in about 64 BC; the last of the people mentioned before 'and in our time' is Philetas, who was active in the late fourth/early third centuries BC. Nicias was tyrant of Cos in 40–31 BC.

Tarán 1981, 733 questions Moraux's arguments but himself suspends judgement on the dating. Barnes 1997, 21–3 discusses the issue and opts for the later dating, partly because of Cicero's silence about both Andronicus and Boethus.

The situation regarding Arius/Areus (I) is complex. As shown by O and by other texts with the longer spelling,[12] Are(i)us was the name of a philosophical courtier of the emperor Augustus. According to a list preserved in two MSS of Diogenes Laertius (= Posidonius T66 EK) there was a Stoic Areius at this period. Areius has commonly, since Diels, been identified with the Didymus identified by the parallel between two passages in Stobaeus (below, 15A(15) and 15B) as the author of a discussion of Peripatetic ethics preserved in the second book of Stobaeus' *Anthology*, translated below as 15A. Eusebius (*Preparation for the Gospel* 15.15.1–9, 15.20.7) attributes two reports on Stoic physics to Areius Didymus, and (11.23.3) one on Plato to Didymus. On this basis Diels attributed to 'Arius Didymus', identified as the courtier of Augustus, a considerable number of fragments on physics preserved mainly in Stobaeus' first book, with some passages from Eusebius and some that appear in both; the fragments on physics include some relating to Aristotle, although none of these are explicitly attributed either to Arius or to Didymus.[13]

The account of Peripatetic ethics in Stobaeus' second book is the third of three accounts of ethics preserved there consecutively; a general ethical doxography arranged by topics, an account of Stoic ethics and the account of Peripatetic ethics, commonly labelled 'Doxography A', 'B' and 'C' respectively. It is, however, questionable whether the second and third are by the same author as the first; at any rate all three cannot be parts of a single *work*, because, as Göransson 1995, 222 points out, following Giusta 1964–7, 140–7, that would involve presenting overlapping material twice in two different arrangements. Kenny 1978, 21–2 observes that Doxography A explicitly quotes the *Nicomachean Ethics* in a way that Doxography C does not do and suggests that inconsistencies between the two are to be explained by the first being the work of Stobaeus himself.[14] Moreover, Göransson 1995, 203–27 has called into question Diels' identification of

---

[12] Listed at Moraux 1973, 261 n. 17.

[13] Their number is increased by Mansfeld and Runia's argument (1996–, 249–54) that Diels attributed some material in Stobaeus to Aëtius (see the Preface above) when its similarities are rather with the material he assigned to Arius Didymus. See the commentary on 12B.

[14] Dillon 1996, 116 (from the first, 1977 edition), followed by Trapp 2007, 34 n. 16, attributes Doxography A to the Platonist Eudorus; in the Afterword to the 1996 edition, 437–8, Dillon is more cautious, though still endorsing this view. At 1996, 124 n. 1 Dillon argues that Doxography C was taken by Arius from Ariston the former pupil of Antiochus (C above).

Areius Didymus with Augustus' courtier. The *Suda* (Δ 871, vol. II, p. 80.30–1 Adler) refers to an 'Ateius Didymus' or 'Attius Didymus' who was an Academic; the collection of the views of a number of schools is more characteristic of Academics, who can use them in sceptical debate, than of Stoics, though typically, as Mansfeld 1988 and 1990 shows, to be useful in such debate the material would be arranged by topics rather than by schools.

Nicolaus of Damascus, the author of the compendium of Aristotle's esoteric works which survives only in fragments of a Syriac version itself further abridged, was probably the associate of Herod the Great and Augustus born in 64 BC (**P**), though the existence of numerous writers of the same name (**Q**) may cause some hesitation, and Fazzo: 2005, 288–9 n. 52, and 2008 has argued that the compendium may have been by a considerably later author of the same name. Nicolaus is commonly said to have been responsible for the *discovery* of Theophrastus' short discussion to which the same name has been given, but **R** actually shows no more than that he knew of it.

T places Aspasius in the first half of the second century AD. **V**, from Porphyry, shows that Adrastus wrote a commentary on Plato's *Timaeus*, and the fact that the same content as in **V** appears shortly after **U** at Theon of Smyrna, *Exposition of Mathematics Useful for Reading Plato* 50.22–51.4, shows that the work by Adrastus on which Theon there drew was this commentary – which is significant in indicating the context of the astronomical material in **21** below.[15] Theon's *Exposition* was earlier than Ptolemy's *Syntaxis* (AD 147), so **U** indicates a date in the first half of the century for Adrastus. The anonymous commentator on *Nicomachean Ethics* 2–5, who seems to have drawn on the work of Adrastus reported in **W**, may have written in the latter part of the second century AD, in the light of the reference in **X** to the Platonist Atticus, active at that time, as a contemporary (see Moraux 1984, 323–30; Mercken: 1990, 419–29).

Sosigenes[16] and Herminus[17] taught Alexander of Aphrodisias, as Aristoteles of Mytilene may also have done (**Aa**; see Accattino 1985, Moraux: 1985, and also below on **27K**).[18] Alexander was appointed to the

---

[15] See Moraux 1984, 294 and 296.   [16] See **8G**, **13F(2)G(1)**, **21KL**, **26D**.   [17] See **Y**, **21J**.

[18] Schroeder and Todd 2008, 680 argue that we cannot be certain that 'our Aristotle' in **Aa** is Aristoteles of Mytilene. There are in fact two issues here. First, if 'our' means 'in our time', then either the Aristoteles in question is Aristoteles of Mytilene or another Aristoteles has to be found; Occam's Razor may come into play here. Second, does **Aa** indicate that the Aristoteles in question was a *teacher* of Alexander? Not explicitly, to be sure. (Schroeder and Todd 1990, 27 argue that it is odd, if Aristoteles was a teacher, that Alexander does not refer to him as often as he does to Herminus and Sosigenes. But much of Alexander's work is only known to us in fragmentary form at second-hand.) However, whether the Aristoteles in question was a teacher of Alexander, or rather a colleague and fellow-student, may be of little importance *except* for the interpretation of **27K**.

post of teacher of Aristotelianism in Athens between AD 198 and 209 (**Ab, Ac**).[19] Although we do not know at what stage in Alexander's career this happened, it suggests that Sosigenes, Herminus and Aristoteles of Mytilene, as Alexander's teachers, are to be dated rather later in the second century than Aspasius and Adrastus.

---

[19] Geta joined Septimius Severus and Caracalla in governing the Empire with the status of 'Augustus' in 209; cf. Todd 1976a, 1 n. 3. On Alexander's date see also Sharples 2005.

CHAPTER 2

The rediscovery of Aristotle's works?

A. Strabo, *Geography* 13.1.54

(1) From Scepsis came the Socratic [philosophers] Erastus and Coriscus[1] and Coriscus' son Neleus, a man who was a pupil of both Aristotle and Theophrastus, and who inherited the library of Theophrastus, which included also that of Aristotle. Aristotle had bequeathed his own [library] to Theophrastus, to whom he also left the school; [Aristotle] was the first known person to collect books, and he taught the kings in Egypt how to arrange a library. (2) Theophrastus left [the collection] to Neleus;[2] he took it to Scepsis and bequeathed it to his descendants, lay-people, who kept the books closed away and not carefully stored. When they became aware of the eagerness of the Attalid kings, to whom the city was subject, in searching for books to furnish the library in Pergamum, they hid the books underground in a trench. Damaged by damp and bookworms, the books of Aristotle and of Theophrastus were eventually sold by the family for a large sum of money to Apellicon of Teos. Apellicon was a bibliophile rather than a philosopher; consequently, when he wanted to put right [the gaps due to] the worm holes and transferred the text to new copies, filling in [the gaps], he did not [do so] well and published the books full of errors.

(3) The early Peripatetics, after Theophrastus, did not possess the books at all, apart from a few, chiefly those published [by Aristotle himself], and the consequence was that they were not able to engage in philosophy in a serious way, but declaimed general theses.[3] Their successors, after those books emerged, [were able] to be better philosophers and Aristotelians, but most of what they said was necessarily conjectural because of the abundance of errors [in the texts].

---

[1] Actually pupils of Plato in the Academy; 'Socratic' is here used as a general term including Platonists.
[2] This is confirmed by Theophrastus' will, recorded at Diogenes Laertius 5.52.
[3] Or, as Hahm 2007, 98 translates, 'were unable to philosophize in a systematic [or substantive] way, but merely prattled on about philosophical propositions'. See the commentary.

(4) Rome too made a great contribution here. For immediately after Apellicon's death Sulla, who captured Athens, carried off Apellicon's library, and when it was brought here the scholar Tyrannio, by cultivating[4] the person in charge of the library, took it in hand, being an enthusiast for Aristotle, [as did][5] also certain booksellers who used poor scribes and did not compare [the copies with the originals], as happens also with other books copied for sale, both here [in Rome] and in Alexandria. Well, that is enough on these matters.

B. Plutarch, *Life of Sulla* 26.1–2

Putting to sea from Ephesus with all his ships, on the third day [Sulla] anchored his fleet in the Piraeus. After being initiated into the Mysteries he took for himself the library of Apellicon of Teos, which included most of the books of Aristotle and Theophrastus, which were not yet then well known to the majority of people. It is said that when [the library] was taken to Rome the scholar Tyrannio did most of the arranging,[6] and that Andronicus of Rhodes obtained copies from him, made them public, and compiled the catalogues that are now current. The earlier Peripatetics were clearly accomplished scholars in their own right, but they did not have either extensive or accurate acquaintance with the writings of Aristotle and Theophrastus, because the property of Neleus of Scepsis, to whom Theophrastus had left the books, was inherited by lay-people who were indifferent about them.

C. Athenaeus, *The Sophists at Dinner* 5.53.214de (Posidonius, fr. 253 EK)

[The tyrant Athenion] did not only seize the property of citizens, but also that of foreigners, laying his hands also on the treasury of the god in Delos. He sent to the island Apellicon of Teos, an Athenian citizen who was a complicated character and had lived a fickle sort of life. At one time he engaged in Peripatetic philosophy and purchased the library of Aristotle and many other [libraries], for he was very rich, and he stole from the temple of Cybele and kept the original copies of ancient decrees, and anything ancient

---

[4] I adopt the nice translation of Gottschalk 1987, 1084.

[5] Strabo's grammatically incomplete sentence is understood in this way by Moraux. Barnes 1997, 19 n. 89 objects that the booksellers did not 'take the library in hand' or 'manage' it, but the looseness of expression, if what is meant is that they published it, may be tolerable. Barnes, however, speculates that part of the text may have dropped out, including a reference to Andronicus.

[6] *enskeuasasthai*, which can imply getting ready or preparing for a purpose. Barnes 1997, 19 interprets its use here as implying preparing for publication.

that had been stored away in other cities too. When this was detected in
Athens he would have been convicted if he had not gone into exile. Not
long afterwards he came back, having conciliated many people. And he
supported Athenion, as belonging to the same sect as him.

D.   Athenaeus *The Sophists at Dinner* 1.4.3ab

[Larensis], [Athenaeus] says,[7] possessed so many ancient Greek books
that he surpassed all those who have been admired for their collecting,
Polycrates of Samos and Pisistratus the tyrant of Athens and Euclides, also
an Athenian, and Nicocrates of Cyprus, and the kings of Pergamum, and
Euripides the poet, and Aristotle the philosopher <and Theophrastus>,[8] and
Neleus who preserved their books; from him, he says, our king Ptolemy,
surnamed Philadelphus, purchased them all and conveyed them to beautiful
Alexandria along with [the books] from Athens and those from Rhodes.

E.   Aulus Gellius, *Attic Nights* 20.5.7–10 (Aristotle, fr. 662 Rose 1886)

When the king Alexander learned that Aristotle had made the books of the
'esoteric' type available to the general public, at the time when he was
holding almost the whole of Asia which was stirred up by warfare[9] and
was pressing hard on king Darius himself by victorious battles, although he
was occupied by such great concerns he sent a letter to Aristotle saying that
he had acted wrongly in making the esoteric studies, in which [Alexander]
himself had been trained by [Aristotle], generally available in published
books: 'For in what other matter shall I be able to surpass others,' he said, 'if
the things which I have learned from you are shared by absolutely everyone?
For I would prefer to excel in learning rather than in armed forces and
wealth.' Aristotle wrote back to him in the following sense: 'Be assured that
the esoteric books, which you complain have been published and not
concealed like secrets, have neither been published nor not published; for
they will be intelligible only to those who have heard me.' I have added
below copies of both letters, taken from a book by the philosopher
Andronicus.

---

[7] Added by the author of the summary which is all that survives of this part of Athenaeus' work.
[8] Added by Adam.
[9] Reading *exercitam* with the Loeb edition (J. C. Rolfe, London: Heinemann and New York: G. P. Putnam's Sons, 1928) for the *exercitum* of the MSS.

F.   Porphyry, *Life of Plotinus* 24

Since [Plotinus] himself entrusted me with making an arrangement and correction of his books, and I both promised this to him while he was still alive and announced to his other companions that I would do it, first I thought it right not to leave the books in the confused chronological order in which they were published. [In this] I have imitated Apollodorus of Athens and Andronicus the Peripatetic: the first collected [the writings of] Epicharmus the comic poet, putting them in ten volumes, and the second divided [the writings of] Aristotle and Theophrastus into treatises, bringing related subjects together.

G.   Dexippus, *On Aristotle's* Categories 21.19–20

First, 'the account of the being' is not present in all the copies, as both Boethus and Andronicus mention.

H.   Cicero, *On Ends* 5.12

(1) The books [of the Peripatetics] about the supreme good are of two kinds, one written to appeal to the public, which they call exoteric, and the other more accurate, which they have left in notebooks. For this reason they do not always seem consistent; but on the doctrine as a whole there is no difference or disagreement, at least among those I have named. (2) But when the question concerns the happy life and the one thing which philosophy should consider and pursue, whether [the happy life] is entirely in the power of the wise person or whether it can be weakened or taken away by hostile circumstances, in this there sometimes seems to be disagreement and doubt among them. This is chiefly the result of Theophrastus' [= 498 FHS&G] book *On the Happy Life*, in which quite a large part is assigned to fortune; if this were so, wisdom [alone] could not guarantee a happy life. This way of thinking seems to me more self-indulgent, if I may say so, and feeble than the power and importance of virtue requires. (3) Let us therefore keep to Aristotle and his son Nicomachus [as our authorities]; [Nicomachus'] carefully written books on ethics are said to be by Aristotle, but I do not see why the son could not have been like the father.

I.   Aspasius, *On Aristotle's* Ethics 151.21–5 (on '*Nicomachean Ethics* 7' = *Eudemian Ethics* 6.1153b9–14)

In the *Nicomachean [Ethics]*, where Aristotle has dealt with pleasure too, he clearly said that it was not the same as happiness but accompanied it, 'as beauty does those in the prime of life'. A sign that this [present text] is not by Aristotle but by Eudemus [i.e. part of the *Eudemian Ethics*] is that in the <…>[10] [Aristotle] speaks about pleasure as if he had not already discussed it.

The story in **AB** (partly supported by **C**) and that in **D** are incompatible in so far as the former suggest that the entire library of Aristotle and Theophrastus was removed from Athens by Neleus, whereas the latter – perhaps attempting to conflate two inconsistent traditions, as Gottschalk 1987, 105 suggests – implies that books remained at Athens and also at Rhodes (the latter presumably in the school of Eudemus). Fortunately, what is important for the history of Aristotelianism is not which of these stories is true, but whether **AB** are right in attributing the decline of the Peripatetic school to Aristotle's esoteric works' not being available; and that they *were* unavailable only follows if the copies inherited by Neleus were the only ones in existence. Eudemus produced a rearranged version of Aristotle's *Physics* (see e.g. Sharples 2002c) and – according to Simplicius, *On Aristotle's* Physics 923.10 (Theophrastus 157 FHS&G) – corresponded with Theophrastus about readings in the text; it seems a reasonable assumption not only that he produced his own version for the purposes of teaching in his school in his native Rhodes, but also that he did so there, and that he had a written text of Aristotle's own *Physics* to refer to. And in this case there were at least two copies of Aristotle's *Physics* in existence soon after Aristotle's own death. Moreover, Strato, who was head of the Lyceum after Theophrastus, from 287 to 269 BC, bequeathed to *his* successor Lyco 'all the books, except those which we have written ourselves' (Diogenes Laertius 5.62), which shows that the Lyceum still had a library. The letters between Alexander the Great and Aristotle referred to in **E** were undoubtedly spurious, like so many letters attributed to famous people in antiquity; but Andronicus cannot, as Barnes 1997, 63 points out, simultaneously have quoted the letters and also have claimed to be publishing the esoteric works for the first time. **E** also, as Barnes 2002, 294 and n. 3 notes, shows that the belief already existed before Andronicus that Aristotle wrote in a deliberately obscure manner, a commonplace later (cf., e.g., Simplicius, *On Aristotle's* Categories 7.6–12; *On Aristotle's* Physics 8.18–20 – quoting the same exchange of letters as **E**, 8.20–9). For Apellicon, referred to in **ABC**, see also 1C; on the reports in **ABCD** see also Moraux 1973, 3–44 and Tarán 1981, 724–31.

---

[10] Barnes 1999, 20 rightly notes that the missing reference must be to what *we* know as *Nicomachean Ethics* 10. But to insert that number here and so imply that *Aspasius* knew it by that description would prejudge the issue of whether Aspasius regarded the *Nicomachean Ethics* as a ten-book whole. See the discussion below.

The assertion in **A**(3) that lack of Aristotelian texts limited the ability of the Hellenistic Peripatetics to engage in philosophy is highly significant. Gottschalk 1987, 1088 noted that it 'would be more appropriate in the mouth of a grammarian than a philosopher' and suggested that it derived from Tyrannio (for whom see **B**). It may rather be characteristic of the new tendency to see philosophy as the interpretation of canonical texts, on which see the Introduction above, and also **4H**. Hahm 2007, 98–101 goes further and sees it as a tendentious dismissal of the philosophical debating between schools that characterised Hellenistic philosophy. If one stops to think about it, the way in which Strabo (not himself a philosopher) *excludes discussion from real philosophising* verges on the outrageous.

A second issue concerns the extent and nature of Andronicus' contribution. It is commonly said (a) that he produced a definitive edition of the esoteric Aristotelian texts, (b), on the strength of **F**, that he constructed at least some of the treatises we have, and notably the *Metaphysics*, by putting together what had previously been separate texts, and (c) that he established the canon of Aristotelian works.[11] Against (a) Barnes 1997, 28–31 has pointed out that later ancient scholars, when they discuss variant readings in the text of Aristotle, never appeal to Andronicus' edition as an authority, and that neither **A** nor **B** says anything against the supposition that Andronicus' text was a lineal descendant of the allegedly inferior text of Apellicon, improved purely on the basis of conjecture. **G** might seem to be a counter-example to the point about variant readings, but Barnes 1997, 30 explains that Dexippus is paraphrasing the larger of Porphyry's two commentaries on the *Categories*, not now extant (only the shorter one survives), and that it is clear from **6A** that what Porphyry said was that *because* Boethus and Andronicus omitted 'of the being', *therefore* some MSS must have omitted the words. Dexippus has turned Porphyry's inference that MSS must have been compared into an assertion.

Comment (b) rests on nothing more than the supposition that someone must have assembled the treatises and that Andronicus is the most likely candidate. The chief evidence for the *Metaphysics'* not being in the form intended by Aristotle is, however, the presence of Δ and K, the former breaking up the natural sequence of BΓE and the latter duplicating material present also in E; if the presence of Δ in its current position and of K are the

---

[11] The list of titles in a life of Aristotle extant only in Arabic and attributed to Ptolemy 'al-ġarīb', 'Ptolemy the Unknown' (Düring 1957, 224–6, 241–6; see Moraux 1951, 289–309; Plezia 1985, especially 9–10; Barnes 1997, 25–6) is thought to derive ultimately from Andronicus.

result of Andronicus' editorial activity,[12] that activity was not of a very high quality. (See also Menn 1995.) Barnes 1997, 39–40 argues that Porphyry in **F** cites Andronicus only for the principle of ordering by subject matter rather than chronologically, and not for the combination of separate works into single ones, which in any case is not what Porphyry himself did with the works of Plotinus. Moreover (Barnes 1997, 60–1) Eudemus already in the fourth century BC used the *Physics* as we have it as the model for his own treatise. As for (c), Barnes 1997, 31–9 notes that Andronicus notoriously differed from subsequent ancient and modern scholars on one issue, the authenticity of *On Interpretation* (11ABCD), and that his rejection of the latter part of the *Categories* (below, 7B) did not lead to its permanent exclusion, even though many since have shared his doubts.

As Barnes 1997, 58–9 points out, **H**(3) is evidence for the existence of two ethical treatises apparently before Andronicus, a *Nicomachean Ethics* (perhaps without its present books 5–7, apparently transferred later from the *Eudemian Ethics*; see below) and, perhaps, the *Magna Moralia* (since there is no reference to Eudemus; and for the influence of the *Magna Moralia* see below on 15A); **H**(1) suggests that by 45 BC Cicero was aware of the contrast between Aristotle's exoteric and esoteric works, but, as Barnes 1997, 48–50 observes, this does not necessarily mean that he had read the latter as well as the former. See also 4I(2) below, which refers to the obscurity of one of the esoteric works – if we accept that it was indeed Aristotle's *Topics* which Cicero had in his library; see the commentary there – but also to 'sweetness of style', which must surely relate to the exoteric works. On **H**(2) see below, commentary on 18.

Kenny 1978, 29–36 argued that what we know as the 'common books' (*Nicomachean Ethics* 5–7 = *Eudemian Ethics* 4–6) originally belonged to the latter and were commented on by Aspasius, to fill a lacuna in the former; Aspasius thus, he suggested, started the trend of treating the 'common books' as part of the *Nicomachean Ethics*, though, as **I** shows, Aspasius did not himself so regard them. See also Barnes 1999, 19–21.

On the issues considered in this section see Barnes 1997; also Gottschalk 1987, 1083–97.

---

[12] Even if he did not originate these features of the arrangement, his perpetuation of them perhaps suggests an undue deference to tradition. *Metaphysics* Λ seems to be an originally independent work but may have been put in its present position to occupy the place of a book which Aristotle did not live long enough to complete (so Donini 1995, 140–1). That parts of *Metaphysics* MN repeat parts of Λ suggests that Aristotle did not intend all three to be part of the same work in their present form; but their incorporation could, again, have occurred soon after Aristotle's death, or even be due to Aristotle himself, if he intended to remove the duplications but did not live to do so.

CHAPTER 3

A Hellenistic account of Aristotle's philosophy

A.   Diogenes Laertius, *Lives and Opinions of Eminent Philosophers* 5.28–34

(1) This is how many books [Aristotle] wrote. In them his views are these: philosophy is twofold, practical and theoretical. To the practical belong the ethical [part] and the political, in which both what concerns the city and what concerns the household are outlined. To the theoretical, physics and logic, of which logic is developed not independently, but as an instrument [*organon*]. He clearly proposed that it has two goals, what is persuasive and what is true. (2) He used two capacities for each of these, dialectic and rhetoric for what is persuasive, analytic and philosophy for what is true; he omits nothing which leads to discovery, to judgement or to utility. (3) With a view to discovery[1] he handed down [to us, in] the *Topics* and the *Methodics*,[2] a multiplicity of premises, from which one may have an abundance of persuasive arguments for [solving] problems. For judgement [he handed down] the *Prior* and *Posterior Analytics*. By the *Prior* the premises are judged, by the *Posterior* their combination is examined. For utility there are the [works] on contests and those concerned with questioning and sophistical refutations and syllogisms and things similar to these. (4) As criterion of truth, in the case of things that actually appear he declared it to be sense perception, but in the case of ethics and things concerning the city, the household and the laws, intellect.[3]

---

[1] That is, discovery in the rhetorical sense of finding points to make, Cicero's *inventio*.

[2] It is not known to what work this refers, but the same title appears at Simplicius, *On Aristotle's Categories* 65.5 (Sorabji 2004, vol. III 3(c)(1)), coupled with the (pseudo-Aristotelian) *Divisions*. Moraux 1951, 66–8 and 1986, 271 n. 75 argued that it was identical with the *Topics*, but that it should be so here where both works are mentioned implies that Diogenes or his source is confused. Cf. Mejer 1992, 3574; Bodéüs 1995, 576 and n. 108; Barnes 1997, 55; Chase 2003, 147 n. 726. On the *Topics* see below.

[3] Cf. below, **14DEFGH**. It is odd that *only* practical matters are mentioned under the criterion of intellect; Barnes 2007a, 554 suggests that they are chosen only as an illustration.

(5) He set forth one [ethical] end, the employment of virtue in a complete life. (6) He said that happiness was a completion made up of three [types of] goods:[4] those concerning the soul, which indeed he calls first in power; secondly those concerning the body, health and strength and beauty and the like; thirdly external [goods], wealth and good family and reputation and things like these. (7) Virtue is not sufficient for happiness; for there is also need of bodily and external goods, since the wise man will be unhappy in pains, poverty, and the like. But wickedness is sufficient for unhappiness, even if it possesses external and bodily goods to the greatest extent possible. (8) He said that the virtues do not imply one another;[5] for it is possible for someone to be wise, and similarly just, but also profligate and lacking in self-control.[6] (9) He said that the wise man is not free from passions [*apathēs*][7] but moderate in passions [*metriopathēs*].[8] (10) He defined friendship as an equality in reciprocal goodwill; of it one [type] is for relations, another erotic and another for strangers. Love is not only for intercourse but also for philosophy. The wise man will fall in love and engage in politics, marry and be the courtier of a king. There are three ways of life, the theoretical, the practical and that devoted to pleasure, and of these he preferred the theoretical. Ordinary studies are useful for the attainment of virtue.[9]

(11) In natural [philosophy] he explained more than anyone else, so that he gave explanations even of the smallest things. And for this reason he wrote not a small number of books of notes on nature. (12) He declared god to be incorporeal,[10] as did Plato. [God's] providence extends as far as the heavenly [bodies],[11] and he himself is unmoved; things on earth are governed by their sympathy with [the heavenly bodies]. (13) Besides the four elements there is another, a fifth, of which the heavenly things are composed. Its movement is of a different sort, for it is circular. (14) The soul is incorporeal, being the first actuality of a natural and instrumental [*organikon*] body potentially possessing life. (15) By 'actuality' he means what has some incorporeal form. This is twofold according to him. One is potential, as the [figure of] Hermes is in the wax which possesses a suitability to receive the shape, and the statue is in the bronze; but the actuality of the completed Hermes or statue is said to be 'in disposition'. [He said] 'of a natural body', since of bodies some are fashioned by hand, like those made by craftsmen, for example a tower or a boat; some by nature, like plants and the [bodies] of

---

[4] Cf. **18H1(1)JK** and contrast **15A(11)(15)**, **18I(2)U**.
[5] On the contrary, *complete* virtues do imply one another: *Nicomachean Ethics* 6.13.1144b32–1145a2.
[6] And so to lack the virtue of temperance.   [7] The Stoic view.   [8] Cf. **15** below.
[9] Contrary to the view of Epicurus: LS 25E–G.
[10] Contrary to the views of the Stoics and Epicureans.   [11] Cf. **22** below.

animals. He said 'instrumental', that is constructed with a view to some end, as sight in order to see and hearing in order to hear. 'Potentially possessing life', as in itself. (16) The potential is twofold, that according to the disposition and that in actuality. In actuality, in the way in which the person who is awake is said to possess soul; according to the disposition, as the one who is asleep. So that the latter too should fall under [the definition], he added 'potentially'.

He declared much else about many things, which it would be a long business to enumerate . . .

This summary of Aristotle's doctrines in Diogenes Laertius' book 5 seems to go back at least in part to the Hellenistic period,[12] and in particular shows affinities with the thought of Critolaus. (See below, **18** and **22** – though, as Hahm 2007, 51 notes, Diogenes Laertius nowhere shows any awareness of Critolaus.) Diogenes' summary is in the order logic–ethics–physics, which was the standard arrangement for Aristotle's works in later antiquity and may have been that adopted by Andronicus.[13] The division of philosophy with which Diogenes introduces the summary is not, however, entirely consistent either internally or in relation to the order of the summary that follows.[14] Moraux 1986, 283 is scathing about Diogenes' account: 'The author piles one absurdity on top of another. It is clear that he is speaking of what is completely unfamiliar to him, and that he has understood nothing in it . . . this fabric of follies . . .'[15] Bodéüs 1995, however, argues that Diogenes' account is not *simply* confused, but rather shows the result of forcing a systematising agenda derived from Stoicism on to the Aristotelian material.

Diogenes' *Organon* – a term he explicitly applies to logic – is the *Topics* and *Analytics*. As noted by Bodéüs 1995, 576, Diogenes' source distinguishes between the two *Analytics* with no actual knowledge of the contents of either. For individual premises are in fact dealt with not in the *Prior Analytics* but in *On Interpretation*; the **Prior Analytics** are concerned with the combination of premises into arguments, and the *Posterior* with demonstrative arguments specifically. Diogenes' source seems not to be aware of either *Categories* or *On Interpretation* as parts of the *Organon*.

In keeping with the relative neglect of ontology by Aristotle's Hellenistic successors, and in sharp contrast with the emphasis in Andronicus and his

---

[12] Cf. Moraux 1986, 268 and 289; Mejer 1992, 3574–6; Sollenberger 1992, 3859.
[13] Cf. Düring 1957, 242 and 244.   [14] Mejer 1992, 3574, cf. Sollenberger 1992, 3857.
[15] Cf. Mejer 1992, 3575; Sollenberger 1992, 3859.

successors (below, **12**) Diogenes' summary contains just enough ontology to give a shaky interpretation of the meaning of the definition of soul in *On the Soul* (see below on **24**), and no more. There is no mention of the doctrine of the categories at all, and the term 'substance', *ousia*, does not appear – in fact it appears *nowhere* in Diogenes' book 5 on the Peripatetics.

In (14) the definition of the soul at Aristotle, *On the Soul* 2.1.412a27–b1 is accurately quoted. Moraux (above) is scathingly critical of the interpretation that follows, but in fact, even if some of the details could be more clearly expressed, the basic doctrine is grasped well enough. What is said in (15) and (16) about potentiality and actuality is confusingly expressed: Aristotle in fact distinguishes three stages, potentiality, first actuality and second actuality, the first being like the child who has not yet learned geometry but can do so, the second like the person who has learned geometry but may not actually be engaged in it at any given time, and the third like the person actually doing geometry at the moment. Soul is an example of the second, Diogenes' 'disposition' (*hexis*, cf. Aristotle, *On the Soul* 2.5.417a32) and not the third, for the reason made clear at the end of (16); a sleeping person may not be *exercising* all soul functions, but is still alive. In the case of a statue (unlike a knife, say, which may not be cutting at the moment) the distinction between first and second actuality does not arise; in the third sentence of (15) Diogenes confuses the distinction between first and second actuality with the more general distinction between potentiality and actuality. The definition of 'instrumental' at the end of (15) is to be contrasted with Alexander's later, influential and arguably incorrect interpretation of the term as 'furnished with organs',[16] 'as in itself' scarcely explains 'potentially possessing life', but the correct explanation follows in (16); the soul is the form that produces *first* actuality, which, in relation to the second actuality of actually performing the functions of life, is itself only potential.

---

[16] Cf. Bos 2001, 191; 2003, 85 n. 75 and 87; 2007, 42; Sharples 2008a, 146.

CHAPTER 4

Philosophy and rhetoric

A.   Sextus Empiricus, *Against the Professors* (*Adversus mathematicos*) 2.12 (Critolaus, fr. 32 Wehrli 1969b)

So just as I would not say that there is an art of burglary which instructs one that this is how one should burgle, or of thieving [which instructs one] that this is how it is appropriate to thieve and snatch purses (for these things are false, and neither appropriate nor scientific principles), just so one should not suppose that rhetoric exists as an art, tossed about on precepts like these. At any rate the followers[1] of Critolaus the Peripatetic, and much earlier those of Plato, with this in mind abused [rhetoric] for being established as a false art rather than an art.

B.   Quintilian, *Education of the Orator* 2.15.19–20, 23 ((2) = Critolaus, fr. 26 Wehrli 1969b)

(1) But those who did not regard everything as the orator's subject matter introduced more careful and lengthy distinctions, as was necessary; among them was Ariston, the pupil of Critolaus the Peripatetic, whose conclusion is 'the knowledge of how to identify and carry out persuasion of the public through speeches in civil disputes.' Being a Peripatetic he does not, like the Stoics, regard this knowledge as a virtue; by including persuasion of the public he is actually rather disparaging of the art of oratory, which he does not think will persuade learned people at all ... (2) Some people have thought that [rhetoric] is neither a power nor a science nor an art, but Critolaus [thought it] experience in speaking (for this is what *tribē* means), Athenaeus an art of deception.

C.   Sextus Empiricus, *Against the Professors* 2.61

And Ariston the associate of Critolaus says that the goal of [rhetoric] is persuasion, its end achieving persuasion.

---

[1] As often, the Greek *hoi peri* may simply be a way of referring to the named person himself.

D.   Cicero, *On the Orator* 1.43

The Peripatetics would prove that even these very things which you think are the orators' own resources and embellishments of speech must be got from themselves, and would show that Aristotle and Theophrastus (667 FHS&G) wrote not only better about these things than all the teachers of speaking, but also much more.

E.   Cicero, *On the Orator* 3.80

If there should ever be anyone who, in Aristotle's fashion, could speak in support of both sides concerning all things, and on every issue by knowledge of [Aristotle's] rules could set out two opposed speeches, or in the manner of Arcesilaus and Carneades could argue against anything that was proposed, and to this principle and practice could add the experience and manner of speaking of an orator, he would be the true, the complete, the only orator.

F.   Cicero, *Tusculan Disputations* 2.9

Therefore I always favoured the custom of the Peripatetics and the Academy, of discussing on opposite sides concerning all matters, not only because in no other way could it be discovered what was plausible in every matter, but also because this provided the most exercise in speaking. Aristotle was the first to practise this, and then his followers. But within my own memory Philo,[2] whom I frequently heard, made it his custom to pass on the precepts of the rhetoricians at one time, those of the philosophers at another.

G.   Cicero, *On Ends* 5.10

[Aristotle and Theophrastus] handed down rules for arguing not only in discussion but also in speeches, and Aristotle first established the exercise of arguing for each side concerning particular matters, so that he should not always speak against everything, like Arcesilaus, but should set forth in all matters what could be said from both sides.

H.   Alexander of Aphrodisias, *On Aristotle's* Topics 27.8–18

Either by 'exercise' [Aristotle] means that which takes place in discussion: for, being given certain problematic propositions by those debating with

---

[2] Philo of Larisa (159/8–84/3 BC), the Academic.

them, people are exercised in trying to defend these, constructing their arguments on the basis of accepted premises [*endoxa*]. Or by 'exercise' he may mean arguing for both sides. For this kind of argument was customary among the early [philosophers], and they conducted most of their meetings in this way, not with reference to books as now – for books of this sort did not yet then exist – but, when a thesis had been proposed, they exercised on this their ability to find arguments, arguing through accepted premises for and against what had been proposed. There are books of this sort written by Aristotle and Theophrastus (135 FHS&G) which contain argument for opposite sides through accepted premises.

I.   Cicero, *Topics* 1–3, 5

(1) When I had started to write on more important matters, and ones that were more deserving of these books of which I have published quite a number in a short time, your wish, Gaius Trebatius, has called me back from the path on which I had already set out. For when you were with me in my villa at Tusculum, and in the library each of us was separately unrolling the books he wanted for his own studies, you chanced upon some *Topics* by Aristotle, which he had set out in several books. Excited by this title, you immediately asked me about the subject of those books. When I explained to you that those books contained a method invented by Aristotle of finding arguments, so that we could arrive at them in a rational way without error, you requested me to pass these things on to you – politely, as always, but in such a way that I could easily see that you were fired with enthusiasm. (2) When I urged you – not so much in order to avoid the work myself but because I thought this was to your advantage – either to read the books for yourself or to get the whole principle from a certain learned orator, you tried both, as I heard from you. But you were driven away from the books [themselves] by their obscurity, and that great orator replied, as I think, that he did not know these Aristotelian [teachings]. I was not at all surprised that a philosopher who is unknown to all but a few of the philosophers themselves should not be known to an orator; [the philosophers] are less deserving of pardon than he, since they ought to have been attracted not only by the things which were said and discovered by [Aristotle], but also by the unbelievable facility and sweetness of his style . . . (3) When I departed from you on my way to Greece,[3] since neither the state nor my friends

---

[3] The date is 44 BC, after the assassination of Julius Caesar. Cicero planned to leave Italy and join the Republican leaders in Greece. In the event he changed his mind and returned to Rome.

were making use of my efforts and I could not honourably become involved in armed conflict, even if it had been possible for me to do so safely, I arrived at Velia and saw your property and your people. I was reminded of this debt and was not willing to fail to meet your demand, even if it was not expressed. So, since I did not have my books with me, I have written what follows from memory during the voyage itself and sent it to you while I was on my way, so that by my carefulness in carrying out your commands I might stir you to be mindful of my affairs, even if you do not need reminding.

Peripatetics of the second and early first centuries BC continued the debate concerning the relative merits of philosophy and rhetoric which can be traced back to Plato and Isocrates. In criticising rhetoric, Critolaus' pupil Ariston (**B**(1), cf. **C**) was following his teacher (**AB**(2)); true, Ariston allowed that rhetoric involved knowledge (**B**(1)) whereas Critolaus saw it as simply a matter of experience (**B**(2); Plato's *Gorgias* 463b, where the same contrast is drawn and the same term *tribē* is used, is in the background here), but Ariston clearly still regarded it as inferior to philosophy; cf. **D**. See further on this issue Reinhardt 2003, 42 and Hahm 2007, 54–61.

    Cicero attributes to Aristotle and his followers the practice of arguing for both sides of a question, and regards it as the best training for an orator (**EFG**) – reasonably enough: a good debater will anticipate an opponent's arguments, and an advocate such as Cicero may in any given case speak either for the prosecution or for the defence. That Aristotle and Theophrastus argued in this fashion is attested by Alexander in **H**,[4] and the collections of 'Theses' attributed to them both (Aristotle: Diogenes Laertius 5.24, Hesychius' list of titles 65–9 (Düring 1957, 85), Ptolemaeus' list of titles 64–7 (Düring 1957, 227); Theophrastus: 68 nos. 34–6 FHS&G) are to be connected with the practice. What is less clear, however, is how far the practice was continued by the Peripatetics of the second and first centuries BC. Long 1995, 52–6 argues that Cicero's view reflects not so much the attitudes or practices of contemporary Peripatetics as those of the Academic tradition and in particular Cicero's teacher Philo of Larisa. Hahm 2007, 91–3 uses Cicero's evidence to argue for a culture of argument (as opposed to commentary) in philosophy in the second century BC, a

---

[4] The most obvious way to take the passage is that Alexander is drawing a contrast between debates on theses conducted without reference to books and those conducted with reference to books, and that the 'early philosophers' are those even earlier than Aristotle. (So Fortenbaugh 2005, 187.) The books in question are presumably written models, rather than records of extempore speeches made after the event. (I am grateful to Bill Fortenbaugh for further correspondence on this issue.)

culture in which he argues the Peripatetics participated, but he does not disagree concerning the role of Philo. As Hahm notes, sceptical Academics would argue on both sides of a question in order to create uncertainty, but Peripatetics would argue in order to defend their own views; arguing on both sides of a question would thus be – as it was for both Aristotle and Cicero – a means to an end, the improving of one's ability to argue for one side rather than the other.

Cicero's *Topics* has long been a mystery, for Cicero in **I**(1) alludes to what seems to have been the Aristotelian work – unless we suppose that Cicero was mistaken about this – but his own treatise, of which this is the introduction, bears little relation to Aristotle's. (Cf. Huby 1989; Barnes 1997, 54–7; Reinhardt 2003, 177–80.) Reinhardt 2003, 9–17, 49–50 suggests that a theory of topics for use in rhetoric was revived and developed by Peripatetics after Critolaus but was taken over by Cicero's *Academic* teacher Philo of Larisa and came to Cicero through Philo; it will be this theory that Cicero draws on in his own *Topics*, and the reference to Aristotle's work is not intended to suggest that Cicero thinks he is setting out Aristotle's own views.

CHAPTER 5

The starting-point and parts of philosophy

A.   Philoponus, *On Aristotle's* Categories 5.15–20

Next is the third heading, where in Aristotle's writings one should start. Well, Boethus of Sidon says that one should start from the treatment of physics, since this is more familiar and knowable for us, and one should start from the things that are more clear and knowable. But his teacher, Andronicus of Rhodes, examining [the issue] more exactly, said that one should first begin with logic, which is concerned with demonstration.

B.   Elias, *On Aristotle's* Categories 117.17–25

Let us investigate three things, where to start on Aristotle's writings, where to end, and the route between. We make this investigation not only because of the number of [the writings] but also because of the disagreement among the ancients; for some said that one should begin with physics, some with logic, others with ethics, others from mathematics. Boethus of Sidon says with physics; Andronicus of Rhodes, the eleventh of the successive heads of the Aristotelian school,[1] said with logic, and of the Platonists some with ethics, others with mathematics.

C.   Elias, *On Aristotle's* Categories 118.9–31

(1) Those who said that one should begin with physics said that natural things are easier, as being grasped by us as familiar from childhood onwards, for example flesh, veins and sinews,[2] and that doctors at the start of their treatment begin with the milder drugs, [and] that Aristotle

---

[1] Cf. **11A**. That Andronicus was in any formal sense the head of Aristotle's school as a continuing institution is uncertain, and the exact number of successors down to his time even more so.
[2] The connection of physics with *living* things is noteworthy – and properly Aristotelian; living things are after all the prime examples of sublunary substances.

40

seems to have a high reputation most of all in his treatments of nature. That is what they say.

(2) Those who say that one should begin with mathematics say that one should read this first because of the confidence of the demonstrations (for this we learn in the strict sense of the term, on other [subjects] we make conjectures rather than 'learning'), and that by this we are taught how one should learn, by geometrical necessities, not contenting ourselves with the credibility of authorities, and because Plato wrote on the front of his school 'Let no one enter who has not studied geometry.'

(3) Those who said that one should begin with logic said that logic is an instrument [*organon*], and that one should first know the instrument and then, on this basis, where the instrument should be used. For that is how it is in the case of the crafts; the trainee carpenter first learns the tools [*organa*], for example the auger and the gimlet, and then on this basis begins on the [craft] of carpentry itself.

(4) Well, that is what these [said]. But let me say in truth where one should start. One should start from ethics, because of those who say one should start from ethics; for we have nothing keener than this. But since we do not learn ethics from habit, like the beasts that are driven by a blow,[3] one should begin from logic, not thus neglecting ethics, but in some way or other ordering ourselves with written or unwritten precepts, for example those of Isocrates, so that reason may find ready for it what has been firmly established in it . . .

D. Seneca, *Letters on Morals* 89.9–10

Most authorities and the greatest say that there are three parts of philosophy; moral, natural and logical. The first calms the mind;[4] the second investigates the nature of things; the third examines the properties of words and their structure and arguments, so that falsity may not substitute itself for truth. However, there are some who divide philosophy into fewer parts, and some who divide it into more. Some of the Peripatetics have added a fourth, political part, since it requires consideration of its own and is concerned with a different subject; some have added to these a part which they call 'household management',[5] the knowledge of how to administer

---

[3] Alluding to Heraclitus, fr. 11.

[4] A distinctively Hellenistic approach to ethics or moral philosophy; but see further below.

[5] The literal meaning of *oikonomikē*. Cf. the first book of the treatise *Oeconomica* attributed to Aristotle, and below, 15A(45)–(46).

one's own property; some have also separated the topic of ways of life. But all of these will be found included in the moral part.

E.   Pseudo-Plutarch, *Summary on the Opinions of the Philosophers concerning Nature* 874D–875A = Aëtius 1, prologue (*Dox.* 273a6–274a15)

(1) Intending to give an account of nature we regard it as necessary right at the start to make a division of the activity of philosophy, so that we may see what it is, and what fraction of it the description of nature [constitutes].

(2) Well, the Stoics said [LS 26A] that wisdom is the understanding of things divine and human, and philosophy [= love of wisdom] the practice of an appropriate art; the single and supreme appropriate art is excellence, and the most generic excellences are three, in nature, in character, in reasoning. For this reason philosophy is divided into three parts, natural, ethical and logical. Natural [philosophy] is when we enquire about the world and the things in the world, ethical is that which is occupied with human life, logical is that concerned with reason, which they also call dialectical.

(3) Aristotle and Theophrastus [= 479 FHS&G] and almost all the Peripatetics divided philosophy as follows: it is necessary for a man who is complete both to speculate about the things that there are and to do what ought [to be done]. This can be seen also from what follows: for example, there is an enquiry whether the sun is alive or not, since it moves.[6] The person who enquires into this is speculating; for nothing is an object of speculation more than what is. Similarly, there is an enquiry whether the world is infinite and whether there is anything outside the world. All these things are matters of speculation.[7] Again, there is an enquiry how it is appropriate to live and to be in charge of children and to rule and to make laws; all these things are enquired into with a view to action, and a person like this is a practical man.

The ordering of the parts of philosophy was much discussed by the Stoics (cf. LS 26). Andronicus' view, that one should start with logic, is the one that has been most influential. Tarán 1981, 743 suggested that Boethus' starting with physics reflects his rejection of form as substance (below, 12F) and what is presented by Platonist witnesses as his conceptualist doctrine of universals (12R). To argue that he was influenced by metaphysical

---

[6] I translate Diels' conjecture for the "since it is seen" of the MSS.
[7] In the sense of theoretical contemplation (*theōrētika*); there is no implication of guesswork.

considerations rather than by those actually indicated in **A** would perhaps be artificial; but one may detect a common tendency. Drossaart-Lulofs 1965, 22 notes that Philoponus' report of Boethus in **A** refers to what is 'more familiar and knowable [not: more knowable] for us', and that in Nicolaus of Damascus (F3 Drossaart-Lulofs) a similar combination of a comparative adjective followed by a positive 'more clear and known' occurs, while the passage of Aristotle on which both are ultimately drawing (*Physics* 1.1.184a16–18) has two comparatives and asks whether this is just coincidence.

In **C**(1) Aristotle's biology is, rightly, taken as typifying his enquiry into nature; physics is not concerned only, or even primarily, with the inanimate.

D shows that Seneca was aware of Peripatetics for whom politics was a distinct branch of philosophy. Their date is unclear. Certainly Aristotle's own treatise on *Politics*, concerned as it is with the classical Greek city-state, is of doubtful relevance to Hellenistic and Roman conditions, and it does not seem to have been of interest to any of the commentators. See further below, on **15A**(47)–(52).

E, which derives from Aëtius writing in about AD 100, distinguishes between (2) the standard Stoic tripartition of philosophy into physics, ethics and logic and (3) the Peripatetic bipartition into physics and ethics only, logic for the Peripatetic tradition being an instrument (*organon*) of philosophy rather than a part (cf. **C**(3) and **3A**(1). See further Mansfeld and Runia 1996–, vol. II, part 1, 67, and for the two topics of whether the heavenly bodies are alive and whether there is anything outside the world see below, **21J** and **21I** respectively.

CHAPTER 6

Commentaries

A. Simplicius, *On Aristotle's* Categories 29.28–30.5

Responding to this difficulty [sc. that 'account of the being/substance' at Aristotle, *Categories* 1a2 implies that homonymy occurs only in the category of substance, an implication for which Aristotle had been criticised by Nicostratus] Porphyry first says that ['of the being'] was not in all the copies. For Boethus did not know [this reading], [for] he says that Aristotle shows what [things] are homonymous by saying 'those are said homonymously which have only the name the same, but the account[1] that corresponds to the name is different'. Boethus, *who interprets each expression*, [thus] left out 'of the being' as not written [in his text]. And Andronicus, *who paraphrases the book*, says 'of things which are said without combination those are called homonymous of which only the name is the same, while the account corresponding to the name is different'. (Sharples 2007a, 511)

In spite of Simplicius' contrast, it is clear that Andronicus too engaged in critical discussion as well as paraphrase; see Moraux 1973, 98, and below, **9C**, **12D**. Simplicius' contrast, in its context, is rather concerned with how closely each commentator followed the details of Aristotle's precise wording, in the context of drawing inferences from their versions about the text of Aristotle that they read. On the particular omission mentioned here see below, discussion of **8A**.

---

[1] Here our texts of Aristotle have 'account of the being/substance (*ousia*) that corresponds to the name'.

Logic and ontology

CHAPTER 7

The Categories: *(i) Placement and title*

A.   Simplicius, *On Aristotle's* Categories 15.27–16.4

(1) But it is worth enquiring into the reason for the title, first, how many titles there are, and which of them is more to be approved. For some gave the book the title *Preliminary to the Topics*, others *On the Kinds of Being*, others *On the Ten Kinds*, others *Ten Categories*, others *Categories*, as is still now the current [title]. (2) Those who gave the title *Preliminary to the Topics* and put the book here in sequence [acted] strangely; for it is preliminary not only to topics, but in logic to the whole consideration of syllogisms and demonstration and to that of premisses, to which they give the title *On Interpretation*, and in the consideration of beings the teaching of the simple ones leads the way in all philosophy, since it teaches [us] about the most fundamental elements. (3) It was not just anyone who placed the *Topics* immediately after the *Categories*, but Adrastus of Aphrodisias, one of the genuine Peripatetics, in his *On the Order of Aristotle's Philosophy* wants the *Topics* to be placed after the *Categories* in order, what persuasive reason is there for the judgement of [this] distinguished man?[1]

B.   Simplicius, *On Aristotle's* Categories 379.6–10

But we must enquire in general concerning [the 'post-predicamenta', chapters 10–15 in modern editions of the *Categories*], first why these are added at the end of the *Categories*, and what use they have. Some, among them Andronicus, say that they were added contrary to the purpose of the book by whoever gave the book *Categories* the title *Preliminary to the Topics*.

---

[1] Adrastus' view is attributed to pseudo-Archytas (see below on **8IJ**) by Elias, *In Cat.* 132.26, but apparently as the result of a confusion (Szlezák 1972, 93–4).

47

C.   Boethius, *On Aristotle's* Categories, *PL* LXIV.263B[2]

(1) Many have asked why, after dealing with all the categories, [Aristotle] entered on this discussion of opposites [in the 'post-predicamenta'], contrary to the purpose of the book. Andronicus thinks that this is not an addition by Aristotle, and at the same time judges that this addition about opposites, about things that are simultaneous, about what is prior, about motion and about the ambiguity of 'having' was added by the person who entitled this book *Preliminary to the Topics*, because he thought these things necessary for that work in the same way as the *Categories* themselves help with understanding the *Topics*; for he was not aware that enough for the arguments is set out in the *Topics* [themselves], both concerning all these things which are added, and concerning the categories. Thus Andronicus.

The *Categories* clearly was, and remains, a puzzle. It has come to be placed at the start of the *Organon* because its discussion of simple terms can be treated as the start of a sequence (as Simplicius shows in **A**(2); and see above on section 2) rather than because it is explicitly formulated in such a way as to belong there. Adrastus in **A**(3) was writing in the second century AD; but **BC** show that the treatment of the *Categories* as preliminary to the *Topics* specifically was already known to Andronicus. It may well be that, due to emphasis on rhetorical argument, the *Topics* was more familiar to late Hellenistic writers, at least by name if not by content, than the *Analytics*. On discussion of 'topics' after Aristotle see van Ophuijsen 1994, and, on the mystery of Cicero's *Topics* and what he knew or understood of Aristotle's (above, **4I**), Huby 1989, and Barnes 1997, 54–7. On the question why there was such interest in the *Categories* in the first century BC see Sharples 2008b, suggesting that it may have attracted attention because it did not fit neatly into the framework of Hellenistic philosophy; however, in arguing thus I may have fallen into the trap of viewing the *Categories* from the perspective of later Peripatetic philosophy (see **12** below) and not taking sufficient account of the fact that much of the early debate about it was concerned with such issues as the nature of relatives, which was a topic of interest to the Stoics (below, **9**. I owe this point to Riccardo Chiaradonna).

---

[2] Text established by Shiel 1957, and reproduced in Moraux 1973, 100 n. 12; the text in *PL* is defective.

CHAPTER 8

The Categories: *(ii) Words or things?*

A.

Andronicus' paraphrase of the opening of the *Categories* as reconstructed by Moraux 1973, 102–3 from Simplicius, *On Aristotle's* Categories 21.22–4, 26.18–19, 30.3–5 (= **6A**) and Dexippus, *On Aristotle's* Categories 21.18–19; what is underlined here is addition, what is not is as in the text of Aristotle (except that the text of Aristotle has 'in common' rather than 'the same', and 'the account *of the being*'; on the latter point see the discussion below).

Of [things] that are said some are said without combination, others with combination.[1] **Of those that do not involve combination,** those are said homonymously which have only the name the same, but the account that corresponds to the name is different. (Sharples 2008b, 280)

B. Simplicius, *On Aristotle's* Categories 18.16–21

Adrastus, in his *On the Ordering of Aristotle's Writings,* records that another book on categories too is in circulation as Aristotle's; it too is short and concise in expression and differs by only a few distinctions; its beginning is, 'One (class) of the things that are . . .' He records the same number of lines in each, so that he said 'short in expression' (meaning) that the arguments of each are set out concisely. (Sharples 2008b, 281)

C. Ammonius, *On Aristotle's* Categories 13.20–25

One should be aware that in the ancient libraries there were found forty [*sic*!] books of *Analytics* and two of *Categories*; [of the latter] one had the beginning 'Of the things that are, some are spoken of homonymously,

---

[1] The former being simple terms, and/or what they refer to; the latter being sentences and/or the states of affairs which they report. Cf. Aristotle, *Metaphysics* E.4.1017b17–25.

others synonymously'; the second is the one that we now have before us. [The latter] has been preferred as having the advantage in order and content, and everywhere proclaiming Aristotle as its author. (Sharples 2008b, 281)

D.   Porphyry, *On Aristotle's* Categories 59.10–27

The followers[2] of Athenodorus and Cornutus, giving priority to the questions about verbal expressions as such, for example the proper [uses] and the metaphorical [uses] – for these are distinctions among verbal expressions as such – and being perplexed as to which category they belong to, said that the classification was incomplete, as not every meaningful verbal expression was included in it.

– So did everyone go wrong about the purpose of recognising the categories?

– No; Boethus in his *On the* Categories, and Herminus, stated this briefly.

– Tell me what Herminus said, since you say it was stated briefly.

– Well, Herminus says that the purpose is not concerned with the first and most general genera of natural things, for it would not be appropriate to teach the young these, nor what are the first and fundamental differences in things that are said, so that the account would appear to be about the parts of speech, but rather about the category of things said that would be appropriate to each kind of the things that are. And for this reason it was necessary to deal in some way at least with the genera, to which the things that are predicated are referred. For it is not possible for the proper meaning of each thing to be known if there is not already a conception of it.

E.   Simplicius, *On Aristotle's* Categories 18.26–19.8

Indeed some oppose [Aristotle], rejecting the division [into the categories], some as pointlessly excessive, others as leaving out many things, for example Cornutus and Athenodorus, who, thinking that the aim is concerned with verbal expressions as such, put forward many of these, some literal, some metaphorical, and think that they are refuting the division on the grounds that it does not include every verbal expression. They also think that a division is being made of names into the homonyms and synonyms and paronyms, and they suppose that the book is a heaping up of observations of

---

[2] See above, 4 n. 1.

all kinds about logic and physics and ethics and metaphysics; for the considerations about homonyms and synonyms and paronyms are logical, as also is that about opposites, but those concerned with movement are physical, those about virtue and vice ethical, and the philosophising about the ten kinds is metaphysical. But this is not true; [Aristotle] is not making a division of names, for he would not [then] have left out heteronyms and polyonyms.[3]

F. Simplicius, *On Aristotle's* Categories 11.23–9

Porphyry also adds the [remarks] of Boethus, which are very shrewd and have the same import as what has been said. For he too says that the division into noun and verb is of the parts of speech, but the division according to the categories is according to the relation of verbal expressions to the things that there are, since they indicate these. 'And for this reason,' he says, 'conjunctions are found in speech, but not among the categories; for they do not indicate any of the things that there are, neither substance nor quality nor anything else like this.'

G. Sosigenes, reported by Dexippus, *On Aristotle's* Categories 6.27–9.14

(1) – Well, that the categories were so named from predication [*kategoreuesthai*], which is being said of some subject, you have shown both well and briefly ... but since it appears perplexing to me what it is that is said, whether it is an utterance or a thing or a thought, try to show this to me clearly.

(2) – I must first answer your question concisely; primarily it is thoughts that are indicated, but incidentally things as well. But since there is a great deal of enquiry about the things that are said, I too want to say more about them. Indeed Sosigenes the Peripatetic set out arguments in parallel about

---

[3] In Aristotle's usage, synonyms are things which share a common definition and are called by the same name (so that human beings and oxen are animals synonymously). Homonyms are cases where the same word is used but the definition is different (the leg of a table is only homonymously a leg, as it cannot be used for walking, and the flesh of a corpse is only homonymously flesh). Paronyms are things that take their name from something else with a change in the form of the word (e.g. 'grammarian' and 'grammar'). Not in Aristotle in this context, but in terminology introduced by Plato's nephew Speusippus (below, **K**), polyonyms are cases where different words apply to something with the same definition – confusingly, what modern usage calls synonyms, such as 'column' and 'pillar'; see the commentary below; and heteronyms are cases where both the definition and the word are different (as for example 'house' and 'dog').

the things that are said, and he did not make a decisive declaration [in favour of] one of them but left the arguments in an equal fight. I want to consider what he says and finally to introduce my own opinion.

(3) Arguing [the case for] things and wanting these to be what are said [Sosigenes] employs reasoning like the following: if things in some way determine speaking and not speaking,[4] and if they do not exist we say nothing[5] but if they do we make a positive statement, it will be things that are said. (4) In reply to this I would say that nothing prevents things being the causes of speaking [truly or falsely], but these are not *proximately* the things that are said, and this is what we are looking for. For example, being in the sun is a cause of fever, and pricking with a needle is a cause of pain, but the needle is not in the pain or being in the sun in the fever. Of causes some are separate, others are present; so things can be the causes of speaking [truly or falsely], but they are not the very things that are said. For we speak also about things that are not present and about things that are past and things that are future, but when the statement that is about them exists, the things would have to exist too. If the things do not exist along with the statement, they will not be what is said. Indeed it is possible to speak of things that do not exist, such as centaurs and goat-stags, and those who are mad and out of their minds speak words, so that if what is said were the things, they too would be speaking about things, and we would not name anything which did not exist.

(5) Moreover [Sosigenes] says that if the statement is true or false as a result of the things, it could not be that what is said is different from what produces falsity and truth, so that these will be what is said, the causes of the complete statement. (6) But I am surprised that Sosigenes, using this argument, did not realise that if every statement is true or false, he would have seemed to be right in constructing his argument that it is the things that are said; but if there is some statement that is neither true nor false,[6] and it is possible to speak without application to any subject, how is it possible to rely on this argument? Next, it is one thing to speak about a thing and to produce a true or false statement *about* it, but now we are enquiring what it is that is *said*. In addition to this, grant that the thing is the cause of the statement [being] true or false; it will not on account of this follow of necessity that it is the things that are indicated. For it is not the case that, because the statement admits of [being] true or false, for this reason it has become true or false on account of the

---

[4] I.e. saying something and not saying something. See the next note.
[5] 'Saying nothing' is Greek idiom for speaking falsely. The argument is that the truth or falsity of what we say depends on the things (facts, states of affairs) to which we refer.
[6] I.e., as the immediate sequel shows, statements about non-existents; 'all centaurs are brown'.

things; for being true or false attaches to it *per accidens*, but indicating a particular thing in a primary way is essential [to it].

(7) But, [Sosigenes] says, even after the things have been said, for example horse or ox or stone, it is clear that it is these that are indicated. For [otherwise] they would not exist when the utterance ceased. (8) Well, I would say the opposite, that on this basis it is not the things that are said, nor does the statement relate to these primarily. For the statement that spoke about them is now past, but the things remain. If it were the things that were indicated, they should not exist when the statement had become past. But as it is, the one who speaks and the one who listens exist, it may be, but the things, about which the statement is, do not exist. And yet if what acts must exist at the time when what is acted on is acted on, it is necessary that what is said should exist at the time when what hears hears. But if the one who speaks and the one who hears exist, but the things do not, in cases where the statement is about what is past, how is it possible for it to be the things that are indicated? (9) Well, concerning [the case for] the things [being what is said], this is how we have determined [the matter]; but if someone says that it is speech that is said (for many people can hear it, and it can exist and be spoken whether the things exist or not), we will say that it is different for something to be indicated through [speech] and for [speech] itself to be indicated by something. If we suppose that 'saying' is uttering with one's voice, it will be speech that is said, for it is uttered through the voice; but if naming is not saying the name, but [saying] something else through the name, [saying] will not be saying the statement, but something else through the statement, so that now we are asking what it is that is indicated by the statement, not what it is that we utter through the voice.

(10) But, [Sosigenes] says, just as walking is the activity of the walker and writing of the writer, so speaking [is the activity] of the speaker, and the speaker goes through statements and parts of speech, and these will be what are said. (11) But I would say that the activity and what the activity produces are different; the building [i.e. the house that is built] is not the same as the activity of the builder, or the painting [i.e. the work of art] the same as the activity of the painter, but the products are different. So speaking, which is the product of the activity[7] of the speaker, is different from what is indicated by the product.

(12) Again, [Sosigenes] says that 'speaking' [*lexis*] is derived from 'to speak' [*legein*] and 'statement' [*logos*], so that in this way too it will result that speech is what is said. (13) Well, from this very point one might refute

---

[7] I follow Dillon 1990, 28 n. 14 in taking 'product of the activity' to be the meaning of *energēma* as opposed to *energeia* 'activity'.

what is now being sought for; for if 'to speak' is derived from 'statement', we would not 'speak statements', if we do not 'walk [the act of] walking' or 'live healthily health', or 'act actions' or 'make makings'.

H.   Simplicius, *On Aristotle's* Categories 13.11–18

So it is clear from what has been said that the aim [of the *Categories*] belongs to the logical treatment of simple, primary and generic expressions as being indicative of the things that are, but certainly it also teaches about the things and the thoughts that are indicated by these, in that things are indicated by expressions. This is the opinion of the Alexanders[8] and Herminus and Boethus and Porphyry, and the divine Iamblichus casts his vote for it and Syrianus makes it clear and my own teachers accept it.

I.   Pseudo-Archytas, *On Universal* Logos *or the Ten* Categories 22.8–21 Thesleff

(1) I will attempt to write about universal *logos* . . . which man uses in interpreting [*hermēneus*] things [*pragmata*] and recognising accurately the things that there are. I say that *logos* is what is composed of thought and speech; thought is what is signified, speech what signifies . . . what are signified are, universally [speaking], ten, and what signify are equal in number to these. (2) I say that what are signified are substance, quality, quantity, what is relatively disposed [*pros ti pōs ekhon*]; also acting, being acted on, having, being situated, where, when. Substance is, for example, man, horse, fire, water and in short all things which subsist [*huphistasthai*] *per se*. Quality, white, black, good [*spoudaios*], bad [*phaulos*] and in short all that exists along with something. Quantity . . . a mina, a talent, two cubits, three cubits, and in short all that signifies concerning number and . . . measure. Relatively disposed, for example double, half, greater, smaller, and in short all that are said in relation to one another and are of a nature not to be named without one another.

J.   Pseudo-Archytas, *On Universal* Logos *or the Ten* Categories 31.30–32.23 Thesleff

(1) The system of universal *logos*, what the things are that exist along with it and how many they are and how they are related to one another by

---

[8] I.e. Alexander of Aegae (above, 1SY; cf. Simplicius, *On Aristotle's* Categories 10.19–20) and Alexander of Aphrodisias.

combination and division, has been shown. From this it is clear, that man is the rule [*kanōn*] and weighing-instrument [*stathmē*] of real knowledge, and has come to be with a view to observing the complete truth of the things that there are. (2) For [otherwise] he would never possess, as naturally cognate with the *logos* of the whole, counting, through which he interprets and indicates divine and human things [*pragmata*], those that have come to be, those that are coming to be, and those that will come to be. For everything is considered either in these or through these or not without these. For *logos* is either about substance or about the things that exist along with it, and either about body or about the incorporeal, and, of the incorporeals, either that [which consists] in quality or in magnitude, and so on.

(3) All knowledge begins from its own elements, which are finite, but comes to know an infinity [of things]. So <great>[9] a power does it possess, if it has knowledge even through a few things. But the knowledge of the things that there are is much greater. For the things that are and have come to be and will come to be are infinite, and it knows these. And this it does reasonably. For man has been constituted with a view to these two things, being and being nobly. For being he has espoused craft, of which the hands are the master craftsmen, while for being nobly he has acquired in addition knowledge and *logos*. (4) All craft and knowledge is ordered and definite, and this [depends] on number. The whole of number is the [number] ten.[10] Reasonably the extremities of the body have ten parts[11] and the elements of the whole of *logos* are in truth ten. [Ordinary] people possess *logos* accidentally, for they use it without knowing it, but the wise [possess it] in themselves. For, grasping what is real and considering the things that exist, they apply fitting indications to them.

K.   Porphyry, reported by Simplicius, *On Aristotle's* Categories 36.25–31

But where the concern is with a plurality of expressions and the varied names for each thing, as in the *Poetics* and the third book of the *Rhetoric*, we need 'synonym' in the other [sense], which Speusippus called 'polyonym'. Boethus is wrong when he says that Aristotle has left out what are called synonyms by the more recent [philosophers], what Speusippus called polyonyms; for they have not been left out but are taken up in other treatises, where the account was appropriate.

---

[9] Suppl. Szlezák.
[10] Standard Pythagorean doctrine: see, for example, KRS 279. 10 = 1 + 2 + 3+ 4, and thus includes the basic harmonic ratios of the octave (1:2), fourth (3:4) and fifth (2:3).
[11] I.e. the ten fingers and the ten toes (Szlezák).

It was much disputed in antiquity whether the *Categories* is about words, things (**BC**), or words in terms of the things they signify (**DFH**); on the issue and its later history see Sorabji 2004, vol. III 3(b). Athenodorus and Cornutus, referred to in **DE**, were Stoics; taking the *Categories* to be concerned with words, in the spirit of the linguistic analysis which was a marked feature of Stoicism, they found its treatment wanting. Boethus in **F** counters their position. Sosigenes as reported in **G** suspended judgement; as reported by Dexippus, his discussion is concerned, not directly with the subject matter of the treatise *Categories*, but with the more general question what it is that we say when we speak, utterances or the thoughts that we express or the things to which we refer. For Peripatetic discussion of the relation between speech, thoughts and things see below, **11**, on Aristotle's *On Interpretation*; Dexippus' report of Sosigenes could have been included there (and is included with the material there by Sorabji 2004, vol. III 7(a)), but as it is included in a commentary on the *Categories* I have placed it here. Sosigenes' discussion in any case reflects a Peripatetic reaction to Stoicism. Aristotle in the first chapter of *On Interpretation* regards written words as symbols of spoken words, spoken words as symbols of thoughts (the way he expresses this point being the cause of the problems in **11ABCD**) and thoughts as likenesses of things. The Stoics, however, distinguished, precisely as 'things that can be said' (*lekta*), what words *mean*, as opposed to the words themselves on the one hand (which differ from language to language) and the things that they refer to on the other (LS 33); a person who does not know the language will hear the words but will not know what they refer to, or can at best only guess, in the absence of an indication by gesture, to which of the things in the vicinity they refer. (The apparently apocryphal story that the Russian word for a large railway station derives from the Czar's envoys arriving at Vauxhall in south London, and mistaking the name of the particular station for a word for the general type, may spring to mind.) Compare, after our period, Ammonius in LS 33N arguing that Stoic *lekta* are an unnecessary addition to Aristotle's theory in *On Interpretation*.

The opening of the *Categories* is notoriously abrupt. Andronicus in **A** expanded it to make the relevance clearer. What, if anything, **A** implies for Andronicus' view on the question whether Aristotle is here concerned with words or things is not immediately clear, for 'saying' may apply to words, to what is said or indicated by using the words, or indeed to both if we suppose that there is a correspondence between them. Where **A** has 'the account', Aristotle has 'the account of the being'; Moraux 1973, 102–3 interprets the omission of 'of the being' by Andronicus and Boethus (Simplicius, *On*

Aristotle's Categories 30.1–5 = **6A** above; Dexippus, *On Aristotle's* Categories 21.19 = **2G** above) as indicating that homonymy was not to be confined to the category of substance, but Tarán 1981, 745 n. 69 suggests that we are not dealing with a deliberate doctrinally motivated omission and that the words were, as Porphyry reported in **6A**, inferred, simply missing from the text of the *Categories* to which Andronicus and Boethus had access.

We also know of one, perhaps two variant texts (**BC**) – for the wording in the two reports is slightly different; Moraux 1973, 103 – which inserted a reference to *beings* at the start, and at least the first of these was earlier than Adrastus in the middle of the second century AD. Philoponus, *On Aristotle's* Categories 7.22–8, noted by Barnes 2005, 30–1, gives the same number of books of *Analytics* and *Categories* as Ammonius in **C** but refers specifically to the library at Alexandria and explains the number by the presence of forgeries produced by those exploiting Ptolemy Philadelphus' love of books.

The treatise of pseudo-Archytas (**IJ**) is an example of the fabrication of what claimed to be early Pythagorean texts which it was supposed had influenced Plato and Aristotle; one may compare the treatise by 'Timaeus Locrus' which is in fact based on Plato's *Timaeus* but claimed to be the original work which had influenced Plato. Pseudo-Archytas sees Pythagorean significance in the fact that there are ten categories (**J**) and uses this to argue that number is the key both to reality and to our understanding of it. The reference to thought in **I**(1) may be compared with Aristotle, *On Interpretation* 1.16a4–5 (what is spoken is a symbol of affections in the soul); for links between pseudo-Archytas and *On Interpretation* see also Szlezák 1972, 142–3, and on the pseudo-Archytas work generally see Huffman 2005, 595–6, arguing for a date in the first century BC.

In **K** Boethus criticises Aristotle for discussing 'synonyms' only in his own technical sense of things which share not only the same name but also the same definition, and not also in the more recent sense – apparently attributed by him to the Stoics, referred to by Simplicius in what precedes **K** (Simplicius, *On Aristotle's* Categories 36.9), and still in use today – of two or more different words referring to the same thing. Porphyry's reply is in effect that Boethus is making the same mistake for which he rightly criticised Athenodorus and Cornutus in **F**; the Stoic distinction is appropriate to a discussion of words, not of things (see also **9E** below).

CHAPTER 9

The Categories: *(iii) Ten categories or two?*

A. Simplicius, *On Aristotle's* Categories 63.22–6

The followers[1] of Xenocrates and Andronicus seem to include everything in what is *per se* and what is relative, so that according to them so great a multitude of categories is superfluous. Others divide into substance and accident;[2] and these in a way seem to say the same as the previous people who say that accidents are relative, since they are always of other things, and that substance is *per se*.

B. Simplicius, *On Aristotle's* Categories 157.18–22

Nor must one follow Andronicus who puts those items which are in relation to something after all the other categories, on the grounds that [relation] is a *skhesis* and a side-growth [*paraphuas*]. For the *skhesis* of the items which are in relation to something, connatural as it is, takes the lead compared with the acquired *skheseis*, which is also Archytas' view. (Reinhardt 2007, 521)

C. Elias, *On Aristotle's* Categories 201.18–27

Andronicus of Rhodes assigns the last place to relatives, giving a cause like this; relatives have no matter of their own, for they are like a side-shoot which does not grow independently but is woven in with those that have their own proper root, but the nine categories have their own matter. So [relatives] ought reasonably to have the last position. Archytas of Tarentum gives them the fourth position, since substance, quality and quantity are *per se*, but relatives are relational, and what is *per se* is prior to what is relational. For first there is a man and then a father, first a number and then double number.

---

[1] See above, 4 n. 1.
[2] Cf., with Mueller 1995, 148, Dexippus, *In Cat.* 31.10–14; Hippolytus, *Haer.* 7.18.5.

D.   Simplicius, *On Aristotle's* Categories 373.7–32

The Stoics thought that 'having' [*ekhein*] should be referred to 'being in a certain state' [*pōs ekhein*].[3] Boethus opposes this, thinking that ['having'] should not be referred either to what is in a certain state or to what is relative, but is an individual category. For it does involve 'having' [*skhesis*], but having is ambiguous and is said in three principal ways. One is in itself and by itself, another is in relation to [something] else, and [the third] is that of [something] else to [the thing] itself. One is considered in itself according to what is in a certain state, as with the man who is shielding himself [from a blow], for this is a *skhesis* that he has to himself. The *skhesis* which is in relation to something else is that of things spoken of in relation to something; for 'father' and 'on the right' are spoken of not according to the relation of something to itself, but [according to] the [relation of something] to [something] else. [The third] is from [the relation] of [something] else to the thing itself, as, for example, that of the person who is armed or shod; for it is the relation of another thing to him, of the arms to the one who is armed, of the shoes to the one who is shod. 'But perhaps', Boethus says, '"having" on the one hand indicates what is equivalent to having anything at all, a part or a place, which is perhaps indicated by the expression put forward by itself, [while] the other and further [indications involve] the combination; for the field which is put forward[4] or the father or the part makes the difference.' And under this there is another meaning of 'having', that which is assigned peculiarly to 'having control over'. 'So if someone sets down the category according to the first meaning, being wise and being sensible and being healthy will be referred to this category (for being wise is having wisdom), but the category of acting and being acted on will be removed from it. And it will also be separated from relation; for the possessor will come under relation, but the possessing under having, and the father under relation, but being a father under having a son. If, however, [someone lays down the category] according to the second [meaning], the other meanings of 'having' will be referred to the other categories, and only as many as involve the control of some possession will fall under this one.' Well, let these things be recorded in addition from the noble Boethus.

---

[3] The standard Greek idiom for 'being in a certain state/condition' (and the name of the third Stoic 'category' – see the commentary) translates literally as 'having in a certain way'; 'to have well' is Greek for 'to be in a good condition'. Consequently, to be in a relation to something is literally, for the Stoics, 'to have in a certain way to something'. Thus the verbal noun *skhesis* can be translated as 'having' in the sense of 'possession', but also as 'being in a state'; and 'shielding oneself', an example of being in a certain condition, can be interpreted as being in a *relation to* oneself.

[4] As an example, by Aristotle in *Categories* 15.

E.   Simplicius, *On Aristotle's* Categories 159.9–22

Proceeding to the text, we say that it was not possible to give a definition of relatives; for it was impossible to give definitions of the primary kinds [of being, i.e. the categories] for the reasons mentioned earlier. But it was possible through a sketch to prompt a notion in us[5] which fits relatives. And [Aristotle] does this, following Plato in the first account, as Boethus says. For [Boethus] says that Plato too gave an account of relatives in this way: 'as many as are said to be what they are *of* other things'. And it looks as if Boethus has forgotten what Plato said (for I would not assert that he did not know it, being a distinguished person). For that [Plato] character-ises relatives not by their being *said* in relation to one another, but by their *being* [so], as Aristotle too thinks, he [Plato] shows both in the *Republic* [438a] by saying '"But," I said, "as many things as are such as to be themselves of certain sorts *of* something of a certain sort"', and in the *Sophist* [255d], wanting to show that the Different is relative, he says 'whatever is different, turns out necessarily to be what it is [i.e. different] *from* [something] else'.

F.   Simplicius, *On Aristotle's* Categories 163.6–9, 15–19

However Boethus, who wrote a whole book about the relative and what is relatively disposed, thinks that the definition was given by Plato as far as 'which are said to be *of* other things' [Aristotle, *Cat.* 6a36–7], but what follows ['or are in any other way relative to something else', *Cat.* 6a37] was added by Aristotle as a correction ... But Boethus also criticises the full definition, saying 'the account in this form too seems to be faulty. For the definition of what is relatively disposed should not include "what is disposed in relation to something else". For this is what was to be defined. Neither "other" nor "something else" should be included in the definition when defining what is relative; for these too are relatives.'

G.   Simplicius, *On Aristotle's* Categories 159.28–160.2

Things that are relative to one another are not single, nor would anyone say 'the [thing] that is relative to one another', but 'the things that are relative to one another'. Thus [one does not say] 'the thing that is relative' but 'the things that are relative'. Noting this, [the followers of Achaicus and Sotion]

---

[5] Literally 'our notion'.

criticise the ancient commentators on the *Categories*, Boethus and Ariston and Andronicus and Eudorus and Athenodorus, for having neither understood nor indicated [this], but having used the terms in a confused way and sometimes speaking of 'the relative' in the singular, whereas Aristotle always does so in the plural.

H. Simplicius, *On Aristotle's* Categories 187.24–188.7

But others say that the distinction involved in such a statement [of two relative terms][6] is absurd. For the wing and the steering-oar and the head, however they are stated [as relatives], ought not to be. For they do not belong among relatives at all, since each of them is a part of a substance and [itself] a substance,[7] and no substance is a relative, as Aristotle himself too thinks.[8] So, whether one follows Athenodorus' view of the relative according to Aristotle, [that it is] the case in which the appellation requires that in relation to which it is said (for the person who hears 'slave' wants [to know] whose), or whether as Cornutus says those things are relative which immediately involve a relation to something else, not grammatically, as in the case of possessors and what is possessed, but in respect of their subsisting, when [a thing] in its very being involves a reference to something else – in neither way is the steering-oar or the wing relative. For they neither require something in relation to which they are said, nor are they spoken of by a relation to something else involving their subsistence. For the steering-oar and the head and the wing are substance. One should consider not just the grammatical notion and that involving an ellipse,[9] but also that of [a thing's] constitution. For it is in this way that the part, too, is related to the whole of which it is a part, in the very [fact] of its being a part. And Boethus rightly allowed that hand and head are relatives insofar as they are parts, but not in that [the hand] is a hand, and [not] that which *is* a hand and that which *is* a head; in this respect [he said] they are substances. So let their relativity be considered as that of parts to wholes, and nothing impossible results.

---

[6] Aristotle's argument at *Categories* 7.7b2–9 that 'wing' should be stated as correlative not to 'bird' but to 'winged'.

[7] Aristotle, *Categories* 7.8b17.

[8] Fleet 2002, 167 n. 154 cites *Categories* 7.8b22. That is, however, the end of an aporetic discussion starting at 8a14; and neither at the beginning nor at the end of this is it clear that Aristotle actually endorses this view; in 8b21–2 he says that *if* heads and hands are not relatives *then* it is true that no substance is a relative. See the discussion below.

[9] As 'slave' involves an unspoken reference to some master.

I.   Simplicius, *On Aristotle's* Categories 167.20–26

But as for the consequence, it is not the case that, as the Stoics say, the relative follows the relatively disposed, but the relatively disposed does not follow the relative, nor that, as Boethus says in their defence, 'the relatively disposed follows along with the relative, for along with being disposed in a certain way in relation to something else, these also possesses their own proper difference. But the relative does not follow the relatively disposed; for not all relatives are spoken of in relation to something else in virtue of their relationship and their having their own proper difference.'

Aristotle in the *Categories* distinguishes ten categories (substance, quantity, quality, relation, where, when (see 10 below), position, 'having' – often called in English 'state' or 'condition', but see the footnote on **D** above– acting and being acted upon), though elsewhere he gives shorter lists. Platonists however favoured a simpler distinction between what is *per se* and what is relative to something else, based ultimately on *Sophist* 255C. Eudorus noted the absence of this distinction from the *Categories*: Simplicius, *On Aristotle's* Categories 174.14; Szlezák 1972, 130. The Stoics had distinguished four 'kinds', commonly referred to by modern scholars as the Stoic 'categories' but in fact not so called in any ancient text; these were (i) being (the most general, applying to everything corporeal just as such), (ii) the qualified (applying to items such as Socrates, this oak-tree and so on, which are for the Stoics body with a certain quality – see further **12** below), (iii) being in a certain condition (see the footnote to **D** above) and (iv) being in a certain condition in relation to something. See LS 27–9, especially 27F and LS's commentary thereon.

  Andronicus in **A** is reported, along with the Old Academic Xenocrates, as adopting the two fold distinction, which raises the question how he distributed the ten Aristotelian categories among the Platonic two. Moraux 1973, 103, followed by Gottschalk 1987, 1105, held that Andronicus distinguished substance on the one hand from all the other categories on the other, thus regarding all the others as relative rather than *per se*, like the 'previous people' mentioned in the second part of **A**. Tarán (1981) 741, however, argued that Andronicus was distinguishing the relative in the *narrow* sense of that term from the other nine categories, all therefore regarded as *per se*, and that he was influenced by the Stoics in this. **BC** seem on the face of it to argue for Tarán's view, but Reinhardt 2007, 521–2, suggests that Andronicus in fact used both a wide notion of 'relative', in which it will include the other, non-substance categories, and a narrow sense, the latter being the one at issue in **B**.

In E Boethus compares Aristotle's account to Plato's, but is criticised by Simplicius for putting the point in terms of being *said* rather than of being. In F Boethus criticises Aristotle's account as circular, but Simplicius goes on to reply that there is no objection to including in a definition something which is only an *example* of what is being defined. In G the point is made against Andronicus, Boethus and others that relatives must always, strictly speaking, be referred to in the plural. The Ariston in G *may* be identical either with the Ariston of Alexandria who left Antiochus' school or with the contemporary of Strabo, if indeed they were different; see above on 1EGH.

Aristotle in *Categories* 7 argues that particular heads and hands, being primary substances, are not relative at all (8a20), and that 'head' and 'hand' as universal, secondary substances are relative in the sense that what they belong to enters into their definition, but not in the narrower sense that their very being consists in being related to something else in a particular way (8a26–35). Earlier in the chapter he has used 'head', along with 'steering-oar' and 'wing', as examples to make the point that correlatives need to be stated correctly; the correlative of 'wing' is 'winged', not 'bird'. Simplicius records various objections to Aristotle's discussion, including the complaint that if heads and hands are substances they cannot be relatives. Boethus in H restates in terms of a whole and its parts Aristotle's contrast between the way in which such things are and are not relatives. It is more likely, as Moraux 1973, 159 supposes, that the Stoics Athenodorus and Cornutus are among the critics to whom Simplicius refers at the start of H, than that he is simply using their accounts of what a relative is to formulate the objection; but in either case the passage is evidence for their interest in the topic of relatives generally. In I Simplicius is attacking, and Boethus is defending, the distinction drawn by the Stoics between relative qualities, such as 'sweet' and 'bitter', and relative dispositions, such as 'on the right of' and 'father of'. See LS 29C.

On the issues raised in this section see further Reinhardt 2007, 518–23.

CHAPTER 10

The Categories: *(iv) Time and place*

A.   Simplicius, *On Aristotle's* Categories 134.5–7

But perhaps, they say, Andronicus did better, making place and time categories in their own right and ranking Where and When beneath these.

B.   Simplicius, *On Aristotle's* Categories 342.21–5

One should note that Aristotle made time and place [types] of quantity and When and Where categories in their own right; but Archytas, and Andronicus following Archytas, ranked When beneath time and Where beneath place and thus established the two categories [of time and place], themselves too preserving the number of kinds as ten.

C.   Simplicius, *On Aristotle's* Categories 359.1–6

Cornutus is puzzled why, if 'where' and 'when', differing from place and time by the form of the expressions, are placed in individual categories because the point at issue is forms of expression, the following too were not added to this category [of 'where'], for example 'from Dion' and 'towards Dion' and expressions like these, which are many; for they are similar to 'from Athens' and 'towards Athens'.

D.   Simplicius, *On Aristotle's* Categories 347.6–15

Archytas and Andronicus, positing a particular individual nature of time, placed When together with this as subsisting concerning time. For [Archytas'] proposal is to take as fundamental the primary and first kinds of subsistence, concerning which the others subsist. So, since time is prior in being to When, and place to Where, reasonably he treats them as primary[1]

---

[1] Reading *prohēgoumenois*; Gaskin 2000, 207 n. 404.

kinds, leaving aside the things included in them as being secondary to them. So it has been shown, from what has been said, how Aristotle places When in a different category [from time], paying attention to the differences in meanings, and how Archytas placed When with Time, having regard to the kinship in the things [themselves].

E.   Simplicius, *On Aristotle's* Categories 347.18–348.7

(1) We must for the rest proceed to the difficulties that are commonly stated against [the category of] When, and bring forward the solutions to them. When the associates of Plotinus and of Andronicus say that yesterday and tomorrow and last year are parts of time, and for this reason think it right that they should be ranked with time, we shall say that they are not parts of time but involve a relation to time of the things that are in time, and these are two different things.

(2) 'But if yesterday', they say, 'is past time or a measure of time, it will be a composite, if "past" is one thing and time is another, and When will involve two categories, not just one.'

(3) But by the same argument we will say that if animal and rational and mortal are three different things, they will not be [one] simple [category], but three. If in this case we apply the three to what is one in kind, time and 'past', too, will amount to one thing and will not produce two categories.

(4) But perhaps 'yesterday' is not simply time that is past, and several concepts do not coincide in the same thing in this case. For 'yesterday' is given its form by the very relation alone of the thing to time.

(5) 'But if When', they say, 'is applied to what is in time, [then] if you say that this "what is in time" is some thing, for example Socrates, because Socrates existed last year, then [this] belongs to another category. If it is a time, this too [belongs to] another [category]. But if it is the combination [of the two], there will not be a single category.'

(6) Rather; the category of When does not derive its form either from the things that are in time or from time or from the combination of the two but is the bare relation of the thing to time. And for this reason we will not include in When either the parts of time or the things [that are in time], but this too will be simple like the other categories.

(7) Boethus, too, supposes that time is one thing, what shares in time or is in time is another; year and month are time, but yearly and monthly share in time, just as wisdom is in one category but what is in accordance with wisdom, namely being wise, in another, the former in Quality, the latter in Acting. In this way time, too, differs from what is according to time.

F.   Boethus(?), *On Aristotle's* Categories, in MS Laurentianus 71.32, folios 84–6, edited in Waitz 1844–6, vol. I 21.35–22.27

(1) Some have put time, like place, not under Quantity, but under Relative, because time is the measure of motion, and place contains body and is the limit of the container, and these things are in relation [*en skhesei*] and for this reason come under things that are Relative [*tois pros ti*]. (2) But we say that measure, whether you interpret it as the account applying to number or to length, is twofold, for it is considered either in itself or with reference to what is measured. In itself it is quantity, and the starting-point of all quantities, but in relation to what is measured, it will be relative. In the same way time, the measure of movement, in itself and having an extension, will be a certain quantity, but with regard to movement, relative, and there is nothing strange in its being referred to different categories according to different notions of it. (3) In the same way too concerning place: in its extension [*diastasis*] it is a surface and accordingly a quantity, but in its relation to what is contained it is no wonder if place too is referred to the [category of] Relative, like time.

(4) So the category of When is not time, and neither is it what is in time; for time is a quantity, and what is in time is a substance. Nor is it the combination of the two; for a category is simple, and it is just the bare relation of the thing to the time that gives form to the category of When, for example: being in time, which is lasting for a time. (5) Just as wisdom is one thing but what is in accordance with wisdom, namely being wise, is another, and the former is Quality, the latter belongs to Acting, just so there is a difference between time and being in time. The former is a quantity, the latter indicates the category of When. (6) For when a thing which is different from time and is not being considered as a part of time has a relation to time and for this reason is in time, like the battle of Salamis [being] in this time, then another category is produced, that of When, being different from quantity, and given its form by its being separate from time but observed in time.

(7) The differentiae of time are past, present and future; those of When, yesterday, tomorrow and today, the first having a special relation to the past, the second to the future, the third to the present, if you consider the period of a night and a day taken together. If you consider the sun's circular path, to the past corresponds last year, to the future next year, to the present this year. (8) It is also possible to take the differentiae of When in an indeterminate way; in relation to the present, 'already' and 'just now', to the past 'a long time ago', to the future 'not yet'. Time is indefinite, since it is coming-to-be continuously,

but When is definite, because what is done in it is definite. And time is not in time, but When indicates being in time.

G.   Boethus(?), *On Aristotle's* Categories, in MS Laurentianus 71.32, folios 84–6, edited in Waitz 1844–1846, vol. I 22.28–23.8

(1) 'In something' has eleven uses: as the attribute is *in* the substance, as the parts are *in* the whole, as the whole is *in* the parts, as the form is *in* the matter, and further as the genus is *in* the species and the species *in* the genus, and in addition to these the affairs of the subjects are '*in*' [= depend on] the ruler and those of the ruler '*in*' the subjects, and as being *in* a vessel or *in* place and time. (2) Well, since there are so many uses of 'in something', it is worth asking why it is only in respect of those two relations that categories have been established. We say: some of the other meanings of 'in something' complement each other, like the parts and the whole and the genera and the species and the ruler and the subjects. (3) Others cannot subsist separately, like the form [*eidos*] in the matter and the attribute in the subject, which is also the shape [form, *morphē*] of the subject; for this reason the subject is given a name with reference to it, such as 'white' and 'having increased', and [so] with the other categories that exist in substance. How then in these cases could the one thing be *in* the other in the strict sense, when they do not even exist substantially in the strict sense separated from each other, but only in the thought in which we separate the genera? (4) For this reason each of the [cases] like this was not judged worthy of a category of its own; but the things that are in time and in place were [judged worthy]. In these alone, since one [thing] contains and the other is contained, each preserving its own nature and neither becoming a part of the other or complementing the other. (5) For in these alone 'in something' becomes a definite nature subsisting in the relation; and for this reason each of them has been judged worthy of a category of its own. For the things that are in time and in place are most clearly different from time and place; that is why things which are numerically identical are at different times in a different place and time.

H.   Simplicius, *On Aristotle's* Categories 302.12–17

For this reason [sc. that the Prime Mover is unmoved, acting but not being acted on] acting is separated by [Aristotle] from being acted on, and they are not both placed in a single kind [= category]; so one should not reduce both of these to a single [kind], but distinguish two, as Aristotle too separated them. This is how both Boethus and Iamblichus objected to the problem that supposes that change should be placed, as a single genus, before both acting and being acted on.

The passages collected here relate to the treatment of time and place in relation to the categories; on their physical nature see below, **19**.

Aristotle treated Where and When as categories in their own right but included time and place within the category of Quantity. Andronicus made Time and Place into categories in their own right, including When within Time and Where within Place (**AB**). Simplicius in **B** presents Andronicus as following (pseudo-)Archytas, but this is in the belief that the treatise of Archytas was a genuine early Pythagorean work; the true relationship is certainly the reverse. In **D** Simplicius, by using the singular, speaks as if the view in question was Archytas' specifically, but Huby 1981, 403 n. 7 argues that, because they do not appear in the text of pseudo-Archytas, the arguments are probably those of Andronicus.

The Stoic Cornutus, whom we have already seen supposing that the *Categories* is concerned with words rather than the realities they signify (**8DE**), interpreted Aristotle's treating When and Where separately from time and place as turning on the form of verbal expression, and he asked why spatial expressions relating to specific individuals should not in that case be included in the category of Where (rather than in that of relation) (**C**). Chronology excludes Andronicus' having adopted his position in response to Cornutus personally, but Cornutus is often coupled with his Stoic predecessor in writing on the *Categories*, Athenodorus (cf. **8DE**), so it is possible that Andronicus was reacting to Athenodorus (second half of the first century BC), especially if we adopt the later dating for Andronicus (above, commentary on **1N**). On the other hand Athenodorus is not mentioned in **C** itself. Gottschalk 1987, 1107, following Simplicius in **D**, connects the change made by Andronicus in **AB** as reflecting an interpretation of the *Categories* as concerned with the things which words indicate rather than with the words themselves (cf. above, **8**), and this may be accepted, provided it does not imply that Aristotle himself was concerned with words rather than things. Andronicus also regarded periods of time referred to by temporal adverbs such as 'yesterday' as parts of time, placing them in his new category (**E(1)**). Boethus (**E(7)F(4)–(8)**), followed by Simplicius in **E(4)** and (6), objects that the adverbs indicate relations to time rather than parts of time, and this indeed is what constitutes the category of When. It might seem that this risks making When a species in the category of Relation, but Boethus in **G** attempts to meet the objection by explaining why When and Where are different from other examples of being 'in' something. One might object that the argument in **G** does not show why there is not a category of (being contained in a) Vessel; but the wine in a vessel is given shape by the container, in a way that Socrates does not, for Aristotle, derive his nature from the place where he is or the time when he is.

Some indeed regarded Aristotle's definitions of time as the number or measure of motion (**F**(1), **19C**; *Physics* 4.11.220a24) and place as the inner-most unmoved limit of what contains a thing (**F**(1); *Physics* 4.4.212a20) as implying that time and place themselves are relations; in **F**(2)–(3) Boethus rejects this by invoking the distinction between measure and what it measures. (**FG** and **19D** are from an anonymous text, attributed to Boethus by Huby 1981, who also reprints Waitz's Greek text.) Boethus also resisted attempts to collapse Acting and Being-affected into species of a single category of change or movement (**H**) – though Gaskin 2000, 193 n. 71 notes that this gains some support from Aristotle, *Metaphysics* Z.4.1029b25 and Λ.1.1069a22.

On the issues raised in this section see further Sorabji 2007c.

CHAPTER II

On Interpretation

A.   Ammonius, *On Aristotle's* On Interpretation 5.24–6.6

None of those who have been seriously engaged with Aristotle's writings
thought it right to raise doubts about this book being a genuine work of
the philosopher . . . except for Andronicus of Rhodes, the eleventh [head
of the school] after Aristotle, when he heard him in the prologue of this
book calling thoughts 'affections [*pathēmata*] of the soul' and adding 'as
has been said about them in the [work] *On the Soul*'. Because he did not
see where in the treatise *On the Soul* the philosopher called thoughts
affections of the soul, he thought that one of the two treatises, this one
and the one *On the Soul*, should be declared as a spurious [work] of
Aristotle, and he thought one should reject this one rather than the
one *On the Soul*. But one should note that in many places in *On the
Soul* we have imagination called by the philosopher 'intellect that can
be affected'.[1]

B.   Philoponus, *On Aristotle's* On the Soul 27.21–8

On the basis of this passage [*On the Soul* 1.1.402a9] we refute
Andronicus of Rhodes, who declared *On Interpretation* to be spurious.
For when Aristotle says there that thoughts are affections [*pathēmata*]
in the soul as has been said in *On the Soul*, Andronicus says that this is
not found anywhere in *On the Soul*, so that it is necessary to regard
either *On the Soul* or *On Interpretation* as spurious. But it is agreed that
On the Soul is by Aristotle; so *On Interpretation* [must be] spurious.
Now we say that here, by 'affections [*pathē*] proper to the soul' Aristotle
meant nothing other than thoughts, so that this was what he meant in
On Interpretation.

---

[1] See the commentary below.

C.   Philoponus, *On Aristotle's* On the Soul 45.7–13

Look, again [Aristotle] called thinking a being-affected [*pathos*] [1.1.403a5–8]! [I say] this against Andronicus of Rhodes, who regarded *On Interpretation* as spurious because there Aristotle said that thoughts were affections [*pathēmata*] of the soul as had been said in *On the Soul*, but it was clear, as Andronicus thought, that nowhere in On the Soul had [Aristotle] said that thoughts were affections. So look! Here too [Aristotle] says that 'thinking seems most like something peculiar to the soul' – like an affection [*pathos*] peculiar [to the soul], clearly.[2] So, [Aristotle] says, if the soul has any affection peculiar to it, this will be thinking.

D.   Boethius, *On Aristotle's* On Interpretation, *Second Edition*, 11.13–12.7 Meiser 1880

For Andronicus thinks that this book is not by Aristotle; Alexander truly and forcefully refutes him. Since the ancient tradition judged [Andronicus] to be precise and careful both in his judgement and in his discovery of books by Aristotle, the reason for his going wrong in his judgement of *this* book is certainly deserving of great wonder. For he tries to show that it is not Aristotle's own work on this basis, that Aristotle in the beginning of this book makes certain points about the mind's [acts of] understanding,[3] and these thoughts he calls affections [*passiones*] of the soul, and says that he has discussed these more fully in the books on the soul. And since they called sadness and joy and lust and other affections of this sort *passiones* of the soul, Andronicus says that this proves that this book is not by Aristotle, because he did not deal with this sort of affections in the books on the soul at all. But he did not understand that in the present book Aristotle used '*passiones* of the soul' not for emotions [*adfectus*] but for [acts of] understanding. To these Alexander adds many other arguments as to why this work very much appears to be Aristotle's. They include that [the things said here] agree with Aristotle's opinions [elsewhere] about statements; that the style, in its brevity and compression, is not inconsistent with Aristotle's obscurity; and that Theophrastus [72A FHS&G], as is his custom elsewhere, when he deals with things similar to those that had previously been dealt with by

---

[2] At 403a6–7 Aristotle has said that most of the ways in which the soul is affected (*paskhein*, the verb from the noun *pathos*), or acts, involve the body: 'what seems most peculiar [to the soul] is thinking'.

[3] I so translate Boethius' plural, 'understandings'. Aristotle at 16a10 speaks of thoughts, *noēmata*. The difference – thoughts may be false, understanding(s) cannot be – will be important in F below.

Aristotle, in his book on affirmation and negation, too, uses some of the same words which Aristotle uses in this book.

E. Herminus reported by Boethius, *On Aristotle's* On Interpretation, *Second Edition*, 39.25–40.9 Meiser 1880

Herminus, however, opposes this interpretation. For he says that it is not true that the thoughts which spoken words indicate are the same for all people. For what, he says, will be said ambiguously, when one and the same mode of expression indicates several things? But he thinks that it is rather the following that is the true reading, so that it will be 'the things of which these are in the first instance indications, these[4] are for everyone the affections of the soul, and the things of which these are likenesses are the following': so that it will seem to be a demonstration of what spoken expressions indicate or what the affections of the soul are likenesses of. And this is to be understood in a straightforward way, according to Herminus, so that we will say: what spoken expressions indicate is the affections of the soul, as if [Aristotle] were saying: affections of the soul are what spoken expressions indicate; and again, what the things contained in thoughts are indications of is things, as if he had said: things are what thoughts indicate.

F. Aspasius, reported by Boethius, *On Aristotle's* On Interpretation, *Second Edition*, 41.13–27 Meiser 1880

On this point, however, Aspasius is very tiresome. For he says: how can it be that the affections of the soul are the same for everyone, when there are such different views about what is just and what is good? He thinks that Aristotle did not speak of affections of the soul concerning incorporeal things, but that he did so concerning only those which can be apprehended by the senses. This is quite false. For the person who is mistaken will never be said to have understanding, but perhaps whoever judges what is good not as it [really] is, but otherwise, will be said to have an affection of the soul, but he is not said to have understanding. But when Aristotle talks about likeness, he is speaking about understanding. It cannot be that the person who thinks that what is good is bad has grasped a likeness of good with his mind.

---

[4] Reading 'these' rather than 'the same' (Sorabji 2004, vol. III 207); in the Greek the difference is in an accent and a breathing only.

Aristotle, at *On Interpretation* 1.10a4–9, says that things that are spoken are symbols or tokens (*sumbola*) of affections or experiences (*pathēmata*) in the soul, and things written are symbols of those that are spoken; what is written and what is said are not the same for all people (i.e. there are different languages), but the *pathēmata* in the soul, and the (actual) things of which these are likenesses, are the same for everybody. He then says that these issues have been dealt with in his writings on the soul.

These remarks gave rise to two problems for Peripatetics in our period. First, the difficulty of locating the reference in *On the Soul* caused Andronicus to dismiss *On Interpretation* as spurious (**A**).[5] Ammonius' reply that 'in many places in *On the Soul* we have imagination called by the philosopher "intellect that can be affected [*pathētikos*]"' in **A** is inaccurate in several respects. Aristotle does refer to *nous pathētikos* once in *On the Soul* 3.5, at 430a24 (so 'in many places' is an exaggeration anyway), but the contrast in that chapter which later interpreters came to formalise as between 'active intellect' and 'passive intellect' is *introduced* by Aristotle as one between intellect which makes everything and intellect which becomes everything (430a14–15), and the terms that were used for the latter by interpreters up until the sixth century AD were rather 'material intellect' and 'potential intellect' – perhaps because *pathētikos* had the established meaning of 'emotional', which would have confused the issue (see below, and Blumenthal 1996, 153–9). But the identification of Aristotle's material, potential or passive intellect with *imagination* is the view of only some late Neoplatonists (Proclus, Philoponus, pseudo-Philoponus; see Blumenthal 1996, 157–62, and pseudo-Philoponus, *On Aristotle's* On the Soul 490.23; the identification was also in modern times advocated by Brentano: 1977 [1867], 141–2), rather than a report of Aristotle's explicit doctrine; indeed at 3.3.428a16–18 Aristotle *denies* that imagination can be identified with intellect, because the former may sometimes be false, the latter not. More straightforwardly, Philoponus in **BC** highlights passages in *On the Soul* where Aristotle calls thoughts 'affections'.

Andronicus' argument for rejecting *On Interpretation* is also reported by Boethius in **D**, but rather differently; according to Boethius, no doubt dependent on Alexander whose counter-argument he reports, Andronicus took 'affections of the soul' in *On Interpretation* to mean *emotions*, which it clearly cannot.

---

[5] The supposed difficulty lives on, in spite of **BC** resolving it; see, e.g., Cooke and Tredennick 1938, 114 n. (a).

Second, granted that affections in the soul are thoughts, the claim that they are the same for everyone seemed problematic to Herminus in **E** (who solved the problem by emending Aristotle's text) and to Aspasius in **F** (whom Boethius answers by invoking the Platonist notion that we only have understanding when we are right in our thinking). See also above on **8G**, which is Sosigenes' reaction to issues prompted by the opening of *On Interpretation*, but it has been placed there because of its relation also to the question of the subject matter of the *Categories*.

CHAPTER 12

Ontology: form and matter

A. Arius Didymus (?), *Fragments on Physics* 3 (*Dox.* 448.13–28)

(1) Aristotle sometimes says that these principles are two, the matter and the form, which he also calls shape and actuality [*entelekheia*] and the-what-it-was-to-be and the being/substance [*ousia*] according to the account, and the activity/actuality [*energeia*].[1] This is how rich and many-named the form is for him. (2) The form is different from the shape in so far as the former extends through the depth, while the latter is on the surface; the one is like the whiteness in painting, while the other gives form to the substance [*ousia*] of milk. But the same is also called form inasmuch as the one gives form to the matter and the other gives it shape. (3) He called it actuality [*entelekheia*] either because it is present completely [*entelekhōs*][2] or because it makes each of the things that participate in it complete [*teleion*]. For the bronze is not yet a statue, except potentially, but when it has been fashioned and has taken on the appropriate shape it is said [to be a statue] in actuality; for then it has received its completion [*telos*]. (4) He called it the what-it-was-to-be because it gives the capacity of being to each of the things that are; and being according to the account because it is different from the [being] according to the matter, as the statue [differs] from the bronze and the cup from the silver and whatever statue it might be from the stone. For that by which these go beyond the matter, from which they have been crafted, is the being according to the account. (5) He called it activity/ actuality because none of the beings could be active/actual without having first been given form.

---

[1] In Aristotle's usage, *energeia* can indicate ongoing activity, as opposed to change; or actuality, as opposed to potentiality; activity and actuality are indeed closely linked in Aristotle's thought. Hence the double translation.

[2] On the reading here see the discussion below.

B.   Stobaeus, *Selections* 1.13.1b
(138.9–12 Wachsmuth 1884) = Aëtius 1.11.4

They say that Aristotle indicated[3] each [cause] by using expressions such as the following, saying that that from which was the matter, that by which the agent, that according to which the form, that on account of which the end.

C.   Seneca, *Letters on Morals* 65.4–6

(1) The Stoics think that there is one [type of] cause, [namely] that which acts. Aristotle thinks that 'cause' is said in three ways: for, he says, 'the first cause is the matter itself, without which nothing can be brought about; the second is the craftsman; the third is that form, which is imposed on each [piece of] work, as on a statue'. For Aristotle calls this *[e]idos*. 'A fourth too', he says, 'is added to these, the purpose of the whole [piece of] work.' (2) I will explain this. The bronze is the first cause of the statue; for it would never have been made if there had not existed that from which it could be cast or wrought. The second cause is the craftsman; for that bronze could not have been fashioned in the condition of the statue if experienced hands had not been applied to it. The third cause is the form; for that statue would not have been called 'spear-carrier' or 'the [boy] binding his hair' if that appearance had not been impressed on it. The fourth cause is the purpose of making it; for if this had not existed, it would not have been made. (3) What is the purpose? What attracted the craftsman, what he was pursuing in making [the statue]. This is money, if he made it with the intention of selling it, or fame, if he was working with a view to his reputation, or religion, if he was preparing a gift for a temple. So this too is a cause, that because of which it came to be; or do you not think that there should be counted, among the causes of the work that was done, that in the absence of which it would not have been done?

D.   Simplicius, *On Aristotle's* Categories 54.8–21

(1) One should note that Andronicus and also certain others say that not only the things that are predicated in the category of 'what it is' [i.e. the category of substance] are predicated of a subject, but also certain other things, as 'musical' of Aristoxenus and 'Athenian' of Socrates. (2) Perhaps the things which we predicate of something saying that it *is* what we predicate (for when we say that Socrates walks we do not say that Socrates is [the action of] walking, but we do say that he is Athenian and a philosopher), and as many

---

[3] Heeren's conjecture for the MSS 'Aristotle said that he indicated'.

things as are predicated of these things when we say that these are those, will be said of a subject. For if Socrates is a philosopher and a philosopher is knowledgeable, Socrates will be knowledgeable.

(3) Again, they say: if the body is white and white is a colour, the body too will be colour. (4) Or rather: 'white' indicates two things, the quality and what is coloured, and it is what is coloured that is predicated of the body (for the body is not *whiteness*, but the colour [that is predicated] of the quality [. . . lacuna] but the whiteness. So it is not the colour that will be predicated of the body, but what is coloured.

E.　Pseudo-Archytas, *On Universal* Logos *or the Ten Categories* 24.17–25.16 Thesleff

(1) Each of these that have been mentioned has certain divisions proper to it. Substance has three divisions: one is matter, one shape [*morphē*], one the combination of these.[4] (2) Of quality there are four divisions; part of it [consists] in being affected, part in disposition, part in potentiality, part in configuration. (3) And quantity: part of it [consists] in weight, for example a talent, part in magnitude, as two cubits, part in plurality, as ten. (4) And of what is relatively disposed [*pros ti pōs ekhon*] there are similarly three [divisions]. For one [part] of it does not involve reciprocity, for example knowledge and perception. For knowledge is said [to be] of what is known and perception of what is perceived, but what is known is not also [said to be] of knowledge or what is perceived of perception. The reason is that what is known and what is perceived can exist without the knowledge and the perception, but the knowledge and the perception cannot exist without what is known and what is perceived. Another [part] of it involves reciprocity, but this is of two sorts. One part of it is similar, the other dissimilar, but both admit reciprocity: similar as with equal and brother, dissimilar as with greater and smaller and heavier and lighter. (5) 'Having'[5] does not admit several differences proper [to it] but is said in many ways. For the knowledgeable are said to have wisdom, and the sick [are said to have] the illness, and possessors [are said to have] the possessing.

F.　Simplicius, *On Aristotle's* Categories 78.4–20

(1) However, Boethus wants to put these enquiries aside at this point; for [he says that] the discussion is not about intelligible substance. (2) Rather, he says,

---

[4] Cf. Szlezák: 1972, 119, and the commentary below.
[5] The eighth Aristotelian category; see **9** n. 2 above.

one should raise the further difficulty that elsewhere where he divides up substance [Aristotle] said that in one way matter is said to be substance, in another form is, and in another the compound of the two; but here he posits substance as a single category. So which is this, and how will he arrange under [substance] these three which are not spoken of according to a single account? (3) In response Boethus says that the account of primary substance fits both matter and the compound. For of both it is the case that they are neither said of some subject nor present in some subject. For neither of them is in something else. (4) But the compound, even if it is not in something else, possesses the form which is in it [as] something which is[6] in something else, [namely the form is in] the matter, while the matter possesses nothing which is in something else. So they have something in common and something different, inasmuch as the matter, as matter, is the matter *of* something, as it is also a subject, whereas the compound substance is not *of* anything. (5) In this way, Boethus says, matter and the compound will be brought under the category of substance; but form will be outside [the category of] substance but will fall under another category, quality or quantity or some other.

G.   Simplicius, *On Aristotle's* Categories 97.28–34

(1) Boethus, however, says that the differentia is properly placed with the species, not with the genus, because the differentiae are often substituted for the species. (2) And all [the differentiae] would be applied together to the genus, but each by itself to all of the things under it, of which it is said, but in no way to the genus. For each does not by itself give form to the genus.[7] (3) [The differentia] is different from the species, because the differentia is coupled with the genus, and the differentia is a sort of form [applied to] the genus, the genus as it were its substrate.

H.   Simplicius, *On Aristotle's* Categories 104.22–31[8]

(1) In which respect shall we say that the individual substance is a this-something,[9] in respect of the form or the matter or the combination of the two? (2) Well, we shall say in respect of all of them; in respect of the matter, inasmuch as it underlies and comes to the actuality of receiving the form,

---

[6] Reading *on ti* for *onti* with de Haas and Fleet 2001. Chiaradonna 2005, 253 n. 39 objects that this requires *hôs;* but this can, I think, be supplied, as by '[as]' in my translation here.

[7] Cf. Dexippus, *On Aristotle's* Categories 48.1–6, but without naming Boethus.

[8] Similarly Dexippus, *On Aristotle's* Categories 51.15–22 , but without naming Boethus.

[9] *tode ti;* in Aristotle's terminology, (roughly) a determinate individual.

but as Plato [says][10] and not as departing from its own proper nature. (3) In respect of the form, again, inasmuch as it is made definite and is one in number; for Boethus too defines in this respect what is one. (4) If someone says that matter, being indefinite, is in no way a this-something, we will remind him that the present discussion is not about matter apart from any relation, but about that which is already related to the form. (5) The compound, which is the individual, clearly admits [the description] 'this'.

I. Philo of Alexandria, *On the Ten Commandments* 30–1

(1) Those who occupy themselves with the doctrines of philosophy say that the categories that are said to exist in nature are ten only: substance, quality, quantity, relation, acting, being acted on, having, position, and those without which all these [cannot exist], time and place. For there is nothing that does not share in these. (2) For example, I share in substance, for I have borrowed from each of the elements out of which this world has been completed, earth, water, air and fire, what is sufficient for my composition. I share in quality, in that I am a human being, and in quantity, in that I am a certain size. I become relative when someone is on my right or left side; I act, rubbing or cutting something, and I am acted on, having my hair cut or being rubbed by others. I am found to be in the [condition] of having, being clothed or armed, and in position, when I sit quietly[11] or lie down. And I am certainly in place and time, since none of the aforementioned can subsist without both of these.

J. Alexander of Aphrodisias, *Supplement to* On the Soul (*Mantissa*) 5.120.9–17

(1) If then the natural form is not in a subject, and the soul is a natural form, neither will the soul be in a subject. For the soul does not come to be in body without qualification, since it would [then] come to be in every body, and so also in the simple [bodies], fire, air, water, earth; and this is impossible. (2) Rather, what is its subject and is its matter is the organic body, which cannot be organic before it possesses a soul, nor, when it has lost the soul, is it organic any more. For no body without soul is organic. So it is, for this reason, not possible to apprehend [sc. without reference to soul itself] what the soul is in. For it is [by] being along with [the soul] that [the

---

[10] Plato, *Timaeus* 50b: de Haas and Fleet: 2001, 48.
[11] So the MS reading *skhedēn* is interpreted by Colson 1937, 20–1 and n. 2.

body that soul is in] is organic, as lead [is lead by being] along with weight. (Sharples 2004, 66)

K.   Alexander of Aphrodisias, *Supplement to* On the Soul (*Mantissa*) 5.120.33–121.7

(1) One should note that Aristotle says in the second book of the *Lecture-course on Physics* (2.1.192b34) that nature, being a form, is in a subject. 'For [what has a nature][12] is always a subject and nature is in a subject.' (2) He also says at the beginning of the second book of *On the Soul* (2.1.412a18) 'for body is not one of those things [that are] of a subject', on the one hand calling 'of a subject' [*kath' hupokeimenou*] what is in a subject [*en hupokeimenōi*], but on the other saying that body is not like this, but soul is. (3) Or rather: is it possible that he is now calling 'of a subject' not what is in a subject, but rather what needs some subject for its being? And this is how the form is in the matter. (Sharples 2004, 68)

L.   Simplicius, *On Aristotle's* Physics 270.26–34

(1) Alexander notes that [Aristotle] says that form and nature are in a subject even though he wants them to be substances and had said in the *Categories* (5.3a7) that no substance is in a subject. (2) [Alexander] softens the objection by saying either that none of the substances mentioned there was said to be in a subject (for [Aristotle] was not there speaking about substance in respect of the form, but about the compound, to which he says there is no opposite), (3) or else that he is not now speaking about what is said to be in a subject in the strict sense, which is what he was referring to in the *Categories*, but he is now calling 'in a subject' what needs some subject in order to exist, as in many places, conversely, he [describes] an attribute as said of a subject.

M.   Simplicius, *On Aristotle's* On the Heaven 279.5–14

(1) Since Aristotle has said 'in general, of all those things whose substance is in some matter as subject', one should note, says Alexander, that he says that the form is in some matter as subject in a more general sense, as needing some subject. For this is a customary usage of his. Or has this been said, he asks, in

---

[12] These words are supplied from the context in the *Physics*, with Fazzo 2002a, 103 n. 223. The natural sense of the quotation as our text gives it, without the context, would be 'for nature is always a subject and in a subject'.

place of 'whose being is bound up with matter'? This is clear and appropriately said. (2) But if, [Alexander] says, the form is in matter as a subject, then the soul too will be in a subject. How then was it stated in the *Categories* (5.3a7) that no substance is in a subject? And [Alexander] solves this well also. For it is, he says, the compound substance, which is enmattered and [an] independent [being], which is there said not to be in a subject.

N.   Simplicius, *On Aristotle's* Physics 211.9–18

(1) But if what underlies is potentially, and [to be] potentially involves privation, how will what underlies not, by its own proper account, be privation? (2) Or rather: we say that it underlies in actuality. For it does not possess *this* too potentially. It attaches to it as an accident that it is able to participate in the forms; so the privation of the forms which it is going to receive, too, will attach to it as an accident. (3) 'For,' says Alexander, 'when it is considered as the matter of something, then it is accompanied by the privation; but when [it is considered] as what underlies, just by itself, it is not accompanied by the privation.' (4) However, Boethus said that 'it is called matter [as] being without shape and form; for matter seems to be named in relation to what is going to be. But when it receives the form, it is no longer called matter, but what underlies. For a thing is said to underlie what is already present in it.'

O.   Themistius, *On Aristotle's* Physics 26.20–4

As Boethus says, the matter in qualified things no longer remains matter; for if it is matter it is in itself without shape and form, but it has now changed to what underlies; for this is accompanied by form and limit and underlies the form and the limit. For matter seems to be named in relation to what is going to be, what underlies in relation to what is already present.

P.   Dexippus, *On Aristotle's* Categories 45.24–31

(1) It is false, too, to say that when what is common is removed the individual is not altogether removed; for if the being of what is common consists in extending to all the things ranked under it, the person who removes this [the being of what is common] immediately removes the whole subsistence [*hupostasis*] of what is common,[13] too. (2) This is how

---

[13] The parallel text in Simplicius (see the next note) has 'individual', and Dillon 1990, 83 n. 34 allows that this may be correct.

one must answer the arguments of the associates of Alexander and Boethus and the other Peripatetics, and it is appropriate for those interpreting the *Metaphysics* to show that Aristotle gives priority to the things that are common even when considering things perceptible by sense.[14]

Q.   Simplicius, *On Aristotle's* Categories 49.29–50.9

(1) But how, they say, will individual substances too, such as Socrates and Plato, not be brought under the account of 'what is in a subject' and be attributes, since Socrates is also in something – for he is in place and time – and [is so] not as a part, and cannot exist apart from place and time, since even if he departs from this place, he will certainly be in another, as was said in the case of fragrance. (2) Well, Boethus judged it right to solve the difficulty based on place by saying that things that move are simply not in the place in which they were; for this has been shown in the discussions of movement. By the same argument they will not be in a particular time; for as time flows continually, it is always different, so that, if [they are in any time], they are in time [considered] universally. (3) But in solving this Boethus says that the universal does not even exist according to Aristotle, and if it did exist, it is not 'something'; but Aristotle said 'in something'. So what is in something cannot be in what is universal.

R.   Syrianus, *On Aristotle's* Metaphysics 106.5–7

Boethus the Peripatetic, too, goes astray as a result of Aristotle's teachings, identifying the Forms [*ideai*] with the generic [concepts].

S.   Seneca, *Letters on Morals* 58.8–9

Our friend, a most learned person, was saying today that [being] is spoken of by Plato in six ways. I will set them all out for you, if first I may explain that there are such things as a genus and a species. We are now looking first for that genus from which the others, the species, depend, from which all division takes its start, in which all things are included. We will find it if we start by tracing back individual [species]; for in this way we will be led to what is first. Human being is a species, as Aristotle says; horse is a species; dog is a species. So we must look for something in common which is the

---

[14] Similarly Simplicius, *In Cat.* 82.22–35, where only Alexander is named as proponent of the rejected view.

link for all of these, which includes them and has them under it. What is this? Animal.

T.   Seneca, *Letters on Morals* 117.11

The Peripatetics hold that there is no difference between wisdom and being wise, since either of them is contained in the other. Surely you do not think anyone is wise except the person who possesses wisdom? Surely you do not think that anyone who is wise does not possess wisdom? The ancient dialecticians distinguished these; from them the distinction descended to the Stoics. I will say what it is. A field is one thing, to possess a field is another. How not so, since to possess a field belongs to the possessor, not to the field?

Aristotle in the *Categories*, notoriously, does not discuss the form–matter contrast, which is why it and related issues have here been treated in a separate section rather than as part of the material relating specifically to the *Categories*.

Plato, and his followers, believed that Forms were separate from material objects and so existed in a separate 'intelligible world'. (Some modern scholars would reject this interpretation of Plato's own view, for charitable reasons, not wanting to attribute to him a view which they find untenable. But it was the prevailing interpretation of Plato in antiquity, and that is the significant point for the present purpose.)

Aristotle rejected the notion that the forms of things that involve matter were separate from them. In his view, the form (here I am not using the capital letter; this gives us a way that was not available in antiquity of distinguishing the Platonic and Aristotelian positions) of human being exists only in flesh-and-blood human beings, and in minds (ours, and *possibly* God's though this is controversial; see below, on **22**) that think of it. There are for Aristotle forms, or at least a form, which do not involve matter – the Unmoved Mover or Movers of the heavens. But they are not the forms *of* any enmattered things. It is convenient to call Aristotelian forms-in-material-things 'enmattered forms' and separate Platonic Forms 'transcendent Forms'.

Consequently, when *Peripatetics* argued about the placing of forms in the categories (see below on **F** and on **J**), or about how many categories there are (**9A** above), *they* are arguing about Aristotelian immanent forms and about the analysis of material things in the world. They are not *themselves in these contexts* concerned with arguments about transcendent Platonic Forms at all (as indeed **F**(1) makes clear). It is true that much of our evidence comes from Simplicius and from other Platonists; but the Platonists (mostly) adopted the view that the Aristotelian categories and Aristotelian immanent form are acceptable *as an account of the material, perceptible world*, provided that it is recognised (as it was not by Peripatetics) that Aristotelian immanent forms themselves derive from Platonic transcendent Forms. Partly for this reason, Simplicius generally reports Peripatetic discussions in a way that reflects the Peripatetics' own concerns; when he and other Platonists attack them or distort their views in the context of a specifically Platonist agenda it is usually pretty obvious (see for example Simplicius, *On Aristotle's* Physics 1262.3–5). See also below on **R**.

Arius in **A** gives a largely accurate account of Aristotle's distinction between form and matter, though there is a problem in the text of **A**(3) relating to an issue which will concern us again in connection with soul (below, **24CL**).[15] **B** was included by Diels as a paragraph in his reconstructed text of Aëtius but in fact appears only in Stobaeus, not in Diels' other witness for Aëtius, pseudo-Plutarch, and is assigned to Arius Didymus rather than to Aëtius by Mansfeld and Runia: 1996–, vol. 1 250–1. It gives a statement of Aristotle's four causes in terms of the 'metaphysics of prepositions' popular in our period, on which see Dillon 1996, 138–9. **C** also relates to the four causes and is notable as being the earliest extant text to adopt the practice, common among teachers of Aristotle from that day to this but not found in Aristotle's own surviving works, of illustrating all four causes by reference to a single example, here the statue. Presumably Seneca did not originate this but took it over from exegetes of Aristotle, though, as Todd 1976b, 321 notes, this could have been by Aristotle's early successors rather than by interpreters in our period. Seneca goes on to say (65.7) that to these four causes Plato adds a fifth, the paradigm or (transcendent) form. That the source of the whole account was regarded by Seneca as Platonist and may actually have been so, the Platonists already regarding Aristotle as part of the Platonic tradition, is suggested by Karamanolis 2006, 274–5.

---

[15] 'Completely' (*entelekhōs*) was emended by Meineke to 'continuously' (*endelekhōs*). Diels in *Dox.* prints *endelekhōs*, commenting only that this is the reading of 'A', his symbol for the common source of MS F and of the MS which served as source for the first printed edition; he does not mention *entelekhōs* at all, and the oddity of giving in the apparatus only the same reading that is printed in the text makes one wonder whether there is a misprint either in Diels' text or, more probably, in his apparatus. Wachsmuth in his edition of Stobaeus says that MSS F and P and the first printed edition have *entelekhōs*, but in his text prints *endelekhōs* none the less. Wachsmuth's edition is *later* than *Dox.*, and he is perhaps unlikely to have contradicted Diels' report of the MSS without being sure of his facts. It is true that, with a preceding *entelekheia*, *endelekhōs* is more likely to have been corrupted to *entelekhōs* than the reverse; but given that *endelekhōs* seems to have no MSS authority at all, I have preferred *entelekhōs*.

(For convergence of Platonist and Aristotelian traditions in our period see also below on **23LMN**). Seneca, however, uses the example of a statue not only in his account of the Platonist position which follows **C** (65.3) but also in discussing the Stoic position in what precedes **C** (65.8); since it may seem unlikely that (i) the Stoic position too was discussed in Seneca's source (the superiority of the Stoic account of causation being the chief point that Seneca *himself* wants to make in this part of the *Letter*), it would seem *either* that (ii) the statue example was not applied to the four Aristotelian causes in the source in the same way that it is by Seneca himself, *or*, if it was, that (iii) he himself then extended it to the Stoic position as well. To be sure, if the 'source' was oral discussion rather than a written text, and oral discussion in which Seneca himself was involved (cf. Inwood 2007b, 158–9, 165; and on the need to allow for such oral discussion compare, in a different context, Dillon 1996, 337–8), the difference between the three possibilities (i)–(iii) becomes less clear-cut. Inwood 2007b, 157; 2007a, 139 and 141 suggests that Seneca was prompted to use the statue example by the well-known account of Plato's position in Cicero, *Orator* 8–10. The statue is used to illustrate all four Aristotelian causes also by Clement of Alexandria, *Miscellanies (Stromateis)* 8.9.26.2–3 (Todd 1976b, who also discusses the resurgence of the practice in modern times; Inwood 2007a, 143 n. 6); if Clement is unlikely to have drawn on Seneca as a *Latin* source, this is *prima facie* evidence for the use not being originated by Seneca himself but in a tradition (written or oral) of which he made use.

Aristotle does in the *Categories* distinguish between secondary substances, which are *said of* primary substances such as the individual man Socrates, and attributes in the other categories, which are *present in* the primary substances. Socrates *is* a man, or putting it another way 'man' is said of Socrates, but there is not a man present *in* Socrates – he simply *is* the man in question. Andronicus and others, according to **D**, extended this point to some other characteristics too – Aristoxenus' being musical and Socrates' being an Athenian and a philosopher. Simplicius in **D**(2) makes the issue turn on linguistic usage – Socrates *is not* (the action of) walking, but he *is* a philosopher. This, however, seems too generous; after all, one could equally well argue that Socrates *is* white but *is not* the act of philosophising. What seems significant about the examples is that 'musical' (or 'expert writing about music') and 'Athenian philosopher' can be seen as *defining* characteristics of the named individuals Aristoxenus and Socrates respectively, in a way that 'walking' cannot be. Cf. Moraux 1973, 104.

Simplicius then, in **D**(3), refers to those who raise the paradox that if body is white and white is a colour, body will be a colour. Moraux 1973, 104

n. 27 suggested that 'others' refers only to the 'certain others' included with Andronicus in D(1), and not to Andronicus himself. Simplicius has no difficulty in showing, in D(4), that the paradox equivocates on 'white' as the (i) colour and (ii) the thing that has it. The connection between this and the point in D(1)–(2) is presumably that if 'musical' is *said of* Aristoxenus, there is no distinction available corresponding to that between (i) and (ii). If so, however, it is odd that Simplicius in D(2) presents 'philosopher is said of Socrates, and therefore what is said of philosopher is also said of Socrates' as part of (his own development of) the view he attributes to Andronicus and others, but then in D(3) attributes the *paradox* 'body is a colour' to some of those same people, and presents the solution in D(4) as his own. For logically it is the difference between the case of white and that of 'musical' – at least as interpreted in D(2) – that gives point to D(2) but also *undermines* the paradox. Or perhaps Simplicius is, characteristically (see, e.g., Rashed 1997, 186), muddying the waters by attributing what is unacceptable to others and the solution to himself?

Aristotle at *Metaphysics* H.1.1042a26–31 and Λ.3.1070a9–13 describes form, matter and the compound of the two as all three being substance. Pseudo-Archytas in E(1) follows him, though he uses the term *morphē* rather than *eidos*. Boethus in F(2) reports Aristotle's view but sees a conflict with the treatment of substance in the *Categories* as a single category, and resolves it (F(3)–(5)) by treating both the compound and matter as primary substance in the *Categories* sense of that expression, but the form as an attribute present *in* the compound and therefore in the category not of substance but of quality, quantity or some other. (In practice it is most likely to be quality; a substantial form–matter compound whose form is *purely* quantitative does not seem easy to envisage. But it may be that there is a risk of circular argument here; we cannot necessarily assume that Boethus drew the boundaries of what are to count as substances narrowly rather than more broadly.)[16] Boethus' expression *en allois*, which I have rendered 'elsewhere', indicates a reference to something other than the *Categories*; but the plural does not necessarily indicate a reference to *several* other works – it could be vaguer than that and indicate one or more passages in a single other work. F is significant, for it indicates that Boethus was ready to interpret the *Categories* in a way that *conflicted w*ith other Aristotelian works.[17] In the spirit of *Metaphysics* Z.12, the differentiae can in Boethus' view be

---

[16] I owe this point to Marwan Rashed.
[17] I was alerted to the importance of F through a discussion by Riccardo Chiaradonna, and I am grateful to him for further discussion of the topic.

substituted for the species (**G**(1)) – man, for example, will be simply 'the two-legged rational', for 'two-legged' itself implies 'animal'. (De Haas and Fleet 2001, 74 n. 115, however, argue that **G**(2)–(3) is no longer Simplicius' report of Boethus' view, but Simplicius' own comment.) Whether **H**(3) shows that Boethus was none the less prepared to allow that his quality-form imparted unity to its possessor or whether he is just being cited for his definition of 'one', is perhaps uncertain.

Boethus' position is closer to that of the Stoics than to Aristotle's.[18] For the Stoics substrate or substance, the first of the so-called Stoic 'categories' (see above, on **9**) indicated matter, the stuff of the world, regardless of its differentiations, and individual things, such as human beings, were portions of this matter that were *qualified* in certain ways. Philo in **I**(1) gives an accurate list of the Aristotelian categories and then proceeds to explain them by applying them all to a single individual; but in doing so he explains substance and quality (**I**(2)) in a way similar to the Stoics, except that he identifies substance not with unqualified prime matter but with the four 'elements', its first differentiations.

Boethus' position was rejected by Alexander in **J** (and in other, parallel discussions; see Sharples 2004, 61–4; Sorabji 2004, vol. III 3(y)). For Alexander form is emphatically not *present in* what possesses it; Socrates' soul is not present in a Socrates who could at least theoretically exist without it, for without soul there is no human being for the soul to be in. The importance of this issue for our understanding of Aristotle cannot be overstated; a Stoicising reading such as that of Boethus points towards an interpretation which assimilates Aristotle to those for whom individuals are simply bundles of qualities (with the modification that there is some underlying matter which, however, in the last analysis, has no qualities of its own); it will also appeal to Platonists *as an account of the sensible world*, since for Platonists real being is confined to the Forms, and all that there is in the sensible world is modifications of the Receptacle in the *Timaeus*[19] – that is, in Aristotelian terms, qualities – which are similarities to the Forms.[20] Alexander's reading, on the other hand, indicates that what is primary both in explanation and in being (since for Aristotle, as for many if not all ancient Greek philosophers, the two go together) is the form which causes the compound to be what it is. (That for Alexander the form includes

---

[18] However, Aristotle does in the *Categories* (5.3b12–23) say that secondary substance appears to be substance because of the words used to refer to it, but it is in fact quality, though in a special way.

[19] Or, strictly, appearances in it (*Timaeus* 52b, 52d). But from Aristotle onwards it was usual to interpret the Receptacle as matter acquiring form.

[20] Cf. Plotinus 2.6 [17] 1.40–2 (Sorabji 2004, vol. III 3(w)(11)).

the characteristics of the species and not also those of the individual, the question of 'essentialism', is a further and distinct issue; see on this Rashed 2007, especially 151–2 n. 435 on how modern philosophical debate has been influenced by Alexander without realising it.) The dispute between Alexander and Boethus is effectively taken up again, without reference to either of them, by Elizabeth Anscombe, taking the side of Alexander, in Anscombe and Geach 1961, 33–4; see also Ellis 1994.

In **K** Alexander deals with two passages in Aristotle which had apparently been interpreted by some of his predecessors as indicating that soul and form are in a subject. The passage from *On the Soul* 2.1 cited in **K**(2) does not actually say in so many words that soul is in a subject but implies it; as Ross 1961, 213 comments, 'the missing but easily supplied part of the proof is "whereas soul (or besouledness) is, as we have seen, not a substance but an attribute"'. (Cf. Wurm 1973, 184 and n. 27.) Fazzo 2002a, 104 and n. 225 well suggests that the clause 'on the one hand calling "of a subject" what is in a subject' reflects a stage of discussion earlier than Alexander himself, in which this passage of Aristotle was used to argue that soul *is* in the body, the thesis which Alexander himself rejects; otherwise it is difficult to see why Alexander should have regarded the implication that soul is *of* a subject as problematic for his own view at all. Alexander solves the problem of the *De anima* passage to his own satisfaction by interpreting 'of a subject' rather as 'needing some subject'; but he says nothing here about the passage from *Physics* that he quoted first. However Simplicius in **L**(3) and **M**(1) shows that Alexander applied a similar solution to that passage as well. As for matter, in **N**(4) and in **O** Boethus distinguishes between matter regarded as such, in the absence of form, and matter combined with form, when it is in his view strictly speaking no longer matter but 'what underlies', or substrate.[21]

In **P** Dexippus as a Platonist insists against the Peripatetics, including Boethus and Alexander, that the universal is prior to the particular, and in **Q** Simplicius records Boethus' somewhat sophistical answers to the problem that if Socrates is in time and in a place he will, by Aristotle's definition of what is in a subject, 'what is in something not as a part and cannot be apart from that in which it is' (*Cat.* 1.1a24–5), be an attribute rather than a substance. (We have seen that Boethus is happy for Socrates' *form* to be an attribute, but that is a different point.) In **R** Syrianus describes Boethus as identifying Forms with generic concepts. Syrianus himself clearly understands the reference as being to Platonic Forms (and uses the term *ideai*, not

---

[21] On these passages see Rashed 2007, 199–201. The present paragraph includes material from Sharples 2004, 68 nn. 208–10.

eidē); his report is part of an account of interpretations of the Forms from Cleanthes the Stoic onwards. However, it is likely enough that Syrianus has included in his account of views concerning Platonic Forms what Boethus originally had to say about forms as Boethus himself understood them; putting it another way, what earlier philosophers have to say about forms is for Syrianus their more or less inadequate account of Forms as they really are, that is to say Platonic Forms. Boethus himself held that the *Categories* is not concerned with intelligible substance (F(1)). But that would only be an objection to his having discussed forms in the context of the *Categories* if the forms in question were Platonic forms. See Moraux 1973, 156 and n. 38.

S is from the beginning of an account by Seneca of six modes of being according to Plato, which Dillon 1996, 135–7 rightly describes as a scholastic construction not to be found in the text of Plato himself in the form Seneca gives it. What is significant is the use made of Aristotle in setting out a Platonic position, whether this is due to Seneca himself or to his (presumably Platonic) source. Inwood 2007a, 115 suggests that the application to Plato of the idea that ' "what is" is said in many ways' (*sex modis hoc* [sc. *quod est*] *a Platone dici*, 58.8) reveals Aristotelian influence in the source, whatever we can – or cannot – profitably say about its identity. Compare **C** above.

In **T** Seneca is defending the standard Stoic distinction between corporeal states and incorporeal predicates (for which see LS 33P) against a Peripatetic denial that there is such a distinction. Since the point is not explicitly made in Aristotle himself and is most naturally understood as a response to the Stoic position, the Peripatetics in question must be later than the rise of Stoicism; beyond that their date cannot be ascertained.

On the issues raised in this section see further Reinhardt 2007, 523–9.

CHAPTER 13

Logic

A. Apuleius, *On Interpretation* 13.193.16–20

However, Ariston of Alexandria and some of the more recent Peripatetics add five other moods besides[1] those with a universal conclusion (three in the first figure and two in the second), in place of which they infer particular [conclusions]. But it is completely absurd to conclude less when more is granted [i.e. to have a conclusion weaker than the premises allow].

B. Aratus, *Philosophy*, in Paris, suppl. gr. 645 fol. 197r., ed. C. Kalbfleisch, *Jahrbuch f. d. klassische Philologie* suppl. 23, 1897, 707

(1) *Problem*: that there should be another syllogistic figure, in addition to these [three], seemed impossible to Aristotle and his associates. For it is impossible that, among three terms, the middle term should be arranged in relation to the two extremes in any other relation besides those stated.[2] Theophrastus [93 FHS&G] and Eudemus [fr. 18 Wehrli 1969a] added certain other combinations to the first figure besides those set out by Aristotle; and about these we will speak in what follows. Some of the more recent [thinkers] thought that these constituted a fourth figure, referring the doctrine to Galen as its father. To establish this they use an argument like the following: if it is possible for the middle term to be arranged in relation to the extremes in some other relation besides those stated, there will also be another figure of the syllogism besides those that have been stated. But the first: therefore the second.[3] (2) The minor

---

[1] Reading *'praeter eos'* for *'praeterea'* (Barnes 2007b, 535 n. 2).

[2] In the first figure the middle term is predicated of the minor and has the major predicated of it; in the second it is predicate of both major and minor; in the third both major and minor are predicated of it.

[3] The argument of the 'more recent figures' is in the standard form of the Stoic first undemonstrated argument, i.e. *modus ponens*. Cf. Gottschalk 1993, 63 and 67, suggesting that the source of the argument is Stoics attempting to find weaknesses in Peripatetic logic.

[premiss of their argument][4] is shown [as follows]: it is possible for the middle term, in the reverse way to the first figure, to be predicated of the major term, and to be the subject of the minor, for example: 'every human being is an animal; every animal is a substance; so some substance is a human being.' The major term is 'human being', because it is the predicate in the conclusion, and the minor [term] is substance, because it is the subject in [the conclusion]; and 'animal', which is the middle term, is predicated of 'human being' [in the major premiss], but is the subject [in the minor premiss] of 'substance', which is the minor term.

(3) *Answer*: The figures set out by the Philosopher are complete, in the opinion of his true disciples also. For if someone pays attention to the arguments of his opponents, he will find that what makes the difference in such syllogisms is not the different relation of the middle [term] to the extremes, but the changed order of the premises and the reversed drawing of the conclusion, which predicates the lesser extreme of the greater. For in other respects they are the same as the syllogisms in the first figure.

C.   Galen, *Introduction to Logic* 8.1

So there are three figures involving categorical premisses, and in each of [the figures] there are several [valid] syllogisms, as in the case of the hypothetical [premisses]; some of them are undemonstrated and primary, others require demonstration.

D.   Galen, *Introduction to Logic* 7.2

And indeed some of the Peripatetics, such as Boethus, call syllogisms from leading premisses[5] not only undemonstrated but also primary. But they are not also prepared to call primary those undemonstrated syllogisms that are from predicative premisses.

E.   Ammonius, *On Aristotle's* Prior Analytics 31.11–15

One should note that Aristotle's opinion was that all the syllogisms in the second and third figures are imperfect, but Boethus, the eleventh [head of

---

[4] Viz. that 'it is possible for the middle term to be arranged in relation to the extremes in some other relation besides those stated'.
[5] I.e. 'certain hypothetical assumptions', Barnes 2007b, 536.

the school] after Aristotle held the contrary opinion to Aristotle about this; his opinion was a good one, and he demonstrated that all [the syllogisms] in the second and third figures are perfect.

F. Philoponus, *On Aristotle's* Prior Analytics 126.7–29

(1) What then? Is it not possible to think of any way of helping Aristotle's argument?[6] We say that it is. For he himself says in *On Interpretation* [9.19a23] that 'necessary' is said in two ways, one [a] in the strict sense and one depending on a hypothesis, and [that the necessary] which depends on a hypothesis is also [said] in two ways. For one [sort] [b] is said to be necessary as long as the subject exists, the other [c] as long as the predicate exists. For example, that the sun moves is said to be necessary in the strict sense [a]. It is hypothetically necessary as long as the subject exists [b] for Socrates to be a living creature; for as long as Socrates exists it is necessary that he be a living creature. This [type] is closer to what is necessary in the strict sense. The third [type] [c] is as when we say that it is necessary that the one who is sitting is sitting. For as long as the predicate [applies], I mean the sitting, it necessarily applies to the one who is sitting, by hypothetical necessity. So, we say that the major premiss is taken as necessary in the strict sense; the conclusion, in that of the hypothetical necessity which applies for as long as the predicate [does]. For as long as A applies to C, it applies to it of necessity. (2) And Alexander [of Aphrodisias], the Commentator on the Philosopher [Aristotle], says in a certain monograph[7] that his teacher Sosigenes too was of this opinion, that it is hypothetical necessity that Aristotle infers here. That this is what [Aristotle] means is, he [Alexander, or Sosigenes?] says, clear from the fact that when he infers an assertoric conclusion, the major [premiss] being assertoric and the minor necessary, the Philosopher sets out terms [*Prior Analytics* 1.9.30a28–32], but when he infers a necessary [conclusion], the major [premiss] being necessary and the minor assertoric [30a15–20], he was not able to set out terms which implied necessity in the strict sense; and from this it is clear, he says, that he himself too understood [the conclusion in terms of] hypothetical necessity.

---

[6] The argument that a first-figure syllogism in Barbara (see below, p. 96) has a necessary conclusion if its major premiss is necessary while its minor premiss is not, but not if the relation is reversed. See the commentary below.

[7] Probably Alexander's (lost) *On the Disagreement between Aristotle and his Associates concerning [Syllogisms with] Mixed [Premisses]*, referred to by Alexander himself in I(6) below.

G.   Pseudo-Ammonius, *On Aristotle's* Prior Analytics 39.24–40.2

(1) Sosigenes the teacher of Alexander says that the necessity that is con-cluded is the [necessity] that involves the distinction.[8] For as long as the middle [term] applies to the minor [term], it is necessary that the major, too, should apply to the minor. (2) But as far as this is concerned, even if the major [premiss] is assertoric the conclusion is necessary. For it is necessary that the major [term] apply to the minor, for as long as the major applies to the middle. (3) And every syllogism has hypothetical necessity in its con-clusion, according to the definition of the syllogism.[9] (4) And in the second figure Aristotle shows that a pairing [of premisses; cf. G(1) below] does not give a necessary conclusion, because the necessity of the conclusion is that which involves the distinction.

(5) Herminus said that the conclusion is not always necessary, but in the case of certain [subject] matter. For if we take living creature, human being, walking, the conclusion is necessary; but if we take living creature, human being, moving, it is contingent. And this [says Herminus] is why Aristotle says 'it sometimes results' [*Prior Analytics* 1.9.30a15]. (6) However, Aristotle made a distinction here, saying 'but not whichever it may be', but rather when it is the major [premiss] that is necessary [30a16–17]. (7) And he made his point [using] letters [as symbols] because it was a general one.

H.   Alexander, *On Aristotle's* Prior Analytics 140.14–141.6

(1) By saying in addition 'but not as long as living creature applies to nothing white, so that the conclusion will be necessary if certain things are so, but not necessary without qualification [*haplōs*]' [*Prior Analytics* 1.10.30b31–2],[10] [Aristotle] showed that in the mixtures [of different modalities in the premisses], when he says that the conclusion is necessary, he is speaking of the necessary without a qualification and not of that with the distinction; [the latter] is what is said by some of those[11] who explain the topic of

---

[8] Literally, 'determination' (*diorismos*) or 'limitation' (so Flannery 1995, 82). It might be thought that this is simply another term for hypothetical necessity; but Flannery argues that Alexander, in modifying Sosigenes' position, introduced a terminological distinction between 'hypothetical neces-sity' and 'necessity that involves the distinction', using the latter to refer to that type of hypothetical necessity which applies to the conclusion of *any* syllogism. See the commentary below.

[9] Aristotle, *Prior Analytics* 1.1.24b19: 'A syllogism is a form of words in which, when certain things have been laid down, something other than what has been laid down follows *of necessity* through these things being so.'

[10] Aristotle is discussing Camestres with an apodeictic major and assertoric minor. (For the technical terminology here and in what follows see the discussion below.)

[11] I.e. Sosigenes (cf. G(1) above); so, rightly, Moraux 1984, 343 n. 38.

the mixture of premisses, thinking that they are coming to the aid of [Aristotle's] opinion; they say that he does not say that the conclusion is necessary without qualification, but with the distinction.

(2) For they say that, when living creature applies to every human being of necessity and human being, in the first figure [of the syllogism], [applies to] everything that moves or walks, the conclusion is necessary with a distinction.[12] For living creature applies to everything that walks or moves, as long as the middle [term] applies to it, that is, human being. But when it is the minor [premiss] that is necessary this conclusion no longer applies;[13] for it is not the case that, if moving applies to every living creature, and living creature [applies] to every human being of necessity, moving too [applies] to every human being of necessity, as long as living creature applies to it (for this is false), but as long as moving applies to every living creature.

(3) But that [Aristotle] does not mean the conclusion [in the first figure] to be necessary in this way [i.e. hypothetically], he himself indicated by showing that a conclusion that is of this sort and necessary in this way [i.e. hypothetically] occurs in the second figure, <if> the positive [premiss], whether the major or the minor, is necessary, but not saying that in this sort of combination the conclusion is necessary without qualification. Now if he was saying that the conclusions [in the first figure and in the second figure] were necessary in a similar way,[14] he would have added to that one too [in the first figure] that it was not necessary without qualification but with a distinction, as in this case [in the second figure] too. (4) And at the same time, that he too himself was aware of the division of the necessary which his colleagues made, he indicated through the addition, which he already indicated first in *On Interpretation* [9.19a23], in which he says, about the contradictory disjunction relating to future time concerning particular statements, 'it is necessary that what is is, when it is, and that what is not is not, when it is not'. For hypothetical necessity is like this.

I.   Alexander, *On Aristotle's* Prior Analytics 125.3–31

(1) To say that Aristotle has not here said that the conclusion is necessary in such combinations [of premisses], but [only] in the case of certain subject

---

[12] I.e. in Barbara LXL the necessity of the conclusion is only hypothetical.
[13] I.e. Barbara XLX is valid, Barbara XLL is not.
[14] Literally: 'that the present [conclusion] was necessary in a similar way to that one'.

matter, and to use as an argument for this the fact that he has said 'it *sometimes* follows when one premiss is necessary' <is absurd>.[15] (2) For 'sometimes' does not apply to a combination of a certain sort, so that in a combination of this sort the conclusion is sometimes necessary and sometimes not, but to the combination generally. For in the combination of a necessary and an assertoric [premiss] the conclusion is *sometimes* necessary; but not always, for [Aristotle] does not say that also when the minor [premiss] is taken as necessary a necessary conclusion is inferred. 'sometimes' indicates the manner of the combination, not that the conclusion is sometimes necessary and sometimes assertoric in the *same* manner and combination. (3) And this [Aristotle] himself clearly showed, through what he adds, saying 'except not whichever it may be [being necessary], but that which relates to the major term', since this is why he added 'sometimes'. (4) For it is ridiculous to think that by this 'sometimes' he is saying that in the case of *some* [subject] matter the conclusion is necessary in such a combination. For in this way there is nothing to prevent our saying that combinations that do not yield a syllogism sometimes do so. For they will be found to imply a conclusion in the case of some [subject] matter. At any rate, in the second figure the combination from two universal positive premisses will give a universal positive conclusion if terms are taken such that the two extreme terms are co-extensive. If every human being is a living creature, and everything capable of laughter is a living creature, it is inferred[16] that every human being is capable of laughter. But it is not the case that, just because something is sometimes inferred in the case of a certain [subject] matter, therefore the combination [of premisses] yields a syllogism. (5) Further, if Aristotle had wanted to show this,[17] he would have shown in the case of *what* [subject] matter this is so. For this was appropriate for one [to do] who added 'sometimes' for this reason. But he does not do this but develops his argument by using letters, in terms of which he makes his points general, because they can apply no less[18] to this matter than to

---

[15] Supplied by Moraux 1984, 391 n. 103.

[16] But no valid mood in the second figure has a positive conclusion (Aristotle, *Prior Analytics* 1.5.28a8). As Mueller and Gould 1999, 119 n. 35 point out, even while rightly challenging Herminus' view that a single mood may sometimes produce one result and sometimes another, Alexander himself speaks as if a sample set of premisses and conclusion all of which happen to be true constitutes an inference, even if the argument-schema is not syllogistic because it does not always give a true conclusion. See the discussion below.

[17] Omitting *hôs edeixen* as due to dittography, with Mueller and Gould 1999, 119–20 n. 36.

[18] The Greek has 'no more', but 'no less' makes the point better in English. An anonymous referee here drew my attention to the use of 'no more this than that' in ancient dialectic to indicate that there is no reason to prefer either of two propositions to the other. See, e.g., Diogenes Laertius 9.74; De Lacy 1958.

that. And for this reason [this interpretation] must be rejected as completely empty. (6) We must also pass over a further examination of what is said [here]; for we have spoken about it in [our] writings *On the Disagreement between Aristotle and his Associates concerning [Syllogisms with] Mixed [Premisses]*.

In **A** Apuleius attributes to Ariston (see above on 1EGH; 9G) and others the recognition of the subaltern moods of the categorical syllogism, which are formed by weakening universal conclusions (A and E) to particular ones (I and O); thus in the first figure Barbara, Celarent and Celantes (see below) give Barbari, Celaront and Celantos, and in the second Cesare and Camestres give Cesaro and Camestrop, respectively. (The conclusions of all syllogisms in the third figure are particular in any case. For an understanding of traditional Aristotelian logic and of the medieval mnemonic names for the moods of the syllogism, see, for example, Kneale and Kneale 1962, 72–3, 100–1.) As Apuleius points out, this is a matter of formal completeness rather than practical utility.

A more significant development was the discovery of the fourth figure. Aristotle did not recognise the fourth figure (Bramantip, Camenes, Dimaris, Fesapo, Fresison) as a separate figure, but he did recognise the inferences involved (cf. Ross 1949, 35). Ariston as reported in **A**, since he includes Celantos from Celantes as well as Celaront from Celarent (direct first figure), shows some awareness of the indirect first figure (Baralipton, Celantes, Dabitis, Fapesmo, Frisesomorum), which is formed by converting the conclusions of first-figure syllogisms and is the equivalent of the fourth figure, differing only in the order of the premisses. The fourth-figure Camenes (B applies to all C; A applies to no B; therefore A applies to no C), for example, is equivalent to the indirect first-figure Celantes (A applies to no B; B applies to all C; therefore C applies to no A). But Ariston is not aware of the fourth figure as such, or at least does not regard it as adding anything to the indirect first figure, for he does not include, among his subaltern moods, Camenop from fourth-figure Camenes as well as Celantos from indirect first-figure Celantes. This is indeed hardly surprising, for the fourth figure and the indirect first figure have historically, and rightly, been regarded as alternative ways of formulating the same inferences, rather than as complementing each other; see on this Gottschalk 1993. The fourth figure is attributed to Galen by those whose views are reported in **B**(1) (**B** = Sorabji 2004, vol. III 8(b)(1)), and also by Averroes, but **C**, at first sight anyway, suggests that Galen was in fact unaware of it (on how a mistaken attribution might have arisen see Kneale and Kneale 1962, 183–4). The evidence of **C** may, however, not be conclusive if we distinguish, with **B**(3) and with Rescher 1966 (see Moraux 1984, 706–7 n. 99), between considering the possible relations of the terms in the premisses, of which there are indeed only three (middle term predicate in one premiss, subject in the other; middle term predicate in both premisses; middle term subject in both premisses), and considering also the placement of the terms in the conclusion. On the other hand, the distinction in **B**(3) is used to argue *against* a fourth figure, Aratus in **B**(1) does not himself endorse the attribution of the fourth figure to Galen, and it may be doubted whether Galen would have expressed himself as he does in **C** if he had recognised a fourth figure as such. Gottschalk 1993, 66 and n. 35, concludes that Galen may have *considered* the possibility of a fourth figure.

The fourth figure can indeed be regarded as the least intuitive, whereas the first is the most intuitive. For in the first figure the middle term is part of the predicate in one premiss, subject in the other, and the relations between the terms, in Aristotle's standard way of presenting them, form a sequence: 'A applies to all B, B applies to all C, therefore A applies to all C.' In the fourth figure, on the other hand, we have 'B applies to all C, A applies to all B, therefore C applies to some A' (Bramantip; 'A applies to all B, B applies to all C, therefore C applies to some A' is Baralipton in the indirect first figure). It is perhaps this feature of the first figure that explains why Aristotle (*Prior Analytics* 1.7.29b1) regards Barbara and Celarent as 'perfect' moods from which those in the other figures can be derived. Boethus, as we learn from **DE**, disagreed, arguing that all the figures should be treated alike; the point of **D** is apparently that, whereas in the case of hypothetical syllogisms Boethus recognised certain 'unproved' (i.e. self-evident) syllogisms as primary, in the case of categorical syllogisms he was not prepared to recognise some as primary, on the grounds that all of them can be derived from others – the first figure from the second as well as the second from the first. (See the detailed discussion in Barnes 2007b, 536–42.) Later on, the emperor Julian (the Apostate) was to decide the issue in favour of Boethus: Ammonius, *On Aristotle's* Prior Analytics 31.11.25 = Sorabji 2004, vol. III 8(c)(1).

A notorious problem in Aristotle's modal logic is the problem of 'the two Barbaras'. Aristotle holds (*Prior Analytics* 1.9.30a15–33) that when (a) the major premiss is necessary and the minor only assertoric, the conclusion is necessary, whereas when (b) the major is assertoric and the minor necessary, the conclusion too is only assertoric.

(a)   (b)
A necessarily applies to all B   A applies to all B
B applies to all C   B necessarily applies to all C
∴ A necessarily applies to all C   ∴ A applies to all C

(Using a conventional notation, where L indicates a necessary premiss and X one that is merely an assertion, I will refer to (a) as 'Barbara LXL' and to (b) as 'Barbara XLX', and similarly for other moods mentioned below; where the modality of a conclusion is in dispute, I write, for example, 'Barbara LX-'.)

Aristotle's reason for taking this view has caused puzzlement from antiquity to the present day; indeed his immediate pupils Theophrastus and Eudemus disagreed and held that the conclusion is assertoric in both cases, never being stronger than the weakest premiss (the *deteriorem* rule; cf. Theophrastus 105–6 FHS&G). Alexander of Aphrodisias wrote a monograph on the topic; characteristically, his inclination is to support Aristotle himself against his successors, though his approach is nuanced. For a detailed discussion see Flannery 1995. Alexander's monograph does not survive, but from **FG** we learn that his teacher Sosigenes had already considered the problem, attempting to solve it by arguing that the necessity of the conclusion in Barbara LX- is hypothetical, applying only when the assertoric minor premiss is true. (See the detailed discussion in Barnes 2007b, 542–6.) Using for hypothetical necessity H as opposed to L, from **H**(2)–(3) it appears that Sosigenes' point was that in Barbara LXH the hypothesis or condition relates to the minor premiss, and the minor premiss and the conclusion both have the minor term following the 'applies to', whereas in Barbara XLH the conclusion would involve what applies to the minor term but the condition would relate rather to what applies to the middle term, so that the connection between the condition and the conclusion of whose necessity it is a condition would be less immediate. (See also Flannery 1995, 79–81. Flannery rightly argues that **H**(3) is still part of Sosigenes' argument, not, as Moraux 1984, 343 supposed, a counterargument by Alexander.) **G**(2)–(3) objects against Sosigenes that the hypothetical necessity would apply even if (apparently) *both* premisses were only assertoric. (Flannery 1995, 77–8 indeed reads **G**(2) as appying to Barbara XL-, so that pseudo-Ammonius is attacking Sosigenes on the very same point to which Sosigenes had already replied, as reported by **H**(2)–(3); but **G**(2) can also be read as applying to Barbara XX-.)

Barnes objects that F(1)'s 'For so long as A applies to C, it applies to it by necessity' is either a truism (if read as 'necessarily, if A applies to C, A applies to C') or false (if read as 'if A applies to C, necessarily A applies to C'). We perhaps can – but perhaps should not – rescue Sosigenes by interpreting his statement as a misleading way of saying 'so long as B applies to C, A applies to C *because of B* of necessity', since A's applying to C *because of B* and B's applying to C are extensionally equivalent. (Flannery 1995, 74 points out that this is what G(1), as opposed to F(1), actually indicates.) But we cannot rescue Sosigenes from Barnes' further objection that his argument in F(2) from Aristotle's setting out terms in one case but not in the other is fatally flawed, since for Aristotle setting out terms is a means of showing that a mood is *invalid*, not, as Philoponus assumes, *valid*; Aristotle sets out terms to show that a *necessary* conclusion *cannot* be drawn in the first figure when the major is assertoric and the minor necessary, not, as Philoponus supposes, to show that an *assertoric* conclusion *can* be drawn. (Moraux 1984, 341 wrongly paraphrases Philoponus here as reporting Aristotle correctly.) – I say 'we cannot rescue Sosigenes', but in fact F(2) does not specify whether the mistaken argument was Sosigenes' or Alexander's. One might be reluctant to attribute the mistake to Alexander rather than to his teacher, but even if Alexander did not himself originate it, he did apparently report it, without rejecting it, as far as Philoponus indicates at any rate. And that Alexander systematically misinterpreted Aristotle's procedure of setting out terms as a way of showing which conclusions *can* be drawn, rather than which *cannot*, is argued by Barnes *et al.* 1991, 12–14, followed by Mueller and Gould 1999, 7; see also note 15 above. (But for an interpretation, though explicitly not in the end a defence, of Alexander's approach see Flannery 1995, 136–42).

Moraux 1984, 341–4 held that Alexander rejected Sosigenes' position and that the argument reported in E(2) was only Sosigenes'. Flannery 1995, 63, 81–3, however, holds that Alexander's rejection of Sosigenes' position was more nuanced, and that Alexander held that in the case of Barbara LX- the conclusion was not absolutely necessary but qualified in a certain way. The objection in H is not, according to Flannery, to Sosigenes' claim that the necessity of the conclusion in Barbara LX- is limited in some way (that is, that Barbara LXH is to be accepted, rather than Barbara LXL) but rather to Sosigenes' identification of the type of limited necessity involved with the hypothetical necessity of the conclusion of any syllogism whatsoever. In the view of Flannery (1995, 104) Alexander wants to insist that where the minor premiss is necessary with type (b) of hypothetical necessity in F(1) (let us call it H!) the conclusion is necessary with the same type of necessity – that is, he is defending not Barbara LXL but Barbara LH!H!. Significantly, a text attributed to Alexander, surviving only in Arabic, and translated at Theophrastus, fr. 100c FHS&G, quotes Galen as attacking Theophrastus for suggesting that the difference between (a) and (b) is a difference in the *meaning* of the term necessity, rather than just in its application. Flannery suggests that this is a fragment of Alexander's work *On Syllogisms with Mixed Premisses*, but Fazzo 2002b, 126–7 well points out that the attribution to Alexander is tenuous; the passage is transmitted in the Arabic as part of another work which, she argues, may not all in its present form derive from Alexander, and the attribution rests on a title in the MS which mis-states the topic as possibility rather than necessity and is thus of questionable reliability. Several of Philoponus' examples in **F**(1) (the sun moving, and Socrates being a living creature), though not exactly the same classification, appear in Ammonius' commentary on Aristotle, *On Interpretation* 9 (Ammonius, *On Aristotle,* On Interpretation 153.13–154.2). On their later history see Rescher 1967.

Herminus, another of Alexander's teachers (above, 1Y) attempted to interpret Aristotle in *Prior Analytics* 1.9.30a15 as saying that a necessary major and an assertoric minor premiss in Barbara would only yield a necessary conclusion in the case of some terms and not others (**G**(5)**I**). Alexander does not in **I** name Herminus as his target, any more than he names Sosigenes in **H**, but it is pretty clear that **G** derives from the work by Alexander referred to in **F**(2) and **I**(6); **G**(6) reflects **I**(3) and **G**(7) reflects **I**(5). Cf. Moraux 1984, 342. (Flannery 1995, 99, however, argues that **I** is directed also against Theophrastus, who has been mentioned just before: fr. 106a FHS&G.) Alexander in **I**(4) objects, in effect, that Herminus disregards the distinction between the truth of a conclusion in a particular case, on the one hand, and the formal validity of a mood of the syllogism, on the other.

On the issues in this section see further Barnes 2007b.

CHAPTER 14

Theory of knowledge

A. Aristocles, *On Philosophy* F4.10 Chiesara, reported by Eusebius, *Preparation for the Gospel* 14.18.19

And when [the Pyrrhonian Sceptics] say that all things are unclear, it is worth asking from where they actually learned this. For they must first know what the clear is; for on this [basis] at least they would be able to say that things are not like this. For it is necessary to know the positive statement first, and [only] then the negative one. But if they do not know what the clear is like, they cannot know what the unclear is, either.

B. Aristocles, *On Philosophy* F6.9–10 Chiesara, reported by Eusebius, *Preparation for the Gospel* 14.20.9–10

(1) But since even now there are some [the Epicureans] who say that every sensation and every impression is true, let us say a little about them also. These people seem to be afraid that if they said that some sensations are false, they would not have a criterion or rule that was firm or reliable. (2) But they do not see that thus they are immediately saying that all opinions, too, are true. For we naturally judge many things by these. But none the less they judge that some [opinions] are true, others false. (3) Next, if someone considered, he would see that not even of the other criteria is any free from falsity always and throughout, I mean, for example, a balance and compasses, and the like. But each of them is sound when it is in one condition, faulty when it is in another, and when it is used in one way it gives the true answer, in another way a false one. (4) Indeed, if every sensation were true, they ought not to be so different. For they are different when close at hand and far away, in the sick and the healthy, in craftsmen and in laymen, in the wise and in the foolish. (5) It would be altogether absurd to say that the sensations of the mad are true, and of those who mis-see and mis-hear. For it would

be simple-minded to say that the person who mis-sees either sees [the object] or does not see it; for one could reply that he sees [it], but [does so] incorrectly.

C. Aristocles, *On Philosophy* F8.5–6 Chiesara, reported by Eusebius, *Preparation for the Gospel* 14.21.5–6

In general, sensations and impressions seem to be, as it were, mirrors and images of things; but affections [*pathē*] and pleasures and pains are changes and alterations of us ourselves. In this way, when we have sensations and impressions we look to external things, but when we experience pleasure and pain we attend to ourselves alone. For our sensations are produced by things outside us, and what these are like [determines] the impressions, too, that they produce, but affections are of a certain sort on account of us and according to the state we are in. Therefore the same things sometimes seem pleasant, sometimes unpleasant, and sometimes more so, sometimes less so.

D. Aristocles, *On Philosophy* F7.9 Chiesara, reported by Eusebius, *Preparation for the Gospel* 14.17. 9

Such [Eleatic] arguments have been pretty well sufficiently tested already; for they have been completely obliterated, as if they had never been stated at all. But we now say confidently that those philosophise correctly who employ both sensations and reason in order to know things.

E. Aristocles, *On Philosophy* F8.6–7 Chiesara, reported by Eusebius, *Preparation for the Gospel* 14.21.6–7 (continuing C above)

These things being so, we will find, if we are willing to consider, that the starting-points of knowledge are best laid down by those who employ both senses and intellect. Sensation is like the traps and nets and the other hunting implements of this sort; intellect and reason are like the hounds which track down and chase [the prey]. One must think that better than [the Epicureans'] is the philosophising of those who neither make use of the senses at random nor employ affections [such as pleasure and pain] in order to determine the truth. It would indeed be a terrible thing for those who are by nature human beings to entrust themselves to irrational pleasures and pains, letting go the most divine judge, [namely] intellect.

F.   Sextus Empiricus, *Against the Professors*
(*Adversus mathematicos*) 7.217–18

(1) The followers of Aristotle and of Theophrastus, and the Peripatetics in general, since the nature of things is at the highest level double, some, as I said beforehand, being perceptible by the senses and others intelligible, themselves too bequeathed [us] a double criterion, sense perception for the perceptibles, intellect for the intelligibles, and for both in common, as Theophrastus said (301A FHS&G), clarity. (2) In order the irrational and indemonstrable criterion comes first, [that is] sense perception, but in power intellect [comes first], even if it is thought to be second in order as compared with perception.

G.   Arius Didymus(?), *Fragments on Physics* 16 (*Dox.* 456.5–12)

(1) Aristotle: imagination [*phantasia*] is a being affected and a change in sensation that is in actuality, but it is named from one of the senses, sight; for to appear [*phainesthai*] derives its name from light [*phaos*], and [light] is proper to sight. [Imagination] extends to all the senses and the movements of thought, for these too are called imaginings [*phantasiai*], in a different use of the term [*homōnumōs*]. (2) Criteria of knowledge of these are intellect and sensation, the former for intelligible things and the latter for sensible ones. For sensation cannot judge the universal, nor intellect the particular, but everything is composed of these and through these.

H.   Sextus Empiricus, *Against the Professors*
(*Adversus mathematicos*) 7.226

It appears from what has been said that the primary criteria for the knowledge of things are sense perception and intellect, the former having the role of an implement and the latter [that of] a craftsman. For as we cannot conduct an examination of heavy and light things without a balance, or differentiate between straight and crooked things without a rule, so intellect is not naturally able to judge things without sense perception. Well, this in summary is what the Peripatetics are like [in their opinions].

I.   Cicero, *On Ends* 5.9

Nature has been investigated by [the Peripatetics] in such a way that no part of it has been passed over, in land or sea or sky (to put it poetically). What is more, when they have spoken about the first principles of things and about the whole world, in such a way that they reach many of their conclusions not just by persuasive argument but by the necessary reasoning of mathematicians, they have applied a great deal of material from the things which they have investigated to the knowledge of things which are obscure.

J.   Stobaeus, *Selections* 1.50.28–9, 476.23–7 Wachsmuth 1884 (Aëtius 4.9.11–12, *Dox.* 397b34–398a4)

Epicurus [says that] pleasures and pains [relate to] things that are sensed; the Peripatetics, that they [relate to] things that are thought. For the same things do not seem pleasant and painful to everyone, as [the same things do seem] white or black.

K.   Galen, *On Anatomical Demonstrations* 1, II.218.4–8 Kühn

I went to Rome, where I conducted very many dissections for Boethus;[1] Eudemus[2] was regularly present with him, as was Alexander of Damascus, who is now recognised as public teacher of Peripatetic arguments at Athens.

L.   Galen, *On Prognosis, Against Epigenes* 5.9–16 (*CMG* V.8.1, 96.5–98.11 Nutton 1979)

The beginning of my association with [the jealous doctors and philosophers] was like this. Flavius Boethus, an ex-consul, loved fine things and learning, as you know. As his teacher in Peripatetic doctrine he had Alexander of Damascus, who also knew the [teachings] of Plato but adhered rather to those of Aristotle. When [Boethus] invited me to teach through dissection how respiration and voice come about, he got ready a number of young goats and pigs. For I said that there was no need of monkeys for the dissection, as not only these animals but virtually all animals with feet have the same arrangement, and those with a loud voice were more suitable than those with a small one for providing demonstrative evidence of what

---

[1] A Roman of consular rank with interests in Peripatetic philosophy (cf. Galen, *On my Own Books* XIX.13.5–7 Kühn, and L below); to be distinguished from the first-century BC Peripatetic philosopher Boethus of Sidon (above, 1N).

[2] Eudemus of Pergamum (Eudemus no. 12 in *RE* 6.1 col. 902; *DPA* vol. III 282–5), probably a teacher and certainly a patient of Galen (cf. Moraux 1984, 226 n. 3 and 687 n. 1), to be distinguished from Eudemus of Rhodes, the pupil of Aristotle and colleague of Theophrastus mentioned in the commentaries to 2 and 13 above.

was proposed. When the demonstration was about to take place, there were present, in particular, Adrianus the orator, not yet a sophist but still an associate of Boethus, and Demetrius of Alexandria, an associate of Favorinus, who daily spoke in public, in the style of Favorinus, on topics proposed [to him]. Before performing the dissection I said that I myself would display what was apparent from the dissection, but I hoped that the teacher Alexander would be more able, not only than me but than all of us, to work out by reason what could be concluded from this. The others all accepted what I said as reasonable, respecting Alexander and at the same time being eager that the whole meeting should take place without contentiousness. For you are aware that Alexander had a general reputation for this failing, as indeed he showed clearly on that occasion. For I said that I would show that there was a certain pairing of very fine nerves like hairs growing into the muscles of the larynx, some from the left side and some from the right, and that, if these were interrupted by a ligature or cut, the animal becomes unable to make a sound, but neither its life nor its activity is adversely affected. But Alexander interrupted before I made the demonstration and said, 'Yes, if we first concede this to you, that we should trust what appears through the senses.' When I heard this I left them and went away, saying just this, that I had been mistaken, in thinking that I was not coming to crude Pyrrhonists; otherwise I would not have come. When I went away, the others condemned Alexander, and in particular Adrianus and Demetrius, who were always hostile to his contentiousness, had good grounds for reproaching him forcefully.

Aristotle himself gives an account of how knowledge is achieved, principally in *Posterior Analytics* 2.19 but also elsewhere, notably in *Metaphysics* A.1 and in *On the Soul*. In *Posterior Analytics* 2.19, however, his principal concern is to explain how apprehension of first principles is possible even if one denies the Platonic doctrine of recollection of prenatal experience of the Forms; he is not chiefly concerned to challenge sceptics who deny the possibility of knowledge at all. In *Metaphysics* Γ, too, his attack is directed against the logical consequences of subjectivism, rather than towards explaining how objective knowledge can be achieved. Indeed, whether knowledge can be achieved at all is an issue concerning which he seems remarkably sanguine when compared with some of his philosophical predecessors and with most of his philosophical successors (cf. *Metaphysics* α.1.993a30–b9; *Rhetoric* 1.1355a14).

In the Hellenistic period, however, the question of the criterion of knowledge and of truth gained a new importance. Both Epicureans and

Stoics maintained that the fundamental criterion of truth was the evidence of the senses, and both were attacked by the Academic Sceptics, who argued that the senses could not bring us certainty (LS 40; and for Carneades arguing against the Epicureans cf. Schofield 1999, 339–40). Epicurus insisted that all sensations were, as such, true, error lying only in our misinterpreting of them (LS 16); the Stoics identified a particular class of 'apprehensive' sense-presentations (*katalēptikai phantasiai*) which could not lead us astray (LS 40) – which simply prompted ingenious Academic challenges against every presentation claimed to be of this type. Antiochus of Ascalon (above, 1EF), though claiming to restore the doctrines of the Old Academy after the scepticism of the Middle and New Academies, adopted the Stoic criterion, which is in itself enough to rule out any claim that he was principally responsible for the return of Platonism from scepticism to dogmatism; after all, Plato had little time for the senses as criteria of truth.

Aristocles of Messene, who is probably to be dated at the end of the first century BC or the beginning of the first century AD (see Chiesara 2001, xvii–xx) wrote a work *On Philosophy* in ten books; what survives is almost entirely criticism of non-Peripatetic epistemologies from Aristocles' eighth book. Aristocles attacks the neo-Pyrrhonian scepticism of Aenesidemus (**A**), the view of Metrodorus, Protagoras, the Aristippeans and the Epicureans that we can apprehend only what affects the senses (**BC**), and the Eleatic rejection of sense perception altogether in favour of reason (**D**); he argues that both sense perception and reason must play a part (**DE**); and this notion of the 'dual criterion' is attributed to Aristotle also by Sextus (**F**) and – if the attribution is correct; see above, commentary to section 1 – Arius Didymus (**G**(2)). Similarly also **3A**(4) above.

Chiesara 2001, 149 points out that in **B**(2) the premiss that we judge by opinions is not Epicurus', but Aristotle's (*On the Soul* 1.2.404b26). In other words, Aristocles is importing his own Aristotelian assumptions into his discussion of a rival philosopher's views – as Alexander was to do later (cf. Sharples 2001b, 514 n. 15). The list in **B**(4) of circumstances in which sensations differ might at first sight seem neo-Pyrrhonist, but Chiesara 2001, 150–1 shows that parallels can be found in Aristotle and in Plutarch. As Chiesara 2001, 165–7 shows, the emphasis on the divinity of intellect [*nous*] in **E** is distinctively Aristotelian.

However, as Barnes 2007a, 554 points out, the claims in **G**(2) that sensation cannot judge the universal, or thought the particular, are questionable, and **F**(2) and **H** suggest that in many cases – specifically, those that are not directly evident to either – sensation or thought should be regarded as co-operating. A rather different combination of direct experience and logical argument is attributed to the Peripatetics in **I**, where Cicero's Antiochean spokesman Piso not only attributes to the Peripatetics the drawing of inferences about what is not accessible to experience from what is but also presents Peripatetic natural science as a deductive system on the model of mathematics, which is certainly what the *Posterior Analytics* indicates it *ought* to be but, as modern scholars have pointed out, is very far removed from what it is in practice. (See on this Lennox 2001, xxii–xxiii.) In **J** the Epicurean view that pleasure and pain relate to sensation is contrasted with a view, attributed to the Peripatetics, that they relate to thought; the basis of this argument, that the objects of sensation seem the same to everyone, would simply be rejected by the Epicureans (cf. LS 161). Certainly for Aristotle different things are pleasant for different people, but this has to do with the moral condition of different individuals (*Nicomachean Ethics* 10. 5.1176a10–25), even if their moral condition is also reflected in their conception of the end.

KL have been discussed by scholars chiefly in the context of a mistaken conflation of Alexander of Damascus and Alexander of Aphrodisias in the Arabic tradition. In a modification of this which has not found general favour, Pierre Thillet suggested that these two people were indeed distinct, but that, in saying that Alexander of Damascus was the appointed teacher of Peripatetic philosophy in Athens, Galen was *himself* confusing him with Alexander of Aphrodisias, who we now know for certain held that position (above, **1Ab,Ac**).[3] However, Alexander was not appointed to it until AD 198 at the earliest, and the post was established by Marcus Aurelius in 176, so there was plenty of time for Alexander of Damascus to have held it first. As for the doctrinal implications of the passage, it has been suggested (Todd 1976a, 8–11) that Alexander of Damascus was a sceptical Platonist rather than a Peripatetic, but Todd 1995 argues that, in spite of Galen's refence to Pyrrhonism in **L**, Alexander of Damascus' question reflects not scepticism but a properly Aristotelian distinction between sense impressions, shared by man with the irrational animals, and the uniquely human use of reason.

On the issues in this section see further Barnes 2007a.

---

[3] Thillet 1984, xli–xlix.

Ethics

CHAPTER 15

An account of Peripatetic ethics: Stobaeus, 'Doxography C'

A. Stobaeus, *Selections* 2.7.13
(116.19–152.5 Wachsmuth 1884)

{13}[1] From Aristotle and the other Peripatetics, on ethics.

(1) He[2] says that character [*ēthos*] took its name from habit [*ethos*];[3] for perfection in those things of which we have the beginnings and seeds from nature [117] is achieved by habit and correct training. For this reason the [science] of character is concerned with habit and is concerned only with living creatures and most of all with human beings. For the others through habituation take on certain characters not through reason but by necessity, but a human being is moulded by reason as a result of habituation, when the <irrational> part of the soul is disposed according to reason. What is [here] called the irrational part of the soul is not that which is simply irrational, but that which can obey reason, and this is what the emotional [*pathētikos*] [part] is like, which is that which can admit virtue.[4]

(2) [Part] of the soul is rational, [part] irrational; rational that which discerns, irrational the impulsive.[5] Of the rational that [part] which contemplates the eternal and divine things is called scientific; that which is concerned with action relating to human affairs and <perishable things> is deliberative. Of the irrational that which has appetition for things which depend on us is desiring; that which, as it were, defends us against our neighbours is spirited. So there are also two kinds of virtues, [118] one

---

[1] {Braces} indicate Wachsmuth's chapter numbers, and also material which he square-brackets as not part of the original text. [Square brackets] indicate Wachsmuth's page numbers, and also material supplied in the translation for clarity. <Angle brackets> indicate Wachsmuth's supplements to the Greek text. My own section numbers are given in (round brackets).

[2] Aristotle? Or the author whom Stobaeus – or his source – is excerpting?

[3] *Nicomachean Ethics* 2.1.1103a17–18, *Eudemian Ethics* 2.2.1220a39–b1.

[4] For the three parts of the soul cf. *Nicomachean Ethics* 1.13.

[5] I.e. that concerned with the instigation of movement. The terminology is Stoic, though the thought is Aristotelian.

rational, the other irrational, since contemplation and action are naturally concerned with these. And for this reason moral virtue is not knowledge, but a <disposition> which chooses noble things.

(3) Virtue is perfected by three things: nature, habit and reason.[6] For the human being, differing in body and soul from the other living creatures on account of being intermediate between the immortal and the mortal, has something in common linking him to both, to the rational [beings] the divine [element] in his soul, to the irrational the mortality of his body, [and so] he reasonably desires the perfection of both.[7] And first he desires being, for he is appropriated [*oikeiōsthai*] to himself by nature,[8] and on account of this he is fittingly pleased in [circumstances] that are in accordance with nature, and annoyed in those contrary to it. Eagerness to secure health and desire for pleasure and clinging to life are because these are in accordance with nature and objects of choice on their own account[9] and goods. Conversely rejecting and avoiding illness and pain and destruction are because these are contrary to nature and objects of avoidance on their own account and evils. For our body [119] is dear to us, and so is our soul, and so are the parts and capacities and activities of these; according to our forethought for the safety of these,[10] the beginning comes about of impulse and of proper function [*kathēkon*][11] and of virtue. For if concerning the choice and avoidance of the aforementioned things absolutely no error occurred, but we continued aiming at good things and having no share in evil ones, we would never have looked for correct and unerring selection among these. But since we often go wrong in choice and avoidance on account of ignorance and reject good things and encounter evils as [if they were] goods, necessarily we look for sure knowledge in choosing, and finding that this was in harmony with nature we called it 'virtue' on account of the splendour of its activity, and wondering at it as if divine we honour it before all other things.[12] For actions and what are called proper

---

[6] Görgemanns 1983, 174, notes that habituation does not appear in the sequel, and that *oikeiōsis* has not appeared in (1)–(2); he therefore suggests that we have here a join between two originally separate souces.

[7] Inwood 1983, 192 argues that the emphasis on body and soul here as *two* objects of *oikeiōsis* is distinctive of Antiochus, by contrast with, on the one hand, the Stoics, for whom *oikeiōsis* is to oneself as a unity, and, on the other, the *three* classes of Peripatetic goods in (9) below.

[8] For 'appropriation' see below, 17.

[9] Görgemanns 1983, 176–7 notes that in the sequel the terminology 'objects of choice on their own account', perhaps because of its Peripatetic origins, appears much more often than 'appropriation'.

[10] Rejecting, with Görgemanns 1983, 169, Usener's addition of *di'* before *hōn*.

[11] I adopt LS's translation of the Stoic term rendered by Cicero as *officium*, 'duty'. 'Appropriate action' might be clearer, but it risks confusion with the *etymologically* unconnected 'appropriation', *oikeiōsis*.

[12] Görgemanns 1983, 175 notes that the intellectualist approach to virtue here conflicts with (2) above and thus provides further evidence that (1)–(2) originally belonged to a different discussion.

functions [*kathēkonta*] have their beginnings from selection of things in accordance with nature and rejection of those contrary to nature; and for this reason correct actions [*katorthōseis*] and wrong actions [*hamartiai*] take place in these and concerning these.[13] Virtually the whole [ethical] outline of the school[14] starts from these, as I will show very concisely.

(4) That children are objects of choice for those who have produced them not just because of usefulness, but on their own account, can be recognised from the evident facts. At any rate, no one is so savage and bestial [120] in nature as not to be eager that after his own death his children should enjoy happiness and continue to live fine lives, rather than the opposite. It is a result of this affection for offspring that people make wills when they are going to die, and that they have care even for those still in the womb, appointing overseers and guardians and entrusting and summoning their closest friends to come to the assistance of [the children], and some, when their children die, even die with them. When children are so loved as being objects of choice on their own account, necessarily parents and she who shares our bed and relatives and others connected with us and fellow-citizens are objects of affection on their own account. For from nature we have certain affinities [*oikeiotētes*] to these too; for a human being is a living creature inclined to mutual affection and community. If it happens that some of our friendships are remote, others close to us, this does not affect the issue; for all [affection] is an object of choice on its own account and not just on account of usefulness. If affection for fellow-citizens is an object of choice on its own account, so necessarily must that be which is for those of the same nation and tribe, and consequently too that for all human beings. For all those [121] who rescue [people] are disposed towards their neighbours in such a way as to act in most cases not with a view to merit, but according to what is an object of choice on its own account. For who would not, if he were able, rescue a human being he saw being overpowered by a wild animal? Who would not give support to a person perishing through poverty? Who, if he came across a spring in a waterless desert, would not by markers indicate it to those who come by the same route? Who does not set

---

[13] The contrast between proper functions and correct, i.e. virtuous, actions is Stoic; in the case of the former it is the action that is at issue, in the case of the latter the moral state of the agent.

[14] So Görgemanns 1983, 175, interpreting *hairesis* as 'philosophical sect'; he says that this requires interpreting the present sentence as a remark by the compiler, interrupting his source, and takes 'outline', each time it occurs, to refer specifically to that source (166 and n. 4). But it is not clear that the sentence has to be taken as an interruption in this way. Inwood 1983, 193 notes that the promise here is not fulfilled, for (3) is concerned with *oikeiōsis* to oneself, what follows rather with *social oikeiōsis*, and argues (199) that the difficulty of relating the two results from the lack of an adequate link between the two in Stoicism.

great store by a good reputation after his life [is over]? Who does not loathe, as contrary to human nature, utterances such as the following: 'When I am dead, let the earth be engulfed in fire; it doesn't matter to me at all, for things are fine as far as I'm concerned.'[15] So it is clear that we have a natural goodwill and affection for everyone, which reveals what is an object of choice on its own account and the rationality of nature; for 'one is the race of human beings and gods; we both draw breath from a single mother'.[16]

(5) Since we have a common affection for human beings, much more is being an object of choice for its own sake apparent in relation to those who are our habitual friends. If a friend is an object of choice on his own account, so too are friendship and [122] goodwill, both that from those who share in everything in life and that from the majority of human beings; so praise, too, is an object of choice on its own account, for we have a natural affinity towards those who praise [us]. If praise is an object of choice on its own account, so too is good reputation. For we do not understand good reputation to be in outline[17] anything other than praise from the majority. So in this way it has been clearly shown that the goods which are external are naturally objects of choice on their own account; then how much more so those which are about us and in us? I mean those concerning the body and the soul.

(6) If a human being is an object of choice on his own account, the parts of a human being, too, will be objects of choice on their own account. The most general parts of a human being are body and soul. So the body, too, will be an object of choice on its own account. For how can our neighbour's body be an object of choice for us on its own account, but not our own [body]? How can a human being who is our neighbour be an object of choice on his own account, and each of us not be an object of choice for himself on his own account? Or how can this be so, but the parts of the body and the excellences of the parts and of the whole body not be objects of choice? So objects of choice on their own account for us are health, strength, beauty, swiftness of foot, good physical condition, keen perception, in general all [123] the excellences of body, so to speak. Indeed no one in his right mind would accept being ugly and damaged in appearance, even if absolutely no [physical] difficulty was going to accompany this ugliness. So it is reasonable to avoid ugliness even apart from [physical] difficulty. If

---

[15] Literally, 'let earth be mixed with fire'. The quotation is from an unknown dramatic source = *Tragicorum Graecorum Fragmenta*, adespota, fr. 513 Nauck², and is also alluded to by the Stoic spokesman at Cicero, *On Ends* 3.64.

[16] Pindar, *Nemean* 6.1–2.

[17] Görgemanns 1983, 170, 'from the outline', taking this to refer to Arius' source; so too Inwood 1983, 191.

ugliness is an object of avoidance on its own account, beauty is an object of choice not only on account of utility but also on its own account. That beauty has an attractive quality of its own is obvious; everyone has a natural affinity to those who are beautiful apart from all utility, and towards being ready to do good to them and benefit them, as a result of which [beauty] seems to create goodwill. So according to this argument, too, beauty is one of the things that are objects of choice on their own account, ugliness one of those that are objects of avoidance on their own account. The same argument applies also to health and disease and strength and weakness and swiftness of foot and slowness and sense perception and being disabled [in one's senses]. So, if the goods of the body have been shown to be objects of choice on their own account, and the evils that are opposites of these objects of avoidance on their own account, it is necessary that the parts of the soul be objects of choice on their own account, and the excellences of these and of the whole soul.

(7) When virtue has made its entrance, as we have indicated,[18] from bodily and external goods and has turned towards and considered itself, because it is itself one of the things in accordance with nature, much more than the excellences of the body, it has developed an affinity to itself, as being an object of choice on its own account, and more to itself than to the excellences of the body. So the excellences of the soul are much more valuable.

[124] (8) Moreover, one could also work this out from what has been gone over already. If the health of the body is an object of choice on its own account, much more is that of the soul. <The health of the soul> is temperance which frees us from the vehemence of the passions. If bodily strength is among goods, much more will that of the soul be an object of choice on its own account and a good. The strength of the soul is courage and endurance, which makes souls strong. So courage too will be an object of choice on its own account, and endurance too. Analogously, if the beauty of the body is an object of choice on its own account, the beauty of the soul too will be an object of choice on its own account, and the beauty of soul is justice; for 'doing no wrong makes us fine'.[19]

---

[18] In (3) above, Wachsmuth. But, as Görgemanns 1983, 177 notes, *external* goods were not mentioned there; he suggests (178–9) that they were omitted to avoid repetition when (as he sees it) (1)–(3), originally from a separate treatise, were combined with (4)ff. Inwood 1983, 193 and n. 8 notes that external goods in (4)–(6) are confined to social relationships, as with Antiochus in Cicero, *On Ends* 5.68, and suggests that we are dealing with a combination of material influenced by Antiochus with more orthodox Peripatetic doctrine.

[19] Menander, fr. 790 Koerte.

{14} {That the three kinds of goods, those concerning the body, those concerning the soul, and the external [ones], have a correspondence to one another, even though they are different.}

(9) A very similar argument also applies to the virtues, since it seems that the three kinds of goods, [in spite of] the very great difference between them, nevertheless have a certain correspondence,[20] [125] which I shall try to show clearly. What health is in the body, that, we say, is called temperance in the soul, and wealth in externals; for [wealth] covers up most errors. What strength is in the body, that courage is in the soul, and in externals, political office. What good perception is in the body, that wisdom is in the soul, and in externals, good fortune. What beauty is in the body, that justice is in the soul, and friendship in externals.[21] So three kinds of goods are objects of choice on their own account, those concerning the soul and those concerning the body and those that are external. And those concerning the soul are far more objects of choice than the others, since the soul is more in command and more an object of choice than the body.

(10) So it is clear that the virtues of the soul are more objects of choice than those of the body and external [goods], surpassing them in a similar way. [People] aim at the others first as objects of choice on their own account, then as being useful for life in a city and a community and also for the life of contemplation. For life is measured by actions in city and community and in contemplation. In this choice, virtue is not self-loving, but involved in community and city. Since we said that virtue has an affinity to itself more than [126] all things, it is clear that it necessarily has a natural affinity to understanding the truth. In accordance with this, remaining in life is measured by activities in community and city and contemplation, and departing from it by the opposites. So it is wrong to consider that departure from life can be reasonable for the wise and remaining in life reasonable for the bad. For those who can accomplish actions in community and city and contemplation, whether they are good or bad [people], it is reasonable to remain in life, while for those who cannot, it is reasonable to depart from life.

(11) Since virtue greatly surpasses bodily and external goods both in what it produces and in being an object of choice on its own account, in

---

[20] Omitting *pros ton logon* with Görgemanns 1983, 172. Moraux 1973, 325–7 questions the authenticity of (9), which repeats and expands the theme of (8), and Görgemanns 1983, 180 argues that it is an interpolation deriving from the pseudo-Aristotle *Divisions*, 56.

[21] Tarán 1981, 747 argues that counting friends as external goods here is Stoic, not Aristotelian. The list is based, as far as the soul is concerned, on the four cardinal virtues temperance, courage, wisdom and justice, a listing which is characteristic of Plato and the Stoics rather than of the Aristotelian tradition.

accordance with the argument the end is not completed by bodily and external goods and is not gaining all of these; rather it is to live virtuously with bodily and external goods, either all of them or most and the most important. So happiness is virtuous activity in actions of a primary sort[22] as one would wish. Bodily and external goods are said to produce happiness because their presence makes a contribution; those who think that they *complete* happiness are ignorant, for happiness is a life, and life is made up of[23] action. No [127] bodily or external good is in itself either an action or an activity at all.

(12) Since this is the account of these things, benefaction will be established and gratitude and favour and fellow-feeling and love of children and of brothers, and in addition to these love of country and of one's father and one's relations and, in accordance with proper function, readiness to share and goodwill and friendship and fairness and justice and the whole divine chorus of the virtues; those who despise this clearly go wrong concerning the choice of goods and avoidance of evils and concerning the acquisition and use of goods, and it is agreed that in choice the error is one of discernment, in acquisition one of the manner [of acquisition], in use one of folly. Concerning choice they go wrong when they choose what is not even good at all, or [choose] what is less [good] more eagerly than they need. With most people this happens when they prefer the pleasant to the advantageous or the advantageous to the noble and follow their impulses immoderately. Concerning acquisition, when they do not determine beforehand either from where they should or how they should or the extent to which they should acquire these things. Concerning use, since all use is referred either to itself or to something else, when [it is referred] to itself, [they go wrong] when they do not acquire them in a way that is proportionate to the things; when to something else, when they do not keep to a proper valuation of what is fitting. If the bad go wrong concerning these things, the good will certainly [128] act correctly concerning their opposites, having virtue as the guide of their actions. For all the virtues, it seems, have in common discerning, choosing and acting. Virtue is not undiscerning or unchoosing or inactive, but wisdom, like a guide, is the beginning of the

---

[22] The MSS have *prohēgoumenais*, 'primary'. Here and in other places both in this and in similar texts Wachsmuth and other editors have changed the text to *khorēgoumenai*, 'provided with resources'. But it has become clear that 'primary' is indeed the correct reading in all these texts, indicating either actions that are undertaken in favourable circumstances, as opposed to those performed only because adverse circumstances require it, or else the favourable, as opposed to unfavourable, circumstances themselves. See Sharples 1990, 64–5 n. 220; 2004, 178 n. 597; Giusta 1961–2, 229–31; Grilli 1969, 439–44, 460–61; Huby 1983, 125–6.

[23] Literally, 'completed out of'. See below, **18HI** and commentary.

things chosen and avoided both by itself and by the others, and done and not done, and more so and less so. Each of the others marks off for itself only those that fall under it.

{15} {On excellence/virtue}[24]

(13) Excellence is the name that has been given to the best disposition or that according to which what possesses it is best disposed. This is clear from an inductive argument; for the excellence of a shoemaker is said to be that by which he is able to make the best shoe, and of a builder that by which he is best disposed for building a fine house. Well, it is agreed that putting a thing in the best disposition belongs to excellence. There are two first principles, as it were, of the excellences/virtues: reason and feeling. These sometimes agree in harmony with each other, sometimes disagree in conflict. Their opposition comes about because of pleasures and pains. The victory of reason has the name 'self-control', derived from 'control', while the [victory] of the irrational through its disobedience to reason [is called] 'lack of self-control'. The harmony and concord of both is virtue, when the one leads to what it should, and the other follows obediently.

{16} {On objects of choice and avoidance}

(14) That is called an object of choice which causes an impulse towards itself when reason agrees; [129] that, an object of avoidance which [causes an impulse] away from itself. For just as what is an object of wish derives its name from wishing, so the object of choice [does so] from choosing. To the ancients[25] what is an object of choice and what is good seemed to be the same thing. For, sketching out the good, they defined it in this way: 'the good is that which all things desire'.[26] Of goods they said that some are objects of choice on account of ourselves, some on account of our neighbours. Of those on account of ourselves some are fine, some necessary. Fine are the virtues and the activities that derive from them, wisdom and being wise and justice and acting justly, and correspondingly in the case of the others. Necessary are being alive and the things that contribute to this and those that count as productive, such as the body and its parts and the uses of these, and of those that are called external good family, wealth, reputation, peace, freedom, friendship; for each of these makes some contribution to the employment of virtue.

{17} {The sources of happiness}

---

[24] The Greek *aretē* can mean 'excellence' in general or 'virtue' more specifically. Hence my alternative translations.
[25] Trapp 2007, 147 n. 52 notes that this reference to 'the ancients' is in the style of Antiochus of Ascalon.
[26] *Nicomachean Ethics* 1.1.1049a3.

(15) Happiness comes from noble and primary[27] actions. For this reason it is altogether noble, just as pipe-playing[28] is altogether a matter of skill. For the involvement of material things [130] does not make happiness depart from pure nobility, just as the use of instruments [does not alter] the activity of medicine [from being] altogether a matter of skill. For every action is some activity of the soul. When the person who acts uses certain things for the completion of his purpose, these should not be considered parts of the activity, even though each of the aforementioned <skills> seeks each thing – but not as a part of the skill, rather as producing it. It is not right to say that those things without which something cannot be done are parts of the activity. For a part is conceived of as completing the whole, but necessary conditions [are conceived of] as productive, by contributing and assisting towards the end.

{18} {How many parts of the good there are; and about the goal}

(16) The good is divided into the noble, the advantageous and the pleasant. These are the goals of particular actions; what results from all of them is happiness. Happiness is 'the primary[29] employment of complete virtue in a complete life' or 'the activity of a complete life in accordance with virtue'[30] or 'the unimpeded employment of virtue in things in accordance with nature'. The same is also the end [of choice and action]. If being happy is the end, happiness is called the goal, and wealth is a good, being wealthy [131] one of the things that is necessary, according to those who define in this way for the sake of accuracy in the names. But we should follow the custom of the ancients and say that the end is 'that for the sake of which we do everything, but itself [for the sake] of nothing [else]',[31] or 'the ultimate among objects of appetition', or 'living in accordance with virtue amid bodily and external goods, either all of them or the majority and the most important'.[32] This, being the greatest and most perfect of goods, has all the others serving it. For it is agreed that we must say that the things that contribute to it are among goods; those that oppose it, <among evils; those that neither contribute nor oppose,> neither among goods nor among evils, but among indifferents. But not every noble action brings happiness.

(17) They said happiness is the employment of *complete* virtue, because they said that some virtues are complete and others incomplete. Complete

[27] See above, n. 22.
[28] So the MSS here, reading *aulois*; the summary in **15B** (see the note there) has 'in other things' (*allois*). The latter gives a better sense in view of the following reference in both texts to medicine as an example; but for pipe-playing as an example in a similar context see Alexander of Aphrodisias, *Supplement to* On the Soul *(Mantissa)* 20.160.16, 33.
[29] See above, n. 22.   [30] Aristotle, *Eudemian Ethics* 2.1.1219a39.
[31] Aristotle, *Metaphysics* α.2.994b9–10; cf. *Nicomachean Ethics* 1.1.1094a18.
[32] Cf. Antiochus in **18Z** and in Cicero, *On Ends* 4.15.

are justice and nobility;[33] incomplete are good natural endowment and moral progress. It is what is complete that is fitting for what is complete. The end, then, is the activity of virtue of this sort, with no part missing. They added 'in a complete life', wanting to indicate that happiness concerns men who have already advanced in life. For a youth is incomplete, and so is his life, and so happiness does not apply to him, nor in general in [132] an incomplete time, but in a complete one. 'Complete' is the maximum time that god has laid down for us; 'laid down' allowing some latitude, as with bodily size. As one line will not make a recitation or one hand movement a dance, and one swallow will not make a summer,[34] so a short time will not constitute happiness, either. For happiness must be complete, involving a complete man and a complete time and complete fortune.[35] The activity of virtue must be 'primary' because it is altogether necessary to be among the goods according to nature; even amid evils the good man will use his virtue nobly, but he will not be blessed, and amid outrages he will display nobility, but will not be happy.[36] The reason is that virtue in itself only produces noble things, happiness both noble things and good ones. For it does not want to endure terrible things, but to enjoy good ones, in addition to preserving justice in sharing and not depriving itself either of the nobilities of contemplation or of the necessities of life.

(18) Happiness is a thing that is most pleasant and most noble, and it is not, like a craft, intensified by a plurality of instruments and equipment. It is not the same for a god and for a human being. Nor is virtue something that cannot be lost by the good [133] at all, for it can be removed by the number and magnitude of evils. Consequently one might be in doubt whether someone who is still alive should[37] be called happy in the strict sense, because of the uncertainty of fortune. Solon's saying is a good one: 'consider the end of a long life'. Life also bears witness to this, calling men happy when they die. The person who is deprived of happiness is not miserable like the one who does not possess [happiness] at all, but sometimes in an intermediate state.[38] Both the wise person and the one who is

---

[33] *kalokagathia*, the quality of a morally good person.
[34] In Greek, 'a spring'. The proverb is quoted by Aristotle, *Nicomachean Ethics* 1.7.1098a18, in a similar context to the present.
[35] Literally 'a complete *daimōn*', fortune in the sense of what is bestowed by the divine and the etymological root of 'happiness', *eudaimonia*; to be contrasted with *tukhē*, what befalls one for no apparent reason, and the root of *eutukhia*, 'good luck'.
[36] Compare Aristotle, *Nicomachean Ethics* 1.10.1100b25–1101a8, quoted in the commentary to 18 below.
[37] The Greek here has 'should not', but English idiom requires 'should'.
[38] The Stoics, on the other hand, would deny that there is any intermediate state between happiness and misery, any more than between virtue and vice: Long and Sedley 1987, 376–7.

not wise sometimes live what is called the intermediate life, that which is neither happy nor miserable. Happiness does not apply to those who are asleep, or at least not in actuality. For the activity of the soul is concerned with being awake, and to this is added 'in accordance with nature', since not all the time good men spend awake is employment of complete virtue, but that is [so] which is in accordance with nature. This is that of the man who is neither mad nor deranged, since madness and derangement, like sleep, exclude him from this employment [of virtue], and perhaps indeed from that of reason, making him [like] a beast. Those for whom living is rational possess happiness; but not even these always, but when their life is primary.[39] As the employment of virtue is called happiness, so the employment of vice is called misery; but while vice is sufficient for misery, [134] virtue is not sufficient for happiness. For the good person to possess good things is beneficial both for him and for others. Life is to be abandoned by the good in excessive misfortune, by the bad also in excessive good fortune; for they go wrong more, and for this reason the bad are not fortunate in the strict sense.

{19} {How many senses there are of 'good'}[40]

(19) Since happiness is the greatest good, we must distinguish how many senses of 'good' there are. They say that the term is used in three ways: that which is the cause of preservation for all existents, and that which is predicated of every good thing, and that which is an object of choice on its own account. The divine is the first, the genus of goods <the second>, <the third> is the end to which we refer everything, namely happiness.[41] And that which is an object of choice on its own account is said in three ways: either the ultimate thing for the sake of which we do certain things, or that for the sake of which [we do] all things, or thirdly what is a part of these. Of things that are objects of choice on their own account some have the character of ends, others are productive. Of the character of ends are primary activities in accordance with virtue; productive are the materials of the virtues.

(20) Of goods some are honourable, some praiseworthy, some capacities, some beneficial. Honourable, for example god, the ruler, a father; praiseworthy, for example justice, wisdom; capacities, for example wealth,

---

[39] Above, n. 22.
[40] For parallels to the following sequence of divisions see Sharples 1983b.
[41] Furley 1983, comparing *Magna Moralia* 1.1, well argues that the point of this is to establish the third of the three applications as the one relevant to ethics; he also rightly compares the way in which the first is here formulated to the account of the role of god in the world in pseudo-Aristotle, *On the World* (*De mundo*).

political office, power; beneficial those that produce and preserve these, for example [that produce and preserve] health and good physical condition.

[135] (21) Moreover of objects of choice and goods some are objects of choice in themselves, others on account of other things. Those that are honourable and those that are praiseworthy and capacities [are objects of choice] in themselves. Capacities too are among things that are good in themselves, for example wealth and political offices, which the good man will use <well> and seek for; and the things which the good man can use well are by nature good in themselves, like those that are healthy, which the doctor will seek for and be able to use. But those that are beneficial [are objects of choice] on account of other things; for it is by producing and preserving other things that they are among goods.

(22) Another division: of things that are good in themselves some are ends, some not. For example justice and virtue and health [are ends] and, to summarise simply, all the things which result from the individual activities, such as health, but not what is healthy or the care of the sick. Good natural endowment and instances of remembering and learning are not ends.

(23) Another division: of ends some are good for everyone, some not. Virtue and wisdom are good for everyone, for they benefit whoever has them; but wealth [136] and political offices and capacities are not good for everyone in any way whatsoever, inasmuch as their being goods is determined by the good person's use of them. For [good people] appear to seek for them and to cause benefit by using them. The things that the good person uses well, the bad person uses badly, just as those which the musical person uses well, the unmusical uses badly. At the same time by using [them] badly [the bad person] is harmed, just as the horseman benefits a good horse, but the person who is not a horseman harms it considerably.

(24) Moreover of goods some concern the soul, some the body, and some are external. Concerning the soul, for instance good natural endowment, skill, virtue, wisdom, practical wisdom and pleasure; concerning the body: health, good perception, beauty, strength, soundness, and all the parts with their capacities and activities; external: wealth, reputation, good family, power, friends, relations, one's country. Of the goods concerning the soul some are always present by nature, such as sharpness and memory, and in general good natural endowment; some come to be present as the result of taking care, such as preliminary education and a way of life suited to a free man; some are present as a result of perfection, for example practical wisdom, justice, and in general wisdom.

(25) Moreover of goods some can be acquired and lost, for example wealth. Some can be acquired but not lost, for example good spirit, not being impressed by things.[42] Some [137] can be lost but not acquired, for example sense perception and life. Some can neither be acquired nor lost, for example good family.

(26) Moreover of goods some are objects of choice on their own account only, for example pleasure and being untroubled; some are productive only, such as wealth; some are <both> productive and objects of choice on their own account, for example virtue, friends, health.

(27) And goods are divided in many other ways, because they do not belong to a single genus, but are spoken of in the ten categories. For 'good' is uttered ambiguously, and all such things have only their name in common, but the account corresponding to the name is different.

{20} {Concerning moral virtue, that it [consists in] means}

(28) Now that these distinctions have been made, it is necessary to consider more accurately what is said about moral virtue. They suppose that this is concerned with the irrational part of the soul, since for the present consideration they supposed that the soul has two parts, of which one possesses reason, the other is irrational.[43] Concerned with the rational are nobility and practical wisdom and sharpness of mind and the like; concerning the irrational, temperance and justice and courage and the other virtues that are called moral.

(29) They say that these are destroyed by deficiency and [138] excess. To show this they use the evidence of the senses, wanting to support [what they say] about things that are unclear on the basis of those that are clear. Now, too much or too little exercise destroys physical strength. And the same applies to drink and to food; taking too much or too little destroys health, but when the aforementioned things are proportionate they preserve both strength and health. Similarly in the case of temperance and courage and the other virtues. The person who is such in nature as not to be afraid even of being struck by lightning is not courageous, but mad; conversely, the person who is afraid of everything, even [his] shadow, is ignoble and cowardly. That person is courageous, by general agreement, who fears neither everything nor nothing.

---

[42] Literally 'absence of wonder'. Fortenbaugh 1984, 185 notes the conflict with (18) above, where it is asserted that virtue can be lost because of overwhelming evils, and points out that in the present passage 'good spirit' and 'absence of wonder' are, respectively, conjectures in place of the MSS readings 'good fortune' and 'immortality'.

[43] See A(1)–(2) above. The exposition now returns to the themes of *Nicomachean Ethics* 2, virtue being concerned with pleasure and pain and being a mean between extremes. However, the sequence: division into virtues of the rational and irrational parts – mean between extremes – pleasure and pain is closer to *Magna Moralia* 1.5.

(30) The same things[44] both increase and destroy virtue: moderate fears increase courage, but those that are too great or too small destroy it. Similarly in the case of the other virtues, too, the excesses and deficiencies corresponding to them destroy them, but moderation increases them.

(31) Virtue is determined not only by these things, but also by pleasure and pain. For it is on account of pleasure that we do base things, and on account of fear that we refrain from noble ones. It is not possible to get either virtue or vice without pain and pleasure. So virtue is concerned with pleasures and pains.

[139] (32) In order to show clearly what concerns these things they thought it necessary to take into account also the things that take place in the soul. They say that the following are present in the souls of human beings: affections [*pathē*], capacities, dispositions. Affections are anger, fear, hatred, longing, envy, pity and things like these, which are accompanied by pleasure and pain. Capacities are those by which we are said to be affected by these things, for example those by which we become angry, are fearful, are envious, and whatever of such things we are affected by. Dispositions are those by which we are in a certain condition in relation to these and as a result of which the activity of these is accomplished well or badly. So if someone grows angry easily, at everything and in every way, he will clearly have the disposition of irascibility. If in such a way that [he does not grow angry] at all or at anything, that of being too easy-going. Both are subject to criticism, while the disposition that is praised is mildness, by which we become angry when we should and as we should and with the person we should. So the virtues are dispositions which result in activities in passions being praised.

(33)[45] Since virtue is concerned with things that are done, and every action is considered as continuous, and in everything that is continuous, as with magnitudes, there is some excess and deficiency and mean, and these are either in relation to one another or in relation to us, in everything the mean in relation to us is best, for this is as knowledge and reason command. The mean is defined not by the issue of quantity but by that [140] of quality, on account of which it is also perfect by being in this extreme condition. The opposites are in a way opposed both to each other and to the mean; for deficiency and excess are opposites, but the mean is related to both as the equal is to the unequal, being more than what is less but less than what is more.

---

[44] Adopting Rassow's emendation for 'these things' of the MSS; so *Magna Moralia* 1.5.1185b27, which our author is following here, and *Nicomachean Ethics* 2.2.1104a27.

[45] Moraux 1973, 381–2 notes that our text here shifts from following the *Magna Moralia* (1.7) to the *Eudemian Ethics* (2.3).

(34) So the mean in relation to us is the best, for example, according to Theophrastus,[46] when we meet people one tells us many things and chatters at length, another [says] little and not even what is necessary, whereas another [says] only what is necessary and hits the mark. This mean is relative to us,[47] for this is determined by us with reason. And for this reason virtue is 'a disposition relating to choice, in the mean relative to us, determined by reason and as the man with practical wisdom would determine it';[48] then adding certain pairings, following his master,[49] considering them individually [Theophrastus] next attempted an inductive argument in the following way. The following were taken for examples: temperance, wantonness, insensibility; mildness, irascibility, lack of feeling; courage, rashness, cowardice; justice . . .;[50] liberality, [141] profligacy, illiberality; magnanimity, small-mindedness, vanity; magnificence, sordidness, pretentiousness. Of these dispositions some are base through excess or deficiency concerning affections, others are good, clearly by being means. The temperate person is neither the one who has absolutely no desires nor the one who has desires, for the former, like a stone, has no appetition even for what is natural, while the other, through excess in desires, is wanton. The person who is in the middle of these, who desires what he should and when and to the extent that he should, and determines these by reason according to what is appropriate, as by a rule, is both said to be temperate and is so by nature. Mild is <neither the person who is not pained and never gets angry at anything> nor the one who gets angry at everything, even if it is very slight, but the person who has the middle disposition. Courageous is neither the person who fears nothing, even if the one attacking him is a god, nor [the one who fears] everything and, as the saying is, [his own] shadow . . .; just is neither the man who distributes too much to himself nor the one [who distributes] too little, but the one [who distributes] what is fair – fair proportionately, not arithmetically.[51] <Liberal> is neither the person who gives at random nor the one who does not give . . .; magnanimous is

---

[46] Theophrastus fr. 449A FHS&G. Wachsmuth regards the whole of (34) as deriving from Theophrastus; FHS&G includes (35) as well, but Fortenbaugh 1983b, 205 makes it clear that this is not intended to suggest a Theophrastean origin for (35), which he regards as later.

[47] Or, with the emendations of Usener and Meurer, 'this is the mean relative to us which is best'.

[48] Aristotle, *Nicomachean Ethics* 2.6.1106b36–1107a2.   [49] I.e. Aristotle.

[50] The text is defective and the extremes corresponding to justice as a mean are missing; but see below in (34), also (42).

[51] The Greek term for 'fair' (*isos*) also indicates 'equal'. While democrats interpreted 'equality' in terms of equal shares for all, anti-democrats hijacked the term by interpreting it as *proportionate* equality; equality required that the better people should get more in proportion to their greater worth. Cf. Isocrates, *Areopagiticus* 21; Plato, *Laws* 757bc; Aristotle, *Politics* 5.1.1301b29.

neither the person who thinks he deserves [142] every great thing nor the person [who thinks he deserves] absolutely nothing, but the one who takes on each occasion what he should and to the extent that he deserves. Magnificent is neither the person who is splendid on every occasion even where he should not be, nor the one who never is, but the one who fits himself opportunely to each occasion.

(35) This then is what the moral kind of virtues[52] is like, concerned with affections and considered in the mean; it is related to <practical wisdom> by mutual implication,[53] but not in the same way: wisdom [belongs to] the moral [virtues] as a *proprium*, but they to it *per accidens.* For the just person also has practical wisdom, for it is reason of a certain sort that gives him [this] form; but the person with practical wisdom is not also just as a *proprium*, but because he does what is noble and good generally, and nothing base.

{21} {Concerning the affections of the soul}

(36) Of affections and impulses some are urbane, some base, some intermediate. Urbane are friendship, gratitude, indignation, shame, confidence, pity; base are envy, malice, arrogance; intermediate are pity, fear, anger, pleasure, desire. Of these some are to be taken at once, others require a determination. Every affection is established concerning pleasure and pain, and for this reason the moral virtues are concerned with these. Love of money and love of pleasure and obsession with sex, and things like these, are dispositions of a different sort concerned with vices. Some love[54] is [desire] for friendship, some for intercourse, some for both; and for this reason the first is good, the second bad, the third intermediate.

[143] {22} {On friendship}

(37) There are four differentiations of friendship, for comrades, for relations, for strangers, and erotic. Whether we should also include that of benefactors and that involving admiration needs to be argued. The beginning of comradely friendship is companionship; of that for relations, nature; of that for strangers, need; of erotic friendship, the *pathos*;[55] of friendship for benefactors, gratitude; of that involving admiration, power. Of all [these types] there are, in sum, three ends [in view]: the noble, the advantageous and the pleasant. For all those who engage in friendship in any way at all choose friendship on account of some one of these or all of them. First, as

---

[52] Literally 'the kind of moral virtues'.
[53] Moral virtue requires practical wisdom; and conversely, without moral virtue, one has not practical wisdom but an amoral 'cleverness'. Cf. Aristotle, *Nicomachean Ethics* 6.12–13.
[54] Greek *erōs*, which is passionate desire in the modern sense of 'passion'.
[55] That is, the emotion that affects one in such cases.

I said before, is friendship towards oneself, second that towards parents; next [friendships] towards other associates and strangers. For this reason, in that towards oneself one should beware of excess; in that towards others, of deficiency. The former is criticised as self-love, the latter as meanness.

{23} {On gratitude}

(38) Gratitude[56] is spoken of in three ways. One is service for the sake of the former benefit itself, the second the exchange of beneficial service, the third the memory of such service. And for this reason common usage has proclaimed the goddesses [the Graces] as three. We also speak of graceful-ness in appearance or in speech; in respect of this the former is called graceful, the second charming.

(39) The good person will choose the way of life that involves virtue, whether he is at some time in a position of leadership, the times inducing him [to this], [144] or if it is necessary to be the courtier of some king or to be a lawgiver or to engage in politics in some other way. If he is not involved in these he will turn to the way of life of ordinary people or to that of contemplation or, intermediate [between these], to that of a teacher. He will choose both to do and to contemplate noble things. If he is prevented by the state of the times from being concerned with both of these, he will follow one of them, giving more honour to the life of contemplation, but involving himself in political actions because of his sense of community. Because of this he will also marry and have children and engage in politics and fall in love with a temperate love and drink socially, even if not as a primary aim. And in general he will remain alive practising virtue, and conversely, if he ever should on account of necessities, he will depart [from life], having given thought beforehand to his burial according to the law and to ancestral custom, and to the other things which it is pious to perform for the departed.

(40) There are three types of lives, the practical, the theoretical and that composed of both. The [life] of enjoyment is subhuman,[57] and the life of contemplation is preferred to the others. The good person will engage in politics as a primary aim, not just in special circumstances; for the practical life is the same as the political. The best life is that according to virtue among things in accordance with nature; second is that according to the intermediate disposition, possessing most and the most important of the things [145] in accordance with nature. These [lives] are objects of choice, that of vice is an object of avoidance.

(41) The happy life is different from the noble one, inasmuch as the former requires the presence of things in accordance with nature throughout, while

---

[56] Greek *kharis* covers both 'gratitude' and 'grace'.   [57] Aristotle, *Nicomachean Ethics* 1.5.

the latter can also be among those contrary to nature. And virtue is not sufficient for the former but is sufficient for the latter. There is a certain intermediate life according to an intermediate disposition, in which appropriate actions [*kathēkonta*] are performed. For correct actions [*katorthōmata*] are in the life according to virtue, wrongdoings in that according to vice, appropriate actions in the life that is called intermediate.

(42) Having considered these things, let us draw the following distinctions. Moral virtue is, speaking generally, a disposition which chooses middling [*mesoi*] pleasures and pains, aiming at the noble *qua* noble, and vice is opposite to this. Common to [virtue] based on opinion and moral [virtue] is a disposition which considers and chooses and does the things that are noble in actions. Intellectual [virtue], the peak of both the knowledgeable [part] <and the deliberative [part]>, considers and does what is rationally structured. Wisdom is the understanding of the first causes. Practical wisdom is a disposition that deliberates about and does good and fine things *qua* <good and> fine. Courage is a blame-free disposition involving middling confidence [146] and fears. Temperance is a disposition in choice and avoidance which makes people blame-free on account of what is noble itself. Mildness is a disposition intermediate between irascibility and insensitivity. Liberality is a mean between profligacy and illiberality. Magnanimity is a mean between vanity and small-mindedness. Magnificence <is a mean between pretentiousness and sordidness. Indignation is> a mean between envy and malice. Dignity is a mean between stubborness and obsequiousness. Shame is a mean between shamelessness and extreme shyness. Wittiness is a mean between buffoonery and boorishness. Friendship is a mean between flattery and hostility. Truthfulness is a mean between mock self-disparagement and boasting. Justice is a mean between excess and falling short and between much and little.

(43) There are also many other virtues, some independent, some among the species of those already mentioned; for example under justice are reverence, piety, goodness, being easy to deal with, fair dealing; under temperance are decency, good order, self-sufficiency; <under courage are cheerfulness and readiness to make an effort.> So it is not out of place also to run through [147] the definitions of these. So, reverence is a disposition to worship gods and *daimones*, intermediate between godlessness and superstition. Piety is a disposition which preserves what is right in relation to the gods and the departed, between impiety and some unnamed [vice].[58]

---

[58] That many moral dispositions have no special name in current usage is noted by Aristotle at, for example, *Nicomachean Ethics* 2.7.1107b7, 1108a5, 17.

Goodness is a disposition which does good to people voluntarily for their own sake, intermediate between wickedness and an unnamed [vice]. Being easy to deal with is a disposition which makes people blame-free in common dealings, intermediate between unsociableness and an unnamed [vice]. Fair dealing is a disposition which is wary of injustice in contracts, intermediate between lack of fair dealing and an unnamed [vice], though the unnamed vice has something to do with excessive legalism. Decency is a disposition which preserves what is fitting in movements and gestures, intermediate between indecency and an unnamed [vice]. Discipline is a disposition which aims at what is fine in order, intermediate between indiscipline and an unnamed [vice]. Self-sufficiency is a disposition which is adequate for what befalls one, accompanied by liberality, intermediate between beggary and extravagance. Cheerfulness is a disposition that is not defeated in enduring terrible things, intermediate between despondency and mania.[59] Readiness to make an effort is a disposition that does not surrender in the face of labours and achieves what is noble, intermediate between weakness and making efforts to no effect. The virtue that is the combination of all the ethical [virtues] is called goodness and is complete virtue, making good things beneficial and fine and choosing fine things on their own account.

(44) {26} Now that sufficient distinctions have been made concerning the virtues, and [148] the majority, roughly speaking, of the headings belonging to the topic of ethics have been taken up, it is necessary to continue by explaining the [topics] of household management and politics, since man is by nature a living creature that dwells in cities.[60]

(45) The first political arrangement is the coming-together of a man and a woman in accordance with the law for the begetting of children and partnership in life. This has the name of 'household' but is the beginning of a city; so we must speak about it too. The household seems to be a sort of miniature city, if the marriage brings the increase that is prayed for and children are added and form pairs with one another, and so a second and a third and a fourth household come into being, and from these a village and a city. For it is when there come to be several villages that a city is completed. And since the household provides the seeds, as it were, for the coming to be of the city, so it does also of the constitution. For the outline of kingship is present in the household, and of aristocracy and of democracy. The

---

[59] Literally 'battle-frenzy'.

[60] Aristotle, *Politics* 1.2.1253a1–2, often rather misleadingly rendered as 'man is a political animal'. What follows in our text is a summary derived from Aristotle, *Politics* 1, which should be consulted for further clarification.

relationship of parents to their children has the character of kingship; that of husbands to wives, aristocratic; that of the children to one another, democratic. For male and female come together in desire to produce children and for the permanence of the race; for each desires to beget. When they have come together and taken in addition [149] a fellow-worker in the partnership, either a natural slave (one who has bodily strength for performing services but is stupid and unable to live by himself), or else one who is a slave by law, then from their coming together for a common aim and forethought in all things directed towards a single advantage, a household is constituted. It is the man who by nature has the rule over this. For the [faculty] of deliberation is inferior in a woman, not yet present in children and completely absent in slaves.

(46) Wisdom in household management, which manages the household itself and those in it, properly belongs to the man. Part of it is to do with being a father, part with marriage, part with being a master [of slaves], part with money. For, as an army needs equipment, a city revenues and a craft tools, so a household needs what is necessary. This is of two sorts, [what is necessary] for a life that is more in common and [what is necessary] for a good [life]. These are the things for which the manager of a household should first have forethought, either increasing the income through ways of obtaining resources that are worthy of a free man, or else reducing the expenses; for this is the chief summary of household management. And for this reason the manager of a household must have experience of many things, agriculture, rearing flocks, mining, so that he can distinguish the results that are both most profitable and most righteous. Of making money there is a better and a worse sort; the better is that which comes about naturally,[61] the worse is that through retail trade. Well, that is enough <about household management>.

(47) [150] Of politics the headings are the following. First, cities are constituted in one way by nature, for human beings form communities, and in another for advantage. Next, a city is the most complete community, and a citizen is someone who shares in political rule. A city is the number of such people that is enough for self-sufficiency in life. The limit of the number is such that the city be neither lacking in fellow-feeling nor easily despised, and that it is equipped with the means of life without shortage and with [the means of defence] against foreign attackers adequately. For of practical wisdom part is concerned with household management, part with legislation, part with politics, part with military strategy. Concerned with household management,

---

[61] Aristotle, *Politics* I.8–9. For criticism of retail trade cf. in particular I.9.1257a17–19.

as I said, is that which manages the household itself and the things around it, with legislation . . . <, with politics . . . with military strategy> that concerned with observing and managing what is to the advantage of the army.

(48) Cities must be ruled by one person, or a few, or all. Each of these can be either correct or bad. Correct, when the rulers aim at the common interest; bad, when at their own. The bad is a deviation from the correct. Kingship and aristocracy and democracy desire what is correct; tyranny and oligarchy and mob rule, what is bad. [151] There is also a certain political constitution which is a mixture of the correct ones and is the best. Political constitutions often change for the better or the worse. In general the best constitution is the one which is arranged in accordance with virtue, the worst, that in accordance with vice. Ruling and deliberating and passing judgement in democracies derives from all, either by election or by lot; in oligarchies, from the wealthy; in aristocracies, from the best people.

(49) Civil strife comes about in cities in some cases through *logos*, in others through *pathos*.[62] Through *logos*, when those who are equal are compelled to have <unequal [shares], or those who are unequal> equal [shares]. Through *pathos*, on account of honour or love of power or gain or wealth. Political constitutions are destroyed on account of two causes, either by violence or by deception. The most permanent are those which take care of the common interest.

(50) Law courts and councils and assemblies and political offices are defined in ways appropriate to the constitutions. The most common political offices are priest of the gods, general, admiral, market superintendent, superintendent of a gymnasium, legal overseer of women, legal overseer of children, overseer of the city, treasurer, guardian of the laws, tax collector. Of these some concern the city, some war, some harbours and trade.

(51) It is the function of a person involved in the city[63] to correct the constitution, too, which seems much more difficult than to establish it, [152] and to distribute the multitude of people partly with a view to what is necessary, partly with a view to what is good. Craftsmen and labourers and farmers and merchants for what is necessary, for these are servants of those involved in the city. The military and deliberative [element] has more authority because of its concern with virtue and eagerness for what is

---

[62] *logos* is 'reason', 'rational calculation'. *pathos* – on which see further **16** below – is often translated into English by 'emotion' or 'passion', but the latter has too specific a meaning in contemporary English, and the former fails to capture the basic idea of the Greek word, which is that of something which happens to a person, something of which the person is not in control.

[63] The Greek could be rendered 'a politician', but at 152.4 below the contrast is between those engaged in economic activity and the citizen class as a whole. Cf. Aristotle, *Politics* 3.5.

noble. Of this [element in the city] the more elderly [part] deliberates, the more aged worships the gods, the young wage war on behalf of everyone. This arrangement is very ancient and was first established by the Egyptians.

(52) It is a part of politics, no less than any other, to set up sanctuaries of the gods on the most conspicuous places, and to arrange the landholdings of private citizens partly near the frontiers and partly near the city, so that, when two holdings have been distributed to each individual, both parts of the territory are considered together. It is also useful to legislate that [the citizens] have meals in common and concern themselves with the public education of the children; and with a view to bodily strength and perfection they should not marry those who are either too young or too old, for in both cases the offspring are imperfect and completely feeble. And to legislate that no malformed [child] should be reared, or perfect [child] be exposed or [pregnancy] aborted is most advantageous. Well, these are the chief headings of politics.

B.   Stobaeus, *Selections* 4.39.28 (918.15–919.6 Hense 1894)

From the Epitome of Didymus.

Happiness comes from noble and primary actions. For this reason it is altogether noble, just as activity in other things[64] is altogether a matter of skill. For the involvement of material principles does not make happiness depart from pure nobility, just as the use of instruments [does not alter] the activity of medicine [from being] altogether a matter of skill. For every action is some activity of the soul. When the person who acts uses certain things for the completion of his purpose, these should[65] be considered parts of the activity, even though each of the aforementioned <skills> seeks each thing, but not as a part of the skill, rather as producing it. It is not right to say that those things without which something cannot be done are parts of the activity. For a part is conceived of as completing the whole, but things without which [something cannot be done, are conceived of] as productive, by contributing and assisting towards the end.

On the origins of the account of Peripatetic ethics in **A** ('Doxography C') see above, commentary on **1I** and **1O**.[66] Its presentation of Aristotelian ethics is influenced by Stoicism both in its terminology and in its approach. The

---

[64] *allois*; the corresponding passage in **15A**(15) refers to pipes (*aulois*). See above, n. 28.
[65] **15A**(15) has 'should not', which fits the context better.
[66] The commentary on **15** is adapted from my chapter on 'Peripatetics' in the forthcoming *Cambridge History of Philosophy in Late Antiquity*, edited by Stephen Gersh.

opening material ((1)–(2)) on the link between 'ethics' and 'habit' and on the parts of the soul echoes Aristotle closely enough, but the following exposition of *oikeiōsis* ((3)–(12)) is Stoic teaching (cf. LS 57, and **17** below) modified in the light of Peripatetic doctrine, distinguishing, as the Stoics did not, between *oikeiōsis* to the body and to the soul ((3), (7)–(8), (10)); this, as Inwood 1983, 192–3 notes, was characteristic of Antiochus and used by him, and others, to criticise the Stoic doctrine of virtue for neglecting the body in favour of the soul. Indeed Inwood 1983, 193 suggests that the discussion of *oikeiōsis* combines material from Antiochus with a more strictly Peripatetic source or sources. The summary also refers ((3)) to appropriate selection not among indifferents, as in Stoicism, but among the three types of goods and evils, those of the soul, those of the body and those that are external. The approach to moral virtue familiar from Aristotle's *own* writings, in terms of a mean disposition in respect of affections in the irrational soul, appears only much later in the discussion, at (28)–(35) and does so in a way that, like much else in the account, is closer to the *Magna Moralia* (1.5) and the *Eudemian Ethics* than to the *Nicomachean Ethics*. Even though in the latter, more Aristotelian part of the account it is possible to identify which Aristotelian or post-Aristotelian treatise is being followed, directly or indirectly, at specific points, it appears that the author did not regard them as his primary source, however strange this may seem to us, and that he drew primarily on late Hellenistic Peripatetic sources (cf. Moraux 1973, 435–6; Gottschalk 1987, 1128–9).

The concluding section ((44)–(52)), on economics and politics, follows the theoretical parts of Aristotle's *Politics* (and not the pseudo-Aristotelian *Economics*) relatively closely, though in a very abbreviated form. Indeed it shows little if any recognition that political systems had changed since the fourth century BC. The list of causes of civil strife in (49) partly reflects *Politics* 5.2, but it shows a characteristic preoccupation of Peripatetics in our period (below, **16**) by classifying the causes under *logos* – reason, or perhaps proportion, since what is at issue, as in *Politics* 5.2.1302a24–31, is unfair distribution of goods – and *pathos*, which here seems to have a wider sense than just 'emotion', including honour, love of power, profit and wealth. (It may indeed be that the emotional aspect was originally explicit in all four of these, not just the second, and that a second stage of summarising (by Stobaeus?) has obscured this.)

Hahm (1983, especially 25) has noted the way in which both this text and the account of Stoic ethics which precedes it use classification or division as a means of evaluative analysis and exposition. In general, while the Aristotelian ideas are present, one has the impression that they are struggling to be heard through a manner of exposition which is that of the textbook and is not suited to the development of complex arguments.

CHAPTER 16

Emotions

A. Philodemus, *On Anger* XXXI.31–9 Wilke 1914

At any rate some of the Peripatetics, as indeed we mentioned previously naming persons, say that those who remove anger and spirit [*thumos*] from the soul are cutting out its sinews; without these there is no punishment or self-defence.

B. Cicero, *Tusculan Disputations* 3.22

For the Peripatetics, associates of ours and unsurpassed in breadth, learning and seriousness, do not at all convince me of their 'moderations' [*mediocritates*] either of disturbances or of diseases of the mind. For every evil, even if it is moderate [*mediocre*] is an evil; but our concern is that there should be no evil at all in the wise person. For just as the body, even if it is moderately ill, is not healthy, so in the mind that 'moderation' is without health.

C. Cicero, *Tusculan Disputations* 4.38–40

Therefore we must regard as weak and feeble the principle and expression of the Peripatetics, who say that it is necessary that our minds should be disturbed but apply a certain limit [*modus*] beyond which one should not go. Do you apply a limit to vice? Or is it no vice to fail to obey reason? . . . And what, finally, will this limit of yours be? Let us ask about the limit of grief, on which most effort is spent. It is recorded by Fannius that Publius Rutilius was grieved when his brother failed to gain the consulship; but he seems to have gone beyond the limit, since for this reason he departed this life. So he ought to have borne it more moderately [*moderatius*]. (Cf. also 4.41–2.)

D. Cicero, *Tusculan Disputations* 4.43–4, 46

(1) What of the fact that the same Peripatetics say that those disturbances, which we think are to be rooted out, are not only natural but also given to

us by nature to our advantage? They speak as follows. First they praise irascibility at length; they say that it is the whetstone of bravery and that those who are angry attack both the enemy and a wicked fellow-citizen much more fiercely, and that trivial is the reasoning of those who think as follows: 'it is right that this battle be fought, it is fitting to contend for the laws, for freedom, for one's country'; these things have no force unless courage glows white-hot with anger. Nor do they argue only about warriors; they think that no orders are stern without some sharpness of anger; and they disapprove of not only the orator who prosecutes, but even the one who defends without some darts of anger; even if this is not present, nevertheless they think it should be feigned in words and gesture, so that the performance of the orator should fire the anger of the hearer. Finally they say that the person who does not know how to be angry is not a real man, and what we call mildness they call slowness [to anger], in a bad sense. Nor do they praise only this desire – for anger, as I defined it just now, is the desire for revenge – but that very kind [of emotion], desire or lust, they say has been given [to us] by nature for its very great usefulness; for no one can do anything with distinction that he does not desire . . . (2) Indeed if anyone removed fear, all carefulness in life would be removed, it being at its greatest in those who fear the laws, the magistrates, poverty, disgrace, death and pain. However, they argue these things in such a way that they think that [the emotions] should be cut back; but that they should be totally uprooted, they say, [this] is neither possible nor necessary, and in almost all things they think that the mean is best.

E.   Cicero, *Tusculan Disputations* 4.57

Moreover, who can rightly praise moderation [*mediocritates*] in evils? . . . For as for their saying that what is excessive should be cut back, but what is natural should be left, what can be natural if it can also be excessive? All these things have their roots in errors, which must be uprooted and removed from the base, not trimmed and cut short.

F.   Cicero, *On Duties* 1.89

One should also take care that the punishment not be greater than the crime, and that some should not be punished for the same offences for which others are not even prosecuted. What is most to be forbidden when punishing is anger; for the person who proceeds to punish in a state of anger will never keep to that moderation [*mediocritas*] which is between too much and too little and is approved by the Peripatetics – and rightly so, provided that they do not praise anger and say that it was a useful gift of nature.[1] Anger is to be rejected in all things, and it is to be wished that those who govern the state should be like the laws, which are led to punish not by anger, but by fairness.

G.   Philo of Alexandria, *On the Migration of Abraham* 147

And for this reason some who pursue the mild and sociable philosophy said that the virtues were means [*mesotētes*], locating them in a border region, since undue pride full of much boastfulness is bad, and adopting the manner of the humble and obscure lays one open to attack, but the mixture that is reasonably between these is beneficial.

H.   Anonymus Londinensis, II.20–4, p. 3 Diels

[The ancients] say that moderations of the passions are the sinews of actions. But the more recent [philosophers], that is the Stoics, leave no affection of the soul as natural.

I.   Pseudo-Archytas, reported by Stobaeus, *Selections* 3.1.106 (56.13–57.6 Hense 1894)

So let them not dare to say that man is free from disease and pain, or be confident in saying that he is free from grief. For as we leave some pains for the body, so [we leave some] pains at [these] for the soul. However, the griefs of the foolish are irrational; those of the wise extend as far as reason allows in defining things. Indeed their [the Stoics'] boast of *apatheia* removes the nobility of virtue, if it withstands death and pain and poverty when these are indifferents and not evils. For things that are not evil are easy to overcome. So one must practise approaching *metrio-patheia*, so that we may avoid insensibility to pain as much as what is emotional [*empathes*], and not say things which go beyond our [human] nature.

---

[1]   Cicero here transfers the notion of a mean between extremes to the *punishment*, while rejecting its application to the emotion; any degree of the latter will hinder attainment of the mean in the former.

J. Seneca, *On Anger* 1.3.1

Aristotle's definition [of anger] is not far from ours;[2] for he says that anger is a desire to pay back pain. The difference between this definition and ours is a lengthy matter to investigate.

K. Seneca, *On Anger* 1.7.1

Although anger is not natural, is it not to be accepted, because it has often been useful? It raises up spirits and urges them on, and without it courage achieves nothing splendid in war, if a flame from it is not applied and if this stimulus does not excite the bold and send them to face dangers. Certain people therefore think it best to moderate [*temperare*] anger, rather than to remove it, and, by taking away from it that part which overflows, to restrain it to a healthy limit [*modus*], while retaining that [part of it] without which action will grow sluggish and strength and vigour of spirit will be undone.

L. Seneca, *On Anger* 1.9.2

'Anger', says Aristotle, 'is necessary, and there can be no victory in battle without it, if it does not fill the mind and fire the spirit; however, it should be employed not as a general but as a soldier.' This is false. For if it listens to reason and follows where it is led, it is not anger, whose characteristic feature is stubbornness; if, however, it resists and does not grow quiet when ordered to but is carried on in its fierce desire, it is a servant of the mind as useless as a soldier who disregards the signal to retreat.

M. Seneca, *On Anger* 1.17

Aristotle says that some emotions, if they are used well, serve as weapons. That would be true, if, like weapons of war, they could be taken up and laid down at the decision of the person who equips himself with them; these weapons which Aristotle gives to virtue fight of their own accord, without waiting for the hand [of the one who uses them], and they possess you rather than being possessed. There is no need for other weapons; nature has equipped us adequately, with reason.

---

[2] Seneca apparently gave three definitions of anger, which have dropped out of his text but are quoted by Lactantius, *On the Wrath of God* 17.13; the first, which provides the closest parallel to Aristotle's, is desire to avenge a wrong. See Cooper and Procopé 1995, 19–20, and the commentary below.

N.   Seneca, *On Anger* 3.3.1

'There is no doubt', you say, 'that [anger] is a great and destructive force; therefore the awful plague ought to be cured in any way possible.' But, as I said in the earlier books, Aristotle takes his stand as a defender of anger and forbids us to remove it; he says it is a spur to courage, and that if it is taken away the spirit loses its weapons and becomes sluggish and idle where great enterprises are concerned.

O.   Seneca, *Letters on Morals* 85.2–3

(1) 'The person who is wise is also temperate; the person who is temperate is also steadfast; the person who is steadfast is unperturbed; the person who is unperturbed is free from sorrow; the person who is free from sorrow is happy; therefore the wise person is happy, and wisdom is sufficient for a happy life.'

(2) To this inference certain Peripatetics reply in the following way, that 'unperturbed' and 'steadfast' and 'free from sorrow' are to be understood so that the person who is said to be 'unperturbed' is the one who is rarely and moderately [*modice*] perturbed, not the one who is never perturbed. Likewise they say 'free from sorrow' is applied to the person who is not prone to sorrow or frequently or excessively subject to this failing. For that anyone's mind should be immune to sorrow is a denial of human nature; the wise person is not [indeed] conquered by grief, but he is affected by it; and [they say] the other things to this effect that are in accordance with [the doctrines of] their school. By these points they do not do away with emotions but moderate them [*temperare*].

P.   Seneca, *Letters on Morals* 116.1

It has often been asked whether it is better to have moderate [*modicos*] emotions, or none. Our school [the Stoics] drive them out, the Peripatetics moderate them [*temperare*]. But I do not see how any moderation [*mediocritas*] in what is a disease can be healthy or advantageous.

Q.   Anonymous, *On Aristotle's* Nicomachean Ethics 127.5–9

[Aristotle] also praises Plato for correctly thinking that right from youth people should become accustomed to feel joy and distress at the right things. For this reason one may be surprised at those of the Platonists[3] who introduce freedom from emotion as a Platonic doctrine and revile pleasure.

R.   Aspasius, *On Aristotle's* Ethics 44.12–19[4]

The Stoics thought that emotion was a vehement impulse or an irrational impulse, but they were not right to suppose 'contrary to right reason'. For not every emotion is vehement and not every emotion is contrary to reason, but some are proper to the good person. At any rate, we criticise those who are inflexible[5] and stubborn in character. Moreover, it is completely impossible to remove the appetitive part of the soul, but it is possible to set it in order, like the rational part. It will be set in order when the emotions are proportionate.

S.   Pseudo-Andronicus, *On the Passions* 19
(271.79–87 Glibert-Thirry 1977)

In every case virtue is in a mean [*mesotēs*], as Aristotle himself says fully in the second book of the *Nicomachean [Ethics]*. If opposites are sought in the excess and deficiency, evil will be opposed to evil, for example boldness and cowardice, the former in excess, the latter in deficiency. But if opposites are sought in proportion [*summetria*] and disproportion [*ametria*], evil will be opposed to good, for the good which is in the middle [*mesotēs*] is proportionate [*summetron*], but the extreme is disproportionate in both directions, that in excess and that in deficiency. One should know that only the generic virtues and liberality are considered as means [*mesotētes*].

T.   Clement, *Miscellanies [Strōmata]* 2.8.32.3
(Critolaus, fr. 24 Wehrli 1969b)

A command forbids by subjecting to fear, through education of those who are susceptible to such admonishment. So fear is not irrational, but indeed rational; how not so, when it advises 'you shall not murder, you shall not

---

[3] Identified by Karamanolis 2006, 189 with Atticus, on the basis that Atticus is named by the same anonymous commentator at 248.26 (Atticus, fr. 43 des Places 1977) as adopting the Stoic doctrine of indifferents while claiming to be a Platonist. The identification is plausible enough, but we cannot be certain.

[4] Often referred to as '*On Aristotle's* Nicomachean Ethics'; but see n. 15 to the Introduction.

[5] *apeitheis*. One might be tempted to read *apatheis*, 'without emotion'; so Hanquet, followed by Donini 1974, 100 (tentatively) and by Moraux 1984, 282 n. 197. But there is apparently no evidence to support this in the MSS.

commit adultery, you shall not steal, you shall not bear false witness'? But if we are to quibble about words, let the philosophers call fear of the law 'caution',[6] being a rational avoidance. Critolaus of Phaselis not inappropriately called them 'fighters about words'.

U. Stobaeus, *Selections* 2.7.1
(38.18–24 Wachsmuth 1884: 'Doxography A')[7]

Emotion [*pathos*] is, according to Aristotle, an excessive irrational movement of the soul. He puts 'irrational' on the level of what does not possess the reason that commands, for it does have [the reason] that is subordinate, in accordance with which it naturally obeys the rational [part].[8] He applies 'excessive' to what is of a nature to admit of excess, not to what is already excessive; for sometimes it is excessive, sometimes deficient.

V. Aspasius, *On Aristotle's* Ethics 44.20–45.16

(1) We do not find a definition of emotion in any of the early Peripatetics, but of the more recent ones Andronicus said that emotion is an irrational movement in the soul on account of a supposition of [something] bad or good, taking 'irrational' not as 'opposed to right reason', as the Stoics [do], but as a movement in the irrational part of the soul.

(2) Boethus [said that] emotion was an irrational movement of the soul with a certain magnitude; he too took 'irrational' as movement of the irrational part of the soul, but added 'magnitude', as there are also other movements of the irrational [part] of the soul which are not long-lasting accompanying appropriations [*oikeiōseis*] to, and alienations from, certain people. He did not think it worth calling the [movements] that accompany these [appropriations and alienations, which are] not long-lasting, emotions. (3) I do not know what he meant by this; for every movement of the emotional part of the soul, if it does not go unnoticed, will be an affection [*pathos*] of the body, and not just the [movement] that has magnitude. 'according to an alteration of something' is added [in Boethus' statement],[9] as is 'every movement in the body which is not according to an alteration, if

---

[6] *eulabeia*, the Stoic term for one of the 'good emotions' or *eupatheiai*.

[7] Sometimes attributed to 'Arius Didymus'; but see above, commentary on **1**.

[8] Cf. Aristotle, *Nicomachean Ethics* 1.13.1102b13–1103a3, and **15A**(1) above.

[9] Inferred to be, rather than explicitly said to be, part of Boethus' text; for the phrases in question do not appear in Aristotle's text. I have followed the construal of this difficult passage in Konstan 2006, 45; for a different interpretation see Sorabji 2007b, 623–4.

it does not go unnoticed that it is an affection of the body', because the change of the soul in the emotions seems to be these.

(4) When Andronicus says that emotion comes about on account of a supposition of good or bad things, first he perhaps did not know that some emotions come about from an impression itself without any assent or supposition; for indeed an emotion in the soul sometimes occurs even in respect of sense perception itself, when [something] pleasant or painful appears. So emotions come about not only after suppositions but also before them. This is indicated most [of all] by desires. For often someone comes to desire qua beautiful that which is beautiful, once he has seen it, without any supposition[10] having been formed first.

(5) Moreover, [emotions] often occur without any supposition that something good is present being formed at all, for example when the irrational part of the soul is moved by a witty remark. For we do not then judge that something good is present to us, but we are altogether moved by what is pleasant. There are times when the supposition of good is followed by being pleased, and that of evil by being pained, the soul clearly being moved, because the good is pleasant and the bad painful. Perhaps then emotion is the movement of the irrational [part] of the soul by what is pleasant or painful; for whether the emotion follows an impression or a supposition, at all events it comes about in respect of [something] pleasant or painful, which indicates that the most generic emotions are pleasure and pain.

W. Aspasius, *On Aristotle's* Ethics 43.14–32

(1) Of emotion there are two kinds; pleasure is one, pain the other. Of pleasures some are of the soul, others of the body, and similarly with pains. Those of the soul involve activity of what is natural in the soul, while those of the body are pleasures of the soul which come about through the body. (2) Of those that are of the soul [Aristotle] will say that one is called by the same name as the genus, 'pleasure', being a certain relaxation [*diakhusis*] in reaction to our own faring well or that of our friends, since[11] good things are present for us or our friends. This is synonymous with and admits the account of the genus; for it too is an unimpeded activity of what is natural. But it is also homonymous, in that it has the same name as the genus.

---

[10] Konstan 2006, 45 takes the point to be that we respond to what appears *beautiful* without forming any supposition about whether it is *good*.

[11] The Greek *hôs* implies 'on the supposition that', but to insert an explicit reference to a cognitive state might risk over-translating, in the present context. See the discussion below.

(3) Another kind of pleasure of the soul is confidence, which is a certain pleasure and relaxation on account of the hope that one will not be in any terrible situation, or that even if one is one will overcome it. (4) And the other emotions too which are spoken of according to pleasure of the soul will be pleasures of the soul; of these some are simply wrong, while others are proper to virtue, if they are moderated, but to vice, if they are excessive. (5) Similarly also with pain of the soul. As a whole it is activity of what is according to nature. Its species are what is called lack, which is pain at our or our friends' faring ill, on the basis that[12] the evils are already present; further, anger, which is pain at thinking one will suffer something contrary to what one deserves, accompanied by the appetite for inflicting pain in return on the one who has caused the pain. (6) And fear is a species of pain which has come about on account of an expected evil.

X. Aspasius, *On Aristotle's* Ethics 46.12–20

(1) Perhaps it is not unreasonable to say that the most generic [emotions] are pleasure and pain, pleasure being unimpeded activity of what is in accordance with nature,[13] pain when what is in accordance with nature is impeded in its activity, and to refer the emotions to these. (2) The species of these are the pleasure and the pain that are spoken of in a particular sense, sharing the names of the genera, [pleasure] being relaxation in reaction to pleasant things that are present, pain being confusion [*sunkhusis*] at painful things that are present. (3) Again confidence is a sort of pleasure on account of the expectation that nothing terrible will occur or that, if it does, one will overcome what is terrible; fear is pain on account of the expectation of terrible things.

(4) In addition to these they[14] are accustomed to count as emotions friendship and hatred . . .

Y. Aspasius, *On Aristotle's* Ethics 45.16–46.6

(1) The Stoics said that the generic emotions are pleasure, pain, fear and desire. They said that the emotions come about on account of a

---

[12] Again, *hôs*. See the previous note.

[13] Aristotle's definition, *Nicomachean Ethics* 7.12.1153a14–15. Sorabji: 2007b, 625 notes that Aspasius does not mention the description at *Nicomachean Ethics* 10.2.1172b32–5 of pleasure as *supervening on* the activity.

[14] The Stoics, or people in general? Y below, which precedes X in Aspasius' text, relates to the Stoics, the intervening material at 46.6–12, omitted here, to Plato's views on the most generic emotions.

supposition of good or evil: when the soul is moved as in relation to present goods, there is pleasure, when as in relation to present evils, pain, and again desire is the consequence of expected goods, being an appetition for an apparent good, and when evils are expected they said that the consequent emotion was fear.

(2) It is worth asking why they took fear as a generic emotion, even though it is a species of pain. For fear is pain at an expected evil – and not at any [evil] whatsoever; for we do not say that the person who expects poverty is afraid; rather, fear seems to be most present, and in its proper sense, when the expectation is of evils that relate to danger concerning one's safety. (3) They omitted the emotion opposite to this, I mean confidence, which comes about in respect of the expectation that nothing evil will occur, or that even if it does, one will overcome it. For confidence is brought about by some such supposition; it is not the expectation itself that is the emotion, but the consequent movement in one's reason.

(4) Although they proposed desire [as one of the genera], they omitted anger. For they say that it is a desire, but it is not; rather, it falls under the same genus [as desire]. For both are appetitions, but desire is for the pleasant, simply, whereas [anger] is for inflicting pain in return. But perhaps not always; for fathers who are angry with their sons do not have appetition for inflicting pain in return. Perhaps then anger is, in general, a movement in the soul [brought about] by the person who is thought to have wronged [oneself].

Z. Aspasius, *On Aristotle's* Ethics 139.15–20

Temperance is a mean with respect to bodily pleasures; both the reasoning and the desire in the temperate person are correct. It is flanked by the profligate person, who exceeds in pleasures, so that both the reasoning and the desire in him are corrupted, and by the insensitive person who is deficient and does not even engage in natural [pleasures] (and in him too both the reasoning and the desire are bad) . . .

Aa. Aspasius, *On Aristotle's* Ethics 137.10–14

The person who lacks self-control is mastered by passion only to the extent of not acting according to right reason, not so as to be persuaded to pursue ignoble pleasures. For his reason is not destroyed by desire, only overpowered. He is better than the profligate person; 'for the best [part] in him is preserved, the principle' [*Nicomachean Ethics* 7.8.1151a25–6]. By 'principle' [Aristotle] means reasoning.[15]

Ab.   Aspasius, *On Aristotle's* Ethics 127.5–18

[Aristotle] says [*Nicomachean Ethics* 7.6.1149a25–36] that anger in a way hears the reasoning, but mishears it, like hasty servants who because of their haste mishear their masters, and dogs which bark when anyone makes a noise. In this way anger too, being hasty by nature and very heated, so to say, because the part of the body[16] is the hottest, through mishearing reason when it is actually saying something else rushes [to action] as if it had heard a command. For the reason or the impression is 'that's an insult', or 'so-and-so has shown contempt [for me]'; but without reason saying it or the impression occurring that one should take revenge on him, anger, as if it had been commanded to take revenge, rushes to do this. It does not draw any conclusion by reasoning [*sullogizesthai*], for reasoning belongs to things that are rational, but it has a similar experience to one who has drawn the conclusion by reasoning that he should attack this person. For reason, as has been stated, only says that 'such-and-such a person has insulted [me]', but anger, as if the universal premiss too had been laid down, 'one should attack people who have insulted [one]', and the conclusion, 'so one should attack this man', gets angry at once and rushes [to do this].

Ac.   Aspasius, *On Aristotle's* Ethics 100.31–101.4

But how did [Aristotle] say [*Nicomachean Ethics* 4.1.1120b9–11] that the one who gives less [when he has less property] is more liberal [than the one who gives more, but less in proportion to his property]? Is it on the basis that one is less liberal, the other more so? But if the other oversteps the mark and does not give in accordance with his wealth or keep to the amount that should be given, he is not liberal. So are there degrees of intensity in the imperfect virtues, for example (supposing that we are talking about liberality), if someone gets it exactly right in giving to those to whom he should and when he should, and for the sake of what is noble, and all the rest, but falls short in the amount? Or did Aristotle say 'more liberal' in this sense,

---

[15] Sedley: 1999, 168 contrasts *Nicomachean Ethics* 7.8.1151a16, from which it is clear that the 'principle' in question is, for Aristotle himself, *not* reasoning, but specifically the goal of action. See the commentary below.

[16] I.e. the heart, where anger is located: Aristotle, *On the Soul* 1.1.403a31–b1.

but rather he is accustomed often to speak [thus] when making a comparison, when one person is so and the other is completely not so, for example that the person who deliberates is wiser, the one who does not is less so, when in fact the former is wise and the latter is not.

Ad. Aspasius, *On Aristotle's* Ethics 1.2–2.4

(1) The treatment of ethics, and especially [its] political [part], is prior to theoretical philosophy in terms of what is necessary, but in terms of what is honourable it is posterior. For in that it is not possible for people to live nobly without being temperate and just, and in general orderly in character and having established the *pathē* of their souls in a certain proportion [*summetria*], in this respect political and ethical [philosophy] would seem to be necessary, and for this reason prior; for it achieves nothing if someone should possess all knowledge and theory, if he has not been educated in his character. (2) But in that wisdom [*sophia*] deals with the most honourable and divine things[17] and engages in theory about the works of nature and also other things which are much better than and superior to those constituted by nature, the things which are contemplated by first philosophy,[18] in this way theoretical [philosophy] may be described as prior and more honourable. For as the subjects are in relation to one another, so is the knowledge of them. The things with which wisdom [*sophia*] is concerned are more honourable than and superior to those that fall under political and ethical [philosophy], so wisdom will be much more honourable than these. (3) If indeed we were without bodies, there would be no need for our nature to have any function other than contemplation; but as it is, the nature of the body, yoked to pleasures and pains, has necessarily caused us to be concerned with temperance and self-control and many other such virtues,[19] which it is not reasonable for god to share in since he has no part in bodily pleasures and pains. So it is from bodily necessity that we appear to get most

---

[17] As Aristotle argues in *Nicomachean Ethics* 6.7.1141b2–3; for the superiority of *sophia* to politics cf. 6.7.1141a20–2.

[18] I.e. the Unmoved Mover or Movers, 'first philosophy' (Aristotle's own term for what later came to be called 'metaphysics') being understood as the study of these, or as the study which has these as its culmination. One may compare, much later, pseudo-Alexander (Michael of Ephesus in the twelfth century AD), *On Aristotle's* Metaphysics 668.3, and contrast the wider view of the subject of metaphysics taken by the *genuine* Alexander: Genequand 1984, 12–15; Salis 2005, 9–10, 48–9, 54, 165, 374–6.

[19] Aspasius' rhetoric has got the better of his philosophy; self-control (*enkrateia*) is *not* a virtue (Aristotle, *Nicomachean Ethics* 4.9.1128b33–4, 7.1.1145a17–18, 1145a36–b2), for the fact that one needs it is a sign that one's disposition in respect of pleasures and pains is not (yet) in a virtuous state.

of our concern with ethics, since justice and practical wisdom [*phronēsis*], in which the divine is thought to share, are far inferior to god. (4) *We* need them because of our injustice and greed towards one another, since it is likely that god employs only theoretical justice towards us,[20] and continues in this. The Stoics regarded emotions [affections, *pathē*] as incompatible with virtue. For orthodox Stoicism emotions were erroneous judgements; distress, for example, is the mistaken belief that some evil is present – mistaken, for wickedness is the only evil, and wickedness cannot be present in a good person – and that it is right for me to react in a certain way (LS 65B). The Stoics did indeed allow that the virtuous person might feel 'good emotions', *eupatheiai,* relating to genuine goods and evils: joy at one's own or another's virtue, wishing for its continuation in the future, and caution to avoid losing it (LS 65F).

Aristotle's view was quite different; for him moral virtue is concerned with emotions (and actions: *Nicomachean Ethics* 2.6.1106b24), not in the sense that it involves eliminating emotions but in the sense that it involves having a disposition which is a mean between excess and deficiency. Not to feel as much anger as one should in a given situation is a fault, just as excessive anger too is a fault (*Nicomachean Ethics* 2.6.1106b18–21, 4.5); and emotion is a useful instrument (fighting spirit, or *thumos*, is a necessary though not a sufficient condition for courage: *Nicomachean Ethics* 3.8.1116b23–1117a9; cf. **ADHKLM** here).[21] This difference in doctrine was one of the main issues that distinguished Peripatetics from Stoics, and so defined Peripatetic philosophy, in the period with which we are concerned (**A–I, K–R**; also **3A** (9) above). Aristotle himself speaks of a middle (*meson*) between excess and deficiency, more often than of what is moderate (*metrion*) in the sense of being limited.[22] The idea that emotion should not be totally eliminated seems, as Pohlenz 1906, 343; 1948–9, vol. II 82, 87 argued on the basis of its presence in Theophrastus (446 FHS&G), to have originated in the

---

[20] What exactly Aspasius intends by this remarkable statement, and whether he himself, in this rhetorical opening to his whole commentary, had any very clear idea of what he intended, is perhaps uncertain. The thought *could* be that god exercises justice towards us in distributing benefits among us, but not in the sense that he is involved in relationships with us in which either party might treat the other justly or unjustly. See below, commentary on 22.

[21] Graver 2002, 163–4 argues that the later position differs from that of Aristotle in that for him it is only the *capacity* for anger, and not actual anger, that is required by bravery.

[22] Pseudo-Andronicus in S argues that the extremes are opposed to each other but virtue is in a different sense opposed to them both (cf. Aristotle, *Nicomachean Ethics* 2.6.1107a6–8), but he does so using the language of what is proportionate, *summetron*; similarly, later, Alexander of Aphrodisias, *Ethical Problems* 27.155.6–28).

Peripatetic school spontaneously rather than as a response to Stoicism, but its predominance in our period clearly has much to do with the contrast between the Peripatetic and Stoic positions.[23] The idea can, however, also be traced back to the Academic Crantor, the pupil of Xenocrates; see Thesleff 1961, 57 and n. 5; Dillon 2003, 226–7. Graver 2007, 102, indeed refers to it simply as a Platonist doctrine,[24] and the notion of moderation and limit is indeed at home in Plato himself.[25] See also Dillon 1983; Moraux 1984, 282–4 n. 197.

In J Seneca gives Aristotle's definition of anger from *On the Soul* 1.1.403a30, but, significantly, only that part of it which Aristotle attributes to the dialectician, not the physiological definition as 'boiling of blood around the heart', Aristotle's point being that a complete account requires both.[26] We should perhaps accept that the reference in O(2) to 'certain Peripatetics' indicates an actual position advanced in debate, rather than simply the construction by Seneca of an argumentative position which he will then oppose; there is no direct indication of exactly when the argument in O(2) may have been advanced, but it is significant that the context is the question whether virtue alone is sufficient for happiness (below, **18**) which is indeed a central theme of this Senecan *Letter*; see below on **18T** and **18Aa**. Indeed Inwood 2007a, 220–39 describes those against whom Seneca is arguing throughout the *Letter* as 'Peripatetics', and notes (229) that 'In *De finibus* 4–5 Cicero makes a Peripatetic speak for Antiochus' "Old Academic" Ethics', expressed in this *Letter* in **18Aa** below. However, that immediately prompts the questions, how far Seneca in *Letter* 85 *as a whole* is recounting arguments actually advanced by Peripatetics, or rather attributing arguments to generally unspecified opponents in order to argue against them, and how far, if the former is the case, he provides us with evidence for actual 'Peripatetic' thought which goes beyond what Antiochus

---

[23] A further difference is noted by Graver 2002, 163–4: whereas *metriopatheia* is concerned with individual occasions and showing a moderate degree of emotion when it is appropriate, Aristotle's doctrine of virtue as the mean rather generalises across instances; he actually identifies with the mean or middle (*meson*: *Nicomachean Ethics*: 2.6.1106b21–3) having emotions at the right time, in relation to the right people and as one should.

[24] But cf. Graver 2007, 128, where the doctrine is called '(loosely) Aristotelian', and the qualification relates to how far it accurately represents Aristotle (see the preceding note), rather than which school it belongs to.

[25] I am grateful to Tony Long and to Malcolm Schofield for emphasising this point. I is probably to be dated to the late first century BC or the first century AD: Huffman 2005, 606–7.

[26] Giusta 1964–7, vol. II 315 takes Seneca's only giving part of Aristotle's definition as evidence that Seneca had not read Aristotle's *On the Soul*. But Seneca may rather have deliberately quoted only the part of the definition that suits Stoic intellectualism.

proposed and Cicero in the *De finibus* labelled as 'Peripatetic'. See the Preface.

In **T** Critolaus is cited by Clement for the view that the Stoic distinction between 'caution' (a *eupatheia*) and 'fear' (a *pathos* to be rejected) is purely verbal. In **U** 'Doxography A' in Stobaeus – whatever its ultimate source and date – gives the Stoic definition of emotion as an excessive irrational movement of the soul (LS 65A(1), but with 'impulse' rather than 'movement'), and then tries to reconcile it with Aristotelian doctrine by relating 'irrational' to the account of the soul in *Nicomachean Ethics* 1.13 and by interpreting 'excessive' in a way that also allows for deficiency. Andronicus and Boethus advanced similar accounts of emotion as irrational movement of the soul, the former adding (**V**(1)) that it was the result of a supposition of harm or good – which is in itself essentially the Stoic account, though with harm and good to be understood in Peripatetic, rather than Stoic terms – and the latter stipulating (**V**(2)) that to count as an emotion the movement must have a certain magnitude. Aspasius, who reports both views, criticises both the stipulation of a certain magnitude (**V**(3)) and the view that every emotion involves supposition or belief (**V**(4)–(5)).[27] Aspasius himself speaks of emotions in terms of relaxation (*diakhusis*) and 'confusion' (*sunkhusis*, literally 'pouring together') (**W**(2)**X**(2)); this language recalls the Stoic physical account of emotions in terms of physical *sustolai* ('contractions') and *diakhuseis* ('relaxations') of the soul-*pneuma* (*SVF* 3.463 = LS 65D(4)) – or perhaps plays on it, given the replacement of *sustolai* by the apparently metaphorical *sunkhusis* which is nevertheless the etymological opposite of *diakhusis* in a way that *sustolē* is not. However, Aristotle himself had described the boiling of blood around the heart as the material component of anger (*On the Soul* 1.1.403a31–b2). Aspasius also, in spite of his criticism of Andronicus in **V**(4)–(5), describes emotions in terms involving beliefs; this is natural enough in the case of confidence (**W**(3)**X**(3)) and fear (**W**(6)**X**(3)), but anger too is described in terms of thought about the future (**W**(5)). As Sedley 1999 has shown, Aspasius interprets Aristotle's account of the difference between the person who undergoes psychological conflict, and the one who is simply wicked, *not* in terms of the former retaining a *moral principle* which the latter does not, but in terms of reasoning *as a whole* being corrupted in the latter (**Z**, **Aa**), and also resists the implication in Aristotle's account of lack of self-control (e.g. *Nicomachean Ethics* 7.3.1147a32–4) that desire, too, has a rational element; rather than just

---

[27] See Sorabji 1999, 104–5. Trapp 2007, 82 notes that Aspasius' objection in **V**(3) will also exclude the Stoic view that initial reactions, the *propatheiai* (LS 65XY), are not truly emotions.

saying with Aristotle that anger jumps to conclusions prematurely, he treats it as incapable in itself of reaching logical conclusions at all (**Ab**. This is from Aspasius' commentary on Aristotle's treatment of lack of self control in respect of anger in *Nicomachean Ethics* 7.6; as Sedley points out, Aspasius' commentary on the more general discussion of lack of self-control in 7.3 is unfortunately lost.) In **Ac** Aspasius rejects the idea that there can be degrees of virtue, and in so doing he aligns himself with the Stoics; see on this Sorabji 2004, vol. I 344–6, vol. II 322, and Ierodiakonou 1999. Donini 1982, 218 argues that the indication in **Ad** that moral virtue is a regrettable necessity is a sign of a Platonising tendency in Aspasius; but on this see above, Introduction p. 5 with n. 17. **Ad** is indeed to a large extent an elaboration of themes already present in Aristotle; see note 17 above.

On the issues in this section see further Sorabji 2007b. On the later history of *metriopatheia* in Neoplatonism see Sorabji 2004, vol. I 13(c).

CHAPTER 17

The primary natural things: oikeiōsis

A.   Cicero, *On Ends* 2.34

Whether or not pleasure is included among the primary natural things is a big question; but to think that nothing but pleasure is included – not one's own bodily parts, not one's senses, not the activity of intellect, not soundness of body, not health – seems to me the greatest ignorance. Necessarily, one's whole account of goods and evils must flow from this as its source. Polemo,[1] and before him Aristotle, thought those things were primary which I have just mentioned. This was the origin of the view of the Old Academy and the Peripatetics, that the ultimate good was to live in accordance with nature, that is, to enjoy the primary gifts of nature while employing virtue.

B.   Cicero, *Lucullus* 131

The Old Academy judged [that the goal of life] is to live honourably while enjoying the primary things that nature grants to a human being, as is indicated by the writings of Polemo, of whom Antiochus very much approves; and Aristotle and his supporters seem to come very close to this.

C.   Alexander of Aphrodisias, *Supplement to On the Soul* (*Mantissa*) 17.151.3–13

(1) Some say that according to Aristotle we ourselves are the first thing appropriate to ourselves. For if the object of love is the object of appetition, and we love no one in preference to ourselves and are not appropriated to anything else in this way (for it is by reference back to ourselves that we lay

---

[1] The fourth head of Plato's Academy. See above, 1B.

claim to other [people] and love someone),[2] accordingly each person will be the first thing appropriate to himself. (2) This is the opinion of Xenarchus and Boethus, on the basis of what is said about love in the eighth book of the *Nicomachean* [*Ethics*] (8.2.1155b17–27), where the beginning of the passage is 'Perhaps it will become clear concerning these things when the object of love has become known' up to 'it will make no difference; for the object of love will be what appears [to be good or pleasant]'. And in the ninth book he says similarly 'The facts disagree with these arguments' up to 'and so it is oneself that should be loved most' (9.8.1168a35–b10). (Sharples 2004, 152–3)

D.   Alexander of Aphrodisias, *Supplement to On the Soul* (*Mantissa*) 17.151.18–27

But there are those who say that according to Aristotle the first appropriate thing is pleasure, they too themselves being prompted by what [Aristotle] says in the *Nicomachean Ethics*. For he says there are three objects of appetition, the noble, the advantageous and the pleasant [*Nicomachean Ethics* 2.3.1104b30–1]. An object of appetition is that to which we are appropriated. But we grasp the noble and advantageous when we advance in age; the pleasant, at once. If these are the only objects of appetition and things that are appropriate, and the first of these is the pleasant, then this will be the first thing that is appropriate to us. Moreover, if all appetition is for the good or the apparent good, but the true good is the end, while the apparent good is not like this, and the apparent good is the pleasant, this will be the first object of appetition for us according to nature. (Sharples 2004, 154–5)

E.   Alexander of Aphrodisias, *Supplement to On the Soul* (*Mantissa*) 17.151.30–152.10

(1) Verginius Rufus and before him Sosicrates say that each thing has appetition for perfection and being in actuality, clearly [meaning by this] being active without hindrance. And for this reason [Aristotle, they say,] says[3] that the object of appetition for us is being in actuality, that is being alive and the activities [deriving] from being alive, which are pleasant. For

---

[2] Or (taking the ambiguous terms as neuter) 'we concern ourselves about other things and love certain things'.
[3] Or just '. . . for this reason [Sosicrates] says'.

such activities in accordance with nature, as long as they are unhindered, are pleasant.

(2) But for each thing it is perfection that is good. The perfection of everything that is in potentiality is to become in actuality what it was in potentiality, and [being] a living creature does not consist in being active, but in having potentiality. For even [those who are] asleep are alive. So, having appetition for being in actuality, [each person] will have appetition for his own proper perfection. This is good for each, so we have appetition for this. It follows, for those who suppose that the first appropriate thing is being and living in activity, that they also say that pleasure is the first appropriate thing and the good.

(3) In fact the end, too, is in harmony with this. For the end is being active in respect of intellect and being intelligent in actuality, which depends on our having been appropriated to what is potential. For the human being when perfected has its being in being intelligent. (Sharples 2004, 155–6)

F.   Alexander of Aphrodisias, *Supplement to On the Soul* (*Mantissa*) 17.152.27–153.8, 153.20–7

(1) But since it is impossible for us to have apprehension of the true good as soon as we come into [existence], we have appetition for the apparent good. And the apparent good is what is pleasant. So it is what is pleasant for us that is the first appropriate thing, that is, the apparent good. Even if it follows, because of the necessity of what follows from [their] arguments, for the others too who have spoken that they speak of [it as] the first appropriate thing, nevertheless they themselves did not make distinctions or differentiations, and some said [that the first appropriated thing] was us, others the external thing which is pleasant, but none of them has put it all together and completed the task. Accordingly both groups speak soundly, and at the same time both speak not soundly.

(2) Or rather: he who says that what is proper for each [person] is being in actuality, and being alive, and activity in accordance with his own being (for what is natural, in accordance with the being of each one, is pleasant and proper and the first object of appetition) does indeed speak in a way that involves a distinction. For the child, through not yet being rational, will not first be appropriated to activity in this respect, but since it has sensation it will be appropriated to the activities of the senses, and also to feeding itself.

(3) In having appetition for unhindered activity in accordance with their being, [things] will have appetition for their own proper good and for

pleasure, if pleasure is unhindered activity of a natural state, and further for its coming about for themselves; for they have appetition for their own personal activity . . .

(4) And the end according to Aristotle is in harmony with such a starting-point, being activity in accordance with virtue. In the tenth [book] of the *Nicomachean Ethics* [10.4.1175a10–17] Aristotle speaks as follows about this: 'One would think that all have appetition for pleasure, because all desire also to be alive. Life is a certain activity, and each is active concerning those things and in those things which he most likes. Pleasure perfects activities, and [perfects] living, for which they have appetition. Reasonably, then, they desire pleasure, too, since for each it perfects living, which is to be chosen.' (Sharples 2004, 157–9)

We have already seen how the summary of Peripatetic ethics attributed to Arius Didymus takes over and modifies the Stoic theory of appropriation or *oikeiōsis* (above, **15A**(3)–(12)). It is not alone in our period in doing this. Antiochus, as reflected by Cicero in **AB**, puts the disagreement between Stoics and Peripatetics on whether virtue is sufficient for happiness (below, **18**) in terms of whether the 'primary things according to nature' are to be included in the goal of life or, as by the Stoics, 'left behind' (as their critics objected: LS 64K(1), (5)). An essay by Alexander of Aphrodisias records and takes issue with the attempts of earlier Peripatetics to identify the 'first appropriate (*oikeion*) thing', that is the first thing to which we develop an affinity. (For the complete text of the essay, including more of Alexander's own discussion of the views given here, see Sharples 2004, 149–59. Striker 1996, 269 notes that this essay provides evidence that Antiochus' Peripatetic contemporaries, like Antiochus himself – cf. **A**[4] – derived the goal of life from the first object of desire, while for the Stoics, as she shows – 1996, 227–31, 263, 268–9, 288–93, 305 – this provided an account of how individuals' development can lead them towards the true goal, but *not* a justification for the identification of that goal.) Xenarchus and Boethus, we are told, held that the first appropriate thing is ourselves (**C**; cf. 'Arius' in **15A**(3) and Philippson 1932, 465; Moraux 1973, 209). Philippson argues that Xenarchus may have been Arius' source (Pohlenz 1940, 42 is doubtful) and comments (1932, 464) that Xenarchus' and Boethus' formulations of the Peripatetic position show more direct Stoic influence – mediated, he suggests, via Antiochus – than those that follow in **DE**. Gottschalk 1987, 1117 comments that the passages cited in **A**(2) do not actually support

---

[4] Cicero is here arguing as an Academic against the Epicureans but is clearly influenced by Antiochus.

Boethus' and Xenarchus' view. The second seems more directly relevant than the first; but what is important is that the appeal to the text of Aristotle shows that Xenarchus and Boethus certainly did not intend to adopt a Stoic rather than a Peripatetic position. (I owe this point to Andrea Falcon.)

Others, unnamed, held that the *first* object of appropriation was pleasure (**D**). Verginius Rufus and Sosicrates held that each thing has appetition for being in actuality (**E**); this is a modification of the view in **C**, in a rather less Stoic and more Aristotelian formulation, which is noteworthy given that Xenarchus and Boethus were Peripatetics but Verginius and Sosicrates probably were not. Buecheler 1908, 190, suggests that Verginius here is L. Verginius Rufus, consul in AD 63 and guardian of the younger Pliny. Lautner 1997, 305 nn. 42 and 44 suggests that Sosicrates may be the author of philosophical *Successions* recorded at Diogenes Laertius 2.84–5, 6.80, 7.163, or the Sosicrates who was a pupil of Carneades (Philodemus, *Index of Academic [Philosophers]* 24.8 Dorandi). The form of the reference suggests that the interpretation is in fact Sosicrates', but Alexander knows it only through Verginius.[5]

Alexander himself objects, in **F**(1), that **C** and **E**, unlike **D**, do not take sufficient account of the fact that what is under discussion is the *first* appropriate thing. He then recognises, in **F**(2), that the view in **E** can be regarded as doing so after all; moreover, by Aristotle's own doctrine pleasure will be involved at the later as well as the earlier stage (**F**(3)–(4)).

On Peripatetic and Platonist treatments of *oikeiōsis* see Trapp 2007, 45–7, 111–12, 145–6.

---

[5] This paragraph includes material from Sharples 2004, 155–6 n. 527.

CHAPTER 18

Bodily and external goods
and happiness

A. Cicero, *On Duties* 3.106

Therefore, those who discuss these things with more vigour dare to say that what is base is the only evil, while those who do so in a more relaxed way do not hesitate to say that it is the supreme evil.[1]

B. Seneca, *Letters on Morals* 88.5

Unless perhaps they persuade you that Homer was a philosopher, when they deny this by the very points which they collect. For now they make him a Stoic, approving only of virtue and shunning pleasures and not abandoning what is honourable even for the reward of immortality; now an Epicurean, praising the condition of a peaceful state where life is spent in banquets and singing; now a Peripatetic, introducing three kinds of goods; now an Academic, saying that everything is uncertain. It is clear that none of these things is present in him, because they all are; for they disagree with one another.

C. Seneca, *On Benefits* 5.13.1–2

There are goods of the mind, of the body and of fortune. The foolish and wicked person is excluded from those goods of the mind; he is admitted to those which he can receive and ought to repay, and, if he does not repay them, he is ungrateful. Nor is this just something *we* have laid down; the Peripatetics too, who extend the boundaries of human happiness far and wide, say that only very small benefits will be received by the wicked; but the person who does not repay them is ungrateful. We therefore do not accept that those things are benefits which are not going to improve the

---

[1] The Stoics and Peripatetics respectively.

mind, though we do not deny that they are advantageous and should be sought for.

D.   Seneca, *Letters on Morals* 87.12–14

'What is good makes people good (for in the art of music, too, what is good makes a [good] musician); chance things do not make a person good; therefore they are not goods.' To this the Peripatetics reply that our first premiss is false. 'What is good', they say, 'does not make people good in every case. In music there is some good such as a pipe or a string or some instrument which is suited to use in playing; but none of these makes a [good] musician.' To this we will reply, 'You do not understand how we posited what is good in music. For we are not speaking of what equips a musician, but of what produces one; you are considering the furnishings of the art, not the art itself. But if something is good in the musical art itself, this will certainly make a [good] musician.' Now I want to make this more clear. 'Good' in the art of music is spoken of in two ways: one, what assists the performance of the musician; the other, what assists his art. The instruments, pipes and organs and strings, are relevant to the performance, but not to the art itself. For he is an artist even without them, though perhaps he cannot use the art. This is not twofold in the same way in a human being; for the good of a human being, and of his life, is the same.

E.   Seneca, *Letters on Morals* 87.38–9 (Posidonius F170 EK)

'Good does not come from things that are evil; wealth comes from much poverty; so wealth is not a good.' This argument is not recognised by us [Stoics]; it is the Peripatetics who both construct it and answer it. Posidonius says that this sophistical argument, tossed around in all the schools of the dialecticians, was refuted as follows by Antipater:[2] 'poverty does not refer to possession, but to subtraction' (or, as the ancients said, privation; in Greek, *kata sterēsin*); 'it does not indicate what someone has, but what he does not have. Many voids cannot fill anything; it is many possessions that produce riches, not much poverty. You are', he says, 'understanding poverty wrongly. Poverty is not what possesses few things, but what does not possess many things; so it does not refer to what it possesses, but to what it lacks.'

---

[2] The Stoic Antipater of Tarsus (head of the school *c.* 152–129); see the commentary below.

F.   Cicero, *Tusculan Disputations* 5.119

But if those philosophers whose opinion is that virtue in itself has no power,[3] and who say that everything that *we* say is honourable and praiseworthy is empty and adorned with empty speech, nevertheless think that the wise person is always happy, what do you judge that philosophers who take Socrates and Plato as their starting-point ought to do? Of these some[4] say that the goods of the soul have such pre-eminence that they eclipse those of the body and those that are external, while others[5] say that the latter are not even goods, and place all [goods] in the soul. Carneades was in the habit of deciding their dispute like an honorary arbitrator; for since some things seemed 'good' to the Peripatetics but 'advantageous' to the Stoics, and the Peripatetics did not attribute more to wealth, good health, and the other things of that sort than the Stoics did, since they judged them by the facts rather than the words, he said that there was no reason for dispute.

G.   Cicero, *On the Nature of the Gods* 1.16

(1) 'Antiochus thinks that the Stoics agree with the Peripatetics in substance but differ only over words. I would like to know, Balbus,[6] what you think about this book of his.' (2) 'What do I think?' he said. 'I am amazed that someone as outstandingly sharp as Antiochus has not seen that there is a very great difference between the Stoics, who separate what is honourable from what is advantageous[7] not [just] by name but by their whole nature, and the Peripatetics, who mix up what is honourable and what is advantageous, so that these things differ from each other in magnitude and, as it were, in degree, not in kind.'

H.   Clement, *Miscellanies* [*Strōmata*] 2.21.129.10 (Critolaus, fr. 20 Wehrli 1969b)

Critolaus, himself too a Peripatetic, said that [the end is] *completion* according to the nature of a well-flowing life, indicating the triple[8] completion made up of the three kinds [of goods]. (Sharples 2007c, 628)

---

[3] Epicurus, and the Peripatetic Hieronymus of Rhodes (c. 290–230 BC). The former identified the goal of life as pleasure, identified as the absence of pain; the latter, as the absence of pain itself. They thus gave wisdom a purely instrumental role, securing happiness by choosing a way of life conducive to these ends (see LS 21OP, and above 1B).

[4] The Peripatetics.   [5] The Stoics.

[6] The character representing the Stoic position in this Ciceronian dialogue.

[7] That is, preferred indifferents: see the commentary, p. 165.

[8] Reading with Bernays *trigenikēn* for the MSS *progonikēn*: White 2002, 86 n. 37.

I.   Stobaeus, *Selections* 2.7.3b, p. 46.10–17 Wachsmuth 1884 ('Doxography A'):[9] Critolaus, fr. 19 Wehrli 1969b

(1) By the younger Peripatetics from [the school of] Critolaus [the end is said to be] 'what is *completed* from all the goods' – that is, from the three kinds [of goods]; but this is wrong. (2) For not all good things are part of the end; bodily goods are not, nor are those derived from outside, but the activities of virtue in the soul alone. So it would have been better to say, instead of 'completed', 'activated', so that it might be apparent that virtue *employs* [these things]. (Sharples 2007c, 628)

J.   Philo of Alexandria, *Questions on Genesis* 3.16

[on Genesis 15:18] As for the deeper meaning, it indicates felicity, which is the fulfilment of three perfections, of spiritual goods, of corporeal goods and of those which are external. This [doctrine] was praised by some of the philosophers who came afterwards, [such as] Aristotle and the Peripatetics. (trans. Marcus 1953, 200, from the Armenian version)

K.   Philo of Alexandria, *That the Worse Usually Plots against the Better* 7

[on Joseph's coat of many colours] [Moses, as author of this passage of Genesis], engaging in philosophy with a view to the political rather than with a view to the truth, leads and gathers the three kinds of goods, the external, the bodily and the soul, though they are separated from one another in their entire natures, into a single [whole], thinking it right to show that each needs each and all need all, and what is composed of them all together is perfect and in reality a complete good, but the things from which this is constructed are parts or elements of goods, but not complete goods.

L.   Hippolytus, *Refutation of All Heresies* 1.20.5–6

(1) Aristotle introduces three kinds of goods and says that the wise man is not complete if he does not have the goods of the body and the external goods. [The goods of the body] are beauty, strength, keen perception, dexterity; the external [goods], wealth, good breeding, reputation, power, peace, friendship. The internal [goods] concerned with the soul, as Plato too

---

[9] See above, commentary on 1O.

supposed, are practical wisdom, temperance, justice, courage. (2) [Aristotle] too says that evils come about by contrast with goods, and [he says] that they exist beneath the region around the moon, but not beyond it.

M.   Cicero, *Tusculan Disputations* 5.50 (Critolaus, fr. 21 Wehrli 1969b)

At this point I ask what is the power of those scales of Critolaus, who thinks that, when he puts the goods of the soul in one side of the scales, those of the body and external ones in the other, the former will weigh more to such an extent that it will outweigh the earth and the seas.

N.   Cicero, *Tusculan Disputations* 5.75–6

As far as I am concerned, may the Peripatetics and the Old Academy eventually stop stammering and dare to say, openly and clearly, that there will be a happy life even in the [bronze] bull of Phalaris.[10] Let there be three kinds of goods, so that we can get out of the snares of the Stoics[11] which I realise I have used more than usual; let there certainly be those kinds of goods, provided that bodily and external goods lie prostrate on the ground and are only called goods because they should be taken,[12] while those other divine goods [of the soul, i.e. the virtues] spread far and wide and right up to heaven; why should I say that the person who has obtained *these* is only happy, and not also most happy?

O.   Cicero, *Tusculan Disputations* 5.23–5

(1) [continuing X] But since they say there are three sorts of evils [of the soul, of the body, and external ones], are we to say that the person who is oppressed by every evil of two of the kinds, so that fortune is opposed to him in everything and his body is overwhelmed and worn out by all sorts of pains, lacks only a little a happy life, let alone the happiest? This is the position that Theophrastus [= 493 FHS&G] was not able to defend; for when he had decided that floggings, the rack, torture, overthrow of one's country, exile and bereavement had great power to make life evil and pitiful, he did not venture to speak in an exalted and eloquent way,

---

[10]   In which Phalaris, tyrant of Agrigento, was said to have roasted his victims alive.
[11]   I.e. the dispute over terminology in **FG** above.
[12]   Or, as the Stoics, would say, 'selected'; virtue alone deserves to be *chosen*.

since his opinions were base and degraded. (2) The question is not whether he was right; at least he was consistent. It is not my custom to criticise the conclusion when one has granted the premises. However, [Theophrastus], the most elegant and learned of all philosophers, is not much criticised when he says that there are three kinds of good, but he *is* attacked by everyone, first for the book which he wrote *On the Happy Life*, in which he argues at length why the person who is tortured on the rack cannot be happy. In this [book] he is also thought to say that the happy life cannot mount the wheel of torture.[13] He does not anywhere say quite this, but what he does say comes to the same thing. So, if I grant him that bodily pains and the shipwrecks of fortune are among evils, can I be angry with him when he says that not all good people are happy, since the things he counts as evils can befall every good person? (3) The same Theophrastus is attacked in the books and the schools of all philosophers, because in his *Callisthenes* he praised the saying 'Life is ruled by luck, not by wisdom.' They say that nothing more feeble has been said by any philosopher. About this they are right, but I do not understand that anything could have been said that was more consistent. For if there are so many goods of the body, and so many outside it that depend on chance and luck, is it not consistent that luck, which is the mistress both of external things and of those that relate to the body, should have more power than judgement does?

P.   Cicero, *Tusculan Disputations* 5.85

And the position of the Peripatetics has been fully stated; apart from Theophrastus [= 499 FHS&G] and any who, following him, show more weakness in shuddering at pain and dreading it, the others can do what indeed they do, exalting the importance and worth of virtue; when they have raised it to the skies, as they customarily do with an abundance of eloquence, it is easy for them to trample on and despise everything else in comparison. Nor is it permitted for those who say that praise should be sought after even at the cost of pain, to deny that those who achieve it are happy. For even if they suffer certain evils, nevertheless this name 'happy' has a wide extension.[14]

---

[13] I.e. anyone who is made to climb onto the torture wheel cannot be called happy.
[14] I.e. it includes not only those who suffer no evil, but also those for whom the great good of virtue far outweighs other evils.

Q.   Cicero, *Academica Posteriora* 1.33

Theophrastus [= 497 FHS&G], a man whose speech was charming and whose character was such that his honesty and uprightness was plain for all to see, in a way damaged the authority of the original teaching even more; for he robbed virtue of her honour and made her weak, because he said that the happy life did not depend on her alone.

R.   Cicero, *Lucullus* 134

I fear that [Zeno the Stoic] grants more to virtue than nature allows [in making virtue sufficient for happiness], especially when Theophrastus [= 492 FHS&G] says a great deal eloquently on the other side. And I fear that [Antiochus][15] is hardly consistent when he says that there are evils both of the body and of fortune but judges that the person who is subject to all these will be happy if he is wise.

S.   Cicero, *On Ends* 5.75

'I approved [what you said] the more because I remember that Staseas of Naples, your notable teacher, certainly a distinguished Peripatetic, was in the habit of making these points somewhat differently, agreeing with those who make much depend on favourable or adverse fortune, and much on the goods or ills of the body.' 'It is as you say,' he said, 'but these issues are discussed by our friend Antiochus in a much better and more courageous way than they were by Staseas.'

T.   Seneca, *Letters on Morals* 85.30–2

'What is evil causes harm; what causes harm to someone makes him worse; pain and poverty do not make someone worse; therefore they are not evils.' 'What you suggest', he says, 'is false; for what causes some harm to someone does not also make him worse. A storm and a squall harm the navigator, but they do not make him worse.' To this some of the Stoics reply that the navigator is made worse by a storm and a squall, since he cannot carry out what he intended or hold to his course; he does not become worse in his skill, but in its execution. To them the Peripatetic says 'So poverty, pain, and whatever else there may be of that sort make the wise person, too,

---

[15] That the reference is to Antiochus is rightly argued by Fortenbaugh: 1984, 217–18.

worse; they will not take away his virtue, but will impede his activities.' This would be correct if the situation of the navigator was not different from that of the wise person. The intention of the latter is not to achieve without fail what he attempts in the course of his life, but to do everything rightly; the intention of the navigator is to get the ship to harbour without fail.

U.   Aspasius, *On Aristotle's* Ethics 24.3–9

Happiness needs external goods not as parts or as things that complete it but as instruments, just as pipe-playing needs instruments for its own end, in order to achieve its particular end. For it is impossible, [Aristotle] says, to do noble things without provision; it is not possible to practise medicine if one is not provided with medical instruments and drugs. Then he reckons up the external goods, at the same time showing how virtue uses them as instruments for happiness. (Sharples 2007c, 630)

V.   Stobaeus, *Selections* 2.7.3d (48.6–11 Wachsmuth 1884: 'Doxography A')[16]

[People] say that happiness [*eudaimonia*] is a synonym of the end. Happiness is the best thing in life, or the greatest of goods, or what is best. These are the simplest of the notions relating to it. And even if someone speaks of blessedness [*makariotēs*] and living a blessed life, it will come to the same thing as [the goods] relating to the end. (Sharples 2007c, 630–1)

W.   Aspasius, *On Aristotle's* Ethics 24.24–25.2

What follows [in the text of Aristotle] seems to some to be said in a rather weak way. For [Aristotle] says [*Nicomachean Ethics* 1.9.1099b2–6] that being deprived of some things spoils blessedness, for example good birth, good children, being handsome. Some would say that one who is of humble birth and not handsome and childless, too, can be active in 'prime' circumstances, and that if he is active he must be happy. In reply to these it should be said that Aristotle too praises such people for correcting the shortcomings in their birth or appearance or certain other things which they lack, but nevertheless there is a certain stain present from exceedingly humble birth,

---

[16] Sometimes attributed to 'Arius Didymus'; but see above, commentary on 1.

for example if someone were the son of a male prostitute. How would this not be a stain? Perhaps a [morally] noble person might wash it away and cleanse it, but nevertheless it is sometimes an impediment to noble activities. For cities do not entrust the greatest affairs to such people to manage. (Sharples 2007c, 631)

X.   Cicero, *Tusculan Disputations* 5.21–3

(1) But your Brutus, on the authority of Aristus[17] and Antiochus, does not hold this view; for he thinks that [the happy life consists in virtue] even if there is something else that is good besides virtue . . . The things that were said were these, which Antiochus also repeatedly wrote in a number of places, that virtue itself can by itself make life happy, but not the happiest. Next, most things are named after their greater part, even if some part is absent, like strength, health, wealth, honour, glory, which are recognised as kinds [of thing], not by numerical [calculation]. So the happy life, even if it is lame in some part, nevertheless gets its name from the much greater part. – (2) It is not necessary to develop these points now, though I do think that they are not stated consistently. For I do not understand what the man who is happy needs in order to be happier; for if there is anything lacking, then he is not even happy [at all]. As for their statement that each single thing is named and considered on the basis of its greater part, there are cases where this applies in this way; but since they say there are three sorts of evils [of the soul, of the body, and external ones], are we to say that the person who is oppressed by every evil of two of the kinds, so that fortune is opposed to him in everything and his body is overwhelmed and worn out by all sorts of pains, lacks only a little for the happy life, let alone the happiest?

Y.   Cicero, *On Ends* 5.95

[Piso, stating the Antiochean view] This then is our position, which seems to you inconsistent. I, however, take account of a kind of heavenly and divine excellence in virtue which is so great that, where virtue is and the great and greatest achievements of virtue, there wretchedness and calamity cannot be, though toil and trouble can; and so I would not hesitate to say that all the wise are always blessed, but nevertheless it can come about that one is more blessed than another.

---

[17] See above, 1EF.

Z.   Cicero, *Academica Posteriora* 1.22

[Varro, stating the view of Antiochus] And so all that ancient philosophy [sc. the Platonists of the Old Academy and the Peripatetics] felt that the happy life depended on virtue alone, but that it was not the happiest [life] unless there were added [the goods] of the body and the other things which have been described above as suitable for employment by virtue.

Aa.   Seneca, *Letters on Morals* 85.19–20

But that point is absurd, when it is said[18] that [a person] will be happy even with virtue on its own, but not *perfectly* happy; how this can happen I cannot discover. For the happy life contains in itself the perfect, unsurpassable good; and if so, it is perfectly happy. If there is nothing greater or better than the life of the gods, and the happy life is divine, there is nothing greater to which it could be raised. Moreover, if the happy life is in need of nothing, every happy life is perfect, and the happy [life] and the most happy are the same.

Ab.   Aspasius, *On Aristotle's* Ethics 16.32–17.17

(1) Well, [Aristotle] says that these things must be considered later. But he adds that happiness is the most choiceworthy of all things, and not as part of a reckoning. What he is saying is like this. A stock theme [*topos*] has been handed down by him saying that the larger number of the goods included in the same reckoning is more choiceworthy – more choiceworthy than [just] one or two, as, for example, wealth and health and virtue are more choiceworthy than any single one. (2) But there is an objection to this *topos*:[19] if this is the end of the goods, then it is for *its* sake that all the things that are to be chosen are more to be chosen than one or two [parts] of the end;[20] for example, healthy things together with health are not more to be chosen than health. Similarly wealth and health and the rest together with

---

[18] The view expressed here, and argued against, is that of Antiochus of Ascalon; see the commentary below. Inwood 2007b, 43 translates 'the further point *they* make' (emphasis mine) and takes the position attacked by Seneca throughout this letter to be that of the Peripatetics; for what exactly this may mean, see above on 16O.

[19] An objection made by Aristotle himself at *Topics* 3.2.117a18, as White: 1990, 139 points out; the example 'healthy things together with health are not more to be chosen than health' is Aristotle's own.

[20] Following White: 1990, 139 and n. 52, who reads *ginetai* with the MSS in 17.4 for Heylbut's *prosginetai*, and *tode* for *to de*, with punctuation after the word rather than before, in the same line.

happiness are not more to be chosen than happiness alone. For when we have happiness we have everything.

(3) Well, this is the stock theme that he is using now. For those goods are said to be included in the same reckoning as one another which are such that, when they are reckoned up, the totality is more choiceworthy than one or a number less [than the total]. But those are said not to be included in the same reckoning which are not more choiceworthy when reckoned up with the others than if they are taken even by themselves.[21] And like this are all ends in relation to the things that produce them. (4) At any rate he says that happiness is 'most choiceworthy not being included in the same reckoning', that is to say not being of such a nature as to be included in the same reckoning as the other goods, as has been said. 'But if it were included in the same reckoning,' that is in the class of things that are reckoned up, 'it would be more choiceworthy [when] accompanied by the least of goods': this does not apply to happiness, and for this reason it is 'most choiceworthy of all things'. ((1)–(3) Sharples: 2007c, 632; (4) Sharples 1999, 89)

Ac.   Aspasius, *On Aristotle's* Ethics 30.13–18

And . . . great good fortune which is added to the good man will, [Aristotle] says [*Nicomachean Ethics* 1.10.1100b26], make his life more blessed; by 'more blessed' he means so that it appears more blessed because of the adornment, as he says. For just as added adornment does not make beautiful bodies beautiful, for they are so already, but adds an accompanying adornment, just so external goods too, when they are added to the noble and happy man, add an accompanying adornment to his life, and provide for noble use. (Sharples 2007c, 632–3)

The Stoics held that virtue alone was good, and sufficient in itself for happiness. So-called bodily goods (such as health and strength) and external goods (such as wealth, friends and reputation) are in the Stoic view only 'preferred indifferents'; it will usually, though not always, be rational to 'select' them (not 'choose' them – only virtue deserves to be *chosen*), that is, to attempt to acquire or preserve them; but failure to do so does not diminish a virtuous person's happiness. For wickedness is the only evil; poverty and sickness are merely 'dispreferred indifferents'. (Cf. **A** and LS 58.) The Peripatetics, on the other hand, accepted Aristotle's view (*Nicomachean Ethics* 1.8.1098b12–14, *Magna Moralia* 1.3.1184b2–4; see

---

[21] Reading *hairetōtera ē ei* in 17.11; cf. the reading of Z in Heylbut's apparatus.

above, **15A**(7), (9–11)) that there are three types of goods (**BC**) and
countered Stoic attempts to argue otherwise (**DE**). On **D** see Inwood
2007b, 244–5. Kidd in EK vol. II.2 637 (cf. Kidd 1986, 17–18) explains
that the argument referred to in **E**, constructed and refuted by the
Peripatetics but also answered by Antipater, was a straw man set up by
the Peripatetics in order to refute it; apparently, by constructing an argument for the Stoic position that wealth is not a good and then refuting the
argument, they thought that they could establish that wealth is a good. If so,
they were badly mistaken, for refuting any number of individual arguments
in favour of a proposition P does not refute P itself – at most, it weakens the
grounds for accepting it. The Antipater who replied to the argument was
presumably therefore the Stoic Antipater of Tarsus (head of the school
c. 152–129), and this places the Peripatetics who constructed the argument in
the middle part of the second century BC at the latest. See Inwood 2007b,
257–8, suggesting on the basis of the reference to Antipater that the
Peripatetic author of the argument in **E** was Critolaus.

Aristotle in *Nicomachean Ethics* 1.5.1096a1 says that anyone who asserts –
as the Stoics (and the Epicureans) were to do (*SVF* 3.586 and LS 22Q(3)
respectively; contrast **O** here) that the virtuous person will be happy even
when being tortured is arguing for the sake of argument. (Plato, in *Republic*
360d–362c, apparently only makes Glaucon challenge Socrates to show that
a virtuous person who is tortured will be happ*ier* than a prosperous wicked
one.) It is not surprising, therefore, that the claim that bodily and external
goods, as well as moral virtue, are necessary for happiness is the other issue,
in addition to that of emotion (above, **16**) which defined the Peripatetic
position in ethics in our period and set it apart from that of the Stoics
(cf. **17AB**).[22] However, the question whether virtue is sufficient for happiness, as a formal topic for debate, belongs to post-Aristotelian philosophy,
and it is not therefore surprising that, even if some of Aristotle's remarks are
relevant to the question, his position is, as we shall see, not easy to pin down
in all its details, and that different formulations were therefore adopted
within the Peripatetic school.

Carneades in **F** and Antiochus in **G**(1) dismissed the disagreement
between Peripatetics and Stoics as simply one of terminology, the issue
being whether bodily and external 'goods' like health and wealth are to be
called goods or not. But this is clearly wrong (**G**(2)**N**); the Stoic Chrysippus
was himself prepared to *call* them goods as a concession to ordinary ways of

---

[22] For the three types of goods cf. also Aristotle, *Nicomachean Ethics* 1.8.1098b13–15, 1099a31–b8, *Politics*
7.1.1323a24–7, with Hahm 2007, 64 and Colson and Whitaker 1929, 493 on **H** above.

speaking (LS 58H), and the substantial issue is whether or not they are necessary for happiness.

Critolaus, characteristically, took the position furthest removed from that of the Stoics, by maintaining that the three types of goods – virtues, bodily goods and external goods – were parts which made up or 'completed' happiness as a whole (**HI**(1); cf. **JKL** and also **A**(6) above). In arguing thus he was perhaps taking a Stoic formulation and subverting it, for the Stoics held that it is the virtues, and *just* the virtues, which 'complete' happiness; cf. *SVF* 3.73, 106, 107.[23] Critolaus' reference to 'a well-flowing life', at any rate, is an echo, hardly accidental, of Stoic formulations (*SVF* 1.184, 1.554, 3.73, 3.144; Hahm: 2007, 64). Conceivably, in speaking of completion, Critolaus was also influenced by Aristotle's references to a 'complete life' (*Nicomachean Ethics* 1.7.1098a18, 1.9.1100a5), which, however, relate to the completion of an individual life over time, rather than to the presence of a multiplicity of components. Critolaus did, however, insist that virtues, the goods of the soul, were by far the most important part (**M**; repeated, without Critolaus being named, at Cicero, *On Ends* 5.91–2 = Critolaus, fr. 22 Wehrli 1969b. Hahm 2007, 80–1 suggests that here as elsewhere Antiochus concealed the similarities between Critolaus' views and his own. Cf. also **NP**). Antiochus, to judge from Cicero (**OPQR** and **2H**(2) above), drew a contrast between Aristotle and his follower Theophrastus, arguing that Theophrastus gave too much weight to external goods, the goods of fortune. Antiochus may have exaggerated the contrast. (See Theophrastus 487–501 FHS&G, and Fortenbaugh's forthcoming commentary on the texts in FHS&G relating to ethics; meanwhile, Fortenbaugh 1984, 219–23.) In our period Staseas (above, **1D**) too, according to Cicero, seems to have taken a similar line to Theophrastus (**S**).

Others, however, held that bodily and external goods were not parts of happiness in their own right, but rather necessary conditions, happiness requiring virtue, and virtuous activity requiring resources (**I**(2)**TU**; cf. **15A** (11),(15), and the reference to *use* in the passage of Aristotle quoted below). The Stoics would disagree; they too regard virtue as necessary for happiness, but for them even a slave with no property of his own, or a philosopher undergoing torture, can behave virtuously, by acting, for the right reason and from a settled disposition, in the way that is appropriate in those circumstances; cf. LS 59F–K. For the wise person, unlike the navigator, what matters is not the success, but the attempt (**T**). On **T** and its sequel in

---

[23] Cf. White 2002, 84–90, especially 87; Hahm 2007, 65. I am grateful to Inna Kupreeva for drawing my attention to this point.

Seneca, where a different response to the Peripatetic argument is preferred, see Striker 1996, 314 and n.22; Sharples 2000, 129–30; Inwood 2007b, 234–9.

Aristotle, indeed, seems to draw back from saying that a virtuous person who lacks bodily and external goods is simply not happy at all. In *Nicomachean Ethics* 1.10.1100b25–1101a8 he writes as follows:

Great and repeated good [fortune] makes life more blessed [*makarios*]; for the good fortune itself naturally adds adornment to life, and the use made of it is fine and excellent. But when the opposite happens it oppresses and spoils blessedness [*to makarion*] ... nevertheless even in [misfortune] fineness shines out, when someone bears many and great misfortunes well, not through lack of feeling but because he is noble and great-souled. If it is actions that are crucial in life, as we said, none of those who are blessed [*makarioi*] will ever become miserable; for they will never do what is hateful and base. For we think that the truly good and wise person will bear all fortune with a good grace and always do the best thing that the circumstances allow ... if so, the happy [*eudaimōn*] person will never become wretched, though he is not blessed [*makarios*] if he suffers the misfortunes of a Priam.

This passage can be read in two ways. If (A) we take 'blessed' (*makarios*) and 'happy' (*eudaimōn*) as synonyms, the difference between them being just a matter of stylistic variation, Aristotle is saying that a virtuous person may lose his happiness because of misfortune, but – because of his virtue – will never become totally wretched; happiness and wretchedness are here seen as extremes, and the virtuous but unfortunate person will be in a middle state between the two. But we may also (B) see 'blessedness' as a higher degree of happiness than mere happiness alone; in that case moral virtue, even in misfortune, will be sufficient for *happiness*, but bodily and external goods will increase happiness to the point of blessedness. (A) is the position indicated by **V** and (in a qualified way) **W**; cf. also **A**(7) and **15A**(17) and (18) above. (B) is close to the position adopted by Antiochus of Ascalon (**X**(1)**YZ**), whether or not he actually linked it to *Nicomachean Ethics* 1 interpreted in this way. It runs into the difficulty that happiness, as the ultimate goal, should by definition be something complete in itself that cannot be increased; cf. **X**(2)**Aa,Ab**(2)–(4). However, Aristotle himself, in the passage quoted above, seems to allow that it is possible to be not just 'blessed' but 'more blessed'. **Ac** is Aspasius' attempt to argue his way out of this difficulty.

On the issues raised in this section see further Sharples 2007c; Trapp 2007, 32–5.

Physics

CHAPTER 19

The nature of time and place

A. Stobaeus, *Selections* 1.8.40b
(103.7–8 Wachsmuth 1884) = Aëtius 1.22.6
(*Dox.* p. 318.22–4) = Critolaus, fr. 14 Wehrli 1969b

Antiphon and Critolaus [said that] time [is] a thought or a measure, not something that subsists [*hupostasis*].

B. Pseudo-Archytas, *On Universal* Logos *or the Ten Categories* 30.9–16 Thesleff

(1) [Time] always was and will be, and the present moment [the 'now'] will never cease becoming different again and again, different in number but the same in kind. (2) But [time] is different from other continua, since of a line and an area and of place the parts subsist, while of time the [parts] that have come to be have perished, those that are coming to be are perishing, and those that will come to be will perish. (3) And for this reason time either does not exist at all or does so in an obscure way and with difficulty. For how could that really exist of which the past no longer exists, the future does not exist yet, and the now is without parts and indivisible?

C. Arius Didymus(?), *Fragments on Physics* 7
(*Dox.* 450.2–7)

The Aristotelians [say that] time is the number of the movements that are marked off by the now, and that the now is a unit of rest in movement. Time is not movement, but it is not independent[1] of movement. For movement is spoken of as slow and fast, but not time; rather [time is spoken of as] much and little. Moreover more and less are judged by number, but

---

[1] Literally: without.

more and less movement by time. So time is not movement but is not separate from movement; for it is the number of movement, continuous in respect of earlier and later.

D. Boethus(?), *On Aristotle's* Categories, in MS Laurentianus 71.32, folios 84–6, edited in Waitz 1844–1846, vol. 1 21.8–20

One number counts, another is counted. We should enquire how we say that time is the number of movement, whether as numbering the movement or as being numbered by it. Well, we say that time is numbered by the first and simple movement, the movement which is in a circle, and numbers it in return. For if a movement of this sort were not numbered by time, by what would it be numbered? So time, which measures the primary and most proper movement which is that in a circle, measures the other [movements] too by this, so that time will be the number of the movement which is in a circle both as numbering it and as being numbered by it, but of the remaining movements only as numbering but not also as being numbered. For time will not be the number of my walking as being numbered [by it]. but only as numbering [it].

E. Themistius, *On Aristotle's* Physics 160.22–8

If then number is said in two ways, [viz.] what is numerable and what is numbered, the one – the numerable, clearly – in potentiality and the other in actuality, and these would not subsist [*huphistasthai*] if what is going to do the numbering did not exist either in potentiality or in actuality, it is clear that time would not exist if soul did not. And yet Boethus says 'nothing prevents number from existing even apart from what does the numbering', as, I suppose, [nothing prevents] the perceptible [from existing] even apart from the perceiver.

F. Themistius, *On Aristotle's* Physics 163.1–7

But in the case of time, how is it reasonable that time should be a notion of our soul but have no nature of its own, as Aristotle seems to grant when he agrees [*Physics* 4.14.223a21–9] that if soul did not exist time would not exist either, since to say that time is measure and number is [the mark] of one who grants such a notion? For as Boethus says, no measure is produced by nature, but measuring and counting are what we do.

G. Aspasius, reported by Simplicius,
On Aristotle's Physics 578.19–29

And at the same time [Aristotle] interprets the purpose of Plato, on account of which [Plato][2] called matter 'space' and 'place'. Next he introduces the arguments, on account of which he [Aristotle] thinks it impossible that matter be place. Wanting, however, to say why the similarity of place to matter is plausible he takes up the proposal in its own terms. For, he says [*Physics* 4.4.211b29–212a2], matter might seem to be place when one considers the things that are in place as being at rest, not as moving in place. For the things that are in matter are at rest in it, not moving. But perhaps Aspasius is more correct when he says that the person who introduces a similarity between matter and place must disregard the fact that matter is in flux, but place is at rest and immobile as long as it exists.

On the treatment of time and place in relation to the categories see above, **10**.

Aristotle defines time as the number of motion (*Physics* 4.11.220a24–6) and seems to suggest in *Physics* 4.14.223a21–9 that time, as the number of motion, would not exist if there were no souls to do the numbering – indeed that in these circumstances motion would not only not be numbered but would not even be numer*able*. The doxographic report of Critolaus in **A** is too terse to indicate whether he thought that time exists *only* in our thought, or whether he was simply denying that it was an independent existent. The Stoics agreed with Aristotle on the latter point, so here at least Critolaus was not directly opposing the Stoics. (For the Stoic position see the discussion in LS 51.)

Pseudo-Archytas in **B** takes up two of the paradoxes concerning time raised by Aristotle in *Physics* 4 but makes significant additions to Aristotle's formulations. To the paradox that the 'now' or present moment constantly changes (Aristotle, *Physics* 4.10.218a8–30), he in effect responds in **B**(1) that it remains the same in kind (*eidos*) (Sorabji 1983, 48); and in stating the paradox concerning the reality of time (**B**(3), with which cf. Aristotle, *Physics* 4.10.217b33–218a3), he adds that the present is without parts. Sorabji 1983, 39–43 points out that Iamblichus was to apply the notion of being without parts to higher, quasi-ideal time as opposed to the flowing time of our experience, but notes that pseudo-Archytas' own text does not indicate such a distinction.

In **D** Boethus considers whether time is number in the sense of what counts or measures, or rather in the sense of what is counted or measured,

---

[2] In the *Timaeus*, as interpreted by Aristotle and his successors.

and replies that in relation to the rotation of the heavens it is both (Sorabji 2007c, 564 compares Aristotle, *Physics* 4.12.220b14–24), but in relation to other movements it is what measures them rather than what is measured by them. The special role given here to the movement of the heavens is noteworthy; Aristotle himself treats the regular movement of the heavens only as the *chief* measure of time (4.14.223b18–23). The short essay *On Time* attributed to Alexander of Aphrodisias, but surviving only in Arabic and Latin versions, follows Boethus in giving the motion of the heavens – specifically, the daily rotation of the outermost sphere, which may be implied by 'first and simple' in **D** as well – a special status in the account of time (Alexander, *On Time* 94.16–23, 95.6–11 Théry 1926, on the grounds that the motion of the heaven is the swiftest movement; cf. 95.6–11 and Sharples 1982, 69–70).

Boethus in **EF** argues that number can exist even if there is nothing to count it. (**F** applies the point explicitly to time; **E** is shown by the context in Themistius[3] to relate to the discussion of time even though the underlying point is more general.)[4] Alexander on the other hand takes Aristotle's suggestion further, adding that in the absence of soul from the universe there would be no movement in the first place.[5]

In **G** Aspasius is commenting on a suggestion in Aristotle's *Physics* 4.4, which Aristotle himself rejects, that place and matter might seem to be identical.

On the issues raised in this section see further Sorabji 2004, vol. II 201–3, 259–63.

---

[3] Themistius' report in **E** is repeated by Simplicius, *On Aristotle's Physics* 759.18–20 = Sorabji 2004, vol. II 11(d)(1); similarly **F** is repeated by Simplicius at 766.13–19, cf. Sorabji 2004, vol. II 11(d)(6).

[4] Notoriously, what Aristotle says in *On the Soul* 3.2.425b31–426a26 implies that a tree falling in a forest makes no actual sound if there is no living creature close enough to hear it. Cf. Sorabji 2007c, 564–5.

[5] Alexander, *On Time* 95.11–15 Théry 1926 = Sorabji 2004, vol. II 11(d)(2); Alexander reported by Themistius, *On Aristotle's* On the Soul 120.17–21 = Sorabji 2004, vol. II 11(d)(7) and by Simplicius, *On Aristotle's Physics* 760.11–18 = Sorabji 2004, vol. II 11(d)(4).

CHAPTER 20

The eternity of the world

A. Philo of Alexandria, *On the Eternity of the World* 55–7 (part = Critolaus, fr. 13 Wehrli 1969b)

Critolaus, one of those who cultivate the Muses, a follower of the Peripatetic philosophy, supporting the doctrine of the eternity of the world used arguments like these: 'if the world has come to be, it is necessary that the earth too has come to be; if the earth is subject to coming-to-be, certainly the human race [will be so too]; but man is not subject to coming-to-be, since the race has existed from eternity, as will be shown. So the world too is eternal.' (2) What has been passed over must now be established, if indeed demonstration is needed for things that are so clear; but it is necessary, as it seems, because of the contrivers of fables, who have filled life with lies and banished truth beyond its boundaries, forcing not only cities and households but each individual also to be bereft of the best of possessions, and who have contrived enticing style, metres and rhythms as a bait to trap people; with these they cast spells on the ears of fools, as ugly and loathsome courtesans bewitch the eyes by attached and spurious adornment for want of the genuine. For they say that the coming-to-be of human beings from one another is a recent work of nature, and that coming-to-be from the earth was more original and older, since she both is and is thought to be the mother of all; the Sown Men of whom the Greeks sing[1] grew as trees do now, the complete and fully-armed sons of Earth. That this is a contrived fable is easy to see from many things . . .

B. Philo of Alexandria, *On the Eternity of the World* 70 (Critolaus, fr. 12 Wehrli 1969b)

Continuing his contention Critolaus also used an argument like the following: 'what is the cause of its own health does not suffer disease. What is the

---

[1] The Theban warriors who sprang from the earth when Cadmus sowed the dragon's teeth.

cause of its own wakefulness, too, does not sleep. But if this is so, what is the cause of its own existence is eternal. But the world is the cause of its own existence, if it is the cause [of the existence] of all other things. So the world is eternal.'

C. Philo of Alexandria, *On the Eternity of the World* 71–3

It is also worth considering this point too, that everything that has come to be must at all events be incomplete to begin with, but as time advances increase to being altogether complete. So, if the world has come to be, it was once, if I may use the terms for stages of life, altogether childish, but advancing with the circling of the years and the length of time it became complete late and with difficulty; the prime of what is very long-lived is necessarily slow to arrive. But if anyone thinks that the world ever passed through these changes, he should know that he is in the grip of an incurable madness. For it is clear that not only its bodily [aspect] will increase, but also its mind will progress, since those who say that it perishes[2] suppose that it is rational. So, like a human being, it will be irrational to begin with, but when it reaches the prime of its life, rational. But it is impious not just to say this, but even to think it. For how is it not right to suppose that the most perfect perimeter of the visible <gods>, which surrounds the particular tenants,[3] is always perfect both in body and in soul, with no share in evils, with which all that comes to be and passes away is linked?

D. Philo of Alexandria, *On the Eternity of the World* 74

In addition to this he[4] says that there are three causes of death laid down for living creatures, apart from external ones – disease, old age and lack [of food], and the world is not liable to any of these; for it has been constructed from the elements as wholes, so that it cannot be forcibly affected by any part falling short or acting independently, and it has control over the powers from which weaknesses come, and those that yield to it keep it free from disease and old age; it is most sufficient for itself and not lacking in

---

[2] I.e. (orthodox) Stoics who accept the periodic conflagration.

[3] The heavenly bodies are thought of as divine, and as occupying particular land allotments in a settlement of which the world as a whole is the outermost boundary.

[4] Philo does not indicate whether this is still Critolaus or not; Mansfeld 1979, 186 n. 94, argues that it is, but Runia 1986, 185 and 197 regards **D** as deriving from Aristotle's lost *On Philosophy*. See Sharples 2008d, 60 and n. 27.

anything, falling short in none of the things that are [needed] for survival, rejecting the successive emptying and replenishment which living creatures engage in on account of their uncultured insatiability, courting death rather than life or, safer to say, [courting] a life that is more pitiful than destruction.

E. Philo of Alexandria, *On the Eternity of the World* 75

Moreover, if no nature is seen to be eternal, those who introduce a destruction of the world would seem to commit an injustice with less[5] good reason, for they would have no example of eternity. But since, according to those who give the best account of nature,[6] fate has no beginning or end but chains together [*eirein*][7] the causes of each thing without failure or interval, why indeed should not the nature of the world also be said to be long-lasting, the order of things that are without order, the fitting together of things that are disconnected, the harmony of things that are unharmonised, the union of things that are separate, the state [*hexis*][8] of logs and stones, the nature of plants and trees, the soul of all living creatures, the intellect and reason of human beings, the perfect virtue of good people? But if the nature of the world does not come to be or pass away, it is clear that neither does the world [itself], being held together and controlled by an eternal bond.

That the world order is everlasting, without beginning or end, is both Aristotle's own view (see in particular *On the Heaven* 1.10–12) and that of all Peripatetics after him. Consequently we do not have, and should not expect to find, evidence of debate within the Peripatetic school about this issue, and our concern is with Peripatetic arguments directed against those who denied the eternity of the world; notably, in our period, the Stoics, for whom the world was periodically turned to divine fire in an apotheosis, its entire history then beginning again (see LS 46 and 52). Within the Platonic school there were disagreements as to whether the establishment of the world order described in the *Timaeus* was to be understood literally[9] or whether it was, as Plato's pupil Xenocrates had argued, merely a device used

---

[5] Logically one would expect: more. Such 'polar errors' were and are not uncommon.
[6] The Stoics, as the following list of points shows; perhaps ironically.
[7] Cf. **22S** and discussion there.
[8] This and the next four items allude to the standard Stoic classification of ways in which the ruling principle of the world is present in various types of intra-cosmic beings. Cf. *SVF* 2.458, 716 = LS 47NPQ.
[9] An interpretation that was, as far as we know, endorsed first *among those who regarded themselves primarily as Platonists* by Plutarch (*On the Generation of the Soul in the Timaeus*); but on Philo see the next note.

in order to explain the structure of a world that was in fact everlasting. Alexander of Aphrodisias was to follow Aristotle (*On the Heaven* 1.10.280a30) in (a) interpreting the *Timaeus* literally as indicating that the world had a beginning and (b) attacking this view (Alexander, *Quaestiones* 1.18, and Alexander cited by Simplicius, *On Aristotle's* On the Heaven 358.27–360.3), but it does not seem that we have surviving traces of Peripatetics between Critolaus and Alexander engaging in this debate either against the Stoics or against the Platonists. On one aspect of the broader history of the debate see however Sedley (forthcoming).

Philo of Alexandria's essay *On the Eternity of the World* survives only in part, if indeed it was ever completed; all we have is a series of arguments for the view, which Philo did not himself share, that the world had no beginning and will have no end.[10] These arguments are in four groups, attributed, at least in part, respectively (a) to Aristotle (generally regarded as partly deriving from his lost *On Philosophy*; frr. 18–21 Rose 1886), (b) to Critolaus, (c) to Theophrastus (= 184 FHS&G) and (d) to dissident Stoics (Boethus of Sidon and Panaetius) who denied the doctrine of the conflagration.[11] It seems possible that the first three groups of arguments, at least, were collected by Critolaus and that he transmitted them to the source which Philo, in what was probably a youthful essay, seems to have used; though it is also clear that at various points in the whole sequence Philo has, characteristically, elaborated what he found in his source and has given it a more literary expression.[12]

This is the case in particular with the argument in A(1), which clearly depends for its validity entirely on the argument, which follows and occupies the whole of sections 56–69, rejecting the mythical origin of the human race from the earth. Wehrli included only A(1) in his collection of the fragments of Critolaus, influenced by the contrast between its compressed logical form and the literary elaboration of what follows. From the latter I have included only enough, in A(2), to show the general direction of the argument; I have attempted in my translation to bring out Philo's distinctive affectation in style and vocabulary.

---

[10] Philo himself endorses the view, which he attributes to Plato, that the world had a beginning; *On the Eternity of the World* 14–16, 19. See Runia 1981, 134 and 2003, 137–9.

[11] This Boethus (above, Introduction, n. 7) is to be distinguished from the later *Peripatetic* Boethus of Sidon (above, 1N, 5AB, etc.).

[12] On this and other aspects of the arguments attributed to Theophrastus see Sharples 1998, 131–42, with references. On Critolaus' contribution to the debate see Hahm 2007, 81–5, and on Philo's work as evidence for Critolaus' arguments see Sharples 2008d, 59–61, and the discussions cited there.

In **B** the claim that the world is the cause of the existence of all other things appears to be *ad homines* use of a Stoic theory against the Stoics themselves; Hahm 2007, 83–7 sees this as the context for Critolaus' substitution for the unitary Stoic cosmos of a traditional Peripatetic distinction between the eternal heavens and the sublunary region characterised by coming-to-be and perishing (below, **22D**(1)–(2)**HIO**). The arguments in **CDE** are not explicitly attributed to Critolaus by Philo, unless 'he' in **D** is supposed still to refer to him; if so, Philo must have regarded **C** too as deriving from Critolaus. The way in which **E** turns Stoic terminology and doctrine against the Stoic doctrine of the periodic conflagration seems to be in Critolaus' manner, though characteristic of the Academic Sceptics too; the argument for attributing **E** to Critolaus depends on this and upon the fact that it is only after it, at 76–8, that Philo introduces the next set of arguments as those of the dissident Stoics.

CHAPTER 21

The heavens

A.   Cicero, *On the Nature of the Gods* 2.44
(Aristotle, *On Philosophy,*
fr. 24 Rose 1886)

Aristotle, too, is to be praised for judging that all things that move are moved either by nature or by force or by [their own] will. The sun and moon and all the stars[1] move; but things which are moved by nature are carried either downwards by their weight or upwards by their lightness, and neither of these applies to the stars, because their movement is round in a circle. Nor can it be said that some greater force brings it about that the stars move contrary to their nature; for what greater [force] can there be? So what is left is that the movement of the stars is voluntary.

B.   Cicero, *Academica Posteriora* 1.26

Aristotle thought that there was a fifth kind [of element], from which were stars and minds; it was unique and unlike the four which I mentioned above.[2]

C.   Arius Didymus(?), *Fragments on Physics* 9
(*Dox.* 450.12–20)

[Aristotle] (1) [The four elements] are surrounded by the aither, where the divine [bodies] are established, distributed in the spheres of what are called the fixed and the wandering stars. The gods that move the spheres are as many in number as [the spheres], and greatest of these [gods] is the one who embraces all [the spheres], being a living creature that is rational and blessed, holding together and exercising providence over the heavenly

---

[1] 'Stars' can include both the 'wandering' planets and the so-called 'fixed' stars. But the latter too were thought to have a daily rotation round the earth; so I have used the more general term.
[2] Earth, air, fire and water.

things. (2) The stars and the heaven are composed of aither, and this is neither heavy nor light, neither generated nor perishable, and neither increases nor diminishes but remains for ever undeviating and unchanging, limited and spherical and ensouled, moving around the centre in a circle.

D.   Simplicius, *On Aristotle's* On the Heaven 13.22–8

Xenarchus, who in his work *Against the Fifth Substance* opposed many of the things said here, also opposed 'the reason is that these magnitudes only are simple, the straight and the circular' [Aristotle, *On the Heaven* 1.2.268b14–20]. 'For', [Xenarchus] says, 'the spiral on [the surface of] a cylinder is also a simple line, because every part of it fits on every [other] equal part. But if there is a simple magnitude besides the two, there will also be a simple magnitude besides the two, and another simple body besides the five, [namely] that which moves with that [spiral] movement.'

E.   Simplicius, *On Aristotle's* On the Heaven 23.31–24.7

Xenarchus also says this: 'Suppose that there are two simple lines, the circular and the straight, and that each of the four [simple bodies], earth, water, air and fire, when it exists, has as its proper natural movement that which is in a straight line. Even if this is accepted, what prevents [movement] in a circle, too, being natural either for one or for more or for all of these? For we did not suppose in addition that the natural [movement] of each is single. Nor *can* this be supposed in addition; for it is clearly false. For each of the intermediates has two natural movements. Water naturally moves upwards out of earth, but in the opposite direction out of fire and air, and air [moves] downwards out of fire, upwards out of water.'

F.   Simplicius, *On Aristotle's* On the Heaven 24.21–7

Xenarchus also states another [objection], as follows: 'It is impossible for movement in a circle to be natural for a simple body, if in simple bodies, the parts of which are uniform, all the parts [move] at an equal speed. In a circle the [parts] near the centre are always slower than those near the circumference, since they move a smaller distance in the same time. And in a sphere the circles around the poles move more slowly than those far away, and swiftest of all the largest of the parallel [circles, i.e. the equator].'

G.   Simplicius, *On Aristotle's* On the Heaven 20.10–36

(1) One should note that Ptolemy too, in his book *On the Elements* and in his *Optics*, and the great Plotinus, and Xenarchus in his difficulties [raised] *Against the Fifth Substance*, say that movement in a straight line belongs to the elements when they are still coming to be and in an unnatural place, and have not yet got their natural [place]. And Aristotle seems to grant this in the fourth [book] of the present treatise when he says 'to move to its own place is to move to its own form' [*On the Heaven* 4.3.310a33–4]; and also in *On Motion*[3] [= *Physics* 3.1.201a15], and Alexander in this context, as will be said. (2) For in fact, if it is desiring their proper places and their proper wholeness that they move from an alien place and an unnatural condition, it is clear that they move not being completely in a natural condition, but, as the people previously mentioned, Ptolemy, Xenarchus and Plotinus say, when they are in a natural [condition] and in their own proper places the elements either remain at rest or move in a circle. (3) Earth remains at rest, clearly, as do water and the stagnant [part] of the air, but fire moves in a circle, as does the bright [part] of the air that moves round with the heaven because of its affinity to it. (4) If this is true, and Aristotle himself in the *Meteorology* [1.7.344a11] says that the fire-sphere moves in a circle, giving as evidence of this the comets and the other appearances in [the fire-sphere] which rise and set with the stars, how does Aristotle here first in a way try to show from the unnatural movement of sublunary things that the heavenly body surpasses and excels them? (5) Well, this difficulty I shall resolve shortly, since it was put forward by Xenarchus; but for the moment we must ask how it is that [Aristotle] says that neither fire nor any other of the four [bodies] moves in a circle either naturally, if each has one natural movement and [in the case] of these it is in a straight line, or unnaturally, if a single thing has a single opposite, and what is opposite to upwards is downwards, not in a circle.

---

[3] Accepting Hankinson's emendation (2002, 114–15 n. 116). The Greek text has 'On Coming-to-be'; but, as Hankinson points out, there is no obvious passage in Aristotle, *On Coming-to-be and Passing Away* to which Simplicius might be referring. Hankinson himself prefers to take the reference as being to an otherwise unknown work by Alexander, 'On Generation', but is thereby compelled to take *en toutois* not as 'in this context' but 'among these people', which in my view is awkward when Aristotle has just been referred to and the mention of others is in the previous sentence.

H. Simplicius, *On Aristotle's* On the Heaven 21.32–22.17

(1) Xenarchus raises a second difficulty in those which he raises *Against the Fifth Substance*, after that concerned with simple lines [= **D**], against the claim that the movement of a simple body is naturally simple. 'For none of the four elements', he says, 'naturally has movement in a straight line when it already *is*, but only when it is coming to be. For what is coming to be does not have being without qualification but is between being and not-being, just as is what is moving; for this too is in between the place that it is acquiring and the one that it occupied before, and coming-to-be is akin to movement, being itself too a type of change. And for this reason we do not say that the fire that is said to move upwards *is* fire in the strict sense, but that it is coming to be [fire]; when, however, it has gone to its proper place and floats on the other [simple bodies] and has come to rest, then it has come to be [fire] in the strict sense. For it is given its form, in so far as it is light, by this position. And earth *is* earth in the strict sense when it is beneath the other [simple bodies] and occupies the central place [in the universe]. And water and air [*are* water and air in the strict sense], in the case of water, when it floats on the earth but is beneath the air, and in the case of air, when it floats on water but is beneath fire. (2) So it is false', [Xenarchus] says, 'that a simple body naturally has a simple movement; for it has been shown that the movement belongs not to [the simple body] when it *is*, but when it is coming to be. If, however, we must assign some movement to [the bodies] when they already *are*, and this [movement must be] simple, we must assign [to them movement] in a circle, if these two are the only simple [movements], that in a circle and that in a straight line, and that in a straight line belongs to the four [simple bodies] when they are coming to be but [do] not [yet have their] being. So it would not be absurd to assign circular [movement] to fire, rest to the other three.'

I. Alexander of Aphrodisias, reported by Simplicius, *On Aristotle's* On the Heaven 285.32–286.6

'But if, [Alexander says] as Chrysippus supposes, there were an infinite [void outside the world], and they say that void is that interval which is able to receive body but has not done so, and of relatives it is necessary that if one exists, so does the other, [then] if what is able to receive exists, there will also be, or [at least] *could* also be, what can be received. But neither do [the Stoics] themselves say that there is an infinite body that can be received by the infinite void, nor [indeed] is there one; so neither is there what is able to receive it. Xenarchus[4] changed "able to receive" into "receptive", as thus resolving the absurdity brought against the position on the basis of the relative. But the change did not achieve anything. For what is receptive is nothing other than what is able to receive, and being like this it remains relative.'

J.   Simplicius, *On Aristotle's* On the Heaven 379.32–380.5

What Alexander says next I think deserves more, or at least no less, attention than what has been said already. 'We enquired,' he says, 'when we got to this part of the second [book], with what movement the soul moves the body that moves in a circle, if it moves in the movement in a circle by its nature. The enquiry is necessary and most certainly deserves to be set as a problem; we must consider the solutions. Well,' he says, 'Julianus of Tralles'[5] opinion was that the soul was responsible for its movement being to the right and even and orderly. Herminus[6] said that [the soul] was responsible for its moving to infinity; for no finite body possesses, by its own nature, a power of movement to infinity.'

K.   Sosigenes,[7] reported by Simplicius, *On Aristotle*, On the Heaven 504.17–506.3

(1) But the [spheres] of Eudoxus[8] do not preserve the phenomena, not only not [the phenomena] apprehended later, but not even those that were known before and believed by those very people themselves. What need is there to

---

[4]   I take it, as does Rescigno 2004, 482, that Simplicius is still quoting Alexander here, as he is certainly doing in what follows this extract; since Xenarchus' argument is presented as a reply to Alexander's – which is *chronologically* impossible, but philosophers did and do often speak of 'replies' in terms of the arguments, rather than in historical terms – it fits the context better for Alexander, rather than just Simplicius, to be reporting and then rejecting it.

[5]   Iulianus no. 1 in *RE* 10.1 col. 9, which is unsure whether he was a Peripatetic or a Platonist. Goulet, 'Iulianus (45)' in *DPA* vol. III 961, is equally uncertain but adds that the following reference to Herminus (who seems to have been active in the middle of the second century AD; see above on 1) suggests that Julianus could have been active in the late first or early second century AD.

[6]   One of the teachers of Alexander of Aphrodisias; above, 1Y.

[7]   Another teacher of Alexander of Aphrodisias. See 8G, 13F(2)G(1), 26D.

[8]   *hoi peri Eudoxon*, an idiom which may refer to Eudoxus and his associates or just to Eudoxus himself. See above, 4 n. 1. Eudoxus was a mathematician and astronomer of the mid fourth century BC, associated with Plato's Academy.

speak of the other things, some of which Callippus of Cyzicus tried to preserve when Eudoxus had been unable to, if indeed [Callippus] did preserve them? But this very thing, which is obvious even to sight, none of them took it upon himself to demonstrate through his hypotheses until Autolycus of Pitane[9], and not even Autolycus himself was able to. This is shown by his disagreement with Aristotherus.[10] (2) What I mean is that [the planets] sometimes appear to us closer, sometimes further away, and that this is apparent to sight in some cases. For the star called 'Aphrodite's' and that of Ares[11] [= Mars] in the middle of their course[12] appear many times [bigger], so that that of Aphrodite causes shadows to be cast by bodies in moonless nights; and it is clear from sight itself that the moon is not always the same distance from us, because it does not always appear to us as having the same size when the same things are set around the place through which it is seen. (3) Moreover the same appears to those who observe with more use of instruments, because sometimes an eleven-inch drum and sometimes a twelve-inch one, set at the same distance from the observer, blocks our sight from it, so that it cannot reach it.[13] (4) In addition to this all the different sorts of eclipses which happen to the sun bear witness to what has been said and are evidence of its truth. For when its centre and that of the moon and our sight happen to be aligned, what happens does not always seem the same, but sometimes the cone which surrounds the moon and has our sight as its vertex also includes the sun in itself, so that for a period of time it continues to be invisible to us, while at other times it falls so short of this that a certain rim of it is left appearing around the outside at the middle of the eclipse. So necessarily the apparent difference in their sizes is on account of the inequality in their distances, the circumstances in the region of the air being similar.

(5) That this happens in these cases is clear to sight; [so] it is reasonable that it happens in the other cases too, even if it is not clear to sight; and not only reasonable, but also true, since their daily movement is seen to be uneven. But no difference in their apparent sizes strikes us, because the change in their position upwards and downwards, which the mathematicians are accustomed to call the movement in depth, is not great. So they did not in any way try to account for this, and so did not show that it changes each day, even though the problem required this. (6) And yet it is

---

[9] In the second half of the fourth century BC.

[10] Identified in ancient biographies of the astronomical poet Aratus as his teacher, but this is uncertain.

[11] The planets Venus and Mars respectively.

[12] Mueller interprets this as referring specifically to their loops of retrogression.

[13] We would say 'blocks its light from reaching us', or perhaps 'blocks it from our sight'. But Simplicius, like many ancient Greeks, assumes that sight travels from the eye of the observer to the thing seen.

possible to say that the inequality of the distances of each from itself [in the daily movement] did not escape their notice. For Polemarchus of Cyzicus[14] clearly knew of it but thought it of little account, not being perceptible, because he preferred the positioning of the spheres themselves around the centre in the whole. (7) Aristotle too in the *Natural Problems* clearly raises a difficulty with the suppositions of the astronomers from the fact that the sizes of the planets do not appear equal [always].[15] So he was not entirely satisfied with the counteracting spheres, even if their being concentric with the whole and moving around its centre won him over.

(8) And indeed,[16] from what [Aristotle] says in *Metaphysics* Λ, he clearly does not think that the astronomers before him and contemporary with him had given an adequate account of the movements of the planets. For he says 'For now, we say what some of the astronomers say, in order to give an idea, so that there may be some definite number [of movements] to grasp in one's thought; but for the future we must make our own investigations into some things and enquire about others from those who investigate them, and, if anything contrary to what has now been said should be apparent to those who deal with such matters, we should respect both parties, but believe those who are more accurate.'[17]

L.   Simplicius, *On Aristotle's* On the Heaven 488.18

Eudoxus of Cnidus, was the first of the Greeks to deal with this sort of hypothesis, as Eudemus[18] records in the second book of his *History of Astronomy*, and

---

[14] A pupil of Eudoxus.

[15] This is one of a considerable number of references to Aristotle's *Problems* in ancient writers which do not correspond to the collection as it has come down to us. (See, e.g., Flashar 1991, 303–16.) It is often said that an original collection of genuinely Aristotelian *Problems* was lost and replaced by the collection that we possess, but with such material, which is intrinsically fluid in its nature, to assume that any reference to a *Problem* of Aristotle which does not correspond to the extant collection must therefore be to a genuinely Aristotelian *Problem* is unsafe. The present reference is Aristotle, fr. 211 Rose 1886.

[16] Sorabji 2004, vol. II 379 says that Mueller regards (8) as still part of Simplicius' quotation from Sosigenes; Heiberg, the *CAG* editor, as Simplicius' own comment. But in Mueller 2005, 44 the text is set out in a way that suggests that the quotation from Sosigenes ends with (7), and at III n. 193 Mueller simply comments that Heiberg ends the quotation there, without saying that he himself disagrees. See the commentary below.

[17] Aristotle, *Metaphysics* Λ.8.1073b11–17. The form of the quotation is, however, tendentious, for it gives the impression that it reflects doubts on Aristotle's part *about the theory of concentric spheres itself* only by omitting Aristotle's preceding words, which are (1073b10–11) "As to how many [the heavenly movements] are . . .'

[18] Eudemus of Rhodes, the pupil of Aristotle and colleague of Theophrastus. See the commentary on 2 and on 13.

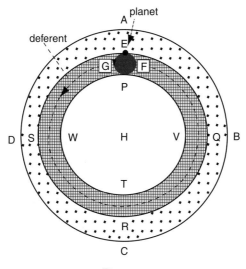

Figure 1

also Sosigenes taking this from Eudemus. It was Plato, according to Sosigenes, who set this as a problem for those concerned with these things: through what suppositions of uniform and ordered movements could the appearances concerning the movements of the wandering [heavenly bodies] be preserved?

M. Adrastus, reported by Theon of Smyrna, *Exposition of Mathematics Useful for Reading Plato* 181.12–182.25

[See Fig. 1.]

Let there be a hollow sphere of the fixed stars, ABCD, around the centre of the universe, H, with depth AE. Its diameters are AC and BD. And let ABCD be understood as the great circle through the middle of the zodiacal signs [i.e. the ecliptic]. Let there be another hollow sphere beneath it, with the same centre, belonging to a planet, EQRSPVTW, with a thickness of EP. In its thickness there is a solid sphere EFPG, carrying the planet fixed in it at E. And let them all[19] travel evenly with simple movements in the same direction from rising in the east to setting in the west, but only that which

---

[19] This is odd, as the sphere of the fixed stars is the *only* one that rotates from east to west, those for all the planets moving along the zodiac in the opposite direction.

delimits the breadth of [the sphere of] the planet [i.e. EQRSPVTW, which defines the diameter of EFPG] travel in the opposite direction, or in the same direction but left behind because of its slowness. For either way the appearances will be preserved.[20] The [sphere] of the fixed stars [moves] around an axis at right angles to <the plane of the equinoctial [circle],[21] the hollow [sphere] of the planet around an axis at right angles to>[22] the same surface in which is also the oblique circle which defines the breadth of [the movement of] the planet in relation to the [circle] through the middle of the zodiacal signs.[23] Let the sphere of the fixed stars move most quickly; more slowly than this the hollow sphere of the planet in the opposite direction, so that in a certain fixed time it goes round the whole [sphere] of the fixed stars in the opposite direction or, as some think, is left behind. Which opinion is more correct has been stated elsewhere. Let it carry with it the solid sphere which holds the planet. The solid sphere, moving evenly round its own centre, will return to the same position, moving in the same direction as the [sphere of the] fixed [stars]. It will return to the same position either [i] in a time equal to that in which the hollow [sphere] of the planet [either] goes round the [sphere] of the fixed [stars] travelling in the opposite direction or is left behind [by one whole revolution], or [ii] more quickly, or [iii] more slowly.[24]

N.   Adrastus, reported by Theon of Smyrna, *Exposition of Mathematics Useful for Reading Plato* 201.20–202.2

(1) The movement of all [the planets] is chosen and unforced, involving the smallest number of movements and in ordered spheres. (2) He criticises all the philosophers who unite the planets[25] with the spheres as if [the planets]

[20] Cf. L above. The easterly movement of a planet along the zodiac can be thought of either as an easterly movement imposed on the daily rotation of the whole heaven to the west, or in terms of the planet moving westwards slightly less slowly than the fixed stars.

[21] I.e. the celestial equator on which the equinoctial points lie, being the intersections of the celestial equator and the ecliptic; L and N in Fig. 2 below (p. 192).

[22] There is a lacuna in the Greek text here. I translate Martin's supplement in the apparatus criticus to Hiller's Teubner edition.

[23] That is, at right angles to the path of the particular planet in relation to the ecliptic, different planets (other than the sun) diverging from this by differing angles.

[24] If the solid sphere, i.e. the epicycle, rotates once for each revolution of the hollow sphere carrying it, i.e. the deferent, the epicycle model is equivalent to a simple eccentric rotation, and there will be no loops of retrogression, as indeed there are not for the sun or the moon.

[25] Here and in what follows Theon has 'stars', but for the Greeks the planets were, literally, 'wandering [stars]', and it is the planets that are relevant here.

were inanimate and introduce multiplicities of spheres for the circlings [of the planets], as Aristotle thinks it right to do, and of the astronomers Menaechmus and Callippus,[26] who introduce some [spheres] that carry [the planets], others that unwind [these].[27]

Aristotle, in his surviving esoteric works, holds that the heavens are composed of an element, *aithēr*, which is different from the four sublunary elements earth, air, fire and water, and is characterised by (a) only admitting spatial movement, and no other form of change, and (b) having as its natural movement not movement upwards (i.e. away from the centre of the world, like that of fire and air) or downwards (towards the centre of the world, like that of earth and water), but movement in a circle. Only thus, he argued, could the heavens rotate for ever in a circle; for time and movement have no beginning or end, as argued in *Physics* 8.1–2 and *Metaphysics* Λ.6, and no unnatural motion can be everlasting, as this would require an infinite power to bring about by force what is unnatural. (Cicero, in **A**, records an earlier stage in Aristotle's thought, from the lost exoteric dialogue *On Philosophy*, where a similar argument by elimination is used to show that the motions of the heavenly bodies are voluntary.)

Aristotle himself, unlike his later interpreters, never refers to the *aithēr* as the 'fifth element', regarding it rather as the *first* (*On the Heaven* 2.12.291b32; Drossaart-Lulofs 1965, 155; Hussey 1983, 121). He draws at least an analogy between it and the 'connate spirit' which is the instrument through which an animal's soul moves its body; this analogy influenced later interpretations of Aristotle's theory of soul (**B**, and below, **24A–D**, cf. **24EF**. Cf. Moraux 1963).

Aristotle's view was exceptional in the history of Greek thought. *aithēr* was standardly used for the bright heavens as opposed to the murky, misty *aēr* in the terrestrial region; but the former was commonly thought of as fire, or a superior form of fire, the latter as air. It has been argued that Theophrastus already abandoned Aristotle's theory of a separate celestial element; this is uncertain (see the discussion in Sharples 1998, 88–93), but it is clear that Strato did so (fr. 84 Wehrli 1969c = 42 in Sharples (in press)).

---

[26] Menaechmus was a pupil of Eudoxus in the middle of the fourth century BC, best known for his contributions to geometry. Callippus was an astronomer of the second half of the fourth century BC; his modifications to Eudoxus' theory of concentric heavenly spheres are discussed, along with that theory, by Aristotle in *Metaphysics* Λ.8.

[27] The theory of *counter-acting* spheres, which negate the effect of those producing the motion of one planet so that there can be a fresh start, as it were, in explaining that of the planet next to it in sequence, is shown by *Metaphysics* Λ.8 to be Aristotle's own, rather than Menaechmus' or Callipus' as 'unwind' might here imply. But the terminology became confused early in antiquity. See the commentary below.

The four-element theory was endorsed by Plato's *Timaeus* 53–61c (though not by the author of the *Epinomis* falsely attributed to Plato, 981c; and some Platonists used the fact that the *Timaeus* mentions five regular solids to suggest that Plato could have accepted Aristotle's fifth element, cf. Sorabji 2004, vol. II 364–6). It was also upheld by the Stoics (LS 47AB).

Aristotle's five-element theory is accurately reported by Diogenes Laertius in **3A**(13) above, and by Cicero and Arius Didymus (?) in **BC** in the present section (for **C** see also below, commentary on **22**). Xenarchus (on whom see also above, **1EI**, **17C**), however, challenged the theory of a separate heavenly element. He argued that Aristotle's list of simple natural motions (upwards for fire and air, downwards for earth and water, circular for the *aithēr*) is incomplete and so cannot be used to argue for there being five elements; for in addition to the motions listed by Aristotle spiral motion too, he argued, is simple (**D**. This is clearly a purely dialectical argument; Xenarchus is not seriously proposing that there is a type of simple body that naturally moves in a spiral.) Moreover, Aristotle's argument, Xenarchus claims, fails to take into account that the intermediate elements, water and air, do not have simple movements; air, for example, rises upwards in water but falls downwards relative to fire (**E**). Circular motion is not simple, for in a rotating solid body the speed of each part is proportional to its distance from the centre (**F**); and the natural movements of the sublunary elements apply only when they are *not* in their natural places (**GH**). Earth moves downwards, but when it gets as close as it can to the centre of the world it remains at rest (it could indeed be objected that it does so not naturally but perforce, being prevented from descending any further by the other earth that is between it and the actual centre); so similarly fire, when it reaches its natural (i.e. the highest) place may, Xenarchus argued, stop moving upwards and rotate around the centre of the world instead – this being all the more plausible since, as pointed out in **G**(4) (cf. Sorabji 2004, vol. II 357), Aristotle himself regarded the fire immediately below the heavens as rotating, since meteors and comets, which Aristotle regarded as meteorological phenomena in the fire layer rather than as strictly heavenly phenomena, apparently follow the rotation of the fixed stars around the earth, in addition to having their own individual movements.[28] **H**(2) suggests that the distinction in **G**(3) between the lower air that is stagnant and the upper air that moves in a circle is not Xenarchus' own. Tarán 1981, 746 suggests that Xenarchus' intention was not to challenge Aristotle's

---

[28] In actual fact, of course, it is the daily rotation of the earth that causes the apparent daily movement both of the fixed stars and of the comets and meteors.

theory of the elements but simply to point to weaknesses in his arguments for the fifth element *as arguments*. However Falcon 2008 rightly emphasises that Xenarchus' position is not just a rejection of the fifth element, but a major modification of Aristotle's whole theory of natural motion; it is from Xenarchus' insistence that we should consider the motion, or lack of it, of the elements *in their own proper places* that it follows both that the only possibilities apart from forced motion are rest and natural movement in a circle (**G**(2)) and that fire is an example of the latter.

In *On the Heaven* I.9.279a13–17 Aristotle argues that there cannot be void outside the heaven, because void is that in which there is no body at present, but could be, and since there cannot be body outside the heaven there cannot by this definition be void either. The Stoic Cleomedes, apparently here dependent on Posidonius, attacked the basic assumption; that there cannot be body in a particular place does not show that there cannot be there that which *could* receive it if there were. (The Stoics, unlike the Peripatetics, required the existence of void outside the heaven because when, in the orthodox Stoic view, the whole world turns to fire at the periodic conflagration, it will need to expand.) Simplicius in **I** reports what seems to be an ineffective attempt by Xenarchus to attack the basic assumption of the argument by substituting 'receptive' for 'able to receive'; but, as Simplicius says, the two terms come to the same thing in this context – what is needed is rather an assertion, like that of Cleomedes, that a thing can be receptive even if what would be received by it cannot in fact exist. (See further on this Sorabji 1988, 132–5; 2007c, 567; and for a later stage in the debate Alexander, *Quaestiones* 3.12 with the notes in Sharples 1994, 138–41).

Even after the introduction of the theory of *aithēr*, Aristotle continued to hold that the heavens have soul, that is are alive. (This statement is controversial, and, in particular, some have held that there was a period in which the theory of *aithēr replaced* that of the heavens being alive and moving of their own volition. See however Guthrie 1939, xxix–xxxv; Sharples 2002b, 4 and n. 10, with references there.) This created a problem for Aristotle's interpreters, in that explanation of the movement of the heavens *both* by their own volition *and* because they were made of a stuff whose very nature it was to revolve in a circle seemed to create redundancy. Various attempts, recorded in **J**, were made to resolve this by assigning separate roles to each of the two factors. Alexander's own solution, given by Simplicius in the sequel (and anticipated in principle, even if only in passing, by Aspasius in **22J**(4) below), was that, since the soul of a living thing is its form, in the heavens soul and nature are identical (Simplicius, *On Aristotle's* On the Heaven 380.29–381.2 = Sorabji 2004, vol. II 1(d)(9); cf.

Simplicius, *On Aristotle's* Physics 1219.1–7 = Sorabji 2004, vol. II 1(d)(11), and for Simplicius' rejection of Alexander's position his *On Aristotle's On the Heaven* = Sorabji 2004, vol. II 1(d)(10), and below on **24AB**).

Aristotle's theory of the heavenly movements in *Metaphysics* Λ.8 and *On the Heaven* 2.12.293a5–10 is based on Eudoxus' theory of concentric spheres. The apparent daily motion of the sun around the earth and the annual motion of the sun along the ecliptic, from furthest north at the summer solstice in the northern hemisphere (Q in Fig. 2, where FEDCBAJIHG is the projection onto the celestial sphere of an observer's horizon) to furthest south at the winter solstice (S) can be represented by the rotation of two circles (respectively KDLMIN, the celestial equator, and QLCSN, the ecliptic) inclined to one another with the earth at their common centre, as in Plato's construction of the world-soul in *Timaeus* 36be. Those circles can be thought of as great circles on two spheres, one inside the other, each circle being at right angles to the axis of rotation of its own sphere, the axes of rotation of the two spheres being inclined to one another, and the earth being at the common centre of both. Eudoxus, and after him Callippus, added further concentric spheres to the model to explain irregularities in the observed planetary motions which are due to the fact that in reality the heavenly bodies, with the exception of the moon, do not revolve around the earth, and the orbits are not in actual fact (and in spite of **L** below) circular, but elliptical.

This model was already obsolete, as far as astronomers were concerned, soon after Aristotle himself; among other problems in accounting for the phenomena, it postulated that the sun, moon and planets are all carried on spheres which have the earth as their centre of rotation, and so, as Sosigenes points out in **K**, it could not account for the variations in their apparent

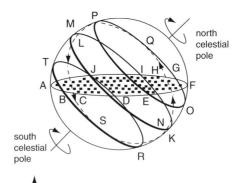

Figure 2

sizes, as demonstrated *inter alia* by the difference between total and annular solar eclipses (Fig. 3).

The *actual* reasons for the variations in distance and hence in apparent size are that (a) the sun, moon and planets do not all in fact rotate round the earth, and (b) the orbits of the heavenly bodies are ellipses, not circles. To solve these and other difficulties in Eudoxus' system, such as variations in the apparent speed of the planets in different parts of their orbits, Hellenistic astronomers postulated the theories of eccentrics (Fig. 4) and epicycles (Fig. 5), the former supposing that the earth was not at the centre of each heavenly body's supposed circular path, and the latter that the planets were carried not on spheres or circles with the earth at or near their centres, but on circular paths (the 'epicycles' or 'additional circles') whose centres *themselves* traced circular paths (the 'deferent circles') with the earth at or near their centres.

This created a problem for interpreters of Aristotle in our period. They were, after all, interested in Aristotle as an authority, not simply as a subject

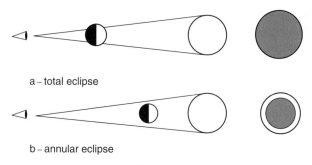

a – total eclipse

b – annular eclipse

Figure 3

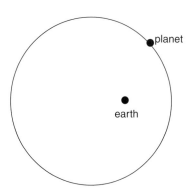

Figure 4

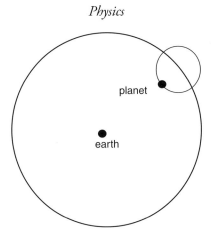

Figure 5

for historical interpretation; and his apparent endorsement of a theory that was now recognised as obsolete was a potential embarrassment. It is true that in *Metaphysics* Λ.8 Aristotle makes it clear that he is interested in the general principle of a combination of several circular movements to account for the apparent movement of each planet, rather than in the precise number and details of such movements, which he explicitly says are a matter rather for experts in astronomy; so ancient interpreters *could* in principle have concentrated on the general implications for Aristotle's ontology, regarding the now superseded details as of purely antiquarian interest. But no one in our period seems to have taken this line explicitly, unless the quotation in **K**(8) is due to Sosigenes rather than to Simplicius.

In **K**(7) Sosigenes claims that Aristotle himself 'in the *Natural Problems*' raised the difficulty of variation in size. But Sosigenes' report here is not parallelled anywhere else, and Schiaparelli 1926, 110–11 n. 3 suggests that it is not a genuine record of something Aristotle himself said, but rather reflects attempts by later Peripatetics to reconcile their own adoption of more up-to-date astronomical theories with continued loyalty to Aristotle. Sosigenes was also responsible for providing an influential, if probably unhistorical, context for our understanding of ancient astronomical theories by preserving the story that Plato set the explanation of the phenomena in terms of regular circular movements as a problem and goal (**L**; on the historical plausibility of and background to this see Zhmud 1998).

Aristotle in *Metaphysics* Λ.8 is commonly regarded as taking the purely mathematical accounts of the heavens given by Eudoxus and Callippus and converting them into a physical account by adding 'counteracting' spheres which negate the effect of the spheres that explain the motion of one planet in order to give a fresh start, as it were, for explaining that of the next in the series.[29] Already before Sosigenes, Adrastus (for whom see above, 1UVW) in M seems to give physical expression to the epicycle theory, by placing each planet on a solid sphere (representing the epicycle) rotating between the inner and outer surfaces of a hollow sphere (the centre-line of the space between the surfaces representing the deferent circle); for the solid sphere is said to *carry* the planet.[30] In N(1) Adrastus insists that the movement of the planets is chosen by them, while also accounting for it in terms of physical spheres. The reference to 'unwinding' spheres at the end of N(2) may seem to be in error, attributing the counteracting spheres of *Metaphysics* Λ.8.1073b38–1074a5 to Callippus rather than to Aristotle; this could reflect a careless reading of Aristotle's text, but confusion over the sense of 'unwinding' started early. Already Simplicius, *On Aristotle, On the Heaven* 491.18–19 applied it, reasonably enough in terms of the meaning of the word, to the spheres *above* that carrying the planet itself, as (in some cases) moving in different directions to the sphere of the fixed stars (cf. Moraux 1984, 345–6, suggesting that the double usage of the term goes back to Sosigenes; Sharples 1998, 107; Salis 2004, 149); and the accounts of pseudo-Alexander (*On Aristotle's* Metaphysics 704.21–705.13; see Salis 2005, 266–70), Averroes (*On Aristotle's* Metaphysics 1672–5 Bouyges; see Genequand 1984, 54–5) and Aquinas (*Sententia libri metaphysicae* 12.10.14, 12.10.16) – the latter two indeed being at the mercy of misleading or ambiguous translations – are even more confused. So it may be that Adrastus is already using the term in a different way from Aristotle.

On the issues raised in this section see further Sorabji 2007a.

---

[29] Wright 1973, however, argues that Eudoxus' model too was not purely geometrical and computational in intention. Drossaart-Lulofs 1965, 156 criticises Nicolaus of Damascus (F32) for saying that each sphere moves the one beneath it, objecting that Aristotle does not say this explicitly and that it would make Unmoved Movers for the subordinate spheres redundant. But it is (a) one thing to say that each sphere moves the *axis* of the one below it, (b) another to say that it causes the *rotation* of the one below it around that axis; it is (b) that would risk making the Unmoved Movers redundant, but (a) is probably all that Nicolaus intended. Cf., on a similar issue in Alexander, Bodnár 1997, 200–1.

[30] MN are not explicitly attributed to Adrastus by Theon, but the context suggests that it is his theory that is being described, and the attribution is generally accepted.

CHAPTER 22

God and providence

A. Cicero, *On the Nature of the Gods* 1.33

(1) Aristotle in the third book of his *On Philosophy* introduces great confusion, disagreeing[1] with his teacher Plato: for now he attributes all divinity to intellect, now he says that the world itself is a god, now he puts some other [god] in charge of the world and assigns to him the role of ruling and preserving the movement of the world by a certain rolling back,[2] then he says that the heat of the heaven is a god, not understanding that the heaven is a part of the world which he himself elsewhere has designated as a god. (2) But how could that divine awareness be preserved in such rapid motion? Where are all the gods [we speak of], if we count the heaven itself as a god?[3] And when he wants god to be without a body, he deprives him of all awareness,[4] and [so] of wisdom. Further, how can [god] move if he does not have a body, or how, if he is always moving himself, can he be peaceful and blessed?

B. Stobaeus, *Selections* 1.1.29b (35.5–6 Wachsmuth) = Aëtius 1.7.21 (*Dox.* p. 303.6–7) = Critolaus, fr. 16 Wehrli 1969b

Critolaus, and Diodorus of Tyre,[5] [said that god is] an intellect from impassible aither.

---

[1] Manutius here conjectured, and Lambinus and many subsequent editors accepted, 'not disagreeing'.
[2] Presumably alluding to the 'counteracting' heavenly spheres of *Metaphysics* Λ.8.1073b38–1074a5 (cf. above on 21N), or perhaps just to the fact that the apparent yearly rotation of the sun round the zodiac is in the opposite direction to its apparent daily rotation round the earth. There could also be a reference to the perpetuation of the world's movement by its 'replication' or repetition.
[3] I.e. the gods of ordinary belief will – absurdly, in the view of the Epicurean Velleius who is speaking here – have to be in a god.
[4] For an Epicurean, sensation and thought are explained as material processes.
[5] Critolaus' pupil. See 1B above.

C. Athenagoras, *Supplication* 6.3

Aristotle and his followers regard [god] as one, as it were a composite living creature; they say that god is composed of a soul and a body, thinking that his body is the ethereal and the planets and the sphere of the fixed stars, [all] moving in circles, his soul the *logos* that applies to the movement of the body, not itself moved but being the cause of [the body's] movement.

D. Hippolytus, *Refutation of All Heresies* 7.19.2–8

(1) According to Aristotle the world is divided into several different parts. One part of the world is this which extends from the earth to the moon; without providence, without government, for which its own nature alone suffices; the other, beyond the moon as far as the surface of the heaven, is ordered with complete order and providence and government. The surface of the heaven, being a certain fifth substance, is separate from all [the] natural elements of which the world is composed and is according to Aristotle the fifth substance, as it were a certain supra-worldly substance. (2) And his account of philosophy is divided according to the division in the world. For he [composed] a certain lecture course on *Physics*, in which the concern is with the things that are administered by nature, and not by providence, from the earth as far as the moon. He also [composed] a certain other separate treatise entitled *Metaphysics* about the things beyond the moon; and he [composed] a separate work about the fifth substance, which is his *Theology*. Such in outline is the division of the discussions in Aristotle's philosophy.

(3) His account *On the Soul* is unclear; for from three whole books it is not possible to say clearly what Aristotle thinks about soul. It is easy to say what is the definition he gives of soul, but what is revealed by the definition is hard to discover. The soul is, he says, the actuality of a natural organic body. To discover what this is requires very much discussion and a considerable investigation. (4) God, who is the cause of all these fine things, is harder to know than the soul, even if one considers at greater length. For the definition which Aristotle gives of god is not difficult to state, but to know [what it means] is impossible. For he says that [god is] thinking of thinking; that is [to say], non-existent. The world is imperishable and eternal according to Aristotle; for there is nothing discordant in it, since it is governed by providence and nature.

(5) Aristotle not only left accounts of nature and the world and providence and god, but he also [left] a certain treatise [containing] arguments

about ethics. This is entitled *Books on Ethics*, and through it the character of those who hear it is made noble instead of being base.[6] ((1) Sharples 2007b, 601)

E.   Aëtius 1.7.32 (*Dox.* 305a2–13)

(1) Aristotle said that the highest god is a separate form,[7] mounted on the sphere of the universe, which is etherial body, what he calls the fifth [body].[8] (2) This is divided into spheres which are contiguous in nature but distinct in account. He thinks that each of the spheres is a living creature composed of a body and a soul; the body is etherial, moving in a circle, while the soul is an unmoved rational [principle], the cause of the movement in actuality.

F.   Alexander of Aphrodisias, *Supplement to* On the Soul (*On Intellect*) (*Mantissa* 2).113.6–15, 16–17

(1) This [divine] intellect either organises things here [in the sublunary region] on its own, in relation to the movement of the heavenly bodies above, and combines and separates them, so that it is itself the craftsman [producing] the potential intellect,[9] as well; or else [it organises things here] along with the orderly movement of the heavenly bodies.[10] (2) For it is by this that things here are brought about, chiefly by the approach and withdrawal of the sun: either they are brought about by [the sun] and by the intellect here, or else it is nature that is brought about by these things [the heavenly bodies] and their movement, and it [nature] organises individual things along with intellect.

(3) It seemed to me to be an objection to this [theory] both that intellect, [though] it is divine, is in even the basest things, as the Stoics thought, and in general that there is intellect and some sort of primary providence in things here . . . (4) also that thinking would not depend on us and would not be our task. (Sharples 2004, 42)

---

[6] Erik Eliasson suggests to me that there may be some confusion here with a report of the *Protrepticus*. This is certainly possible, but one might also think of *Nicomachean Ethics* 2.2.1103b27–9.

[7] Stobaeus, one of our two witnesses for Aëtius, but not the other, pseudo-Plutarch, adds here 'similarly to Plato'.

[8] The sequel only in pseudo-Plutarch, not in Stobaeus.

[9] See below, 27I, to which this is the sequel.

[10] The difference between the options here is not immediately obvious. See the commentary below.

G. Alexander of Aphrodisias, *On Mixture*
11.226.24–30

How is it not unworthy of our conception of the divine to say that god goes through all the matter that underlies all things and remains in it, of whatever sort it is, and has as his primary task the constant production and fashioning of some one of the things that can come to be from it, and to make god the artificer of grubs and gnats, just like a modeller devoting himself to clay and making everything that can come to be from it?

H. Aëtius 2.3.4 (*Dox.* 330.5–12)

Aristotle [says that the world] is neither ensouled throughout nor endowed with sense perception[11] nor rational nor intellectual nor governed by providence. For the heavenly things share in all of these, since spheres which are ensouled and alive surround [the world]; but the things in the region of the earth [share in] none of them, and have a share in good order accidentally, not in a primary way. (Sharples 2007b, 601)

I. Adrastus, reported by Theon of Smyrna, *Exposition of Mathematics Useful for Reading Plato*
149.4–150.4

(1) But of the things beneath the moon and in our region and extending to us there is every change and movement and, as he says, 'there are wrath and slaughter and the tribes of the other cares'[12] and coming-to-be and passing away are about all the things here, and growth and diminution and alteration of every sort and varied spatial movements. The causes of these, he says, are the wandering stars. (2) These things might be said not on the basis that the things that are more honourable and divine and eternal and ungenerated and imperishable exist for the sake of those that are lesser and mortal and perishable, but on the basis that the former are always as they are on account of what is finest and best and most blessed, while things here follow them accidentally.[13] For in order that the circular motion of the

---

[11] 'nor endowed with sense perception' was deleted by Diels, but Mansfeld and Runia: 1996–, vol. ii, part 2, 340–4 retain it.

[12] Empedocles, fr. 121.

[13] The parallel text in Calcidius, *On Plato's* Timaeus 124.4–5 expands this: 'the latter, as the result of a certain accidental partnership which agrees with them [the heavenly bodies] up to a certain point, imitate the divine happiness as far as they can'.

whole may always come about in the same way, being as it were some activity and divine life of this, the earth must remain at the centre, and what moves in a circle will rotate around it. If it is necessary for the earth to remain below, it is also necessary for fire to occupy the opposite place to it, positioned below the ethereal substance which moves in a circle. And with these being separated in this way it is necessary for the other elements, water and air, to occupy the space in between, as is reasonable. These things being so, it is necessary also for there to be change in the things here, because their matter is altogether changeable and has opposite potencies. And the change is brought about in them by the complex movement of the planets.

J.   Aspasius, *On Aristotle's* Ethics 71.16–31

(1) Of things some are eternal and always the same, such as the world, for it is ungenerated and eternal, and the diagonal which is incommensurable with the side of square. No one deliberates about such things, nor about how the diagonal might become commensurable, but if he does [enquire at all], he enquires whether it *is* incommensurable but does not in any way deliberate. (2) There are other things which are not always but come to be in the same way always, like the rising and setting and turnings[14] of the planets; and there is no deliberation about such things either. [Aristotle] says [*Nicomachean Ethics* 3.3.1112a24–5] that it is from necessity, either by nature or because of some other cause, that such things come about in the same way, meaning by 'necessity' not the [necessity] of force.[15] (3) For nothing of the things in the heavens comes about by force. But he has given the name of 'necessity' to the providence of the one who always causes movement in the same way, because he causes movement altogether without qualification and cannot ever do so otherwise. For what cannot be otherwise is said to be necessary. By such necessity, at any rate, the movements and risings and settings and turnings of the planets are either by nature or according to nature. (4) For the things in the heavens are moved either according to nature <or by nature>[16] or both; for the providence of the one who causes

---

[14] In the case of the sun the 'turnings' are the solstices, the furthest points north and south in its annual path. The reference here must therefore be to the similar northmost and southmost points reached by the other planets, in the ancient sense of that term including sun and moon; consequently at the end of this clause I have rendered by 'planets' the Greek term which can refer either to what we call 'stars' (and the ancients, 'fixed stars') or to the planets.

[15] Aristotle in fact treats necessity, nature and some other cause as three co-ordinate possibilities, But the sequel shows that Aspasius treats the second and third as two alternative explanations of the first.

[16] Adopting Konstan's supplement (Konstan 2006, 194 n. 153).

movement is most in agreement with the nature of the things that are moved.

K. Plutarch, *Precepts for Managing Affairs of State* 15.811c (Critolaus, fr. 37a Wehrli 1969b)

Others, among whom is Critolaus the Peripatetic, think that Pericles' [approach] is more solemn and dignified: judging that the Salaminia and the Paralos, the [state] galleys at Athens, were not launched for every task but [only] for the necessary and major activities, he employed himself for the most important and greatest [tasks], like the sovereign of the universe: 'for god takes hold of what is greater, but the small matters he lets go and leaves to chance' according to Euripides.[17]

L. Plutarch, *Life of Pericles* 7 (Critolaus, fr. 37b Wehrli 1969b)

In the assembly, avoiding continuity and satiety, [Pericles] was present as it were at intervals, not speaking on every matter and not always coming forward to speak to the multitude but assigning himself like the trireme Salaminia, as Critolaus says, to occasions of great need, he dealt with other things by sending speakers who were his friends and companions.

M. Cicero, *Academica Posteriora* 1.28–9

(1) That force which we have called quality[18] moves in such a way and thus moves back and forth . . . this force [the Peripatetics and the Old Academy] say is the soul of the world, and is also perfect mind and wisdom, which they call god, a sort of forethought[19] for all the things that are subject to it, caring most of all for heavenly things, but then for those on earth which concern human beings; (2) this sometimes they also call necessity, because nothing can be otherwise than it has been established by it within, as it were, a fated

---

[17] Euripides, fr. 974 Nauck². The Greek can also mean 'too great', and this fits the original tragic context; that the proud and overweening are in *danger* from the gods is a constant theme of tragic choruses. But what Pericles, Critolaus and Plutarch have in mind is presumably rather *beneficent* concern for greater matters while disregarding smaller ones.

[18] The Stoic Active Principle, in Antiochus' identification of the physics of the Stoics, the Old Academy and the Peripatetics. See the commentary below.

[19] *prudentia*, but perhaps with a wordplay on the etymologically related *providentia*.

and unchangeable sequence of an eternal ordering; (3) and sometimes indeed they call it fortune, because it brings about many things that are unforeseen and unexpected by us because of the obscurity of their causes and our ignorance of them.

N.   Atticus, fr. 3.7–10 des Places 1977

(1) Similarly to [Epicurus] the Peripatetic [Aristotle]. For it is not eagerness for pleasure that reinforces injustice, as much as lack of belief that the divine is concerned about it. 'What then,' someone might say, 'are you ranking Aristotle with Epicurus?' Certainly, as far as the point at issue is concerned; for what difference is there for us in evicting the divine from the world and leaving no connection between us and it, [on the one hand,] and keeping the gods in the world but keeping them apart from affairs on earth [on the other]? For the lack of concern from the gods for human beings is equal in both, as is the immunity from the gods for those who commit injustice. (2) To say that, although they remain in heaven, we derive some benefit,[20] is something that we share with irrational and inanimate things, and in this way there is some benefit for human beings from the gods according to Epicurus as well; at any rate [the Epicureans] say that the better effluences from them are, for those who have a share in them, the accessory causes of great goods. (3) But it is not right to reckon either [Epicurus] or [Aristotle] as [upholding] providence; if providence is abolished according to Epicurus, even though the gods according to him exercise all care for the preservation of their own good things, then according to Aristotle too providence is abolished, even if the things in heaven are disposed in a certain ordering and pattern. (4) For we are looking for a providence that makes a difference *to us*, and he who does not admit *daimones* or heroes or the possibility of the survival of souls at all has no share in this.

O.   Epiphanius, *On Faith* 9.35, 39 (vol. III, p. 508.4–9 and 15 Holl and Dummer = 3.31, 35 in Diels, *Dox.* 592.9–14 and 20. Critolaus, fr. 15 Wehrli 1969b)

(1) Aristotle, son of Nicomachus, was a Macedonian from Stagira according to some, but a Thracian in race according to others. He said that there are two principles, god and matter, and that the things above the moon are objects of divine providence, but the things below the moon exist without

---

[20] Compare Epicurus, *Letter to Menoeceus* 124 (LS 23B(3)-(4)).

providence and are borne along in some irrational way as chance has it. He says that there are two world orders, that above and that below, and that which is above is imperishable, but that which is below is subject to passing away … (2) Critolaus of Phaselis held the same opinions as Aristotle. (Sharples 2002b, 22; FHS&G 162)

P. Epictetus, *Discourses* 1.12.1–3

(1) Concerning the gods there are some who say that the divine does not exist at all, (2) and others who say that it exists, but is idle and free from care and exercises no providence over anything. (3) Third are those who say that it both exists and exercises providence, but over great and heavenly things, not over any of the things on earth; (4) fourth those [who say that it exercises providence] over things on earth and human affairs, but only with a view to what is common and not also over each separate individual. (5) Fifth, including Odysseus and Socrates, are those who say 'I do not escape your notice in my movements' [from Odysseus' prayer to Athena at Homer, *Iliad* 10.279–80].

Q. Pseudo-Aristotle, *On the World* (*De mundo*) 6.397b30–398a1

And so it is reasonable that earth and the things on earth, being furthest from the assistance that comes from the divine, should be weak and discordant and full of confusion; nevertheless, inasmuch as the divine naturally penetrates to the whole, the things among us happen in a similar way to those above us, receiving assistance more or less according as they are nearer to or further from god.

R. Pseudo-Aristotle, *On the World* (*De mundo*) 6.398b4–22

(1) If it was unseemly for Xerxes to seem to do everything himself and to bring about whatever he wanted and to stand over it and manage it, it would be much more unseemly for god. It is more fitting and more seemly for him to be established in the highest place, and for his power, penetrating throughout the entire world, to move the sun and moon and cause the rotation of the whole heaven and to be the cause of the preservation of things upon earth. (2) He has no need of contrivance or of the service of others, as those who rule among us need many hands because of their weakness, but

this above all is divine, to bring about all sorts [of things] easily and with a simple movement, as indeed those who make machines do, bringing about many different actions through a single triggering of the machine. Similarly puppeteers, pulling a single string, make the neck and hand of the creature move, and its shoulder and eye, and sometimes all its parts, with a rhythmical [movement]. (3) So too the divine nature, from a certain simple movement of what comes first, transmits its power to what is adjacent and from those things to what is further off, until it permeates the whole.

S. Pseudo-Aristotle, *On the World* (*De mundo*) 7.401b8–14

I think that Necessity [*Ananke*] is a name for nothing other than [god], as being an invincible [*aniketos*] cause; Fate [*Heimarmene*] because he connects [*eirein*] everything and proceeds without hindrance; Destiny [*Pepromene*] because everything has been determined [*peperatosthai*] and nothing that is is unlimited; Doom [*Moira*] from things having been divided into portions [*memeristhai*], Retribution [*Nemesis*] from the distribution [*dianemesis*] to each person, Adrasteia as being by nature an inescapable [*anapodrastos*] cause, Aisa as always existing [*aei ousa*].

T. Alexander of Aphrodisias, *Quaestiones* 1.25.40.30–41.19

(1) The reason for this double motion they [the heavenly spheres] have is the need for there to be some other body apart from that which is eternal and divine, [a body] subject to coming-to-be and passing away – for this sort of body too contributes to the eternal rotation of [the heavenly spheres] – [together with the fact that] this sort of body cannot remain eternal in species if it is not governed by the complex movements of [the heavenly spheres]. (2) These things being so, [then], if someone wanted to say that everything was an object of providence which in any way possesses change and movement on account of something and deriving from it, all corporeal being, both that which is eternal and that which is subject to coming-to-be and passing away, would be an object of the providence of the first being, which is eternal and unmoved and incorporeal.

(3) But if one were to say that objects of providence are only those things for the sake of which that which is said to exercise providence over them performs certain activities in moving, [then] only the body which is below the moon would be an object of providence according to Aristotle, and this is that which is enmattered and subject to coming-to-be and passing away.

(4) For it is established that it is for the sake of the orderly change of this, and of its eternal preservation in species, that the seven spheres of the body that moves in a circle, after that which is first and is called 'undeviating', move with the second movement; it was because the things that come to be and pass away needed a complex movement. (5) For it was not possible for all the divine [bodies], if they were in the same state, to be causes simultaneously of orderly coming-to-be and passing away for the things here (and it is on account of these comings-to-be and passings away, coming about in this manner, that these things too remain eternal in species), if there was not some complex motion also in those [divine bodies]. (Sharples 1992, 85–6)

U. Alexander of Aphrodisias, *On Providence* 87.5–89.12[21]

(1) The divine nature or providence concerning earthly things is, in so far as it appertains to them, also directed towards the generation of the substance of these things ... (2) This power, then, moves things in accordance with the pattern of the movement of the heavenly bodies, inasmuch as it lets the individuals that come to be on the earth, or their succession based on their form, be long-lasting, indeed eternal. (3) In this context 'succession' is identical with 'universal', since the coming-to-be of individuals results from the preservation of the species which exhibit what is comprehensive or universal. Socrates only exists in order that Man should exist, and Xanthus, Achilles' horse, in order that Horse should exist. (4) The universal and its continuance, to be sure, are located in the individuals; for the beings that are subject to coming-to-be and passing away, since they are not rotating heavenly bodies, have their imperishability – given through the species – only through propagation. (5) In earthly beings, in so far as they can share in permanence and eternity, this imperishability is produced by Nature in so far as it proceeds from [Nature] and leads to the goal pursued by [Nature], and in so far as in these beings participation in the species is possible.

V. Justin Martyr, *Dialogue with Trypho* 1.4

And they also try to persuade us that god cares for the whole and for the genera and species themselves, but not also for me and you and particular

---

[21] On this work see the note in the Index of sources.

[things]. For [if he did] we would not pray to him throughout both night and day.[22] (Sharples 2003b, 116)

Medieval thinkers, both Islamic and Christian, took Aristotle's account of the Unmoved Mover, or Unchanged Changer, in *Physics* 8 and in the second half of *Metaphysics* Λ as a basis for the development of a philosophical theology.[23] Modern interpreters have questioned whether what Aristotle is doing in these works is properly described as his 'theology' at all, and whether it is primarily to these texts that we should look for his views about the divine and its relation to human affairs.[24] It has also been debated just how much the divine intellect[25] described in Λ is aware of; but what seems clear is that, even if its thought includes unchanging truths such as the theorems of mathematics and, perhaps, the natures of sublunary species,[26] it cannot be aware of the changing fortunes of individuals. Its effect on the world, moreover, is as an object of appetition, a final cause,[27] rather than as performing specific actions in order to change the course of events, for that would involve it in change itself.

Consequently, *if* it is to Λ that we should look for Aristotle's definitive thinking about theology, any notion of divine providential care for the world would seem to be excluded. It is true that elsewhere in Aristotle's works there are passages that imply this – passages which it is unsound methodology to dismiss as only passing references and/or concessions to popular ways of thinking[28] – and that even in Λ itself the analogy of the

---

[22] This last clause is to be explained as based on the assumption that, if god *were* concerned with individuals, prayer would be superfluous: so van Winden 1971, 38, interpreting this as originally an *ad homines* argument against the Stoics.

[23] Bodéüs 1992, 67 n. 34 notes that the treatment of Λ as Aristotle's 'theology' goes back at least to Alexander, *On Aristotle's* Metaphysics 171.5–11. See the next note.

[24] This has been questioned notably by Bodéüs 1992. Lang 1993, 277 n. 34 and Donini 2002, 188 n. 15 note that the term *theologia* and its cognates are not in Λ applied to Aristotle's own views at all. The application of the term *theologia* to the study of immaterial substances derives from *Metaphysics* E.1.1026a19.

[25] And indeed how far Λ.9 is about divine intellect and how far about intellect in general. See, for example, Brunschwig 2000.

[26] Cf. Norman 1969; Sorabji 1983 146–9; Frede 2000, 42–3. Ross 1924, cxlii and Wedin 1988, 229–45 argue that thinking of thinking has the minimal 'narcissistic' (the term is due to Norman 1969) sense of awareness of a thought which has no content beyond the fact that it is a thinking. Brunschwig 2000, 304 argues that god's thought is narcissistic in Λ.9, but not in Λ.7 which he regards as later.

[27] Even if it is also *in this sense* a productive cause. Cf. Brentano 1977[1867], 162–80; Ross 1924, cxxxiii–cxxxiv; Broadie 1993, 378–9 and n. 4; Judson 1994, 164–7; Berti 1997 and 2000, 186–7, 202–6; Natali 1997; Frede 2000, 43–7.

[28] As is argued spiritedly by Bodéüs 1992, 22–4. Cf. *Nicomachean Ethics* 10.8.1179a24, with Bodéüs 1992, 23 (Verdenius 1960, 60 and 66 n. 28 comments on this passage that Aristotle 'accepts divine providence without any discussion', but subsequently recognises some uncertainty on Aristotle's

world as a household at the start of Λ.10 on the face of it implies a rather different view.[29] Certainly, interpretations of Aristotle's views on the nature of god and of divine providence in the Hellenistic and Roman periods are not what we might expect if we take account only of *Physics* 8 and *Metaphysics* Λ; it is debatable how far they were influenced by Aristotle's published works, those now lost to us.

Aristotle himself links divinity with the heavens, as was customary in Greek thought in the non-Atomist tradition, to the extent of specifying a spatial location for the spatially unextended Unmoved Mover (*Physics* 8.10.267b6–9). Interpreters of Aristotle are still in conflict over whether the souls of the divine heavenly spheres and the Unmoved Movers that cause the spheres to move are to be distinguished or not;[30] and already Theophrastus seems to have rejected the doctrine of a separate Unmoved Mover and to have regarded the heaven as the highest principle in the world.[31] It is not therefore surprising, especially given the Stoic identification of the ruling principle of the world either with the heaven or with the sun (LS 47O), that we find the heaven identified with god for Aristotle (the last option in **A**; **BC**. In **A** the alleged contradiction in 'not understanding that the heaven is a part of the world which he himself elsewhere has designated as a god' may reflect the fact that the Greek *ouranos* can refer either to the world as a whole, or to the heaven as opposed to the sublunary region. This passage is in any case spoken by Velleius, the Epicurean character in Cicero's dialogue, who is presented as attempting to put all non-Epicurean doctrines about the gods in the worst possible light. He does in **A**(2) recognise god for Aristotle as incorporeal but uses this simply to generate absurdities by combining it with the identification of god with the *moving* heaven and with the Epicurean view that thought is a material process. What exactly is meant in **B** by saying that god is an intellect **from** *aithēr* is unclear. **D**(1)–(2), later than our period but reflecting popular tradition (see below), distinguish between the heavens in general and their 'surface' – that is, presumably, the outermost sphere – but speak of theology in terms of the corporeal fifth element, though Hippolytus in **D**(4) is also aware of the definition of god as 'thinking of thinking' in *Metaphysics* Λ.9.

---

part); also *Nicomachean Ethics* 1.9.1099b9–18 (which is explicitly aporetic) with Verdenius 1960, 60 and 67 n. 31 and Bodéüs 1992, 22, and 10.9.1179b21–3 with Verdenius 1960, 68 n. 44. (I am grateful to Philip van der Eijk for drawing my attention to the foregoing references.) See also below, n. 33. The Aristotelian principle normally formulated as 'nature does nothing in vain' appears in the form '*god and* nature do nothing in vain' at *On the Heaven* 1.4.271a33.

[29] Though the point can be and has been argued either way; see Sharples 2002b, 10–11, and references there.

[30] Cf. Sharples 2002b, 4–7 and references there.   [31] See the discussion at Sharples 1998, 87–8.

1074b34–5. E(2) identifies the Unmoved Movers with the souls of the spheres; E(1) is less clear, for it both makes the highest god a *separate* form but also says that he is 'mounted on' the sphere of the universe – which, however, may not indicate any closer identification of Unmoved Mover and sphere-soul than does *Physics* 8.10.267b6–9 (above). In **21C** above Arius clearly has some knowledge of the theory of heavenly movers in *Physics* 8 and *Metaphysics* Λ, but his account is too compressed for it to be clear whether 'the gods that move the spheres' are the souls of the spheres or separate Unmoved Movers which those souls desire, and whether 'the greatest of these gods, the one who embraces all the spheres' is the outermost sphere itself, regarded as a soul–body compound, or a separate Unmoved Mover which it desires. **3A**(12) above asserts that god for Aristotle is incorporeal.

Divine providence is not an issue on which Aristotle explicitly formulates a position, as opposed to passing references (above, n. 28). It was, however, an important issue of philosophical debate in the Hellenistic period; the Epicureans denied that it existed at all (LS 13DFH), while the Stoics insisted that God was present in and fashioned every detail of the world (LS 54J–U, and cf. **FG** here). It is hardly surprising, therefore, that positions on the issue were formulated and attributed to Aristotle. Hellenistic, and later popular, tradition emphasises the distinction that was indeed drawn by Aristotle between the heavenly and the sublunary regions and argues that he confined divine providence to the former (**DHINO** and **3A**(12), **18L**(2) above, **23PQ** below), in **O** where Critolaus is said to agree with Aristotle.[32] The view that there is no sublunary providence is no doubt once again advanced in deliberate contrast to the Stoic view, since for the Stoics the world, heavenly and sublunary, was a single unified system, even if, as has just been seen, the heavens had a particular and special role.

Formulations of the limitation of providence to the heavens vary. The sublunary region may be governed by separate principles (chance, in **O**; nature, in **D**(1)–(2), and below, **23O**) or be an object of divine providence only accidentally (**HI**. On **H** see Mansfeld and Runia 1996–, vol. II, part 2, 340–44, 670–1). Sometimes the limitation of divine providence is more nuanced; **3A**(12) above speaks of 'sympathy' between the sublunary and the

---

[32] The way in which Epiphanius' account of the opinions of five Peripatetic philosophers (Aristotle, Theophrastus, Strato, Praxiphanes, Critolaus) is structured as a whole (**O** and **24L** between them only include a part) may indicate that what it gives us is in fact Critolaus' interpretation of Aristotle; see on this Sharples 1998, 104, and Hahm 2007, 87–9 n. 66.

heavens, and the pseudo-Aristotelian treatise *On the World* (*De mundo*; probably from the second half of the first century BC or the first half of the first century AD) speaks rather of god delegating his powers and acting through intermediaries, and of a divine *power* that penetrates the entire world (**QR**). In arguing thus, *On the World* is in a tradition – the world is an ordered system, but with different degrees of ordering at different levels – that is already present in *Metaphysics* Λ.10 and in the work by Theophrastus that we know as his *Metaphysics*, and that would continue in Alexander of Aphrodisias (see below on **23TU**). Donini 1974, 112–13 notes that Aspasius combines the idea that providence has the heavens as its object (**J**) with that of a more direct relation of the gods to human beings (above, **16Ad**(4) and note).

The idea that the divine is not involved in the management of every detail is attributed to Critolaus in **K** (with which cf. **L**); that Critolaus should adopt a view opposed to that of the Stoics is no surprise, but unfortunately it is not possible to press Plutarch's reference to the point of determining whether what Critolaus had in mind was providence only for the heavens and not for the sublunary, or for major sublunary affairs too but not minor ones.

In **M** Varro, as a character in Cicero's dialogue, is presenting Antiochus' view of the philosophy of the Old Academy and the Peripatetics and, not surprisingly (see above, Introduction p. 2), attributes to them the Stoic doctrine of two principles, the active and the passive, god and matter. Interestingly, though, in this account the providence of the divine principle is limited to the heavens and to those terrestrial matters that affect human beings. The account of chance in **M**(3) is distinctively Stoic (cf. *SVF* 2.965–6, 971); Aristotle indeed notes the existence of the view that chance is a cause obscure to human reasoning (*Physics* 2.4.196b5–7), but himself explains chance rather in objective terms, as accidental causation (*Physics* 2.5–6). In **M**(2) the active principle is described very much in the terms of Stoic fate; cf. LS 55JKL. In **S** the author of the *De mundo* applies to god both descriptions and etymologies applied by the Stoics to fate (cf. LS 55 JKL and **23X**(4) below).

Aristotle's supposed confining of divine providence to the heavens came under attack, especially from the Platonist Atticus (**N**), for whom Aristotle differs from Epicurus only in lacking the courage of his convictions. In response to this attack Alexander of Aphrodisias developed a theory of divine providence, attributed by him to Aristotle, which sought to find middle ground. Characteristically, he did so by taking a central Aristotelian doctrine – that the complex movements of the heavens, by causing the seasons, preserve the continuity of sublunary coming-to-be

(*On Coming-to-be and Passing Away* 2.10, especially 336b27–337a7;[33] cf. *Metaphysics* Λ.6.1072a10–17, and, already before Alexander, Adrastus in I) – and interpreting it as a doctrine of divine providence concerned with species rather than with individuals (T(3)–(5)U); that idea was already current in other, non-Peripatetic contexts, see P(4)V, and Sharples 2003b, and on Alexander's theory of providence see further Sorabji 2004, vol. II 79–84. To suppose, with the Stoics, that god was involved in every occurrence in the world, however trivial, would be demeaning to the divine (G); interestingly, Alexander sees an unknown Peripatetic predecessor's doctrine of divine intellect (F(1)–(2) here, and see below, 27I and commentary) as committing the same error: F(3). On the other hand, *accidental* providence, which is after all a contradiction in terms, is rejected (Alexander, *On Providence* 63.2, *Quaestiones* 2.21.65.25–66.2). In an unfinished philosophical dialogue, too long to reproduce here,[34] Alexander indicates ways in which human forethought can be neither a primary concern nor yet purely accidental – if the agent is aware of the benefit though it is not a primary aim, if the agent benefits from caring for something else, and if the individual benefits from care for the universal. It seems likely that he intends all three to apply to divine providence too; where the second is concerned, the heavens gain benefit from the preservation of sublunary coming-to-be, because it maintains the eternity of the earth and thus gives them a centre round which to rotate (T(1), also Alexander, *Quaestiones* 1.23.36.22–3 and *On the Principles of the Universe* §58 in Genequand 2001.

On the issues raised in this section see further Sharples 2007b, 595–600.

---

[33] Significantly, Aristotle in this passage explicitly says that '*god* completed the universe in the remaining (possible) way, by making coming-to-be continuous (*endelekhēs*: cf. 24CL). For this is how being could most be connected (*suneiroito*: compare 22S), because the constant coming-to-be of coming-to-be is closest to being.' (My emphasis.) So, even if it is strictly true that Aristotle does not explicitly put forward a doctrine of divine providence, it is hardly surprising that Alexander found one in this passage.

[34] Alexander, *Quaestiones* 2.21; translation in Sharples 1994, 19–26.

CHAPTER 23

Fate, choice and what depends on us

A. Aëtius 1.29.2 (*Dox.* 325b5–15)

(1) [Aristotle says] . . . that there are four causes in the whole according to which everything is constituted: intelligence, nature, necessity and chance. And each of these is double, one sort being in human affairs and the other in other things. Some things are fulfilled in every case, others for the most part, others differently at different times. (2) Fate is not a cause, but a manner [*tropos*] of cause, which attaches in a way to the ordered things that belong to necessity. (Sharples 2007b, 597)

B. Anonymous, *On Aristotle's* Nicomachean Ethics 149.33–150.4

(1) Having said that deliberation is concerned with things that can be done and depend on us–for these alone are left–[Aristotle] added as an indication that of the things mentioned the cause of some is nature, of others necessity, of others chance (placing the spontaneous too under chance), and of others intelligence. These are the things that come about through a human being and have a human being as their origin; and for this reason they are also up to us. (2) Fate too would be said to be placed under nature according to these men. For what is fated is neither inevitable nor necessary. (Sharples 2007b, 596)

C. Aspasius, *On Aristotle's* Ethics 74.10–15

From what has been said it is clear that a human being is always a source of his own actions, and that everything is not determined of necessity or fated. For if he deliberates and seeks and chooses, it is clear that [this] depends on him; if not, all deliberation, and consideration concerning things that can be done, is done away with. So each human being is the source and cause of the things that he does.

D. Aspasius, *On Aristotle's* Ethics
76.11–16

If virtue depends on us, so does vice; for in the cases in which acting depends on us, not acting too depends on us. For if not acting does not depend on us but has been necessitated, it is clear that acting too has been necessitated. For if acting has been necessitated, <neither> will not acting depend on us. So it is clear that in the cases in which acting depends on us, not acting, too, depends on us.

E. Aspasius, *On Aristotle's* Ethics
61.5–16

[Aristotle] says that such actions[1] are mixtures of the voluntary and the involuntary. In that the source of the action is outside, for example the tyrant or the despot and his threat, these things are involuntary, but in that, [when] it is possible for them to suffer anything rather than perform a shameful action, in not suffering what they fear they endure doing the shameful things, in this way they seem to be voluntary. Nevertheless, [Aristotle] says that they are more like voluntary [actions]. For actions of this sort are objects of choice, and the end of such an action is judged according to the occasion when it is done. For it is not possible to reach a determination concerning any action in general, but why it is done and how it is done are judged at the time when it is done. And [the agent] acts willingly at the time when [the action] is done, and he prefers [*protiman*] one thing to another and contributes not a little to the action. For the beginning of the movement of the limbs, which are instruments of the soul, is in the agent himself, when he performs the actions.

F. Aspasius, *On Aristotle's* Ethics
64.6–15

[Aristotle] speaks of ignorance in choice, when someone makes a wicked choice through ignorance of what is advantageous. He calls the same also

---

[1] Those performed under duress, which we would not normally choose to do, but do choose in certain circumstances in order to avoid a greater evil.

'general ignorance', because it is not concerned with one thing, nor is such ignorance concerned with a single action, but in general the person who is ignorant in this way lacks knowledge of everything that is advantageous. On account of such ignorance certain errors are not said to be involuntary. Here is the evidence: those who have performed involuntary actions receive pardon both from the laws and from the judges, but ignorance in one's character is an object of hatred. And reasonably so; for people are the causes of their own ignorance of this sort, through not taking care to distinguish which things are truly advantageous, and [to recognise] that wickedness and injustice are of all things the most harmful to their possessor.

G.   Aspasius, *On Aristotle's* Ethics
70.28–71.2

And some adult men too do many things suddenly without having deliberated and are not said to choose [*prohaireisthai*] any of these. But the person who has deliberated about something and has assented to it as to be chosen – and appetition follows on this – is said to choose [*prohaireisthai*] it. And for this reason [Aristotle] says that what has been deliberated about beforehand is voluntary, showing that choice [*prohaeresis*] is located in prior deliberation, and that first one must have deliberated and reasoning must occur, and then appetition follows. For what is prior is prior to something, and it is clear that appetition is what the deliberation precedes.

H.   Alexander of Aphrodisias, *On Fate*
11.178.15–28

(1) That deliberating is in vain if everything comes to be of necessity can easily be realised by those who know the use of deliberating. It is agreed by everyone that man has this advantage from nature over the other living creatures, that he does not follow appearances in the same way as them, but has reason from her as a judge of the appearances that impinge on him concerning certain things as deserving to be chosen. (2) Using this, if, when they are examined, the things that appeared *are* indeed as they initially appeared, he assents to the appearance and so goes in pursuit of them; but if they appear different or something else [appears] more deserving to be chosen, he chooses that, leaving behind what initially appeared to him as deserving of choice. (3) At any rate [there are] many things [which], having seemed different to us in their first appearances [from what they appeared to us subsequently], no longer remained as in our previous notion when reason put them to the test;

and so, though they would have been done as far as concerned the appearance
of them, on account of [our] deliberating about them they were not done
– we being in control of the deliberating and of the choice of the things that
resulted from the deliberation. (Sharples 1983a, 55–6).

I.   Aspasius, *On Aristotle's* Ethics
73.9–25

Further, we deliberate not about ends, but about the things that lead to the
ends ... so when several ways are apparent they consider through which
they may most easily and best attain the end. For example, a general who
wants victory deliberates [as follows]: it is clearly possible to achieve victory
by using both the power of infantry and that of cavalry and sea-power. After
this he enquires with which this will come about most easily and with least
danger, and whichever of the ways the finds to be like this, this one he
prefers. If there is one way, either preferred to all or apparent from the
beginning, we enquire how the end will come about through this, for
example how the war can be successfully concluded on account of the
cavalry, and through what this [will come about], for example how we
will get cavalry, for instance that we need money for this. Where will the
money come from? So [we conclude that it will come if] there is a financial
levy on the citizens. When this opinion has been formed, from this point
onwards [people] start on the action, which is last in the discovery through
consideration, but the first cause in the action.

J.   Aspasius, *On Aristotle's* Ethics
68.26–30

Wish [*boulēsis*] seems to be close to choice [*prohairesis*], but it is not choice.
It seems close, because first, it is in the rational part of the soul, where the
principal [part] of choice [is located], and next because it is a part of choice.
For whenever the intellect, having deliberated, approves [*sunainein*] and
chooses, then wish, which is [an] appetition, shares in impulse with it.

K.   Aspasius, *On Aristotle's* Ethics 75.6–15

Since what is chosen is what is an object of deliberation and appetition
among things that depend on us, choice will be a deliberative appetition of
things that depend on us [Aristotle, *Nicomachean Ethics* 3.3.1113a10–11].
[Aristotle] shows how he takes this account of choice; for [he does] not

[take it] as an accurate definition.[2] For neither deliberation nor appetition is the genus of choice, but [it is] the [product] of both, as it were a composite. And for this reason [Aristotle] says that, judging as a result of having deliberated, we have appetition according to our wish [*boulēsis*] [1113a11–12]. There is a variant reading '[according to our] deliberation' [*bouleusis*], since deliberation comes first, appetition follows, and the result of this is choice. Like this account is 'an animal is an ensouled body'. For there too body is not the genus of animal, but what is being said is like this, that the animal is the composite of body and soul.

L.   Pseudo-Plutarch, *On Fate* 6 571cd

Again in the case of the contingent one [sort] is for the most part, one for the least part, and a third equally and however it chanced. It is clear that this is opposed to itself, while what is for the most part and what is for the least part are opposed to each other. These mostly depend on nature, while the one that is equal depends on us. That it should be hot or cold at the time of the Dogstar, of which the former is for the most part and the latter for the least, both come under nature; but going for a walk or not, and things like this, where each [occurs] equally, come under human impulse, which is said to depend on us and to be according to choice.

M.   Calcidius, *On Plato's* Timaeus 156
190.8–13 Waszink 1975

There are several different sorts of uncertain outcomes. For some are frequent, some equally frequent, like growing a beard, being literate or pleading cases in court. Further, opposed to those that are frequent are those of which instances are rare, and opposed to those which occur equally those which are not equal. The choice of those which are uncertain in an equal way is under a human being's control; being a rational animal, he refers everything to reason and judgement.

N.   Nemesius, *On the Nature of Man* 34
104.1–11 Morani

Of the contingent some things are said to be for the most part, some rarely, some with an equal possibility: for the most part is for example a sixty-year-old

---

[2] I.e., as the sequel shows, one through genus and differentia.

having grey hair; a sixty-year-old not having grey hair is rare; and going for a walk and not going for a walk, and simply doing something or not doing something have an equal possibility. So it is only about those contingent things that have an equal possibility that we deliberate. That is contingent with an equal possibility which we are able to do and its opposite: for if we could not do both, both it and its opposite, we would not have deliberated. For nobody deliberates about what is agreed upon or the impossible. If we had been able to do only one of the opposites, that would have been agreed upon and in no way in doubt, and its opposite impossible. (Sharples and van der Eijk 2008, 183)

O.   Atticus, fr. 8.2 des Places 1977

[Aristotle says] that nature is not soul, and that the things in the region of the earth are managed by nature alone. For for each thing there are different causes. Of the heavenly things which are always in the same state and condition he supposes that fate is the cause; of the things beneath the moon, nature; of human affairs, wisdom and forethought and soul. He provides elegance in such divisions, but fails to see what is necessary. (Sharples 2007b, 597)

P.   Theodoret, *Remedy for Greek* [i.e. *Pagan*] *Attitudes* 5.47

And whereas he [sc. Plato] had said that God takes forethought for all things, this man [sc. Aristotle] deprives the earth, as far as it entered into his account, of divine care. For he said that God guided things as far as the moon, but that the rest was subordinated to fate. (Sharples 2007b, 597–8)

Q.   Theodoret, *Remedy for Greek* [i.e. *Pagan*] *Attitudes* 6.7

But the son of Nicomachus [i.e. Aristotle] supposed that God presides as far as the moon, but that he has no care for all the things after this and has handed over the guardianship of these things to the necessity of fate. (Sharples 2007b, 598)

R.   Cicero, *On Fate* 39

There were two opinions among the old philosophers; one that of those who judged that all things came about by fate, in such a way that that fate imposed the force of necessity. This was the opinion of Democritus, Heraclitus, Empedocles and Aristotle. The other was the opinion of those who thought that there were voluntary movements of minds not involving fate at all. (Sharples 1991, 85)

S.   Alexander of Aphrodisias, *On Fate*
6.168.18–171.17

(1) We are left with saying that fate is in the things that come to be by nature, so that fate and nature are the same thing. For what is fated is in accordance with nature and what is in accordance with nature is fated. It is not the case that man comes to be from man, and horse from horse, in accordance with nature but not in accordance with fate; rather, these causes accompany each other as if differing only in name. (2) It is for this reason, too, that men say that the first causes of the coming-to-be of each thing in accordance with nature (that is, the heavenly bodies and their orderly revolution) are also causes of fate. For the beginning of all coming-to-be is the heavenly bodies', in their motion, being in one type of position or another in relation to things on earth.

(3) As fate is located in these things and is of such a nature, it is necessary that, as are the things that come to be in accordance with nature, so should those be too that come to be in accordance with fate. (4) But the things that come to be in accordance with nature do not do so of necessity; the coming-to-be of things that come to be in this way is sometimes hindered. And for this reason the things that come to be in accordance with nature come to be for the most part, but not of necessity. For that which is contrary to nature, too, has a place in them and comes to be when nature is hindered in its proper working by some external cause. (5) It is for this reason that man does not come from man of necessity but for the most part, and neither does each of the things that come to be in accordance with nature always come to be in accordance with the fixed time that seems to be laid down for the things that come to be in this way.

(6) If there is, in the things that come to be in accordance with nature, also that which is contrary to nature, as in the things in accordance with craft, then what is contrary to fate will also have a place in the things that come to be in accordance with fate; so that if what is contrary to nature has a place and is not an empty expression, what is contrary to fate, too, will have a place in the things that come to be. (7) And for this reason one might reasonably say, too, that it is the proper nature of each thing that is its beginning and cause for the ordered pattern of the things that come to be in

it in accordance with nature. For it is from this, for the most part, that the lives of men and their deaths derive their pattern.

(8) At any rate we see that the body, through being like this or like that in nature, is affected both in disease and in death in accordance with its natural constitution, but not of necessity; for treatments and changes of climate and doctors' orders and advice from the gods are sufficient to break such a pattern. And in the same way in the case of the soul too one would find the choices and actions and way of life of each individual differing from, and contrary to, his natural constitution.

(9) For 'people's character is their guardian spirit' according to Heraclitus, that is, their nature. For people's actions and lives and endings can for the most part be seen to be in accordance with their natural constitutions and dispositions. The man who loves danger and is by nature bold meets some violent death for the most part; for this is the fate in his nature. For the man who is licentious by nature, what is in accordance with fate is spending his life in licentious pleasures and the life of those who lack self-control, unless something better comes to be in him and shakes him out of the life that is in accordance with his nature; and for the man who is of an enduring nature, again, it is putting up with troubles, and persistence, and ending life in such circumstances. And for those who are illiberal by nature and insatiable in the acquisition of goods the results of fate, too, are in accord; they spend their life for the most part in wrongdoing, and the end of life for those who act in this way is in accordance with this. And people are accustomed to reproach such men, when they are in the circumstances that follow on their way of life and are in accordance with fate, as being themselves the causes of their present troubles.

(10) Moreover, someone who wanted to come to the aid of those who profess the art of prophecy might give this as the cause of their not always hitting the mark; while the nature and fate of each individual does not have a free passage in all things, but some things come to be contrary to it as well, the prophets reveal the things that come to be in accordance with fate, as indeed do the physiognomists. (11) At any rate, when Zopyrus the physiognomist said certain extraordinary things about the philosopher Socrates, which were very far removed from his chosen manner of life, and was ridiculed for this by Socrates' associates, Socrates said that Zopyrus had not been at all mistaken; for he would have been like that as far as his nature was concerned, if he had not, through the discipline that comes from philosophy, become better than his nature. – (12) And this is, to state it in a summary fashion, the opinion concerning nature of the Peripatetic school. (Sharples 1983a, 46–8)

T.   Alexander of Aphrodisias, *On Fate*
25.195.8–18

And we see that night and day, too, which have a certain order in relation to one another, have one and the same cause, as does similarly the changing of the seasons. Winter is not the cause of summer, but both the former things and the latter things are caused by the motion and rotation of the divine body and the inclination along the ecliptic; the sun, moving along this, is the cause of all alike of the things mentioned above. Nor indeed does it follow that, because night is not the cause of day nor winter of summer, and these things are not intertwined with one another in the manner of a chain, they therefore come to be without a cause, or if they did not come to be in this way the unity of the universe and of the things that are and come to be in it will be torn apart. For the heavenly bodies and their rotation are sufficient to preserve the continuity of the things that come to be in the universe. (Sharples 1983a, 74)

U.   Alexander of Aphrodisias, *On Fate*
25.196.7–12

Nor does every transgression of an established order do away with the things in which it occurs; for it is not impossible that some things should come to pass in a way that conflicts with the monarch's order but not therefore be altogether destructive of his monarchy. Nor, if something of the sort happens in the universe, does it at once follow that it altogether destroys the happy state of the universe, just as that of the house and its master is not [altogether] destroyed by some negligence or other on the part of the servants. (Sharples 1983a, 75)

V.   Alexander of Aphrodisias, *Supplement to* On the Soul (*Mantissa*)
25.185.8–186.31

(1) However, we see that there are the following causes in the things that come to be and pass away besides the nature which puts them together and fashions them: choice and the fortuitous and luck (for that which is in accordance with skill is not [present] in these). But that which is [a matter] of fate does not seem to be the same as any of these. (2) We are left, then, with fate being nothing other than the proper nature of each thing. For that which is [a matter] of fate is not in what is universal and common, for

example simply [in] living creature or human being, but in the individuals, Socrates and Callias. (3) And in these the nature that is peculiar to them is, [through] being of a certain sort, the beginning and cause of the ordered pattern that comes to be in accordance with it. For it is from this, in general, that [people's] lives and their endings result, when it is not impeded by certain things.

(4) At any rate we see that the body too, through being like this or like that as a result of nature, is affected both in disease and in death following its natural constitution. But not of necessity; for treatments and changes of climate and doctors' orders and advice from the gods are sufficient to break this pattern. And in the same way in the case of the soul too one could find actions and choices and lives becoming different from, [and] contrary to, the natural constitution.

(5) For 'people's character is their guardian spirit' according to Heraclitus [fr. 119], that is, their nature. For people's actions and lives and the endings of their lives turn out for the most part to follow their natural constitutions and dispositions. The person who is eager for battle and loves danger by nature [meets] some violent death for the most part, for this is his fate and nature; and the person who is licentious and spends his life in pleasures [for the most part meets death] in intemperate behaviour, he who is of an enduring [nature] that through excess of labours and persistence in troubles, the person who is illiberal that from eagerness over what is indifferent [i.e. external, material goods], on account of which they act unjustly and neglect themselves and labour beyond their power. It is on this account, at any rate, that it is customary to reproach such people, [saying that] the person himself became the cause of his own death.

(6) If what is in accordance with fate is like this, we shall not say any longer that prophecy is useless, either, [as] it foresees what will result in accordance with nature and assists [us] through advising and ordering us to resist the natural sequence [when it inclines to] the worse. (7) Neither will the nature of luck be done away with, but, coinciding with the things that come to be in accordance with choice, it will be responsible for certain things. (8) And still more will the divine and the assistance that comes from it, and prayers and entreaties from us, keep their proper place, when that which is [a matter] of fate is like this. (9) And in agreement with these things, too, will be the saying that many things come to be contrary to destiny and contrary to fate, as the poet some-where shows saying

Lest you come to the house of Hades even before it is destined [Homer, *Iliad* 20.336].

(10) And this opinion might also be established by the [fact] that the prophets do not hit the mark in everything that they foretell.

(11) It is in no way remarkable that people do not turn out to hold this opinion concerning fate. For the majority do not aim badly concerning things in outline, but [when it comes to] the particular [details] and defining [them] and making [them] exact they make many errors. For the former is the work of nature, the latter of understanding.

(12) Aristotle already mentions the name of fate in the first book of the *Meteorology* [1.14.352a28] as follows: 'but the cause of all these things must be supposed to be that at fated times there comes about, just as winter does in the seasons of the year, a Great Winter in some great cycle'. And it seems that in these words he is saying that fate is nature (for the fated times, the winter and [that] of the other things, are those which have a reciprocal succession which is natural, but not inevitable and necessitated). (13) And in the fifth book of the *Physics* [5.6.230a32], too, he again mentions fate as follows: 'are there then comings-to-be which are forcible and not fated, to which those that are in accordance with nature are opposite?'; through which it is again clear that he uses the name of fate in connection with the things that come to be in accordance with nature. For if he says that what is in accordance with nature is opposite to what is not fated, and what is contrary to fate is opposite to what is in accordance with fate, what is in accordance with fate will be the same as what is in accordance with nature. For it is not possible to say that several things are opposite to what is not in accordance with fate, [if] this last is one thing; [firstly] what is in accordance with fate, which clearly is opposite to it, and [secondly] what is in accord-ance with nature, [this] being other than what is in accordance with fate. (14) And Theophrastus very clearly shows in his *Callisthenes* [fr. 504 FHS&G] that what is in accordance with fate is the same as what is in accordance with nature, [as does] also Polyzelus in the book that is entitled *Concerning Fate*. (Sharples 2004, 234–7)

W.   Eusebius, *Preparation for the Gospel* 4.3.1–14 (parts = *SVF* 2.939)

From Diogenianus: that [the Stoics'] divination is non-existent and false in most things and that its prediction, according to them, is useless and harmful.

[Chrysippus] introduces another demonstration in the aforementioned book, like this. He says that the predictions of the diviners would not be true if everything were not contained in fate. This too is full of great simple-mindedness. For on the basis that it is clear that all the predictions of the so-called diviners are true, or on the basis that this would more readily be agreed by someone than that all things happen according to fate, and that this statement would not also itself similarly be false, since there is clear evidence of the opposite, I mean that not all of the things predicted come about, or rather most of them [do not come about] – on this basis Chrysippus introduced his demonstration, showing each thing through the other. For it is from the existence of divination that he wants to show that everything happens according to fate, but that divination exists he could not show if he did not first suppose that everything happens according to fate. What more faulty method of demonstration could there be than this? (2) For that some of the things that the diviners predict clearly come about is not a sign that divination is a science, but of the fact that through chance the outcomes happen in accordance with the predictions; and this does not indicate any science to us. For we would not call the man who hits the target once but frequently misses it a good archer, nor a [good] doctor the one who kills most of those he treats but has on occasion been able to cure one. Nor, in general, do we call what is not successful in all, or most, of its own proper actions a science. That the so-called diviners go wrong in most things, the whole of human life declares, and so too do the very people who profess the art of divination, who do not use it to assist themselves in the issues of life, but use their own judgement and counsel and the assistance of those who are thought to have experience in each matter. But that this, which we have called divination by our preconception,[3] does not exist, we will set out more fully elsewhere, adding what Epicurus thought about this too. For now we will add this much to what has been said, that the truth of what the so-called diviners say in their predictions is the result not of a science, but of a chance cause (for we who have distinguished the clear notions arranged under each name[4] by our preconception apply 'a result of chance' not to having never yet achieved an aim, but to not doing so always or for the most part or as a result of science, whenever someone does sometimes achieve it).

(3) Next, even if, as an assumption, it were true that divination sees and foretells all future things, it would be concluded in this way that everything is in accordance with fate, but the usefulness and benefit in life from divination, on account of which Chrysippus seems most to sing its praises, would not be shown. For what benefit would it be to us to learn beforehand

---

[3] The use of *prolambanein* in this way is Epicurean.
[4] This too is Epicurean; cf. Epicurus, *Letter to Herodotus* 38 = LS 17C.

the bad things that are certainly going to happen, which it would not be possible to take precautions against beforehand? For how could anyone take precautions against the things that happen in accordance with fate? So there would be no benefit to us from divination, or rather it would be a disadvantage, enabling people to be grieved in vain in advance at the foretold evils which would necessarily occur. For no one will say that the foretelling of future goods brings equal good cheer, since human beings do not naturally rejoice at expected goods as much as they are troubled by [expected] evils. In particular, we do not expect that [evils] will happen to ourselves until we hear about them; for we all, more or less, expect good things more [than bad ones], because of our natural affinity[5] to them. The majority expect things greater than is possible. From this it results that the prediction of good things does not greatly intensify joy, because, even *without* the prediction, each person of his own accord expects what is better; or else it intensifies it [only] slightly through the supposed assurance, while often it diminishes joy, when what is heard is less than was hoped for. But the prediction of evils causes great anxiety both because they naturally cause aversion and because they are sometimes predicted contrary to expectation. (4) Nevertheless, even if this did not happen, that the prediction would be useless will be clear to everyone. For if someone says that the usefulness of divination will be preserved because it foretells the evil that will certainly occur if we do not guard against it, he will no longer be showing that everything happens in accordance with fate, if it depends on us to take precautions against it or not. And if someone should say that this too is necessitated, so that fate does extend to everything that exists, again the usefulness of divination is done away with; for we will take precautions if it is fated [that we will], and, clearly, we will not take precautions if it is not fated that we will, even if all the diviners there are predict the future to us. At any rate Chrysippus himself says that, although their parents contrived in many ways to kill Oedipus and Alexander [= Paris] the son of Priam, so that they might avert the evil it was foretold would come from them, they were not able to do so. Thus he says that, because of fate, there was no benefit even to them from the prediction of evils. Let this, then, be said, from an abundance [of possible points], to show that divination is not only non-existent, but also useless.

(5) This then the philosopher [Diogenianus says]. But you consider for yourself how it is that Greeks who have been brought up in Greek culture

---

[5] *oikeiōsis*, the Stoic term (but widely used by other schools too); see above, **17**. Diogenianus could be deliberately using Stoic language against the Stoics; cf. 'intensify'(*epiteinein*) below.

from a young age and know their ancestral traditions about the gods more
than anything, all the Aristotelians and Cynics and Epicureans and as many
as think like these, ridicule the oracles that the Greeks themselves shout
about.

X.   Eusebius, *Preparation for the Gospel* 6.8.1–38 (parts = *SVF* 2.998–9)

(1) On the same topic [sc. fate]: from the [writings] of Diogenianus the
Peripatetic.

It is worth putting alongside all this the opinion of Chrysippus the Stoic
about this argument. For in his first book *On Fate*, wanting to show that
everything is determined by necessity and fate, he employs witnesses
including what Homer the poet said as follows: 'But the hateful destiny
engulfs me, which was allotted to me at my birth' [*Iliad* 23.78–9] and 'Later
he will suffer whatever things fate span in his thread when he was born'
[*Iliad* 20.127–8] and 'I say that no man has escaped his destiny' [*Iliad* 6.488],
not considering that the things said elsewhere by the poet are absolutely
opposed to these, things which [Chrysippus] himself uses in his second
book wanting to establish that many things are brought about by us, for
example 'they perished by their own folly' [~ *Odyssey* 1.7] and 'alas, how
mortals blame the gods! For they say that evils come from us, but they,
through their own folly, have griefs beyond what is fated' [*Odyssey* 1.32–4].
For these things and those like them are opposed to everything coming
about in accordance with fate. (2) Nor was he able to see that Homer in no
way supports his opinion even in those former verses. For he will be found
to suggest through them not that *everything* comes about in accordance with
fate, but that *some* things do. For 'But the hateful destiny engulfs me, which
was allotted to me at my birth' says not that everything happens in
accordance with destiny, but that the fact that one will die does. For in
very truth it is fated that every living creature that has been born will die.
And 'Later he will suffer whatever things fate span in his thread when he was
born' means the same. For it does not say that everything after this will
happen to him in accordance with fate, but that *some* things will happen to
him in accordance with necessity. For what other than this does the
distinction in 'whatever' indicate? For many things are imposed on us by
necessity, even if not all are. And 'I say that no man has escaped his destiny'
is very well said. For who could escape what by necessity happens to every
living creature? (3) So not only will Chrysippus not have the support of
Homer in thinking that all things happen in accordance with fate, but he

will actually have him as an opponent, if [Homer] often said clearly that many things are brought about by us, but that all things happen according to necessity he will nowhere be found to say in so many words. And for one who is a poet but does not undertake to tell us the truth about the nature of reality but represents all sorts of emotions and characters and opinions of human beings, it would be fitting often to say things that contradict one another; but for a philosopher [it is fitting] neither to say things that contradict one another, nor, for this very reason, to use a poet as evidence.

(4) – And after some other points [Diogenianus] says:

Chrysippus thinks that he is advancing another strong piece of evidence that fate is in everything in the application of names like these. For he says that Destiny [*peprōmenē*] is a defined [*peperasmenēn*] and completed organisation, and that fate [*heimarmenē*] is continuous [*eiromenē*], whether as a result of the will of god or of whatever cause it may be. And the Fates [*Moirai*] he says are named from the fact that certain things have been apportioned [*memeristhai*] and allotted to each of us. And in this way 'what must be' is applied to what befalls and comes to [us] in accordance with fate. He suggests that the number of the Fates is the three periods of time in which all things return and through which they are accomplished.[6] Lachesis is so called because what is destined is assigned [*lanchanein*] to each person, Atropos because the apportioning is unchangeable [*atreptos*] and unalterable, and Clotho because all things have been interwoven [*sunkeklōsthai*] and connected, and there is one ordered progression of them all. (5) Saying these things, and other similar nonsense, he thinks that he is demonstrating the necessity that is present in all things. But my reaction is to be amazed that, in saying such things, he did not realise the emptiness of his words. For grant that it was with such ideas as he etymologises in mind that people applied the names that have been listed, thinking that fate determines all things and that the causes that have been predetermined from eternity in all the things that are and come to be are unalterable; why, Chrysippus, do you follow all the opinions people have, and none seems to you mistaken about anything, but all can perceive the truth? How then do you say that there is no person who does not seem to you to be as mad as Orestes[7] and Alcmaeon,[8] apart from the Sage?[9] You say that only one or two have been sages, but the rest,

---

[6] I.e. past, present and future.

[7] Who in his madness thought that his sister Electra was one of the Furies: LS 39G.

[8] Alcmaeon, like Orestes, was pursued by the Furies after killing his mother. The present text is the only passage referring to him in *SVF*.

[9] For Chrysippus everyone who is not a Stoic Sage is equally mad and bad: LS 61N.

as a result of their folly, have been as mad as those mentioned. How do you demolish their opinions as being in error, for example those concerning wealth and reputation and tyrannical power and, in general, pleasure, which the vast majority think are goods? How do you say that all the established laws and constitutions are in error? Or why did you write so great a quantity of books, if people do not have mistaken opinions about anything? (6) For we will not say that they are in their right minds when they think the same things as you, mad when they think different ones. For first, you do not say that even you are wise, let alone us, so that we might make it a criterion of people's sometimes thinking aright that they agree with your opinion; and next, even if this were true, why should you say that all are equally mad, and not praise them in so far as they clearly think the same as you, on the grounds that they have grasped something correct, but in so far as they disagree, suppose that they are wrong? But even so you should not think that their opinion is sufficient evidence of the truth, since even if they are not mad, as you suppose, yet everyone would agree that they are far from being wise. (7) So it is in a ridiculous way that you too use them as witnesses through their application of the names, people whom you would say are no different from you yourself in understanding,[10] unless indeed it happened that those who originally applied the names were wise[11] – and *that* you will in no way be able to show. (8) But let it be granted to you that these things are so and that those names were applied with the meanings that you wish, and that this did not come about in accordance with false opinions; where then is it indicated that all things are according to fate without qualification, and not – if this is so – just those things to which fate applies? For the number of the Fates and their names, and Clotho's spindle and the thread which is wound on it and the spinning of it and all the other similar things said about these, indicate that the causes are inescapable and come from eternity, in the case of as many things as have been compelled of necessity to come to be in this way and as many as have been prevented from being different. And there will be many things like this. (9) But as many things as do not come to be in this way, of some of these people have named the gods as managers and craftsmen, of some they have supposed that we ourselves are the causes, of others again nature, of others chance; wanting to indicate her readiness to change and her instability and that she is now like this, now like that, they created an image of this way things befall and portrayed Chance on top of

---

[10] Because Chrysippus too does not claim that he himself is wise.
[11] On the Stoic belief in primitive wisdom preserved in mythology cf. Boys-Stones 2001, especially 31–59.

a sphere. (10) Are these too not opinions that people have held? For even if they sometimes mix up the causes and think that the things that come about in accordance with fate or chance are the result of divine power, and that the things that are brought about by us are in accordance with fate, nevertheless that they think that all these causes are present in things is, I suppose, clear to everyone. So it turns out that neither people's suppositions, nor the application of such names, support Chrysippus' opinion.

(11) And following on from this [Diogenianus] says:

So, in the first book *On Fate* [Chrysippus] uses proofs like these, but in the second he attempts to resolve the difficulties that seem to follow on the account that says that everything has been necessitated, which we too set out at the beginning: for example, that it does away with our eagerness concerning blame and praise and encouragement and all the things which are clearly brought about by our causation. So, in the second book [Chrysippus] says that it is clear that many things come about from us, but that these are none the less co-fated[12] with the administration of the whole. He uses examples like these:[13] that the cloak should not be lost, he says, was not fated *simpliciter*, but along with its being looked after, and that a certain person would be saved from the enemy [was fated] along with his fleeing from the enemy, and that children should be born [to someone was fated] along with his willing to sleep with a woman. (12) For just as, he says, if someone were to say that the boxer Hegesarchus would finish the bout without receiving a blow, it would be absurd of someone to think that Hegesarchus should fight with his hands lowered[14] since it had been fated for him to finish without receiving a blow – for the person who said this did so because of the man's exceptional guard against being struck – so it is also in the other cases. For many things cannot come about without our willing them and contributing our strongest eagerness and desire concerning them, since it is along with this, he says, that they have been fated to come about.[15] (13) Here too one might again be amazed at the man's failure to consider and to take into his reckoning both the things that are obvious and the connection of his own arguments. For I think that, as what is called sweet is most opposed to what is called bitter, black to white and hot to cold, so what is in accordance with fate [is most opposed] to what [is brought about]

---

[12] On this term see Bobzien 1998a, 212 and nn. 92–3.

[13] On these examples, and their relation with the partly overlapping set recorded by Cicero, *On Fate* 30 (LS 55s), see Bobzien 1998a, 208–17; Sharples 2007e, 177–8.

[14] Salles 2005, 14 and n. 28 notes that by the rules of ancient Greek boxing this would be an impossibility; if one neither punches one's opponent nor keeps up one's guard one is not *fighting* at all.

[15] (11)–(12) = LS 62F.

by us, if his conception[16] of what he calls 'in accordance with fate' is all the things that come about both if we are willing and if we are not, but of 'brought about by us' all the things which come to completion through our eagerness and activity, or are not completed as a result of our disregard and idleness. (14) So if as a result of my eagerness to look after the cloak it was preserved, and as a result of willing to sleep with a woman children are born, and as a result of willing to flee from the enemy [someone] is not killed by them, and as a result of fighting courageously against one's opponent and guarding against the attacks of his fists [the boxer] finishes the bout without receiving a blow, how will what is in accordance with fate be preserved here? For if these things come about in accordance with [fate], they would not be said to come about through our [agency], and if through our [agency], clearly not in accordance with fate, as these things are not compatible with each other.

(15) But they will be by our [agency], [Chrysippus] says, but with our [agency] being included in fate. *How* included, I would say, if both looking after the cloak and not looking after it were results of my power? For thus it is clear that *I* would be in charge of its being preserved. And from the very distinction which Chrysippus makes it is clear that causation by our [agency] is separate from fate. For it has been fated for the cloak to be preserved, he says, if you look after it, and for there to be children, if you wish it, but otherwise none of these things will be. (16) But in the case of things that are included in fate we would never use this sort of assessment. So we do not say that every human being will die if a certain thing should happen, but not if it does not; rather, that he will die, unconditionally, even if absolutely *anything* should happen which in general prevents dying;[17] and [we do not say] that some man will not be able to feel pain, if he does certain things, but unconditionally that every man is capable of feeling pain, whether he wishes it or not. And [so with] all the other things that are fated to be thus and not otherwise. (17) So if it is necessary that a certain thing happen if we should wish it, but otherwise not, it is clear that our wishing and not wishing has not been constrained in advance by any other cause but was in our power; but if this was not necessitated, it is clear also that the coming about of [the consequence] was not constrained in advance from eternity, unless our actually wishing to look after the cloak,

---

[16] See above, n. 3.
[17] Following Bobzien 1998a, 213. That is: there are many things that may prevent – in other words postpone – death in particular circumstances, but there is none of them which can postpone it for ever.

too, or not wishing, came about as a result of some fate and necessary external cause. But on *that* basis our power of self-determination is completely done away with, and the preservation or loss of the cloak will not be caused by *me*. As a result, if it is lost I will not be reasonably subject to reproach (for there was some other cause of its being lost), and again, if it is preserved [I will] not in any way [reasonably] be praised, since *I* did not accomplish this.

As with providence, so with fate: it was not a topic on which Aristotle had formulated a position (though attempts were made to find authority for one in his works; see V(12)–(13). Apart from the *Poetics*, which is clearly a special case, the passages considered in **V** are the *only* occurrences of the adjective 'fated' in Aristotle's extant works; the noun 'fate' does not occur outside the *Poetics* at all.) But, once again, the issue was an important one in Hellenistic philosophy, the Stoics identifying fate with the divine providence which in their view determined everything that happened in the world (LS 54U, 55R, cf. 55J–N; **22** above).

For Aristotle, the efficient or productive cause is only one of the canonical four causes (above, **12C**). But, as Frede (1980) showed, the Stoics introduced a narrower sense of the term 'cause', closer to that with which we are now familiar, confining it to efficient causes. Each thing does, for the Stoics, have an immediate efficient cause of its own, and these causes are different in type; but they are all part of the network of causes which constitutes fate, so in a sense fate is the single cause of everything (Seneca, *Letters on Morals* 65.11 = *SVF* 3.246a). Characteristically, the Aristotelian tradition drew distinctions where the Stoics did not. As Bobzien 1998b, 143–6 has shown, a starting-point for classifications of different causes (in the later, Stoic sense of that term) in Aristotle was the list of things about which we do not and do deliberate in *Nicomachean Ethics* 3.3. **A** is one of the passages which attempts such a classification; significantly, fate, which is not mentioned in the *Nicomachean Ethics* passage at all, has, it seems, been added to an original list, presumably because it was felt that some account needed to be taken of it in the classification. See also Mansfeld and Runia 1996–, vol. I 254, arguing that the part of Stobaeus' report included here probably came from Arius Didymus rather than from Aëtius, and their vol. II, part 1, 68. **B** is from the anonymous commentary (see above on **IX**) on this passage of the *Nicomachean Ethics* (but on the reference to fate in **B** see further below), and **C** (and **22J**) from Aspasius' commentary on the same chapter; **D** is from Aspasius' account of the argument concerning responsibility at 3.5.1113b3–14. What is striking about **CD**, as Bobzien 1998b, 145 points out, is not that they unambiguously indicate a view of what depends on us that is incompatible with determinism, any more than Aristotle himself does (although this will be the natural reading both of **CD** and of Aristotle for those who reject the compatibility of something's being dependent on us and everything's being predetermined, unlike the Stoics and like Alexander later on). Rather, **CD** are significant because they recast Aristotle's discussion in terminology derived from discussion of necessity and what depends on us, prompted by the Stoic view.

Aspasius adds to Aristotle's reason for saying that 'mixed' actions – those chosen under duress – are voluntary, namely that the origin of the movement is in the agent (*Nicomachean Ethics* 3.1.1110a15–18) the fact that there is a possibility for alternatives and that the agent exercises a preference (**E**: Alberti 1999, 115–16, and cf. 134, arguing that Aspasius here comes closer than Aristotle to formulating a concept of the will, and 136, arguing that on this issue Alexander is closer to Aristotle). Aspasius, however, anticipates Alexander (*Supplement to* On the Soul 23.175.9–32, *Ethical Problems* 9.129.3–19, 18.139.9–14, 29.160.34–161.29) in arguing, more clearly than Aristotle himself does in *Nicomachean Ethics* 3.5, that we are responsible for our characters and for our knowledge or ignorance of general moral principles, and that character is consciously chosen (**F**: Alberti 1999, 120–3). To be sure, Aspasius may be seen here as only spelling out more clearly the implications of what Aristotle says, which is after all the role of a commentator; but certainly the argument 'people are not responsible for their actions, for their conception of the end of action depends on their upbringing and that was not in their control' is one for which he has little time.

In **G**, as Alberti 1999, 128 and Natali 2007, 77 note, Aspasius anticipates Alexander in **H** by incorporating the Stoic notion of assent into his account of Aristotelian deliberation, even though, contrary to the emphasis in Alexander and following Aristotle's text (*Nicomachean Ethics* 3.3.1112b11–31),[18] he approaches the topic in terms of the choice of means to an end (**I**), not in terms of reaction to an immediate stimulus. Aspasius also, in **JK**, recasts Aristotle's distinction between wish and choice (people can *wish* for what they cannot attain, but not choose it, *Nicomachean Ethics* 3.2.1111b20–3) in terms of wish being the *result* of deliberation and choice (Alberti 1999, 125–7).

---

[18] Cf. Donini 1987, 83.

Alexander's clear treatment of what depends on us in terms of the *unrestricted* ability to choose the opposite (cf. Bobzien 1998b, 138–9) is, Bobzien argues (1998b, 146–52), influenced not by developments such as the foregoing but rather by a treatment of contingency which draws on various passages of Aristotle including not only *Nicomachean Ethics* 3.3 but also *On Interpretation* 9 and 13 and *Metaphysics* Θ, and which survives for us only in the Platonist witnesses **LMN**. She comments (148) that 'the original author could be equally well a Peripatetic or a Platonist – if indeed such a distinction made sense at the time'; consequently it seems appropriate to include **LMN** here, even though our primary concern is with the Peripatetics. It should be noted, though, that **MN** at least are late enough (*c.* AD 400) for their formulations to have been influenced also by Alexander. See further Sharples 2008c.

In **L** one might expect rather 'where each is equally possible', as in **N**, rather than 'where each [occurs] equally'; but in the case of what is for the most part and what is for the least part the reference is clearly to occurrence, rather than to possibility, and I have interpreted accordingly even though the treatment of human choice in frequentative terms is clearly flawed (people do not go for a walk 50 per cent of the time, or even on 50 per cent of the occasions when they consider whether to do so or not). **L** is also somewhat compressed in placing both what is for the most part and what is for the least part under 'nature'; the point that is actually being made is that both occur in the natural, rather than the human sphere, though only the first of them is natural as opposed to unnatural. Calcidius, in **M**, seems confused about the idea in **L** that what happens and does not with an equal frequency is opposed to itself.

Given that fate is being inserted into an Aristotelian theory where it did not originally belong, it is not surprising that we find conflicting views about where fate operated. Sometimes it is linked with the entirely regular and unvarying movements of the heavens (**O**); sometimes it is linked rather with the sublunary region (**PQ**, which are much later in date – Theodoret wrote in the first half of the fifth century AD – but may, like **MN**, reflect the thought of our period). In the sublunary context fate may, in particular, be linked with nature (**B**, where, however, the reference to 'these men' may suggest that (2) originated as an added marginal comment by some reader, rather than being part of the original text). But nature, for Aristotle, applies for the most part, rather than always (*Physics* 2.8.198b35). Therefore, whereas the Stoics held that fate was inexorable and something that could not be altered or avoided (LS 55KJLR), the way was open for an opposing, even if counterintuitive, Peripatetic concept of a fate that admitted exceptions.

Q indeed refers to the *necessity* of fate; however, 'necessity' can[19] indicate both what is regular and what is opposed to purpose, and the preoccupation of **PQ** is with the denial of *providence* in the sublunary region. The reference to fate in **A** is sufficiently vague that it could be interpreted either as indicating that fate is itself a non-necessary product in the sublunary region of the necessary movements of the heavens, or as indicating that fate is the necessary product of those movements. Why Cicero in **R** treats Aristotle as a determinist is not known; see Sharples 1991, 186 and references there.

We may find a hint as to how a non-deterministic Peripatetic concept of fate developed in a logical discontinuity, even if not an inconsistency, in a passage of Alexander of Aphrodisias. **S** is concerned to argue that fate admits of exceptions. In **S**(1)–(5) the example considered is animal generation, which does not always occur in the same way; there can be monstrous births, when, according to Aristotle's analysis (*Generation of Animals* 4.3.769b8–10), an animal is produced, but not an animal of the same species as the parent; the period of gestation can vary (this is presumably the point of **S**(5)); and, as Alexander points out later on in the same treatise (*On Fate* 24) while all children have adult parents, not all adults are parents of children. In **S**(7)–(9), however, what is at issue is exceptions to the natural tendencies of *individuals*, on a level below that of the whole species. This may suggest (Donini 1977, 182–3) that Alexander has taken over an earlier anti-Stoic discussion which focussed on exceptions to individual character and has imperfectly fitted it to its new context. The story about Socrates in **S**(11) had, we know, been in circulation – and apparently not just in Peripatetic circles – for some time; it occurs in Cicero, *On Fate* 10 and *Tusculan Disputations* 4.80, and may have originated as a protreptic to philosophy, possibly in a dialogue by Phaedo of Elis, rather than in anti-determinist argument. (Cf. Rosetti 1980.) If the identification in **S**(1)–(5) of fate with *specific* nature is Alexander's own addition, it fits well with his theory of providence too as concerned with species rather than with individuals (above, **22TU**). In *On Fate*, too, Alexander invokes the movement of the heavens as a way of giving the universe unity (**TU**); the Stoics sought to establish the unity and coherence of the universe by arguing that everything was determined by fate (e.g. Alexander, *On Fate* 22 = LS 55N), but Alexander's account allows for exceptions at the sublunary level, with an explicit echo of the household example in *Metaphysics* Λ.10 (though the use of the example was widespread in such discussions; see Sharples 2003b). It is, however, stated in terms of efficient rather than final causes, which is

---

[19] In principle; for the Peripatetic what is regular will often or always coincide.

significant for the shift in the notion of 'cause' identified in Frede 1980. Significantly, the term *suneiroito*, which appears in *On Coming-to-be and Passing Away* 2.10.336b33 (see above, 22 n. 33), was etymologically connected by the Stoics with *heimarmenē*, fate (cf. *SVF* 2.914, 986; also X(4), 20E and 22S. To infer from 22S that the author of the *De mundo* intended to adopt a determinist position might be over-hasty; his concern is with taking over the Stoic etymologies rather than, necessarily, with all their implications).

S(7)–(9), but *not* S(1)–(5), also appear, in a compressed version, in V(3)–(5). In both texts there is a further internal awkwardness, in that the reference to Heraclitus and the material that follows it on the face of it present an argument for identifying fate with nature because it obtains for the most part, rather than an argument for its admitting of exceptions, though the latter point is indeed implied by the former. Putting it another way, in 'And in the same way in the case of the soul too one would find the choices and actions and way of life of each individual differing from, and contrary to, his natural constitution. *For* "people's character is their guardian spirit" according to Heraclitus, that is, their nature' (my emphasis), the logic of 'for' is at best elliptical. But V avoids the other incongruity in S, for V(2), unlike S(1)–(5), focusses on *individual*, rather than specific nature. For various reasons (see Sharples 1980) it seems likely that V was composed *after* S, which raises a difficulty for the view that V simply reproduced an earlier theory and S reused this earlier material in a more ambitious but not entirely successful way; we should perhaps rather think of V, as the later text, avoiding the difficulty in S by omitting the reference to exceptions to the nature of the species.

As already mentioned, V attempts to find support for its view of fate in Aristotle's own writings (V(12)–(13)) and also (V(14)) in a work by Theophrastus, now known only through this and other second-hand reports (Theophrastus 493, 504 FHS&G; cf. also 505), and a work by a Polyzelus who is otherwise completely unknown. If we ask whether V(12)–(13) relate to exceptions to specific nature or to individual nature, the answer will have to be the former; however, to conclude from this that these appeals to the Aristotelian texts are due to Alexander himself, rather than being taken over by him from the earlier tradition, would be to press the distinction too far onto passages which do not in themselves suggest it. In V(12) the point is that winter or spring may come earlier or later; it is not being suggested that, for example, winter might be followed by summer without spring intervening at all.

Eusebius (*Preparation for the Gospel* 6.8.1) describes Diogenianus, whom he quotes in **WX** for criticism of the deterministic views of the Stoic Chrysippus, as a Peripatetic. The general view has been that Eusebius' description is inaccurate and that Diogenianus was an Epicurean;[20] but even if we do regard Diogenianus as a Peripatetic, what we have of his work in Eusebius' reports is more significant for its anti-Chrysippean arguments, and as evidence for Chrysippus' own arguments, than for its positive doctrine. On **W**(4), where Diogenianus seems to slide from the argument that whether we take precautions or not will itself be fated, to the argument that examples used by Chrysippus show that taking precautions is in any case futile, see Sharples 2007e, 182–3, suggesting that from Diogenianus' perspective, where determinism excludes anything being up to us anyway, the distinction is unimportant; see also 176, comparing Diogenianus' presentation of the argument with what we find in Cicero and in Seneca. The end of **X**(16) connects fate with what cannot be otherwise, but this may be *ad hominem* against Chrysippus rather than evidence for Diogenianus' own view.

On the issues raised in this section see further Sharples 2007b, 601–5.

---

[20] Diogenianus in **W**(2) says that he will go on to give Epicurus' view on divination. The admission of fate as the cause of some things in **X**(2) and **X**(8) goes against Epicurus, *Letter to Menoeceus* 133, though in each case Diogenianus is reporting the views of others for the sake of argument without necessarily endorsing them himself. The listing of Peripatetics along with Cynics and Epicureans in **W**(5) as rejecting divination presumably reflects Eusebius' belief that Diogenianus was a Peripatetic. Gottschalk 1987, 1142–3 n. 305 accepts Diogenianus as a Peripatetic; Amand de Mendieta 1973, 120 n. 4, 124 n. 1 also inclines to this view. However Isnardi Parente 1990, T. Dorandi in *DPA* vol. II 833–4, and Bobzien 2000, 304 n. 33 reject the Peripatetic identification, and LS vol. 1 495 simply describe him as a 'critic of Chrysippus with Epicurean leanings'. Material in this note and the text to which it relates is taken from Sharples 2007b, 600.

CHAPTER 24

Soul

A. Macrobius, *On the Dream of Scipio* 1.14.20 (Critolaus, fr. 18 Wehrli 1969b)

Critolaus the Peripatetic [teaches] that [the soul] is constituted of the fifth substance.

B. Tertullian, *On the Soul* 5.2 (Critolaus, fr. 17 Wehrli 1969b)

Nor do I speak only of those who fashion [the soul] from things that are clearly corporeal, as Hipparchus and Heraclitus do from fire, Hippo and Thales from water, Empedocles and Critias from blood, Epicurus from atoms (if atoms too produce corporeities from their coming-together), as Critolaus and his Peripatetics do from some fifth substance (if it too is a body, since it includes bodies), but I adduce also the Stoics, who call the soul spirit, virtually [agreeing] with us, in that breath and spirit are very close to each other, but nevertheless will easily persuade [us] that the soul is body.

C. Cicero, *Tusculan Disputations* 1.22

Aristotle, who far surpasses everyone – I always make an exception of Plato – both in talent and in application, when he had grasped those four well-known kinds of principles, from which all things have their origin, holds that there is a certain fifth nature, from which mind is [constituted]; for it thinks and exercises foresight and learns and teaches and discovers things and remembers and does so many other things, loving and hating, desiring and fearing, feeling pain and joy. He thinks that these and things like them are not present in any of these four kinds; he makes use of a fifth kind with no name and thus calls the mind itself by a new name, *endelekheia*, as it were a certain continued and perpetual movement.

D.   Cicero, *Tusculan Disputations* 1.65–6

(1) If, however, there is a certain fifth nature first introduced by Aristotle, this is [the nature] both of gods and of minds. This view we followed and expressed with the exact following words in our *Consolation*:[1] (2) 'No origin of minds can be found on the earth; for there is nothing mixed or combined in minds that has its origin from earth or is made from it, and nothing that is moist or windy or fiery. For in these natures there is nothing that has the power of memory, mind or thinking, which retains past things and foresees future ones and can grasp present ones; these things alone are divine, and nor will there ever be found anywhere from where they can come to a human being, if not from god. (3) For there is a certain unique nature and power of the mind, distinct from these customary and familiar natures. Thus whatever it is that is aware, has wisdom, is alive and is vigorous must necessarily be heavenly and divine and for that reason eternal. (4) Nor indeed can god himself, who is understood by us, be understood in any way other than as a certain mind that is unrestrained and free, separate from every mortal addition, aware of and moving all things and itself endowed with eternal motion.'

E.   Galen, *On the Opinions of Hippocrates and Plato* 7.7.25 (474.22–7 De Lacy 1980)

If it is necessary to make a declaration on the substance of the soul, it is necessary to say one or other of two things; either it must be said to be the light-like, as it were, and etherial body, [a view] at which the Stoics and Aristotle arrive by logical implication even if they do not want to, or [the soul] itself is an incorporeal substance, but its primary vehicle is this body, through which as an intermediary it has partnership with other bodies.

F.   Hippolytus, *Refutation of All Heresies* 1.20.4, 6

(1) Plato [says that] the soul is immortal, Aristotle that it persists, and subsequently it too disappears into the fifth body, which he supposes comes after the other four, rarer than fire and earth and water and air, like spirit [*pneuma*]. [18L follows here] . . . [2] [he says that] the soul of the whole

---

[1] Cicero's *Consolation* to himself on the death of his daughter Tullia, a work now lost.

world is immortal, and the world itself eternal, but that individual [soul], as we said earlier, disappears.

G. Aëtius 4.2.6 (*Dox.* 387a1–4)

Aristotle [declared the soul to be] the first actuality of a body that was natural, organic and potentially possessing life; actuality [*entelekheia*] should be understood as form and *energeia*. (Sharples: 2007d, 607)

H. Alexander of Aphrodisias, *On the Soul* 16.10–12

So [the soul] is the first actuality of a body which is natural and *organikon*. An *organikon* body is one which has a plurality of differing parts which can serve the faculties of the soul.

I. Philo of Alexandria, *Allegories of the Laws* 1.3–4

So when [Moses] says '[God] completed his works on the sixth day', one should understand that he is not considering the number of days, but six as a perfect number, since it is the first to be equal to its own parts, the half and the third and the sixth,[2] and is composed of an oblong, twice three. The dyad and the triad proceed from the incorporeality of the one, since [the dyad] is an image of matter, being divided and cut like it, and the triad [an image] of solid body, since the solid can be divided in three ways. But indeed [six] is also akin to the movements of *organika* living creatures. For *organikon* body naturally moves in six directions, forwards, backwards, upwards, downwards, to the right and to the left. So [Moses] wanted to show that mortal kinds and also imperishable ones were constructed according to their own proper numbers, measuring the mortal ones, as I said, by the hexad, the blessed and happy ones by the hebdomad.

J. Philo of Alexandria, *On Drunkenness* 111

And correspondingly Moses, when he saw that the king of Egypt ([that is] the excessively proud mind) with his six hundred chariots ([that is] the six

---

[2] $6 = 3 + 2 + 1$.

movements of *organikon* body) which are governed by the officers who preside over them (who, [though] nothing of the things subject to coming-to-be is naturally at rest, think they should make declarations about all things as being firmly established and not admitting any change) had suffered a worthy punishment for his impiety . . .

K.   Stobaeus, *Selections* 1.49.1b (320.5–8 Wachsmuth) = Aëtius 4.3.10

Xenarchus the Peripatetic and certain others of the same school [say that the soul is] the perfection and actuality according to the form, which is *per se* and at the same time is united with the body. (Sharples 2007d, 607)

L.   Epiphanius, *On Faith* 9.35 (vol. III, p. 508.9 Holl and Dummer = 3.31 in *Dox.* 592.14)[3]

[Aristotle] says that the soul is the continuous activity [*endelekheia*] of the body. (Sharples 2002b, 22; FHS&G 162)

M.   Arius Didymus (?), *Fragments on Physics* 15 (*Dox.* 455. 33–4, 456.1–3)

(1) Aristotle: the perceptive [part of soul], which is proper to all animals in common (for it is by sense perception that animal differs from plant) seems to be fivefold . . . (2) There is also a certain composite sense, in which everything takes place that is to do with *phantasia* and memory and opinion, which indeed is not without a share in intellect . . .

N.   Arius Didymus (?), *Fragments on Physics* 17 (*Dox.* 457.1–3)

Of [the part of the soul] that produces movement in place, which we called impulsive [*hormētikon*], the first mover both in us and in other animals is unmoved.

---

[3] Continuing the first part of 22O.

O.   Hippolytus, *Refutation of all Heresies* 7.24.2

Aristotle says that the soul is produced and perfected by the body,[4] [being] the actuality of a natural organic body.

P.   Galen, *That the Character of the Soul Follows the Temperament of the Body* (*Quod animi mores*) 4.44.12–20 Müller 1891

<As for Andronicus the Peripatetic>,[5] in general I praise him for having the courage to declare the being of the soul, [speaking] like a free man and not veiling the matter in obscurities (for I find him to be like this in many other matters); but in that he says that it is either a tempering or the power which follows on the tempering, I criticise the addition of 'the power'. (Sharples 2007d, 610)

Q.   Galen, *That the Character of the Soul Follows the Temperament of the Body* (*Quod animi mores*) 3.37.16–24 Müller 1891

And indeed, if all such [i.e. natural] bodies are composed of matter and form, and Aristotle himself thinks that natural body comes to be when the four [primary] qualities are present in the matter, it is necessary to make the blending of these the form, so that in a way the substance of the soul too will be some blending of the four – if you want to say of qualities, of hotness, coldness, dryness and moistness; or if [you prefer to say of bodies, of the hot [body] and the cold and the dry and the moist.

R.   Themistius, *On Aristotle's On the Soul* 32.22–31

(1) We must set what Andronicus says against what [Porphyry] says, inasmuch as it is both clearer and more convincing in establishing Xenocrates' position. 'They [i.e. Xenocrates (and his followers?)] called the soul a number,' [Andronicus] says, 'because no living creature is formed from a simple

---

[4] Literally: is the work and perfection of the body.
[5] The addition to the Greek text of the reference to Andronicus is justified by the Arabic version.

body, but from the primary elements blended according to certain formulae and numbers. (2) So they stated almost the same as those who made [the soul] a harmony, except in so far as these [Xenocrates and his followers] made the account clearer by what they added, defining the soul not as every number, but as a self-moving one, as if [those who made the soul a harmony] too [had defined it] not as every harmony, but as a *self-harmonising* one. For the soul itself is the cause of the blending and the formula and the mixture of the primary elements.' (Sharples 2007d, 610–11)

S.   Pseudo-Galen, *On Seed* 11, in *Galeni opera omnia*, ed. J. Cornarius (Basel, 1549) vol. VIII, col. 142C

Porphyry does not consider the soul [to be corporeal] but considers an ensouled rational spirit [to be so], showing in his *Introduction* [*Eisagogē*] that this spirit is bodily [and serves] the work of the soul, not the soul itself. But Socrates, Plato, Aristotle, Theodorus the Platonist, Andronicus the Peripatetic and Porphyry and very many others unanimously assert that it is not bodily, is not confined by the law of location and is not divided ... (Sharples 2007d, 612)

T.   Pseudo-Galen, *On Seed* 22, 152D–153A Cornarius

(1) On account of this Andronicus the Peripatetic asserts that (i) we are[6] according to our own will; we also (ii) walk apart from our own will, and even (iii) contrary to our own will, when (iv) we are led by our own soul or when (v) we are moved accidentally as a result of the nature of our body, or (vi) by the madness of anger or by another impulse. (2) He also advises that it is in a secondary way or through compulsion by the nature of the body that [we] turn our awareness towards evil. For just as a musician cannot give a [tuneful] sound from a false [= untuned?] string, just so the soul cannot by its reason rule a body which is bad, that is, lustful or something else; and [in such cases] the tuning [*sumphonia*] of the skilful soul's instrument, that is to say of the body, is displeasing. (3) Andronicus therefore asserts that the movements and combinations of the planets are truthful, and the other faults are not natural to the soul, and the soul is not composed of the nature of the body, as certain people wished. For if it were of the same nature, there would be nothing to prevent the soul subduing the body by spiritual principles [*rationibus*], that is to say subduing the vices of the body by acts of fasting and the other virtues. (Sharples 2007d, 612–13)

---

[6] *Sic*: but see the commentary.

U. Pseudo-Simplicius, *On Aristotle's On the Soul* 247.23–6

[Aristotle] rightly added 'eternal' [*aïdion*], as Plato in the *Phaedo* [106ae] added 'indestructible', so that we should not, like Boethus, think that the soul, like the being-ensouled [*empsukhia*] is indeed undying, in that it does not itself endure death when that approaches, but withdraws when [death] comes upon the living creature and so perishes. (Sharples: 2007d, 608)

V. Porphyry, *Against Boethus on the Soul*, fr. 242F Smith (Eusebius, *Preparation for the Gospel* 11.27.20–11.28.5)

(1) Porphyry explains the meaning [of *Phaedo* 79a–81c] in the first [book] of *Against Boethus on the Soul*, writing as follows:

(2) Now an argument which seems to Plato to be powerful in establishing the immortality of the soul, the [argument] from similarity. For if [the soul is] similar to the divine and immortal and formless and undispersed and indissoluble and substantial and what exists indestructibly, how would it not belong to the kind of the exemplar? (3) For whenever there are two extremes which are clearly opposed, for example rational and irrational, and there is a dispute concerning something else, as to which part it belongs to, one manner of demonstration is this, through showing to which of the opposites it is similar. For in this way, although the human kind is confined in irrationality in its early years and many have an abundance of irrational errors until old age, nevertheless, because [the human kind] has many similarities to what is purely rational, it has been believed to be rational from the beginning. (4) So, since there is a constitution which is clearly divine and unmixed and unpolluted, that of the gods, and again one which is clearly earthy and soluble and subject to destruction, and there is among some a dispute as to which of the aforementioned parts the soul belongs, Plato thought it right to track down the truth from the similarity.

(5) And since [the soul] is in no way like what is mortal and soluble and lacking intelligence and with no share in life, and for this reason tangible and perceptible and subject to coming-to-be and passing away, but [like] what is divine and immortal and formless and intelligent and living and akin to truth, and all the things that [Plato] reckoned up concerning it, it seemed right not to be willing, while allowing that the other similarities to god were in it, to remove from it the likeness to substance, on account of which it resulted that it possesses these. (6) For as the things which are dissimilar to

the activities of god are immediately different from substance in their constitution also, just so it follows that the things which participate in some way in the same activities have a similarity to substance. For it is on account of the being-of-a-certain-sort that the activities are of a certain sort, since they flow from it and are offshoots of it.

W. Porphyry, *Against Boethus on the Soul*, fr. 243F Smith (Eusebius, *Preparation for the Gospel* 11.28.6–10)

(1) Boethus, taking away the power of this argument – listen – in the beginning of the argument which he constructed writing as follows:

(2) Whether the soul is immortal and some nature superior to all destruction is something that one needs to show by patiently setting out many arguments. (3) But that nothing of the things about us is more like god than the soul, [this] someone would believe without needing much discussion, not only because of the continuous and unceasing nature of the motion which it produces in us, but because of that of the mind in itself. (4) It was with this in view that the natural philosopher of Croton [Alcmaeon] said that [the soul] was immortal and by nature avoided all rest, like the divine among bodies [i.e. the heavenly bodies].[7] (5) And once for all, when one has noted the sort of thing the soul is, and especially how great are the deliberations and of what sort the impulses that are often set in motion by the mind that rules in us, a considerable similarity to god will be apparent. (Sharples 2007d, 609)

X. Porphyry, *Against Boethus on the Soul*, fr. 244F Smith (Eusebius, *Preparation for the Gospel* 11.28.11–12)

(1) And continuing [Porphyry] says:

(2) For if the soul is shown to be most similar of all things to god, what need is there still of other arguments, having made [this] prelude to show its immortality, and not counting this as one [argument] among many, [since] it is sufficient to persuade those of good judgement that it would not share in the activities that are divine if it were not also divine itself? (3) For if, although it is bound in what is mortal and soluble and lacking intelligence and is itself a dead body and always perishing and flowing away into the transformation of destruction, it [nevertheless] fashions it and holds it together and displays its own divine substance, although it is obstructed

---

[7] Alcmaeon, 24A12 DK.

and impeded by the utterly ruinous image that has been added to it – how, if it is separated from the irrational, like gold that has been covered in mud, would it not there and then display its own form as being like god alone, and also participating in him, preserving the similarities in its activities and [even] in its most mortal [state] (as when it is confined in what is mortal) not being dissolved on account of this, because it is of a nature that has no share in destruction?

Y. Porphyry, *Against Boethus on the Soul*, fr. 245F Smith (Eusebius, *Preparation for the Gospel* 11.28.13–16)

(1) And further down [Porphyry] says:

(2) Reasonably it seems both divine, from its similarity to what is without parts, and mortal, from its affinity to mortal nature; and it descends and ascends and is of mortal form and like the immortals. (3) For even the one who fills his belly and is eager to be sated like the beasts is a human being; so too is the one who can save a ship in peril on the sea through his knowledge and [the one who can] save in diseases and the one who desires the truth and proceeds to apprehension of knowledge and discovery of firesticks and observations of horoscopes and who criticises imitations of the things made by craftsmen. (4) For a human being contrived how to construct the conjunctions of the seven [planets] with their movements, imitating the things in the sky by means of mechanical devices. And what has he not contrived, displaying the mind in him which is divine and equal to god? (5) As a result of this, displaying the daring of what is Olympian and divine and in no way mortal, he persuaded the majority who on account of their self-love are not able to see into the depths, to think from what appears externally that he is of mortal form in the same way as them; this being the one consolation for their badness, [namely] to consider, by equating their own wretchedness, as the things which appear externally, and to persuade them-selves that all human beings are internally such as they are externally.

Z. Porphyry, *Against Boethus on the Soul*, fr. 246F Smith (Eusebius, *Preparation for the Gospel* 14.10.3)

(1) Also in what he wrote *Against Boethus on the Soul* [Porphyry] agrees [that there are many disputes among philosophers], writing as follows, word for word:

(2) Some ideas and enquiries establish the immortality of the soul indisputably. But the arguments introduced by the philosophers to

demonstrate it seem to be easily overturned, on account of the ability of the disputatious to find arguments concerning everything. For what argument in philosophy is not open to dispute by those who think differently, where some people have thought it right to suspend judgement even about the things which seem obvious?

Aa.   Porphyry, *Against Boethus on the Soul*, frr. 247F–249F Smith (Eusebius, *Preparation for the Gospel* 15.10.9–11.4)[8]

[fr. 247] (1) Since we have recounted what Plotinus [says], it is not inappropriate to see what Porphyry says in the [books] *Against Boethus on the Soul*.

(2) Against the one who said that the soul is an entelechy and who supposed that, being altogether unmoved, it causes movement, one should say, where does inspiration come from, when the living creature understands nothing of what it sees and says, but the soul sees what is future and not present and is moved in a corresponding way? From where, in the case of the living creature's own constitution too, [come] the deliberations and considerations and wishes of the soul as belonging to the living creature, which are inclinations of the soul, and not of the body?

[fr. 248] (3) Then he says, continuing:

To liken the soul to heaviness or to uniform bodily qualities which cannot be changed, according to which the subject either is moved or is of a certain sort, was [the doctrine] of one who, willingly or unwillingly, completely missed the true worth of soul and in no way saw that it is by the *presence* of soul, indeed, that the body of a living creature comes to be alive, as it is by the presence of fire that the adjacent water comes to be hot, being cold in itself, and by the rising of the sun that the air is illuminated, being dark without illumination by this; (4) but the heat of the water is neither the heat of the fire nor the fire [itself], and the light in the air is not the light that is cognate to the sun. In just the same way the *presence* of soul (*empsukhia*) in the body, which is like the heaviness and the quality of the body, is not [itself] the soul that has been assigned a place in the body, on account of which the body has a share in a certain breath of life.

[fr. 249] (5) Then, continuing, after some other [points] he adds:

The other things which other people say about it make us ashamed. For how is the account not shameful which makes the soul the actuality of an organic natural body? How is [the account] not full of shame which states

---

[8] I am grateful to George Karamanolis for bringing this passage to my attention.

that it is *pneuma* in a certain state, or intelligent fire, kindled or tempered by the chilling and, as it were, immersion in the air, and the one which makes it a collection of atoms or in general that declares that it is produced from the body? [Plato] showed in the *Laws* [book 10] that this is the impious argument of impious people. So all these accounts are full of shame. But no one would be ashamed of the one that says that it is self-moved. (Sharples 2007d, 613–14)

Ab. Alexander of Aphrodisias, *On the Soul* 22.7–12

As heaviness is the cause of downwards movement for earth and moves it in this respect, though it is not moved in itself (for how could heaviness be moved in itself, being a form and the nature of the body that possesses it?), so the soul of living creatures is the cause of all the movements of the living creature, since it is by it that [the creature] has the power of moving in this way; itself not being moved in itself, [the soul] in this way moves the body.

Ac. Alexander of Aphrodisias, *On the Soul* 24.21–3

Soul is not a certain sort of mixture of bodies, that is an arrangement [*harmonia*], but the power that is created supervening on a certain sort of mixture.

Aristotle in *On Soul* 2.1 defines soul as the first actuality (*entelekheia*) of an organic body potentially possessing life, and as the (incorporeal, immanent) form of such a body. However, in his zoological works he emphasises the role of 'connate *pneuma*' as the instrument through which an incorporeal soul affects a corporeal body (*Movement of Animals* 10.703a9–28), and in *Generation of Animals* 2.3.736b30–737a8 he draws an analogy between the *pneuma* and vital heat of animals and the stuff of which the heavens are made, the *aithēr* (above, 21). His successors Theophrastus (346 FHS&G) and more particularly Strato (frr. 128, 129 Wehrli 1969c = 66, 67 in Sharples (in press, b)) emphasised the role of *pneuma* in animal functioning, encouraged by new anatomical discoveries relating to the nervous system (cf. Solmsen 1961; Sharples 1995, 28–9). It is perhaps uncertain whether Strato actually *identified* soul and *pneuma*, as has often been thought on the basis of fr. 108 Wehrli 1969c = fr. 59 in Sharples (in press, b); cf. fr. 94 Wehrli 1969c = 70 in Sharples (in press, b), but the Stoics certainly did so

(LS 47N–R, 53BG). It is therefore not surprising that Hellenistic writers, including Critolaus in **AB**, and those influenced by them (**CDE**; cf. also **21B** above) attributed to Aristotle a corporealist theory of soul identifying it with the stuff of the heavens. Galen in **E** regards this as the logical implication of Aristotle's views. Apart from the eternity of the world, the position attributed to Aristotle in **F** is Stoic (cf. LS 46EF, LS 53W); this may have more to do with confusion on Hippolytus' part than with widely held interpretations of Aristotle.

We do indeed find reports which show some knowledge of the definition of soul in Aristotle, *On the Soul*, though how well it was understood is another matter; see **GKL**, and above 3A(14)–(16), 22D(3). We may note, in particular, with Bos 2001, 191; 2003, 85 n. 75 and 87; 2007, 42, that the standard modern interpretation of 'organic', that is 'instrumental', in the definition as meaning 'equipped with parts which serve as instruments', was popularised by Alexander of Aphrodisias (**H**; cf. *Supplement to* On the Soul (*Mantissa*) 1.103.38–104.8) and that this use of the term cannot be traced back in extant literature before Philo of Alexandria (**IJ**; Bos 2001, 200 n. 28; 2003, 98. In **IJ** '*organikon* body' is used to distinguish animate bodies from inanimate ones, which have fewer natural directions of movements; since in **I** it would make no sense to speak of *living creatures* as 'instruments' (of what?), *organikon* must have the sense of 'equipped with organs' in both its occurrences in **I** and, because of the parallel, in **J** as well). Bos indeed argues not only that the more natural meaning of the word is 'serving as an instrument', but also that Aristotle himself in the definition was referring not to the whole body of the animal, as has been supposed at least since Alexander, but to the *pneuma* functioning as soul's instrument, and that the absence from Hellenistic discussion of the hylomorphic account of soul in Aristotle as now generally understood is not so much evidence of a lack of interest in Aristotle's position as a reflection of the fact that this account was not in fact Aristotle's at all. However, the point about the understanding of the term 'organic' is independent of these further issues, for the whole body, too, might reasonably be seen as itself the instrument of soul.

One oddity is that Aristotle's *entelekheia* is sometimes replaced by *endelekheia*, 'continuity', or cognate terms (**CL**). In modern Greek pronunciation the two words would be identical, and that change may already have been under way. Aristotle may himself have used the term *endelekheia* in work now lost to us; cf. Huby 1999, 18–20, with further references. The last clause of **D** may suggest that Cicero too had *endelekheia* in mind there, and that, in the context of Antiochean assimilation of Aristotelianism and Platonism, another factor may, at least for Cicero, have been the argument for the immortality of the soul in Plato's *Phaedrus* 245c, which he himself translated twice (*Republic* 6.27; *Tusculan Disputations* 1.53–4).

Arius(?)[9] in **M** appears to combine *phantasia* (the image-forming faculty; see above, **14G**), memory and intellect into a single faculty, and possibly to identify it with Aristotle's 'common sense' (*On the Soul* 3.1.425a27). For Aristotle himself *phantasia* and intellect are capacities of the soul distinct from sense perception. But he does make remarks indicating that human thought necessarily involves *phantasia* (*On the Soul* 3.8.432a13, cf. 3.7.431a14, 431b2; *On Memory* 1.449b31), and these may perhaps lie behind Arius' account. **N**, asserting that for Aristotle animal impulse starts from an unmoved mover, the object of appetition, is an accurate report of Aristotle's view (*On the Soul* 3.10.433b15–17).

Hippolytus in **O** interprets Aristotle's definition of soul in *On the Soul* as implying that the soul is *produced by* the body. It is true that in Aristotle's view a soul requires a body of a certain sort, just as other forms too may require matter of a certain suitable sort (*Physics* 2.9.200a5–9, 200a24–b8). But that leaves open the question of explanatory and indeed ontological priority. Aristotle explicitly rejects the notion that the soul is a 'harmony', or arrangement or tempering, of the bodily elements (*On the Soul* 1.4.407b27–408a28*)*, though his followers Aristoxenus (fr. 120a–d Wehrli 1967) and Dicaearchus (fr. 21AB Mirhady 2001) accepted it (cf. Caston 1997, 339–42). Andronicus, according to Galen in **P**, considered both this possibility and the possibility that the soul was a *power resulting from* the harmony; Galen himself in **P** opts for the former, his own argument for interpreting Aristotle in this way being given in **Q** (and see further Sorabji 2004, vol. 1 6(a)(12)–(19)). But that Andronicus wanted to give the soul more independence can be inferred from **R**, where Andronicus is reported as approving of the definition of soul by Xenocrates, the third head of Plato's school, not just as a number, in Pythagorean fashion, but as a *self-moving* number; Plato's argument for the priority of soul to body in *Laws* 889a–899d can be seen in the background here. Caston 1997, 347–54 has interpreted Andronicus, and Alexander of Aphrodisias of whom more below, as attempting to restore an emergentist view of soul by contrast with the epiphenomenalist view of Aristoxenus and Dicaearchus, and as thus more in agreement with Aristotle himself than they were.

Two problematic reports of Andronicus appear in a pseudo-Galenic work, *On Seed*, which exists in a medieval Latin version but may derive

---

[9] See above on 1IO.

from late antiquity (ST).[10] S is followed in its context by the familiar comparison of the soul to the sun, which illuminates but is not itself affected in so doing; cf. Nemesius, *Nature of Man* 3.40.22–41.5 Morani; Priscian, *Answers to Chosroes* 51.33–52.5; Dörrie 1959, 74–9 (arguing that the source of these passages is Porphyry); Schroeder 1987; Sorabji 2004, vol. 1 204–10. How much significance should be attached to the presence of Andronicus in the list in S is questionable; confidence is not increased by the fact that previously the view that the soul is corporeal has been attributed not only to Democritus but also to 'Ammonius'. T follows a discussion of the effect of the planets on the human body. In T(1) it appears that (iv) refers back to the rather awkwardly phrased (i), (v) to (ii), and (vi) to (iii).

Andronicus' pupil Boethus, as we have seen, argued that form was not substance but quality (above, **12F**). If he followed Aristotle in regarding soul as form, this might suggest that he is unlikely to have emphasised the superiority of the soul to the body or the control of the former over the latter; the Stoics indeed combined the notion that individuals were only portions of matter *qualified* by their soul-*pneuma* (LS 27–8; above, commentary on **12**) with the notion of a (limited) survival of the soul after the death of the body, but this was in the context of a view of *pneuma* as the *corporeal* active principle fashioning the body. We do not, however, have any direct evidence for Boethus' view on the placing of soul in the categories. What we do have instead is reports of his criticisms of the arguments in Plato's *Phaedo* for the immortality of the soul, arguments which had already been attacked by Strato (frr. 118, 122–7 Wehrli 1969c = 76–81 in Sharples (in press)); these reports of Boethus, however, require careful interpretation.

The final argument in the *Phaedo* (105b–107a) is, in essence, that soul, as the source of life, is incompatible with death; the soul cannot therefore die when the body does, but must withdraw elsewhere. Strato objected, in effect, that to argue that there can be no such thing as a 'dead soul' does not prove that the soul is everlasting; there are two ways in which soul can avoid being dead, one indeed being to continue to live after the death of the body, but the other being to cease to exist altogether. A *non-existent* soul cannot *be* a dead soul. Plato's Socrates does indeed already attempt to block this objection by arguing that what cannot admit death is the best candidate for being everlasting (*Phaedo* 106a–107a).

A common response of later Platonists was to distinguish between the *presence* of soul, or the *fact of the body's being ensouled*, on the one hand and *the soul itself* on the other, and to argue that, even if the former ceased to

---

[10] My attention was drawn to these by Vivian Nutton. See his (in press). There is an incomplete Middle English version of the treatise edited in Pahta 1998, which contains only S, at p. 217, and not T.

exist with the death of the body, this did not mean that the same applied to the latter (cf. Damascius, *On Plato's* Phaedo, second version, 78.8–12 (p. 331 Westerink 1977); also Karamanolis 2006, 296 n. 178, and 2007, and **Aa**(3)–(4) below. Simplicius uses this distinction in reporting Boethus in **U**, but it does not seem likely that Boethus himself made the distinction. Rather, Boethus' point seems to have been Strato's: when the body dies the soul does not itself *die*, but that does not mean that (as Plato argued) it withdraws and *survives*, for it may equally well withdraw and *cease to exist*, though not by a process of itself *dying*.

VWXYZ and **Aa** are cited by Eusebius from a work of Porphyry the Platonist *Against Boethus on the Soul*. There is some doubt whether the Boethus in question is the Peripatetic, or rather the Stoic (also from Sidon; second century BC. See above, **20** n. 11). Moraux 1973, 172–6 indeed argues that all our evidence for 'Boethus' on the soul relates to Boethus the Stoic. Beatrice 2005, 271–2 n. 57 argues that the Boethus in question is a Platonist and that *pros* in the title indicates not 'against' but 'in reply to'.

In **V** Porphyry, quoted by Eusebius, paraphrases the Affinity Argument of *Phaedo* 79a–81c. In **W** and **X**, which in his account follow immediately, Eusebius reports Boethus as undermining this argument; but what Eusebius actually quotes seems rather to repeat the argument for the superiority of soul to body and its quasi-divine status. Eusebius does not indeed indicate whether **X** is Porphyry reporting Boethus or Porphyry stating his own view. Gottschalk (1986, 246–8; 1987, 1117–18) argues that **W** is selective quotation by Porphyry; Boethus went on to argue none the less that the soul is *not* immortal, but Porphyry uses Boethus' concession to argue against him that it is.

In **Y** Porphyry notes that human beings can display either (i) affinity to the gods or (ii) affinity to the lower animals (their position between the two being a traditional theme; see, for example, Aristotle, *Nicomachean Ethics* 7.1.1145a18–27; Sallust, *Catiline* 1; Galen, *Exhortation to Study the Arts* 9 (vol. 1, p. 21.4–6 Kühn)), and then apparently gives as an example of (i) the daring of an unnamed individual – perhaps Boethus – who used (ii) to persuade people that the soul was as perishable as the body. Porphyry's presentation of human achievements is in a general way reminiscent of Sophocles, *Antigone* 332–64; lists of human achievements were indeed commonplace (cf. Cicero, *On the Nature of the Gods* 2.147–53), but the fact that the Sophoclean list notes that death is the one thing human beings have not overcome (361–2) provides a particular connection with the context here.

By distinguishing between soul and the property of being ensouled, **Aa**(3)–(4) provides a counter to Boethus' argument against immortality in **U** above.

The natural inference is that it is indeed Boethus who is being attacked in (3)–(4) by Porphyry, and from this one might infer, with Movia 1968, 199 and n. 4, that **Aa**(4) shows that Boethus also anticipated Alexander's analogy between the soul and heaviness (**Ab**). Gottschalk 1986, 250–3; 1987, 1118), however, pointed out that Boethus is not the only person whose views were attacked in Porphyry's treatise, and Moraux 1973, 175 n. 12 argues that it is in fact against Alexander that **Aa**(3)–(4) are directed. Another possibility is that Porphyry used Alexander's analogy between soul and heaviness to formulate his argument against Boethus, transferring Alexander's analogy from soul to 'being-ensouled' (*empsukhia*) precisely in order to point out the difference between immortal soul and the property of being alive to which Peripatetic soul, from a Platonist standpoint, in fact reduces. Alexander's identification of the soul of the *heaven* with its nature was rejected by Simplicius (see above, commentary on **21J**) on the grounds that for Aristotle nature is – though interpreters from Alexander to the present have often forgotten it – a principle of *being moved* rather than a principle that causes movement (Sorabji 2004, vol. II 49–51); the same objection may be raised against the analogy between soul and heaviness in **Ab**.

Aa(5) is attributed to Atticus the Platonist, as a dubious fragment, by des Places 1977 (as Atticus, fr. 7 *bis*), following Merlan 1970, 73 n. 3 (noted by Gottschalk 1986, 245 n. 6), who argued that the reference to shame in **Aa**(5) is in the style of Atticus rather than of Porphyry. Gottschalk himself argues against the attribution of **Aa**(5) to Atticus, on the grounds that this contradicts what Eusebius says, and also that Atticus, arguing against the Peripatetics, would have no reason to introduce Stoic and Epicurean views (*pneuma* and atoms, respectively) into the discussion. Karamanolis 2007, 97 argues that **Aa**(5), criticising Aristotle's definition of soul, cannot be an expression of Porphyry's own view, since **U** shows that Porphyry himself regarded Aristotle as agreeing with Plato rather than with Boethus.

Des Places gives no explanation of why he supposes only **Aa**(5), and not **Aa**(2) and (3)–(4) come from Atticus, when Eusebius attributes all these extracts to Porphyry. If **Aa**(5) is indeed from Atticus and **Aa**(2)–(4) are not, we would have to suppose either that Eusebius muddled his sources, or else that Porphyry cited Atticus and that Eusebius included the material from Atticus in his quotation from Porphyry, either inadvertently or, as George Karamanolis suggests to me, deliberately in order to present Porphyry himself as sympathetic to Eusebius' own anti-Aristotelian position. On Porphyry's habit of including extended citations from earlier authors see Smith 2007, 13. An argument similar to that in **Aa**(2) is reported by Themistius, *On Aristotle's* On the Soul 16.19–25; Themistius does not name the source, but a marginal note in one MS refers to Porphyry; see Todd 1996, 160 n. 8. On **Aa** see further Karamanolis 2006, 296–8; Sharples 2007d, 613–15.

Alexander of Aphrodisias in **Ac** (cf. also Sorabji 2094, vol. 1 6(a)(31)) takes over Andronicus' definition of the soul. Alexander has been accused both in antiquity and in more recent times for adopting an un-Aristotelian, materialistic position which subordinates soul to body; but these criticisms have generally been from those who adopted a Platonising or Thomistic reading of Aristotle, and as with Andronicus, so with Alexander it is reasonable to see his treatment of soul as an attempt to reinstate the priority of soul to body and of form to matter. Detailed discussion of the nuances of Alexander's position is beyond the scope of the present work (cf. Donini 1971; Caston 1997, 347–54; Sharples 2004, 20 n. 34 and further references there); but it may be noted that, as with form (above, **12K** and commentary), so with soul he insists that soul is not present in a subject that exists independently (above, **12J**). Karamanolis 2007, 96–7 attributes to Alexander, as well as to Boethus, the view that soul is 'a mere quality of the living body'; this is wrong as far as Alexander is concerned, though from the *Platonist* perspective that Karamanolis' discussion takes as its starting-point there may be little to choose between Alexander's view and Boethus'.

On the issues raised in this section see further Sharples 2007d, 607–15.

CHAPTER 25

Generation

A.   Galen, *On Seed* 1.1 (*CMG* V.3.1 64.4–14 De Lacy 1992)

What is the usefulness and what is the power of the seed? Does it count as two principles, material and efficient, as Hippocrates supposed, or only as the second, the efficient, as Aristotle thinks, judging that it is a source of change for the menses, but not allowing that the living creature is fashioned from it? It is worth considering and deciding a disagreement among such great men, not entrusting it to persuasive arguments, which the majority of doctors and philosophers take delight in, but demonstrating [the facts of the case] from clear [principles] and through clear [arguments]. Since Aristotle too thinks that one should take premises for demonstrations from experience concerning each of the things enquired into, let us first consider this accurately, whether the seed remains within the women who are going to conceive, or whether it is ejected.

B.   Galen, *On Seed* 1.3 (*CMG* V.3.1 68.3–70.24 De Lacy 1992)

(1) This [that the womb retains and indeed sucks in the seed] I have said on account of some of the contemporary philosophers, Aristotelians and Peripatetics as they call themselves. For I would not myself call them so, when they are so ignorant of Aristotle's opinion as to think that he judges that the male's seed, deposited in the female's womb, imparts a beginning of change to the menses, but after that is ejected, not becoming any part of the bodily substance of what is conceived.[1] (2) They are misled by the first book of *On the Generation of Animals*, which is the [only] one of the five that they have read. For in this it is written: 'As we said, one might posit as the principles of generation not least the female and the male; the male as

---

[1] As the sequel shows, Galen's objection is to the interpretation of Aristotle as saying that the seed is ejected; he agrees that it does not become part of the bodily substance of the embryo.

possessing the principle of the change and the generation, the female [as possessing the principle] of the matter' [1.2.716a4–7]. This, then, is not long after the beginning. (3) Later on in the work [Aristotle] also writes as follows: 'But it comes about as is reasonable, since the male provides the form and the principle of the change, the female the body and the matter, as in the setting of milk the body is the milk, but the fig-juice or rennet is what has the principle that causes the setting' [1.21.729a9–13]. (4) Taking these remarks as their starting-point, some think that the seed, having provided the menses with the principle of change, is ejected again; (5) but some say that [Aristotle] is not saying what all of us who take [what he says] in the natural way supposed, but rather that the female contributes only the matter to what will be conceived, the male both matter and also form. Consequently one of them greatly ridiculed me for thinking that the seed is ejected again from the female, or remains inside but is dissolved into nothing. For they say that this follows, if we think that the bodily substance [of the male seed] is not mixed and blended in the matter of what is conceived.

(6) Well, we will show to both of them in common the following passage from the *second* book of *On Generation of Animals*: 'It follows on from this to raise and answer this question: if there is no part of the seed ejaculated into the female that enters into the conception that is generated, where does the bodily [substance] itself go, if it produces by the power which is present in it?' [2.3.736a24–7] (7) Then having drawn distinctions in what follows concerning soul and intellect,[2] at the end of what he says [Aristotle] writes as follows: 'the body of the semen – in which the seed[3] also travels from its origin in soul, being in part separable from body, [the part] in which the divine is contained (and like this is what is called intellect) and in part inseparable, the seed[4] of the semen – is dissolved and turned to *pneuma*, having a moist and watery nature. And for this reason one should not look for its being emitted outside, nor for its being any part of the shape that is constituted, just as neither [is] the fig-juice that sets the milk. For this too changes and is no part of the bulk that is set' [2.3.737a8–16]. (8) This passage shows that both groups are ignorant of Aristotle's opinion, those who think that the fluid is completely emitted and those [who think] that it is[5] a part of the conception. (9) The second group are separately [refuted] by what follows in sequence after what I quoted earlier,

---

[2] See the commentary on **27**.
[3] So most of the MSS of Aristotle. Michael Scot's medieval Latin translation has 'the *pneuma*'. Peck in the Loeb Aristotle follows Wimmer in deleting 'the seed': 'in which the soul-principle also travels, being in part . . .'
[4] Wimmer, followed by Peck, reads 'the body' here.
[5] Kühn, following the Basel edition, has 'is not a part', but that is clearly wrong.

which begins like this: 'But it comes about as is reasonable, since the male provides the form and the principle of the change, the female the body and the matter' [1.21.729a9–12]. For in everything that follows he shows that, as the bed comes from the wood and the carpenter, and the sphere from the wax and the form, in the same way the conception is constituted from the menses and from the source of change from the male. And for this reason he says that some creatures do not emit semen but simply impart soul-heat to the female; like this are some of the insects in which the female inserts the member into the male, staying with it for a long time and receiving in the coupling nothing bodily, but only the power which gives shape and form to the shape.[6]

C. Lactantius, *On the Divine Creation* 12
(vol. II 44.5–10 Brandt and Laubmann
1893 = *PL* 7 54ab)

Varro and Aristotle, then, think that conception comes about in the following way. They say that seed is present not only in males but also in females; and that for this reason offspring often resemble their mothers. But the females' seed is purified blood, and if this is mixed with the male [seed] in the right way, both of them condense and congeal together and take on form.

D. Pseudo-Plutarch, *Summary on the Opinions of the*
Philosophers concerning Nature 5.5 905C
(Aëtius 5.5.2, *Dox.* 418a10–13)

Aristotle and Zeno [say that females] eject moist matter like the sweat from exercise, but not seed that has the power to concoct.

E. Pseudo-Plutarch, *Summary on the Opinions of the*
Philosophers concerning Nature 5.4 905B
(Aëtius 5.4.2, *Dox.* 417a21–5)

Pythagoras, Plato and Aristotle [say that] the power of the seed is incorporeal, like the intellect that causes movement, but that the matter that is ejected is corporeal.

---

[6] The point of 'for a long time' is, as Aristotle's account makes more explicit (especially *Generation of Animals* 1.21.729b31–2), that if the male does not insert a substance into the female that can work on the matter but simply affects the material in the female from outside, separation of the pair cannot occur until the process is complete.

F.   Galen, *On Seed* 2.1 (*CMG* V.3.1 150.14–18 De Lacy 1992)

And for this reason Athenaeus is not convincing when he says that the seed-producing parts in females are like the nipples in males, the correspondence alone of the parts occurring in the initial shaping, but the activity not being preserved.

G.   Galen, *On Seed* 2.1 (*CMG* V.3.1 152.8–22 De Lacy 1992)

And it would be much better to believe on the basis of what is evident that females have seed, but to consider by reason what its power is. What is evident has been stated previously and will now be stated again. The spermatic ducts that are full of seed eject it without the coming together of the male with the male, and in their effusions during sleep females experience this in a similar way to males, and as was said previously in the case of the widowed woman. And in animals [seed] is found at the extremity of the allantoid membrane. That this is evidently so refutes Aristotle, and not least Athenaeus too, and as many of the more recent doctors as say that the seed-producing parts grow into the Fallopian tubes, but, being perforated with certain sideways perforations, eject the seed outside, below the womb. Someone might grant that they are right, seeing more keenly than Lynceus himself in seeing the smallest perforation, and more dimly than sufferers from cataract in not seeing what is greatest; but one might reasonably find fault with them for not even enquiring at all from where what is in the extremity of the allantoid membrane is gathered, and why [in their view] what is ejected below the womb is wasted.

Aristotle in *Generation of Animals* argues, as reported by Galen in **A** and in **B**(1), that in animal generation the female parent provides the matter for the embryo, matter which would, if no conception takes place, be ejected as the menstrual blood, but the seed of the male parent provides only form. In adopting this position Aristotle was consciously rejecting the prevailing Hippocratic view, also alluded to by Galen in **A**, that both parents contribute to the embryo in a similar way. Aristotle's theory is motivated by a desire to introduce his standard distinction between form and matter, which he regards the Hippocratic theory as in effect disregarding, though he was also influenced by erroneous inference from observed facts (females who have conceived do not menstruate; the volume of the menstrual blood is much greater than that of the male semen), by analogies with artificial production (the curdling of milk to make cheese – cf. **B**(3) (7)) – and by culturally conditioned assumptions of the superiority of the male to the female.

Unfortunately for Aristotle, or rather for his would-be loyal followers, the existence of female ovaries, unknown to him, was discovered soon after his death with the development of anatomical dissection in Alexandria, and the analogy between female ovaries and male testes suggested that both parents contributed in a more similar way than Aristotle had allowed. (The existence of actual sperm cells and egg cells was unknown, in the absence of microscopes.) The polymath Varro (116–27 BC), who is apparently Lactantius' source for his information about Aristotle in **C** (cf. Diels, *Dox.* 198), seems to have attributed the Hippocratic theory of seed from both parents to Aristotle too. In **D** Aëtius, reported by pseudo-Plutarch, reports Aristotle's view more accurately; the male seed has the power to concoct, that is, to fashion the matter from the female into an embryo, but the fluid from the female lacks this power. Galen in **B**(5) indicates that some, unnamed, Aristotelians, presumably in our period, attempted to update or modify Aristotle's position so as to allow at least that the male contributed matter as well as form. (One might compare Adrastus' updating of Aristotle's astronomy, in **21M** above). Galen himself rightly insists in **B**(6)–(9) that both the view that male semen becomes a physical part of the embryo (**B**(5)) and the view that it is ejected by the female (**B**(4)) are misreadings of Aristotle, whose view is rather that it dissolves within the womb; this although Galen himself holds that the male makes a material contribution (De Lacy 1992, 48).

Athenaeus of Attaleia, founder of the Pneumatist school of medicine in the first century AD, argued that female ovaries, like male breasts, had no actual function (**F**). Whether Athenaeus in arguing thus was motivated specifically by a desire to reconcile the authority of Aristotle with the anatomical facts now known is not clear, but in **G** Galen couples him and Aristotle together. De Lacy 1992, 232 suggests that Galen's use of the argument from waste against 'the more recent doctors' suggests that these may have been Peripatetics; this may be so, but Peripatetics were not alone in holding that 'nature does nothing in vain'.

On the issues in this section see further Accattino 1988 87–93; Sorabji 2004, vol. II 44.

CHAPTER 26

Sensation

A. Galen, *On the Opinions of Hippocrates and Plato* 7.7.1–5 (*CMG* V.4.1.2 470.3–21 De Lacy 1978)

(1) Now since it was necessary for the organ of sight to be able to discriminate colours, it was made like light, since only such bodies are naturally altered by colours, as is made clear by the surrounding air, when it is most pure, being altered by colours. One can at any rate see, when someone is lying under a tree in such air[-conditions], the colour of the tree surrounding him. And bright air which touches the coloured surface of a wall often receives [the colour] and transmits it to another body, especially when the colour is deep blue or yellow or some other bright colour. Indeed, just as the light of the sun at sunrise makes all the air like itself just by touching it, in the same way [air] is immediately changed by colour. (2) These things, then, were stated most correctly by Aristotle, concerning the immediate change, close to instantaneous, of things that alter in this way, and, concerning this [change], that the bright air, when altered by colours, naturally transmits the alteration right up to the organ of sight. (3) But Aristotle did not say how we know the position or size or distance of each of the things we perceive. Many of his followers, reasoning about his doctrine, are caught out as wrong, since neither odours nor voices indicate the place from which they come,[1] as has been shown in the fifth book of [my] *On Demonstration*.

B. Alexander of Aphrodisias, *On the Soul* 42.11–19

That light and transparent things that are illuminated are changed in some way by colours is clear from the fact that we see that [the light] becomes the

---

[1] Aristotle in *On the Soul* (see the commentary below) explains sight not in terms of visual rays that travel in straight lines, but in terms of a change in the intervening air, as with sounds that are heard and odours that are smelled.

same colour as many of the colours which are seen through it and takes on their colour. Gold makes it too seem golden, and purple purple, and pale green things grass-green. It is often possible to see the walls opposite such a colour,[2] and the floor, as it were, stained with the colour of those things,[3] and any people who may happen to be standing nearby, since what is illuminated, through being affected by those things, transmits such a colour to these too.

C. Alexander of Aphrodisias, *Supplement to On the Soul* (*Mantissa*) 15.145.25–30

Moreover certain colours appear also in the intervening transparent, since it itself receives the forms and acts as a messenger. At any rate certain things appear to be coloured by the colours of what is placed alongside them. What is [placed] on red or purple appears like this in colour, if such colours are placed alongside, since the colours are transmitted through the air, but are not seen there. (Sharples 2004, 137–8)

D. Alexander of Aphrodisias, *On Aristotle's Meteorology* 142.34–143.14

(1) [Aristotle is explaining solar and lunar haloes] What is beyond [the limit of the mist] condenses more, and being uniform and with very small parts it makes a continuous [band] of very small mirrors around the circumference of the circle. According to those who give the bending-back[4] of [our] sight [*opsis*][5] as the cause, [our] sight falls upon this and, being bent back towards the heavenly body [the sun or the moon] creates the impression of the halo; but in truth the light of the heavenly body, falling on the aforementioned mirrors and then being bent back and transmitted to the sight which sees it, creates the impression of the halo. For in the aforementioned mirrors, because of their smallness, there is a reflection of the colour only.[6] (2) And this, in summary, is what Aristotle's opinion concerning the [solar and lunar] halo is like [sc. that it is formed by symmetrical reflection from mist]. He was followed by Posidonius [F133 EK], while almost all the others give

---

[2] One would rather expect a reference to being opposite a wall of a particular colour. Fotinis 1979, 56 supposes a reference to a mural.

[3] The plural is unexpected, but Accattino and Donini 1996, 180 explain it by the preceding reference to pale green things in the plural.

[4] *anaklasis*, often translated 'reflection'; but here and in what follows I have used 'reflection' rather to translate *emphasis*, literally the appearing in the mirror of the thing reflected.

[5] See the discussion below.   [6] See G(6) below.

the explanation not as reflection, but as breaking-up of our sight, as happens in the case of things seen through water. For they suppose that the cloud is spherical and hollow, and then they say that the heavenly body [sun or moon] which is above it is seen in it broken up in a circle. (3) But that such opinions about the halo are wrong was adequately shown by my teacher Sosigenes in the eighth [book] of his [work] *On vision*.

E.   Galen, *On the Opinions of Hippocrates and Plato* 7.7.10–15 (*CMG* V.4.1.2 472.3–24 De Lacy 1978)

(1) And yet it seems to me that Aristotle noticed in his thinking the absurdity of the reflection that he says comes from the sense objects,[7] for he nowhere dares to use it but always drags it in as unconvincing. For in explaining how the rainbow occurs and halos around the sun and the moon and what are called 'counter-suns' and 'mock suns', and things seen in mirrors, he refers everything to reflection of the sight, saying [*Meteorology* 3.4.374b22–3][8] that it makes no difference whether we think it is [i] the sight that is reflected or [ii] the alteration in the air that surrounds us, brought about by the things seen, engaging in sophistry in a way very like Asclepiades,[9] who uses the term 'attraction' instead of 'motion'. For he realised that 'motion' was not convincing and had the nerve to change the name. (2) In this way Aristotle too, since he clearly understood that he would be stating unconvincing reasons for particular visual [phenomena] if he preserved his own opinion, came to the other [opinion], saying it made no difference which way [the explanations] were expressed. (3) And yet someone might justly say to him, 'if it makes no difference to say it this way or that, why do you leave aside the true opinion which is yours[10] and adopt another which is false? For the sophistical argument will turn back against *you*, since you have given no reason for your irrational change of opinion; so you will be an object of suspicion rather than of trust. (4) If indeed you say that it is because you are more convinced by what is said that you adopt

---

[7] I.e. explanation [ii] below. See the commentary.

[8] De Lacy 1984, 681 identifies this as the passage Galen has in mind. See, however, the discussion below.

[9] Presumably Asclepiades of Bithynia, the medical writer from (probably) the second century BC. (Rawson 1982, 360–3 argues that Asclepiades died before 91 BC; Polito 1999, that he may have lived *c*. 216–120 BC.) As De Lacy 1984, 681–2 points out, Galen unfortunately does not tell us in what context Asclepiades made this verbal substitution; De Lacy suggests that he too was probably discussing sight, but this seems speculative.

[10] I.e. [ii] – not in fact the 'true opinion' in Galen's own view, but Galen is presenting the matter from Aristotle's supposed standpoint, the better to represent him as inconsistent. If both views are equally acceptable, Galen is saying, why use [i] rather than [ii]?

opinions which are not yours [i.e. [i]], then you will again be asked why this is convincing. For if the false opinion explains all the particular cases more convincingly than the true one, all your books of *Problems* will not be believed.'[11]

F.   Alexander of Aphrodisias, *On Aristotle's* Meteorology 155.24–30

And this [Aristotle] says happens very clearly and obviously. For the bending back is the cause of things seen through water being seen like this. For they are not seen exactly, but in the manner of things a long way off. For it makes no difference whether [we] see placing what is seen far away from our sight or whether we make the sight itself seen across a large intervening distance; for sight sees the things that are seen through a bending-back across a greater interval than if it had looked at them directly.

G.   Alexander of Aphrodisias, *On Aristotle's* Meteorology 141.3–142.20

(1) [Aristotle] does not accept the theory that says that we see through the emission of rays, as the mathematicians say, a theory which has as its consequence the one which says that we see everything that we see through reflection by means of the bending-back of these rays. For neither can rays which are emitted from [our] sight and fall on what is visible be the causes of [our] seeing, nor again can these same [rays], bent back from mirrors and all things that are seen through such things[12] be the cause of our seeing these things, with the bending-back of the rays being by equal angles.[13] That these things are impossible was shown in *On How We See*,[14] and [Aristotle] himself, too, mentioned them in *On the Soul* [3.12.435a5–10]. (2) For he thinks that the things which are seen in a straight line are not seen by means of rays, but because[15] the transparent between the thing seen and [our] sight

---

[11]   It is not clear why Galen refers to the *Problems* here, or, given the absence of any specific detail, whether what he has in mind is the original collection, now lost, or the collection we now possess, the contents of which are for the most part later than Aristotle himself (though Louis 1991, 149–55 argues that book 10 of the surviving *Problems* is by Aristotle himself; I owe this reference to John Dudley). Issues in optics are discussed in the *Problems* (see below, n. 421), but Galen's reference to 'all your books' may suggest that he does not have anything very specific in mind (unless indeed the rhetorical point is 'if you admit that you are wrong on this, no one will accept your authority anywhere else in the *Problems* either').

[12]   One might rather expect 'and from all such things through which things are seen'.

[13]   Which is a correct statement of the law of reflection on the ray theory.

[14]   A treatise by Alexander, now lost, referred to in his *On the Soul* 43.16, 18. Moraux 2001, 365 n. 216, following Rose, regards the present reference as due to a scholiast rather than to Alexander himself.

[15]   Literally 'by the transparent ... being affected'; and similarly in the next sentence.

is affected by the colour that is seen and imparts this affection to [our] sight, which is also itself transparent. For this is what it is to be transparent. The things that seem to be seen through the bending-back [of visual rays] are seen because the impression of what is seen first comes to be, through the transparent in between, in the mirrors and all the things like them, and then from this comes in turn to [our] sight through the transparent between the mirror and [our] sight. (4) It makes no difference to the argument whether [we] say that the sight, bent back from the mirror by equal angles, whenever what is seen happens to be in the path of [rays] bent back in such a way, falls on it and [so] sees it,[16] or whether we say that the visible thing itself, through being in a certain sort of relation to the mirror, appears in it by the transparent in between being affected, [the mirror] being such as to be able not only to be affected in this way by the colour [of the thing seen], but also to preserve[17] the impression on account of its smoothness and brightness, so that it in turn affects the transparent between itself and [our] vision, as a coloured thing would.

(5) [Therefore Aristotle] uses the theory of rays, as it is agreed and is accepted by the mathematicians. For this reason, as he is going to speak about 'mock suns' and 'rods',[18] and also about the halo and the rainbow, and all of these are seen through reflection and in the manner of reflections in mirrors, he first says [*Meteorology* 3.2.372a30–3], concerning the bending-back, that one should accept from the study of optics 'that our sight is bent back from air and from all things that have a smooth surface, in the way that it is from water'. For it is in that [context] that the account of bending-back is stated by the mathematicians, who say from what things it takes place and in what way, and to things in what positions. (6) But [Aristotle] also [says: 372a33–b6] that since in mirrors that are indivisible to [our] perception[19] only the colours of things that are seen by means of them are reflected, and not also the shapes; for every shape is divisible for perception and has parts that can be distinguished, but such mirrors are indivisible for perception. So, since there must also be a reflection in [such a small mirror] too, since it is a mirror, but it is impossible for the shape to appear in it on account of its smallness, what remains is the colour only. For these [i.e. the colour and the

---

[16] The assumption is that the visual ray proceeds *from* our eyes to the mirror, is bent back there, and so falls upon the object whose reflection we see in the mirror. See the commentary.

[17] Not in the sense of preserving over time, for the reflection disappears when the object that is being reflected is moved away. The point is rather that the appearance as it were *survives* contact with a polished surface in a way that it does not survive contact with a rough one.

[18] Visual phenomena that appear alongside the sun; Aristotle, *Meteorology* 3.6.

[19] I.e. that are so small that our vision is unable to resolve the image of them into several parts.

shape] are the [aspects] of things seen that appear in mirrors. (7) Having said that it is only the colour of the things that are seen that appears in small mirrors, [Aristotle] goes on to speak [372b6–9] about what the colour that appears in mirrors is like. He says that sometimes when it comes from bright things it [too] appears bright, but sometimes, when what is seen is bright, the mirror does not show it like this, but either through the colour from the thing that is seen being mixed with that of the mirror, which is not bright though [the colour of the thing seen] is [so] itself, or through the weakness of the sight that sees it, the appearance of another sort of colour [is perceived] through [the colour of the thing seen]. (8) He says [372b9–11] that the account of these things belongs to that concerning sense perception and has been indicated there. And he says that he has spoken about these things in the [work] entitled *On Sensation and Things Sensed*. For this reason he says that we must make use of some [points] as having been indicated and established, those concerning bending-back, mirrors and colours, but must state others; the latter are the things he proposed [to speak] about.

H. Stobaeus, *Selections* 1.50.3, 473.1–3
(Aëtius 4.8.4, *Dox.* 394b21–5)

According to the Peripatetics [sensation has] four [aspects]: that from which is the ruling principle [of the soul],[20] that through which is the instrument [*organon*] and the sense organ, that according to which is the activity [of the sense organ], that for the sake of which is the object of sensation.

I. Stobaeus, *Selections* 1.50.16, 474.22–3
(Aëtius 4.8.14, *Dox.* 396b8–10)

The Peripatetics [say that] sensations [are] not without assent, but [are] not [themselves] acts of assent.

In his *On the Soul* (2.7) Aristotle explains vision by an instantaneous alteration produced by coloured objects in the intervening transparent medium (air or water) which affects the organ of sight (directly the eye jelly, and thence the primary sense organ in the heart). This theory, as Galen notes in A(2), explains why both vision and illumination are apparently instantaneous. However, unless one assumes that the effect on the medium is for some reason restricted to taking place in a rectilinear fashion, which is

---

[20] *hēgemonikon*, the standard *Stoic* term for the ruling principle in the soul.

certainly not the case with sound or smell, to which Aristotle's account in terms of an effect on a medium might in *this* respect seem more suited,[21] the account of vision in *On the Soul* fails to explain certain obvious facts, for example that we cannot see round corners.[22] In the centuries after Aristotle's death there were considerable advances in the scientific study of optical effects, such as reflection and refraction on the basis of a theory of light travelling in straight lines; and here as elsewhere (above, sections **21** and **25**) Aristotle's followers were confronted with the question how to reconcile his statements with new scientific discoveries.

The situation concerning vision was, however, rather different from that applying in the case of astronomy (**21** above) and animal reproduction (**25**). For in the case of optics Aristotle himself is apparently inconsistent. Alongside the theory of *On the Soul*, there are passages in which he speaks in terms of what is apparently thought of as a visual ray proceeding (as commonly, though not always, in ancient Greek thought) from the eye of the person seeing to the object seen.[23] The term used for this is the non-committal 'sight' (*opsis*), but it seems clear that what is intended is a visual ray, and that it is even sometimes understood as something bodily that can be affected by external forces. It may be that this was an earlier theory which Aristotle himself initially followed but then abandoned[24] – it does after all bear a certain similarity to that of Plato's *Timaeus* 45–6, 67–8; but we have no explicit evidence that it was abandoned, and it continued to be held by members of Aristotle's school.[25]

Galen in **A**(1) cites, in support of Aristotle's *On the Soul* theory, the way in which bright colours can be seen to affect the apparent colour of nearby objects. (It is not clear that the example of the tree is in fact a good one; the foliage of the tree does not so much colour the air beneath it as prevent light of colours other than its own from reaching the person and so contributing to our vision of him. The Atomists explained a similar phenomenon by particles from a coloured awning becoming mingled with those emitted by the people beneath it: Lucretius 4.75–86.) Alexander makes a similar point in **B** and **C**, and Moraux 1984, 757–8 has argued that it is likely that both Alexander and Galen derive from a common source, which must be earlier than the composition of book 7 of Galen's *On the Opinions of Hippocrates*

---

[21] Although in these cases the propagation of the effect is evidently not instantaneous.

[22] Except with the help of suitably placed mirrors: Lucretius 4.302–7.

[23] *Meteorology* 3.4.373a35, 373b3; *On the Heaven* 2.8.290a17–24. Cf. also Theophrastus, *On Dizziness* 7–8 and [Aristotle], *Problems* 3.9, 15.6. Preus 1968, 177–8; Lindberg 1976, 217–18 n. 39; Simon 1988, 49; van der Eijk 1994, 189; A. Jones 1994, especially 60–72; Berryman 1998, 184–6; Sharples 2003a, 217–20.

[24] So Preus and Lindberg cited in the previous note.   [25] See n. 23 above.

and Plato (*c.* AD 169–75) and, since it is defending the theory of Aristotle's *On the Soul*, is likely to be Peripatetic. Given the interest in vision of Alexander's teacher Sosigenes, his *On Vision* (**D**(3)) seems an obvious candidate, but the connection cannot be proved, and Moraux does also suggest as another possible source a commentary on *On the Soul*, now lost, but earlier than Alexander's.

In **E** Galen notes that Aristotle himself, in the *Meteorology*, uses the ray theory (as indeed the phenomena he is considering require) while (as Galen here interprets Aristotle) maintaining that both it and the theory of *On the Soul* are equally able to explain the phenomena. It is important that the point Galen is attributing to Aristotle in **E**(2) is *not* the familiar, and true, one that in a ray theory it makes no difference whether light is thought of as travelling from the object to the viewer or vice versa. Ptolemy believed that the latter was the case, with the consequence that in discussing refraction he uses the terms 'angle of incidence' and 'angle of refraction' in a way that reverses that familiar to us; but this did not have any adverse effect on his experimental investigation of the relation between the two angles for different pairings of transparent media (water, air and glass; cf. Ptolemy, *Optics* 5.8.227.5 Lejeune 1956, and Lloyd 1973, 133–5). Rather, what Galen at least seems to attribute to Aristotle – though whether this is actually a correct reading of *Meteorology* 3 is another matter – is the view that it makes no difference whether [i] our visual ray is reflected, or rather [ii], in accordance with the theory of *On the Soul*, the thing seen affects the medium in the vicinity of the viewer, and it is *this* effect that is then reflected. Galen in effect charges Aristotle with recognising the superiority of [i] in practice, but refusing to admit it in theory.

De Lacy identifies *Meteorology* 3.4.374b22–3 as the passage Galen has in mind in **E**(1). What Aristotle says there is that clouds reflected in water appear darker than when they are looked at directly, because the *opsis* is weakened by the reflection, and that it makes no difference whether the change is in the actual object or in our sight of it. The context refers to objects appearing darker when further away, and Lee in the Loeb edition cites a note in the Oxford translation explaining Aristotle's point as that, even if the clouds are not actually further away, the reflection means that the 'sight' extends over a further distance.[26] This does not seem the same as what Galen attributes to Aristotle in **E**(1). At *On the Soul* 3.12.435a5–10, cited by De Lacy 1980, 472, Aristotle attempts to explain reflection by the effect of a smooth surface on the medium rather than the bending back of a visual

---

[26] So too Alexander in F, commenting on this passage of Aristotle.

ray; but first, this does not seem quite the same as Galen's [ii], and second, Aristotle does not say here that either explanation is equally acceptable.[27] But *Alexander* does in **G**(4), commenting on Aristotle, *Meteorology* 3.2.372a29–b11 (cf. **D**(1)) say that it makes no difference whether we accept the ray theory or the explanation of reflection in Aristotle, *On the Soul* 3.12. In **G**(1) Alexander asserts that Aristotle does not accept the ray theory; in **G**(5) he says that he none the less uses it because 'it is agreed and is accepted by the mathematicians' – a statement which, if we take it to refer to Aristotle's own time rather than to Alexander's, may be anachronistic. Galen's criticism in **E**(1) thus seems to fit Alexander in **G**, even if not perfectly, better than it fits Aristotle himself; and Moraux 1984, 759–60 therefore again suggests that Galen and Alexander are drawing on a single source later than Aristotle himself.

In **H** the 'metaphysics of prepositions' (see above on **12B**) is applied, in a way that incorporates Stoic terminology, to the Peripatetic account of sense perception. In **I** the Peripatetic position is contrasted with the view that all sensation *is* assent, attributed to the Stoics just before in 1.50.14 (474.18–19 Wachsmuth). What is said about the Stoics here is not strictly correct – in the Stoic view sense perception by a rational being, namely a human, produces a rational *impression*, but we have a choice whether to assent to that impression or not (see LS 39–40). Nevertheless, the contrast does reflect, even if inaccurately, the fact that for the Stoics psychological activities in human beings are reducible to reasoning in a way that they are not for Peripatetics; compare **18** above. On the general issue of the place of reason and opinion in sensation see Sorabji 2004, vol. 1 1(a) and 2(a).

---

[27] Where Aristotle does actually say that the ray theory and the theory of *On the Soul* are both equally able to explain the phenomena is at *Generation of Animals* 5.1.781a3–12, in connection with creatures with sunken eyes being able to see better at a distance (De Lacy 1984, 681. I am grateful to Philip van der Eijk for this reference). However, Galen's reference to meteorological phenomena clearly suggests that it is *Meteorology* 3 that he has in mind.

CHAPTER 27

Intellect

A. Alexander of Aphrodisias, reported by Philoponus, On Aristotle's On the Soul 3[1] 15.65–9 Verbeke 1966

Alexander said that Aristotle says that the intellect exists only in potentiality, but in no way in actuality. Since moreover Aristotle accepts, according to Alexander, those who say that the soul is the place of forms, Xenarchus was deceived by these [words] and suspected that Aristotle was saying that prime matter was intellect; [Xenarchus] judged badly [in this].

B. Alexander of Aphrodisias, Supplement to On the Soul (On Intellect) (Mantissa 2).106.19–26

(1) Intellect is according to Aristotle of three [types]. One is material intellect. I say 'material' not because it is something that underlies like matter – for I say 'matter' of something which underlies and is able to become a 'this-something' through the presence of some form. (2) Rather, since matter's being matter [consists] in its having the potentiality for all things, [it follows that] that in which there is potentiality and indeed that which is potential, insofar as it is such, is 'material'. (3) And so the intellect which is not yet thinking but has the potentiality to come to be like this, is 'material', and it is this sort of potentiality of the soul that is the material intellect, not being in actuality any of the extant things, but having the potentiality for becoming all of them, if indeed it is possible for there to be[2] thinking of all the extant things. (Sharples 2004, 24–5)

---

[1] Philoponus' commentary on On the Soul 3 is preserved only in Latin; the text that is extant in Greek is spurious.
[2] Literally: 'to come to be'.

C. Cicero, *On Divination* 1.70–1

(1) I have explained as briefly as possible oracles from a dream and from [prophetic] madness, which I had said do not involve an art. For both of these kinds there is a single reason, which our Cratippus is accustomed to use; [he says that] the minds of human beings are in part drawn and derived from outside (and by this it is understood that there is a divine mind outside us, from which the human [mind] is drawn). (2) Now of the human mind that part which has sensation, movement and appetition is not separate from the action of the body;[3] but the part of the mind which has a share in reason and intelligence is strongest when it is most withdrawn from the body.

(3) And so Cratippus, after setting out examples of prophecies and dreams that came true, used to draw his conclusion as follows: 'if the function and service of the eyes cannot exist without the eyes, and if the eyes sometimes cannot perform their function, the person who has used his eyes even once to see true things is aware that the eyes see true things. (4) In the same way then, if the function and service of divination cannot exist without divination, but someone who has [the power of] divination can sometimes go wrong and see things that are not true, it is sufficient to establish [the existence of true] divination that something should on one occasion have been divined in a way that did not involve any chance coincidence. But there are countless [cases] like this; so we must admit that divination exists.'[4]

D. Cicero, *On Divination* 1.113

The human mind does not ever divine naturally, except when it is so freed and unoccupied that it has absolutely no dealings with the body, and this happens either to prophets or to those who are asleep. And so those two kinds [of natural divination] are approved by Dicaearchus [fr. 31B Mirhady 2001] and, as I said, by our Cratippus.

E. Cicero, *On Divination* 2.100

This argument of the Peripatetics influenced me more [than the super-stitions of the Stoics], both of Dicaearchus [fr. 31C Mirhady 2001] a long

---

[3] This could mean either that it cannot act without the body also acting (cf. Aristotle, *On the Soul* 1.1.403a3), or that it cannot escape being itself acted on (i.e. influenced by) the body.

[4] One may contrast the diametrically opposite argument of Diogenianus in 23W(2) above.

time ago and of Cratippus, who is eminent now. They judge that there is in the minds of human beings a certain oracle, as it were, from which they are aware of future things beforehand, if the mind is moved in a free and unconstrained way either because it is aroused by divine madness or because it is relaxed in sleep.

F.   Cicero, *On Divination* 1.5

From the philosophers certain ingenious arguments have been collected as to why there is truthful divination. Of these, to speak of the earliest, Xenophanes of Colophon is the only one who says that the gods exist but completely rejects divination; all the others, apart from Epicurus, who stutters about the nature of the gods, have shown that divination exists, but not in a single way. Socrates and all his followers, and Zeno and those who take their starting-point from him, continued to hold the opinion of the early philosophers, with the Old Academy and the Peripatetics in agreement; Pythagoras, who even wanted to be a prophet himself, had already previously assigned great authority to this matter, and in very many places Democritus, a weighty author, endorses awareness of the future. But Dicaearchus the Peripatetic [fr. 31A Mirhady 2001] rejected the other types of divination but left those from dreams and [prophetic] madness, and my acquaintance Cratippus, whom I judge the equal of the greatest Peripatetics, trusts the same [types] but rejects the other types of divination.

G.   Pseudo-Plutarch, *Summary on the Opinions of the Philosophers concerning Nature* 5.1 904E (Aëtius 5.1.4, *Dox.* 416a1–5)

Aristotle and Dicaearchus [fr. 30B Mirhady 2001] allow only [divination] due to inspiration, and [prophetic] dreams; they do not think that the soul is immortal, but that it has a share in something divine.

H.   Atticus, fr. 7.13 des Places
(Eusebius, *Preparation for the Gospel* 15.9.13)

What then intellect is in its substance and nature, from where it is and from where it is introduced [*epeiskrinomenos*] into human beings and where again it departs, [Aristotle] himself might know, if he understands anything of what he says about intellect and does not put himself beyond refutation by cloaking himself in the obscurity of his argument, in the way in which cuttlefish make themselves hard to capture by the darkness [of their ink].

I. Alexander of Aphrodisias, *Supplement to* On the Soul (*On Intellect*) (*Mantissa* 2).112.5–113.6

(1) He wanted to show that the intellect is immortal, and to avoid the difficulties which they bring against the 'intellect from without', which must necessarily change its place but cannot, if it is incorporeal, either be in place or change its place and be in different places at different times. (2) So, following his own individual idea, he said things like the following about the intellect that was said to be in every mortal body. He said that intellect is in matter as one substance in another substance and [is so] in actuality and always performs its own activities. (3) When, from the body that was blended, there comes to be fire or something of this sort as the result of the mixture, which is able to provide an instrument for this intellect, which is in this mixture – for it is in every body, and this too is a body – then this instrument is said to be intellect potentially, supervening on this sort of blending of bodies as a suitable potentiality for receiving the intellect that is in actuality. (4) When [the intellect that is in actuality] takes hold of this instrument, then it is active as through an instrument and in relation to matter and through matter, and then we are said to think. For our intellect is composed of the potentiality, which is the instrument of the divine intellect [and] which Aristotle calls intellect in potentiality, and of the activity of that [divine intellect]. And if either of these is not present it is impossible for us to think.

(5) For straight away, at the first depositing of the seed, the intellect which is in actuality is there, going through all things and being [there] in actuality, as also in any other body whatsoever. But when it is also active through our potentiality, then this is said to be our intellect and we think; just as if someone thought of a craftsman who sometimes is active in accordance with his craft without instruments, and sometimes with instruments when his activity in accordance with the craft is in relation to the matter. (6) In the same way the divine intellect, too, is always active – which is why it is in actuality – and it [is also active] through an instrument when, from the combination of bodies and their satisfactory blending, an instrument of this sort comes to be. For then [the divine intellect] is active with a certain activity involving matter, and this is our intellect.

(7) And it departs in the [same] way as it enters [*eiskrinetai*]. It does not change place being somewhere else but, since it is everywhere, it remains

also in the body, which is broken up as a result of its departure, [though] the instrumental [intellect] is destroyed; just as the craftsman who has cast away his instruments is active then too, but with an activity which is not concerned with matter or by means of instruments.

(8) So, he said that, if one should suppose that intellect is divine and imperishable according to Aristotle at all, one must consider [that it is so] in this way, and not otherwise. (9) And, fitting the passage in the third book of [Aristotle's] *On the Soul* to this [theory], he said that both the 'disposition' and the 'light' must be applied to this [intellect] that is everywhere. (Sharples 2004, 38–42)

J. Alexander of Aphrodisias, *Supplement to* On the Soul (*On Intellect*) (*Mantissa* 2).113.18–24

(1) Rather, what comes to be in something through being an object of intellect does not change place. For neither do the forms of things perceived by the senses come to be in the sense organs as their *places* when we perceive them. (2) The intellect from outside is called 'separate' and is separated from us not as going away somewhere and changing its place; rather, it is separate because it exists in itself and without matter, and it is separated from us by not being intelligised, not by going away. For that is how it came to be in us, too. (Sharples 2004, 44)

K. Anonymous interpreter[5] reported by Alexander of Aphrodisias, *Supplement to* On the Soul (*On Intellect*) (*Mantissa* 2).110.4–25

(1) I also heard, about the intellect from without from Aristotle, [things] which I preserved:

(2) The things that prompted Aristotle to introduce the intellect from without were said to be these: the analogy from things perceptible by the senses, and that applying to all things that come to be. For in all things that come to be there is something that is affected, something that produces, and thirdly, from both of these, what comes to be. It is similar in the case of sensible things; for what is affected is the sense organ, what produces is the sensible [object], and what comes to be is the apprehending of the sensible thing through the sense organ. (3) In the same way in the case of the intellect too [Aristotle] supposed that there must be some productive intellect, which

---

[5] See the commentary.

would be able to lead the potential and material intellect to actuality; and actuality is making intelligible to itself all the extant things. For as there are sensible things which are themselves in actuality and produce sensation in actuality, so there must also be things which produce intellect, being intelligible in actuality themselves. For it is not possible for anything to be productive of anything if it is not itself in actuality.

(4) But none of these things which are thought by us is intelligible in actuality. For our intellect thinks the sensible things which are intelligible potentially, and these are made intelligible by the intellect. For this is the activity of intellect, by its own power to separate and abstract the things which are sensible in actuality from those things in the company of which they are sensible, and to define [them] in themselves. (5) If then this is the activity of the intellect that previously existed potentially, and what is brought to be and is led from potentiality to actuality must be brought to be by something that exists in actuality, there must also be some productive intellect which exists in actuality and will make that, which at one time existed potentially, able to be active and to think. And this is what the [intellect] that comes in from outside is like. These then are the things that prompted [Aristotle]. (Sharples 2004, 32–4)

Aristotle in *On the Soul* 3.4.429a18–29 argues that intellect has no bodily organ. For intellect's thinking, like the senses' perceiving, involves taking on the form of the object thought or sensed, without the matter. The organ of sight, for example, has matter – transparent matter – which is suited to the range of things we can see, namely colours. But since we are able to think of every sort of thing, intellect itself must have no material component, as this would limit the range of things of which we can think.

Xenarchus (above, 1EI), according to **A**, was led by this to identify intellect with prime matter. Philoponus' source for this statement was Alexander, and in **B** Alexander[6] takes care to point out that intellect is like matter in its potentiality, rather than itself being identified with matter. It is a reasonable supposition (made by Accattino 2001, 39) that Alexander is here guarding against the error which he himself reported in Xenarchus. (For the background of the concept of material intellect see further Accattino and Donini 1996, 271, and on **A** see Moraux 1973, 207–8.)

---

[6] I am here assuming, partly in order to clarify what is necessarily an already complex exposition, that *On Intellect* (*Mantissa* 2) as we have it, though clearly a combination of originally different elements, is all in some sense due to – i.e. written by, or reported by – Alexander himself. But this is disputed. See the next note.

Alexander in *On Intellect* (= *Supplement to* On the Soul (*Mantissa*) 2) and also in his own treatise *On the Soul* interprets Aristotle, *On the Soul* 3.5 in terms of an active, divine intellect, itself pure actuality, which is required if each individual human's intellect is to develop to (first) actuality. So Philoponus' statement in **A** that for Alexander himself intellect is only potential, and not actual, must therefore be understood as relating only to the individual human intellect in its initial condition, not actually thinking of anything, or to the individual human intellect as it is in its own nature; where Aristotle (*On the Soul* 3.4.430a1) compares the latter to a blank writing tablet, Alexander went one better and compared it to the *blankness of* a blank writing tablet (Alexander, *On the Soul* 84.24–7).

Since intellect has no bodily organ, Aristotle argues that it cannot, like other soul faculties be transmitted to the foetus in the father's seed, even as a potentiality, and must therefore be divine and come 'from outside': 'So it remains that intellect alone enters from outside [*thurathen*] and is alone divine; for bodily activity has no share in [intellect's] activity' (*Generation of Animals* 2.3.736b27–9). It is possible, as Moraux 1973, 231 suggests, that this phrase influenced Cratippus (above, 1EJJKLM) in **C**(1). Cratippus, according to Cicero in **C**(1)–(2) and **DE**, explained prophetic dreams and prophetic madness in terms of the mind (*animus*) being separate from the body. (**C**(3)–(4) is repeated and challenged at Cicero, *On Divination* 2.107–9.) On this basis, Cicero says (**F**, cf. **CDE**), Cratippus rejected 'artificial' divination, the observation of supposed correlations between certain events (such as the flight of birds, or the state of a sacrificed animal's liver) and future events, which was endorsed by the Stoics (LS 42CE), but accepted the 'natural' divination thought to involve direct awareness of the future. Aëtius, reported by pseudo-Plutarch in **G**, attributes a similar view to Dicaearchus and also to Aristotle himself but couples it with their denial of the immortality of the soul.

It is not entirely clear whether what Cicero attributes to Cratippus is to be understood in terms of spatial separation – 'psychic excursions', to use Dodds' term (1951, 141) – or simply in terms of the mind's not being preoccupied with the body. Cicero in **DEF** couples Cratippus with the early Peripatetic Dicaearchus, which is problematic since Dicaearchus adopted a theory of the soul as a harmony of the bodily elements; see above on **24O**, and Sharples 2001a. Aristotle himself in his surviving works gives some recognition to divination in sleep, but sees this as a *sub*-rational functioning of the soul (*On Divination through Sleep* 2.463b14–22; cf. van der Eijk 1994, 91 and 293–5; 2005, 186–201, 238–58). However, in *On Philosophy*, fr. 10 Rose 1886 (Sextus Empiricus, *Math.* 9.20–2, cf. van der

Eijk 1994, 60 n. 43) Aristotle not only says that 'when the soul comes to be on its own in sleep, then it gets back its own proper nature and divines and foretells the future' but also compares this with the notion that those at the point of death can foresee the deaths of others, explaining that the soul 'is also like this when undergoing separation from the body in death'. The fact that the soul is spoken of only as *undergoing* separation, in the present tense, may suggest that what is at issue is a lessening of the connection between the soul and a body in which it is still located, rather than its already travelling elsewhere, though it is possible that it might be thought of as partly still in the body and partly elsewhere. Glucker 1999, 40–2 interprets both the Aristotle fragment and C(2) in this way, and suggests that in the latter the soul, when freed from the body, 'communes again with the divine mind outside the body'.

The idea that mind or soul came to humans from elsewhere, and specifically that it had a connection with the divine heavens, was a widespread one; compare for example Pindar, fr. 116 Bowra = fr. 131b Maehler: 'Everyone's body encounters mighty death, but an image of life is left alive. It alone is from the gods; it sleeps when the limbs are active, but to those who are asleep it reveals in many dreams the approaching determining of joyful and difficult [fortunes]'; Macrobius, *On the Dream of Scipio* 14.19 (22A15 DK; see KRS p. 205): '(Heraclitus said that the soul is) a spark of the essential substance of the stars'; the epitaph on the Athenian dead at Potidaea in 432 BC (IG^2 1.945.6, KRS 222): 'The *aithēr* has received their souls, <the earth> their bodies'; Aristophanes, *Peace* 832–3: 'So isn't it even true then what they say, that we become stars in the sky when we die?'; also above, **24ABCDEF**. Aristotle's 'from outside' (above) was, however, the specific basis of a later controversy. For the Platonist Atticus, whom we have seen attacking Aristotelian doctrines elsewhere (**22N, 23O**, and perhaps **24Aa(5)**), objected, against Aristotle's theory, that if intellect was incorporeal it could not move from one place to another and so could not 'come from outside' (**H**, cf. **I(1)**). In response to Atticus – for Rashed 1997, 194 draws attention to the coincidence in vocabulary between **H** (*epeiskrinomenos*) and **I(7)** (*eiskrinetai*) – an unidentified author (henceforth referred to as Anonymous₁), earlier than Alexander and reported by him in **I**, suggested that divine intellect is always present everywhere in the world, and that its becoming active in us does not therefore involve spatial movement at all; rather, when and where there is an instrument – the human potential intellect – fitted for its use, it operates through this in a particular way, but elsewhere and at other times it just 'performs its own activities' (**I(2)**). This theory at first sight seems reminiscent of Stoic pantheism (LS 46A, 47O, 54B), but with the important difference that there is no suggestion that the divine intellect in question is corporeal, though it is spatially extended. The idea in I(4) that our intellect is a *combination* of the active or productive intellect on the one hand, and of the potential intellect on the other, goes back to Theophrastus (320A FHS&G; Sorabji 2004, vol. 1 3(g)(2)). As Alexander objects in 22F(4) above, it is at least questionable whether the theory in I can be said to provide an account of *our* thinking at all, rather than of god's thinking through us; there is also no suggestion in it, by contrast with other theories to which we will come, that the divine intellect in any way acts on or transforms our intellect from a potential to an actual state – it simply *uses* it. And it is left unclear exactly what the activities are that the divine intellect performs when not operating through human intellects. Rejecting Anonymous₁'s theory, Alexander gives his own solution to the apparent problem of intellect's motion in J, to which there is a parallel in the fragments of Alexander's *Physics* commentary: see Rashed 1997, and Sorabji 2004, vol. 1 218.

Accattino 2001, 14–15 has suggested that *On Intellect*, as we have it, is a combination of several early compositions by Alexander;[7] Rashed 1997, 194 has shown that I and J are earlier than Alexander's commentary on the problem of incorporeal things moving in *Physics* 6.4.234b10–20. Anonymous₁ is therefore earlier in date than Alexander; but he remains unidentified, for I starts abruptly, without even a connecting particle. I follows directly on Alexander's own development of the interpretation of Aristotle that he reports in K, and it has sometimes been supposed that I and K reflect the views of the same person. But the theory in I and that in K are so different that it is hardly plausible to suppose that they were advanced by the same person, even though this has sometimes been suggested in the past (see Sharples 2004, 38 n. 92, and further references there).

Alexander further reports in I(9) that Anonymous₁ connected his theory with Aristotle, *On the Soul* 3.5. This report is the more likely to be authentic because, while Anonymous₁ correctly notes that Aristotle in that passage applies the term *hexis*, state or condition, to the active or productive intellect,[8] Alexander himself, in developing the theory reported in K below, applies *hexis* rather to the state of the individual potential intellect

---

[7] Schroeder 1997, and Schroeder and Todd: 2008, however, argue that the first part of *On Intellect*, preceding K below, and the development that follows K, show the influence of Plotinus and are therefore much later. However, what is of primary importance in the present context is that Anonymous₁, whose views are reported in I, does seem earlier in date than Alexander; Rashed's argument, in the text above, indicates this, and there is nothing in Anonymous₁'s theory to suggest a later date.

[8] 'Since in all nature there is on the one hand matter in each kind – this is what is all these things potentially – and different from this [that which is] the cause and agent, by making everything – and this is the relation of art [*tekhnē*] to matter – it is necessary that these distinctions should be present in

once it has become capable of actual thought (Alexander, *On the Soul* 86.16; *On Intellect* (*Mantissa* 2).107.29–34, 111.29–34).

Alexander's account of Anonymous₁'s theory continues, after **I**, with a series of possibilities for the way in which the omnipresent divine intellect might govern the universe (above, **22F**(1)–(2)). It is not clear how far this range of options represents Anonymous₁'s own views, and how far it is rather that Alexander himself has tried to read a theory of divine providence into Anonymous₁'s theory; the emphasis on the influence of the heavens is in accordance with Alexander's own (later?) theory of divine providence (above, on **22TU**), and, while providence was another issue on which Atticus had attacked the Peripatetics (**22N**), it has little *direct* connection with the issue of mind's spatial movement from which **I** takes its starting-point. For Alexander's criticism of the theory of providence which he attributes to Anonymous₁, see **22F**(3).

Aristotle, *On the Soul* 3.5, along with the view in *Generation of Animals* 2.3 that intellect comes 'from outside', is the starting-point for a further theory of intellect reported by Alexander, that in **K**. On the strength of **K**(1) this theory has been attributed, by Moraux 1967 and 1985, followed by Accattino and Donini 1996, xxvii and Accattino 2001, 13–15, to Alexander's teacher Aristoteles of Mytilene (above, **1Z**, **1Aa**). It may, however, be that **K**(1), like **K**(2), is simply referring to Aristotle himself (so Moraux 1942, 148; Thillet 1984, xi–xxxi, especially xv–xix; Schroeder and Todd 1990, 23–4, 28–31, and 2008;[9] Opsomer and Sharples 2000), and in that case the identity of the person who advanced the theory reported in **K** – let us call him Anonymous₂ – remains unknown. Anonymous₂'s theory, unlike Anonymous₁'s, shares important features with the views that Alexander himself was to develop; indeed, whereas **I** is followed by Alexander's *rebuttal* in **22F**(3)–(4) and his own alternative solution in **J** here, **K** is followed rather by his *development* of what his predecessor had said (*On Intellect* 110.25–112.5). Anonymous₂'s theory shares with Alexander's own, in *On Intellect* 107.29–34, 111.29–34, the view that the productive intellect of *On the Soul* 3.5 acts *on the potential intellect* – which is not a *necessary* reading of what Aristotle says there – in order to bring it to a state where it is capable of independent thought.

On the issues raised in this section see further Sharples 2007d, 615–20.

---

the soul too; and one sort of intellect is like this by becoming everything, the other *by making everything, as a certain disposition, like light*; for in a way light makes the colours that are potentially, colours in actuality.' (Aristotle, *On the Soul* 3.5.430a10–17).

[9] Schroeder and Todd however argue, against Opsomer and Sharples, that the text in **K**(1) requires emendation.

Bibliography

For editions of ancient texts see also the Index of sources and the Index of passages cited.

Accattino, P. 1985. 'Alessandro di Afrodisia e Aristotele di Mitilene', *Elenchos* 6: 67–74.
  1988. 'Alessandro di Afrodisia e la trasmissione della forma nella riproduzione animale', *AAT* 122: 79–94.
  2001. *Alessandro di Afrodisia:* De Intellectu. Turin.
Accattino, P. and Donini, P. L. 1996. *Alessandro di Afrodisia: L'anima.* Rome and Bari.
Algra, K., Barnes, J., Mansfeld, J. and Schofield, M. (eds.) 1999. *The Cambridge History of Hellenistic Philosophy.* Cambridge.
Alberti, A. 1999. 'Il volontario e la scelta in Aspasio', in Alberti and Sharples (eds.): 107–41.
Alberti, A. and Sharples, R. W. (eds.) (1999) *Aspasius: the Earliest Extant Commentary on Aristotle's* Ethics. Berlin.
Amand de Mendieta, E. 1973. *Fatalisme et liberté dans l'antiquité grecque.* Amsterdam. Reprint of the original edition as D. Amand. Louvain, 1945 (Recueil de travaux d'histoire et de philologie, sér. 3, fasc. 19).
Anscombe, G. E. M. and Geach, P. T. 1961. *Three Philosophers: Aristotle, Aquinas, Frege.* Oxford.
Barnes, J. 1997. 'Roman Aristotle', in *Philosophia Togata,* vol. II: *Plato and Aristotle at Rome,* ed. J. Barnes and M. Griffin, Oxford: 1–69.
  1999. 'An introduction to Aspasius', in Alberti and Sharples (eds.): 1–50.
  2002. 'Ancient philosophers', in *Philosophy and Power in the Graeco-Roman World,* ed. G. Clark and T. Rajak, Oxford: 293–306.
  2005. 'Les *Catégories* et les catégories', in *Les Catégories et leur histoire,* ed. O. Bruun and L. Corti, Paris: 11–80.
  2007a. 'Peripatetic epistemology: 100 BC – AD 200', in Sorabji and Sharples (eds.): 547–62.
  2007b. 'Peripatetic logic: 100 BC – AD 200', in Sorabji and Sharples (eds.): 531–46.
Barnes, J., Bobzien, S., Flannery, K. and Ierodiakonou, K. (tr.) 1991. *Alexander of Aphrodisias: On Aristotle's* Prior Analytics *1.1–7*. London.
Beatrice, P. F. 2005. 'L'union de l'âme et du corps: Némésius d'Émèse lecteur de Porphyre', in *Les Pères de l'Église face à la science médicale de leur temps,* ed. V. Boudon-Millot and B. Pouderon, Paris: 253–85.

Berryman, S. 1998. 'Euclid and the sceptic: a paper on vision, doubt, geometry, light and drunkenness', *Phronesis* 43: 176–96.

Berti, E. 1997. 'Da chi è amato il motore immobile? Su Aristotele, *Metaph*. XII 6–7', *Méthexis* 10: 59–82.

2000. 'Unmoved mover(s) as efficient cause(s) in *Metaphysics* Λ 6', in Frede and Charles (eds.): 181–206.

Blumenthal, H. J. 1996. *Aristotle and Neoplatonism in Late Antiquity*. London.

Bobzien, S. 1998a. *Determinism and Freedom in Stoic Philosophy*. Oxford.

1998b. 'The inadvertent conception and late birth of the free-will problem', *Phronesis* 43: 133–75.

2000. 'Did Epicurus discover the free will problem?', *OSAPh* 19: 287–337.

Bodéüs, R. 1992. *Aristote et la théologie des vivants immortels*. St-Laurent, Québec and Paris.

1995. 'L'influence historique du stoïcisme sur l'interprétation de l'oeuvre philosophique d'Aristote', *RSPh* 79: 553–86.

Bodnár, I. M. 1997. 'Alexander of Aphrodisias on celestial motions', *Phronesis* 42: 190–205.

Bos, A. P. 2001. 'Aristotle's *De anima* II.1: the traditional interpretation rejected', in *Aristotle and Contemporary Science*, ed. D. Sfendoni-Mentzou, D. Johnson and J. Hattiangadi, New York: vol. II 187–201.

2003. *The Soul and its Instrumental Body: a Reinterpretation of Aristotle's Philosophy of Living Nature*. Leiden.

2007. 'The "vehicle of the soul" and the debate over the origin of this concept', *Philologus* 151: 31–50.

Bouyges, M. (ed.) 1952. *Averroes: Tafsīr mā ba'd at-tabī'at*. Beirut.

Boys-Stones, G. R. 2001. *Post-Hellenistic Philosophy*. Oxford.

Brandt, S. and Laubmann, G. 1893. *L. Caeli Firmiani Lactanti opera omnia*, vol. II. Vienna.

Brentano, F. 1977. *The Psychology of Aristotle*, ed. and tr. R. George. Berkeley. (Originally published as *Die Psychologie des Aristoteles*. Mainz, 1867.)

Broadie, S. 1993. 'Que fait le premier moteur d'Aristote?', *RPhilos* 183: 375–411.

Brunschwig, J. 2000. 'Metaphysics Λ 9: a short-lived thought-experiment?', in Frede and Charles (eds.): 275–306.

Buecheler, F. 1908. 'Prosopographica', *RhM* 63: 190.

Bussemaker, U. C. (ed.) 1857. *Aristoteles, Opera omnia*, vol. IV.1. Paris.

Caston, V. 1997. 'Epiphenomenalisms: ancient and modern', *PhR* 106: 309–63.

Chaniotis, A. 2004. 'Epigraphic evidence for the philosopher Alexander of Aphrodisias', *BICS* 47: 79–81.

Chase, M. 2003. *Simplicius, On Aristotle* Categories *1–4*. London.

Chiaradonna, R. 2005. 'Plotino e la corrente antiaristotelica del Platonismo imperiale: analogie e differenze', in *L'eredità Platonica: studi sul Platonismo da Arcesilao a Proclo*, ed. M. Bonazzi and V. Celluprica, Naples: 235–74.

Chiesara, M. L. 2001. *Aristocles of Messene*. Oxford.

Colson, F. H. (ed.) 1937. *Philo*, vol. VII. Cambridge, MA and London (Loeb Classical Library).

Colson, F. H. and Whitaker, G. H. (eds.) 1929. *Philo*, vol. II. Cambridge, MA and London (Loeb Classical Library).

Cooke, H. P., and Tredennick, H. (eds.) 1938. *Aristotle:* Categories, On Interpretation, Prior Analytics. Cambridge, MA and London (Loeb Classical Library).

Cooper, J. M. and Procopé, J. F. 1995. *Seneca: Moral and Political Essays.* Cambridge.

Corcoran, T. H. (ed.) 1971–72. *Seneca:* Naturales Quaestiones. London and Cambridge, MA (Loeb Classical Library).

De Lacy, P. 1958. '*Ou Mallon* and the antecedents of ancient scepticism', *Phronesis* 3: 59–71.

   (ed.) 1980. *Galenus:* De Placitis Hippocratis et Platonis, *CMG* vol. v.4.1, part 2. Berlin.

   (ed.) 1984. *Galenus:* De Placitis Hippocratis et Platonis, *CMG* vol. V.4.1, part 3. Berlin.

   (ed.) 1992. *Galenus:* De Semine, *CMG* vol. v.3.1. Berlin.

Des Places, E. (ed.) 1977. *Atticus: Fragments.* Paris.

Dillon, J. 1983. '*Metriopatheia* and *apatheia:* some reflections on a controversy in later Greek ethics', in *Essays in Ancient Greek Philosophy*, vol. II, ed. J. P. Anton and A. Preus, Albany, NY: 508–17.

   (tr.) 1990. *Dexippus: On Aristotle:* Categories. London.

   1996. *The Middle Platonists*, 2nd edn. London.

   2003. *The Heirs of Plato.* Oxford.

Dodds, E. R. 1951. *The Greeks and the Irrational.* Berkeley.

Donini, P. L. 1971. 'L'anima e gli elementi nel *De Anima* di Alessandro di Afrodisia', *AAT* 105: 61–107.

   1974. *Tre studi sull' aristotelismo nel II secolo d.C.* Turin.

   1977. 'Stoici e megarici nel *De fato* di Alessandro di Afrodisia?', in *Scuole socratiche minori e filosofia ellenistica*, ed. G. Giannantoni, Bologna: 174–94.

   1982. *Le scuole, l'anima, l'impero.* Turin.

   1987. 'Aristotelismo e indeterminismo in Alessandro di Afrodisia', in *Aristoteles: Werk und Wirkung, Paul Moraux gewidmet*, ed. J. Wiesner, Berlin: vol. II 72–89.

   1995. *La metafisica di Aristotele: introduzione alla lettura.* Rome.

   2002. 'Il libro Lambda della *Metafisica* e la nascità della filosofia prima', *Rivista di storia della filosofia* 2: 181–99.

Dooley, W. E. and Madigan, A. (tr.) 1992. *Alexander of Aphrodisias, on Aristotle* Metaphysics *2 and 3.* London.

Dörrie, H. 1959. *Porphyrios' 'Symmikta Zêtêmata'.* Munich.

Drossaart-Lulofs, H. J. (ed.) 1965. *Nicolaus Damascenus* On the Philosophy of Aristotle. Leiden.

Düring, I. 1957. *Aristotle in the Ancient Biographical Tradition.* Göteborg and Stockholm.

Eijk, P. J. van der (tr.) 1994. *Aristoteles*, De Insomniis, De Divinatione per Somnum. Berlin.

2005. *Medicine and Philosophy in Classical Antiquity*. Cambridge.

Ellis, J. 1994. 'Alexander's defense of Aristotle's categories', *Phronesis* 39: 69–89.

Falcon, A. 2008. 'The pre-history of the commentary tradition: Aristotelianism in the first century BCE', *LThPh* 64: 7–18.

Fazzo, S. 2002a. *Aporia e sistema: la materia, la forma, il divino nelle Quaestiones di Alessandro di Afrodisia*. Pisa.

2002b. 'Alexandre d'Aphrodise contre Galien: la naissance d'une légende', *Philosophie Antique: Problèmes, Renaissances, Usages* 2: 109–44.

2005. 'Aristotelismo e antideterminismo nella vita e nell'opera di Tito Aurelio Alessandro di Afrodisia', in *La catena delle cause: determinismo e antideterminismo nel pensiero antico e in quello contemporaneo*, ed. C. Natali and S. Maso, Amsterdam: 269–95.

2008. 'Nicolas, l'auteur du *Sommaire de la philosophie d'Aristote:* doutes sur son identité, sa datation, son origine', *REG* 121: 99–126.

Fazzo, S. and Zonta, M. (eds.) 1998. *Alessandro d'Afrodisia, Sulla Provvidenza*. Milan.

Flannery, K. L. 1995. *Ways into the Logic of Alexander of Aphrodisias*. Leiden.

Flashar, H. (tr.) 1991. *Aristoteles:* Problemata Physika, 4th edn. Berlin.

Fleet, B. (tr.) 2002. *Simplicius, On Aristotle*, Categories 7–8. London.

Fortenbaugh, W. W. (ed.) 1983a. *On Stoic and Peripatetic Ethics: the Work of Arius Didymus* (*RUSCH* 1). New Brunswick, NJ.

1983b. 'Arius, Theophrastus, and the *Eudemian Ethics*', in Fortenbaugh (ed.): 203–23.

1984. *Quellen zur Ethik Theophrasts*. Amsterdam.

2005. *Theophrastus of Eresus: Sources for his Life, Writings, Thought and Influence, Commentary*, vol. VIII: *Sources on Rhetoric and Poetics*. Leiden.

Fortenbaugh, W. W. and Schütrumpf, E. (eds.) 2001. *Dicaearchus of Messana* (*RUSCH* 10). New Brunswick, NJ.

Fotinis, A. P. (tr.) 1979. *The* De Anima *of Alexander of Aphrodisias*. Washington, DC.

Frede, D. and Laks, A. (eds.) 2002. *Traditions of Theology: Studies in Hellenistic Theology, its Background and Aftermath*. Leiden.

Frede, M. 1980. 'The original notion of cause', in *Doubt and Dogmatism*, ed. M. Schofield, M. Burnyeat and J. Barnes, Oxford: 217–49. Reprinted in M. Frede, *Essays in Ancient Philosophy*, Oxford, 1987: 125–50.

1999. 'Epilogue', in K. Algra *et al.* (eds.): 771–97.

2000. 'Introduction', in Frede and Charles (eds.): 1–52.

Frede, M. and Charles, D. (eds.) 2000. *Aristotle's Metaphysics Lambda*. Oxford.

Furley, D. J. (tr.) 1955. 'Aristotle, *On the Cosmos*', in *Aristotle*, On Sophistical Refutations, On Coming-to-be and Passing Away, tr. E. S. Forster; On the Cosmos, tr. D. J. Furley. London and Cambridge, MA (Loeb Classical Library).

1983. 'Comments on Dr Sharples' paper: a note on Arius and *Magna Moralia* 1.1–2', in Fortenbaugh (ed.): 160–4.

Gaskin, R. (tr.) 2000. *Simplicius: On Aristotle* Categories 9–15. London.

Genequand, C. (tr.) 1984. *Ibn Rushd's Metaphysics: a Translation with Introduction of Ibn Rushd's Commentary on Aristotle's* Metaphysics, *Book Lam*. Leiden.

   2001. *Alexander of Aphrodisias* On the Cosmos. Leiden.

Giusta, M. 1961–2. 'Sul significato filosofico del termine προηγούμενος', *AAT* 96: 229–71.

   1964–7. *I dossografi di etica*, 2 vols. Turin.

Glibert-Thirry, A. (ed.) 1977. *Pseudo-Andronicus de Rhodes; édition critique du texte grec et de la traduction latine médiévale*. Leiden.

Glucker, J. 1998. 'Theophrastus, the Academy, and the Athenian philosophical atmosphere', in *Theophrastus: Reappraising the Sources*, ed. J. M. van Ophuijsen and M. van Raalte (*RUSCH* 8). New Brunswick, NJ: 299–316.

   1999. 'A Platonic cento in Cicero', *Phronesis* 44: 30–44.

Göransson, T. 1995. *Albinus, Alcinous, Arius Didymus*. Göteborg.

Görgemanns, H. 1983. '*Oikeiōsis* in Arius Didymus', in Fortenbaugh (ed.): 165–89.

Gottschalk, H. B. 1986. 'Boethus' Psychology and the Neoplatonists', *Phronesis* 31: 243–57.

   1987. 'Aristotelian philosophy in the Roman world', *ANRW* II.36.2, 1079–1174.

   1993. 'Towards a prehistory of the "fourth" syllogistic figure', in *Tria lustra: Essays and Notes Presented to John Pinsent*, ed. H. D. Jocelyn and H. Hurt, Liverpool: 59–70.

Goulet, R. (ed.) 1989–. *Dictionnaire des philosophes antiques*. Paris.

Graver, M. 2002. *Cicero on the Emotions: Tusculan Disputations 3 and 4*. Chicago.

   2007. *Stoicism and Emotion*. Chicago.

Grilli, A. 1969. 'Contributo alla storia di προηγούμενος', in *Studi linguistici in onore di V. Pisani*, ed. G. Bolognesi, Brescia: 409–500.

Guthrie W. K. C. (tr.) 1939. *Aristotle:* On the Heavens. London and Cambridge, MA (Loeb Classical Library).

Hahm, D. E. 1983. 'The diaeretic method and the purpose of Arius' doxography', in Fortenbaugh (ed.): 15–37.

   2006. 'In search of Aristo of Ceos', in *Aristo of Ceos*, ed. W. W. Fortenbaugh and S. A. White (*RUSCH* 13). New Brunswick, NJ: 179–215.

   2007. 'Critolaus and late Hellenistic Peripatetic philosophy', in *Pyrrhonists, Patricians, Platonizers: Hellenistic Philosophy in the Period 155–86 BC*, ed. A. M. Ioppolo and D. Sedley, Naples: 47–101.

De Haas, F. A. J., and Fleet, B. (trs.) 2001. *Simplicius: On Aristotle* Categories *5–6*. London.

Hankinson, R. J. (tr.) 2002. *Simplicius: On Aristotle's* On the Heavens *1.1–4*. London.

Hense, O. (ed.) 1894. *Ioannis Stobaei Anthologii libri duo posteriores*. Berlin.

Huby, P. M. 1981. 'An excerpt from Boethus of Sidon's commentary on the Categories?', *CQ* 31: 398–409.

   1983. 'Peripatetic definitions of happiness', in Fortenbaugh (ed.): 121–34.

   1989. 'Cicero's *Topics* and its Peripatetic sources', in *Cicero's Knowledge of the Peripatos*, ed. W. W. Fortenbaugh and P. Steinmetz (*RUSCH* 4), New Brunswick, NJ: 61–76.

1999. *Theophrastus of Eresus: Sources for his Life, Writings, Thought and Influence, Commentary*, vol. IV: *Psychology*. Leiden.

Huffman, C. A. 2005. *Archytas of Tarentum*. Cambridge.

Hussey, E. (tr.) 1983. *Aristotle's* Physics *Books III and IV*. Oxford.

Ierodiakonou, K. 1999. 'Aspasius on perfect and imperfect virtues', in Alberti and Sharples (eds.): 142–61.

Inwood, B. 1983. 'Comments on Professor Görgemanns' paper: the two forms of *oikeiōsis* in Arius and the Stoa', in Fortenbaugh (ed.): 190–201.

(ed.) 2007a. *Seneca: Selected Philosophical Letters*, Oxford.

2007b. 'Seneca, Plato and Platonism: the case of *Letter 65*', in *Platonic Stoicism –Stoic Platonism*, ed. M. Bonazzi and C. Helmig, Leuven: 149–67.

Isnardi Parente, M. 1990. 'Diogeniano, gli epicurei e la *tukhē*', in *ANRW* II.36.4, 2424–45.

Jones, A. 1994. 'Peripatetic and Euclidean theories of the visual ray,' *Physis* 31: 47–76.

Jones, H. L. (tr.) 1932. *The Geography of Strabo*, vol. VIII. Cambridge, MA and London (Loeb Classical Library).

Judson, L. 1994. 'Heavenly motion and the unmoved mover', in *Self-motion from Aristotle to Newton*, ed. M. L. Gill and J. G. Lennox, Princeton, NJ: 155–71.

Kapetanaki, S. and Sharples, R. W. (eds.) 2006. *Pseudo-Aristoteles (Pseudo-Alexander): Problemata Alexandri Aphrodisiei*. Berlin.

Karamanolis, G. E. 2006. *Plato and Aristotle in Agreement?* Oxford.

2007. 'Porphyry's notion of *empsuchia*', in Karamanolis and Sheppard (eds.): 91–109.

Karamanolis, G. E. and Sheppard, A. (eds.) 2007. *Studies on Porphyry* (*BICS* supplement 98). London.

Kenny, A. 1978. *The Aristotelian Ethics*. Oxford.

Kidd, I. G. 1986. 'Posidonian methodology and the self-sufficiency of virtue', in *Aspects de la philosophie hellénistique*, ed. H. Flashar and O. Gigon, Geneva: 1–21.

1992. 'Theophrastus' *Meteorology*, Aristotle and Posidonius', in *Theophrastus: His Psychological, Doxographical and Scientific Writings*, ed. W. W. Fortenbaugh and D. Gutas (*RUSCH* 5). New Brunswick, NJ: 294–306.

Kneale, W. and Kneale, M. 1962. *The Development of Logic*. Oxford.

Konstan, D. (tr.) 2006. *Aspasius: On Aristotle,* Nicomachean Ethics *1–4, 7–8*. London.

Laks, A. 2000. '*Metaphysics* Λ 7', in Frede and Charles (eds.): 207–243.

Lang, H. S. 1993. 'The structure and subject of Metaphysics Λ', *Phronesis* 38: 257–80.

Lautner, P. 1997. 'λέγει oder λήγει? Amelios und Sosikrates(?) bei *Timaios* 37a6–7 (bei Proklos, *In Tim.* II.300.23–301.5 Diehl)', *Hermes* 125: 294–308.

Lejeune, A. (ed.) 1956. *L'optique de Claude Ptolémée dans la version latine d'après l'arabe de l'émir Eugène de Sicile*. Louvain.

Lennox, J. G. 1994. 'The disappearance of Aristotle's biology: a Hellenistic mystery', in *The Sciences in Greco-Roman Society*, ed. T. D. Barnes (*Apeiron*

27.4, special issue), South Edmonton, Alberta: 7–24. Reprinted in Lennox 2001, ch. 5.

    2001. *Aristotle's Philosophy of Biology: Studies in the Origins of Life Science.* New York.

Lindberg, D. C. 1976. *Theories of Vision from Al-Kindi to Kepler.* Chicago.

Lloyd, G. E. R. 1973. *Greek Science after Aristotle.* London.

Long, A. A. 1995. 'Cicero's Plato and Aristotle', in *Cicero the Philosopher*, ed. J. G. F. Powell, Oxford: 37–61.

Long, A. A. and Sedley, D. N. 1987. *The Hellenistic Philosophers.* Cambridge.

Louis, P. (ed.) 1991. *Aristote: Problèmes*, t.I, sections I à X. Paris.

Lynch, J. P. 1972. *Aristotle's School.* Berkeley.

Marcus, R. (tr.) 1953. *Philo, of Alexandria: Supplement.* Questions and Answers on *Genesis.* London and Cambridge, MA (Loeb Classical Library).

Mansfeld, J. 1979. 'Providence and the destruction of the universe in early Stoic thought', in *Studies in Hellenistic Religions*, ed. M. J. Vermaseren, Leiden: 129–88.

    1988. '*Diaphonia* in the argument of Alexander *De fato* chs.1–2', *Phronesis* 33: 181–207.

    1990. 'Doxography and dialectic. The Sitz im Leben of the "Placita"', *ANRW* II.36.4: 3056–3229.

Mansfeld, J. and Runia, D. T. 1996–. *Aëtiana.* Leiden: Brill.

Meiser, K. 1880. *Anicii Manlii Severini Boeti commentarium in librum Aristotelis Peri Hermēneias.* Leipzig.

Mejer, J. 1992. 'Diogenes Laertius and the transmission of Greek philosophy', *ANRW* II.36.5: 3556–3602.

Menn, S. 1995. 'The editors of the *Metaphysics*', *Phronesis* 40: 202–8.

    1998. *Descartes and Augustine.* Cambridge.

    2003. 'The *Discourse on the Method* and the tradition of intellectual autobiography', in *Hellenistic and Early Modern Philosophy*, ed. J. Miller and B. Inwood, Cambridge: 141–91.

Mercken, H. P. F. 1990. 'The Greek commentators on Aristotle's *Ethics*', in Sorabji (ed.): 407–43.

Merlan, P. 1970. 'Greek philosophy from Plato to Plotinus', in *The Cambridge History of Later Greek and Early Medieval Philosophy*, ed. A. H. Armstrong, Cambridge: 14–132.

Mirhady, D. C. (ed.) 2001. 'Dicaearchus of Messana: the sources, text and translation', in Fortenbaugh and Schütrumpf (eds.): 1–142.

Moraux, P. 1942. *Alexandre d'Aphrodise: exégète de la noétique d'Aristote.* Liège and Paris.

    1951. *Les listes anciennes des ouvrages d'Aristote.* Louvain.

    1963. 'Quinta essentia', in *RE* 24.1: 1171–1263.

    1967. 'Aristoteles, der Lehrer Alexanders von Aphrodisias', *AGPh* 49: 169–82.

    1973. *Der Aristotelismus bei den Griechen von Andronikos bis Alexander von Aphrodisias*, vol. I: *Die Renaissance des Aristotelismus im I. Jh. v. Chr.* Berlin.

1984. *Der Aristotelismus bei den Griechen von Andronikos bis Alexander von Aphrodisias*, vol. II: *Der Aristotelismus im I. und II. Jh. n. Chr.* Berlin.

1985. 'Ein neues Zeugnis über Aristoteles, den Lehrer Alexanders von Aphrodisias', *Archiv für Geschichte der Philosophie* 67: 266–9.

1986. 'Diogène Laërce et le Peripatos', *Elenchos* 7: 247–94.

2001 (ed. posth. J. Wiesner). *Der Aristotelismus bei den Griechen von Andronikos bis Alexander von Aphrodisias*, vol. III: *Alexander von Aphrodisias*. Berlin.

Movia, G. 1968. *Anima e intelletto*. Padua.

Mueller, I. 1995. 'Hippolytus, Aristotle, Basilides', in *Aristotle in Late Antiquity*, ed. L. P. Schrenk, Washington: 143–57.

(tr.) 2005. *Simplicius: On Aristotle* On the Heavens *2.10–14*. London.

Mueller, I. with Gould, J. (trs.) 1999. *Alexander of Aphrodisias: On Aristotle* Prior Analytics *1.8–13*. London.

Müller, I. 1891. *Galeni scripta minora*, vol. II. Leipzig.

Natali, C. 1997. 'Causa motrice e causa finale nel libro Lambda della Metafisica di Aristotele', *Méthexis* 10: 105–23.

2007. 'La causa dell'azione umana secondo Alessandro d'Afrodisia, *Mantissa*, 23 e *De fato*, 15', *ΦΙΛΟΣΟΦΙΑ* (Athens) 37: 71–91.

Norman, R. 1969. 'Aristotle's philosopher-god', *Phronesis* 14: 67–74. Reprinted in *Articles on Aristotle*, ed. J. Barnes, M. Schofield and R. Sorabji, London, 1979: vol. IV 93–102.

Nutton, V. (ed.) 1979. *Galen: Problems and Prospects*. Cambridge.

(in press) 'Greek medical astrology and the boundaries of medicine', in *Medicine and Astrology: East and West*, ed. C. Burnett.

Ophuijsen, J. M. van 1994. 'Where have the Topics gone?', in *Peripatetic Rhetoric after Aristotle*, ed. W. W. Fortenbaugh and D. C. Mirhady (*RUSCH* 6). New Brunswick, NJ: 131–73.

Opsomer, J. and Sharples, R. W. 2000. 'Alexander of Aphrodisias, *De intellectu* 110.4: "I heard this from Aristotle." A modest proposal', *CQ* 50: 252–6.

Pahta, P. 1998. *Medieval Embryology in the Vernacular: the Case of* De Spermate. Helsinki.

Philippson, R. 1932. 'Das "Erste Naturgemäße"', *Philologus* 87: 447–66.

Plezia, M. 1985. 'De Ptolemaei vita Aristotelis', in *Aristoteles: Werk und Wirkung, Paul Moraux gewidmet*, ed. J. Wiesner, Berlin: vol. I 1–11.

Pohlenz, M. 1906. 'Das dritte und vierte Buch der Tusculanen', *Hermes* 41: 321–55.

1940. *Grundfragen der Stoischen Philosophie*. Göttingen.

1948–9. *Die Stoa*. Göttingen.

Polito, R. 1999. 'On the life of Asclepiades of Bithynia', *JHS* 119: 48–66.

Preus, A. 1968. '*On Dreams* 2 459b24–460a33 and Aristotle's *opsis*,' *Phronesis* 13: 175–82.

Radt, S. (ed.) 2002–. *Strabons Geographika*. Göttingen.

Rashed, M. 1997. 'A "new" text of Alexander on the soul's motion', in *Aristotle and After*, ed. R. Sorabji (*BICS* supplement 68). London: 181–95.

2007. *Essentialisme: Alexandre d'Aphrodise entre logique, physique et cosmologie*. Berlin.

Rawson, E. 1982. 'The life and death of Asclepiades of Bithynia', *CQ* 32: 358–70.

Reinhardt, T. (ed.) 2003. *Cicero's* Topica. Oxford.

2007. 'Andronicus of Rhodes and Boethus of Sidon on Aristotle's *Categories*', in Sorabji and Sharples (eds.): 513–29.

Rescher, N. 1966. *Galen and the Syllogism*. Pittsburgh.

1967. *Temporal Modalities in Arabic Logic*. Dordrecht.

Rescigno, A. (ed.) 2004. *Alessandro di Afrodisia: Commentario al* De caelo *di Aristotele. Frammenti del primo libro*. Amsterdam.

Rose, V. 1886. *Aristotelis Fragmenta*. Leipzig.

Rosetti, L. 1980. 'Ricerche sui "Dialoghi Socratici" di Fedone e di Euclide', *Hermes* 108: 183–99.

Ross, W. D. (ed.) 1924. *Aristotle*: Metaphysics. Oxford.

(ed.) 1949. *Aristotle's* Prior and Posterior Analytics. Oxford.

(ed.) 1961. *Aristotle:* De Anima. Oxford.

Runia, D. T. 1981. 'Philo's *De aeternitate mundi*: the problem of its interpretation', *VChr* 35: 105–51. Reprinted in D. T. Runia, *Exegesis and Philosophy: Studies on Philo of Alexandria*, Aldershot, 1990: ch. 8.

1986. *Philo of Alexandria and the* Timaeus *of Plato*. Leiden.

2002. 'The beginnings of the end: Philo of Alexandria and Hellenistic theology', in Frede and Laks (eds.): 281–316.

2003. 'Plato's *Timaeus*, first principle(s), and creation', in *Plato's* Timaeus *as Cultural Icon*, ed. G. J. Reydams-Schils, Notre Dame, IN: 133–51.

Salis, R. 2004. 'I movimenti dei corpi celesti nel commento dello pseudo-Alessandro alla "Metafisica" di Aristotele', *Atti e memorie dell'Accademia Galileiana*, III: *Classe di Scienze Morali*, Padua: 137–68.

2005. *Il commento di pseudo-Alessandro al libro* Λ *della* Metafisica *di Aristotele*. Soveria Mannelli.

Salles, R. 2005. *The Stoics on Determinism and Compatibilism*. Aldershot.

Schiaparelli, G. 1926. 'Le sfere omocentriche di Eudosso, di Callippo e di Aristotele', in Schiaparelli, G., *Scritti sulla storia della astronomica antica*, par I, vol. II, Bologna. Originally published in *Memorie del Reale Istituto Lombardo* (Classe di scienze matematiche e naturali 13), 1877.

Schofield, M. 1999. 'Academic epistemology', in K. Algra *et al.* (eds.): 323–51.

Schroeder, F. M. 1987. 'Ammonius Saccas', *ANRW* II.36.1: 493–526.

1997. 'The provenance of the *De Intellectu* attributed to Alexander of Aphrodisias', *Documenti e studi sulla tradizione filosofica medievale* 8: 105–20.

Schroeder, F. M. and Todd, R. B. (eds.) 1990. *Two Aristotelian Greek Commentators on the Intellect*. Toronto.

2008. 'The *De intellectu* revisited', *LThPh* 64: 663–80.

Sedley, D. N. 1999. 'Aspasius on akrasia', in Alberti and Sharples (eds.): 162–75.

2002. 'The origins of Stoic god', in Frede and Laks (eds.): 41–83.

(forthcoming) 'Cicero and the Timaeus', in *Plato, Aristotle and Pythagoras in the First Century BC*, conference papers 13–16 July 2009, Cambridge.

Sharples, R. W. 1980. 'Alexander of Aphrodisias' second treatment of fate? *De anima libri mantissa*, pp. 179–186 Bruns', *BICS* 27: 76–94.

1982. 'Alexander of Aphrodisias, *On Time*', *Phronesis* 27: 58–81.

(ed.) 1983a. *Alexander of Aphrodisias* On Fate. London.

1983b. 'The Peripatetic classification of goods', in Fortenbaugh (ed.): 139–59.

1990. *Alexander of Aphrodisias: Ethical Problems*. London.

(ed.) 1991. *Cicero:* On Fate *and Boethius:* The Consolation of Philosophy *IV.5–7, V*. Warminster.

(tr.) 1992. *Alexander of Aphrodisias* Quaestiones *1.1–2.15*. London.

(tr.) 1994. *Alexander of Aphrodisias* Quaestiones *2.16–3.15*. London.

1995. *Theophrastus of Eresus: Sources for his Life, Writings, Thought and Influence, Commentary*, vol. v: *Sources on Biology*. Leiden.

1996. 'Ariston (4)', in *Der neue Pauly, Enzyklopädie der Antike*, ed. H. Cancik and H. Schneider, Stuttgart: vol. i, col. 1117.

1998. *Theophrastus of Eresus: Sources for his Life, Writings, Thought and Influence, Commentary*, vol. iii.1: *Sources on Physics*. Leiden.

1999. '*Aspasius on Eudaimonia*', in Alberti and Sharples (eds.): 85–95.

2000. 'The sufficiency of virtue for happiness: not so easily overturned?', *PCPhS* 46: 121–39.

2001a. 'Dicaearchus on the soul and on divination', in Fortenbaugh and Schütrumpf (eds.): 143–73.

2001b. 'Schriften und Problemkomplexe zur Ethik', in Moraux (ed. Wiesner): 513–650.

2002a. 'Alexander of Aphrodisias and the end of Aristotelian theology', in *Metaphysik und Religion: zur Signatur des spätantiken Denkens*, ed. T. Kobusch and M. Erler, Munich: 1–21.

2002b. 'Aristotelian theology after Aristotle', in Frede and Laks (eds.): 1–40.

2002c. 'Eudemus' *Physics*: change, place and time', in *Eudemus of Rhodes*, ed. I. Bodnár and W. W. Fortenbaugh (*RUSCH* 11). New Brunswick, NJ: 107–26.

(ed.) 2003a. 'Theophrastus, *On Dizziness*', in *Theophrastus of Eresus On Sweat, On Dizziness and On Fatigue*, ed. W. W. Fortenbaugh, R. W. Sharples and M. Sollenberger, Leiden: 169–241.

2003b. 'Threefold providence: the history and background of a doctrine', in *Ancient Approaches to Plato's* Timaeus, ed. R. W. Sharples and A. Sheppard (*BICS* supplement 78). London: 107–27.

(tr.) 2004. *Alexander of Aphrodisias: Supplement to* On the Soul. London.

2005. 'Implications of the new Alexander of Aphrodisias inscription', *BICS* 48: 47–56.

2006. 'Natural philosophy in the Peripatos after Strato', in *Aristo of Ceos*, ed. W. W. Fortenbaugh and S. A. White (*RUSCH* 13), New Brunswick, NJ: 307–27.

2007a. 'Aristotle's exoteric and esoteric works: summaries and commentaries', in Sorabji and Sharples (eds.): 505–12.

2007b. 'Peripatetics on fate and providence', in Sorabji and Sharples (eds.): 595–605.

2007c. 'Peripatetics on happiness', in Sorabji and Sharples (eds.): 627–37.

2007d. 'Peripatetics on soul and intellect', in Sorabji and Sharples (eds.): 607–20.

2007e. 'The Stoic background to the Middle Platonist discussion of fate', in *Platonic Stoicism – Stoic Platonism*, ed. M. Bonazzi and C. Helmig, Leuven: 169–88.

(ed.) 2008a. *Alexander Aphrodisiensis, De anima libri mantissa*. Berlin.

2008b. 'Habent sua fata libelli: Aristotle's *Categories* in the first century BC', *AAntHung* 48: 273–87.

2008c. 'L'accident du déterminisme: Alexandre d'Aphrodise dans son contexte historique', *Les Études philosophiques* 86: 285–303.

2008d. 'Philo and post-Aristotelian Peripatetics', in *Philo and the post-Aristotelian Philosophical Schools*, ed. F. Alesse, Leiden: 55–73.

(in press) 'Strato of Lampsacus: the text, sources and translation', in *Strato of Lampsacus, Text, Translation and Discussion*, ed. M. L. Desclos and W. W. Fortenbaugh (*RUSCH* 16), New Brunswick, NJ.

Sharples, R. W. and Eijk, P. J. van der (trs.) 2008. *Nemesius, On the Nature of Man*. Liverpool.

Shiel, J. 1957. 'Boethus and Andronicus of Rhodos', *VChr* 11: 179–85.

Simon, G. 1988. *Le regard, l'être et l'apparence dans l'optique de l'antiquité*. Paris.

Smith, A. 2007. 'Porphyry: scope for a reassessment', in Karamanolis and Sheppard (eds.): 7–16.

Sollenberger, M. G. 1992. 'The Lives of the Peripatetics: an analysis of the contents and structure of Diogenes Laertius' *Vitae philosophorum* book 5', *ANRW* 11.36.6: 3793–3879.

Solmsen, F. 1961. 'Greek philosophy and the discovery of the nerves', *MH* 18: 169–97. Reprinted in F. Solmsen, *Kleine Schriften*, vol. 1, Hildesheim, 1968: 536–82.

Sorabji, R. 1983. *Time, Creation and the Continuum*. London.

1988. *Matter, Space and Motion*. London.

(ed.) 1990. *Aristotle Transformed: the Ancient Commentators and their Influence*. London.

1999. 'Aspasius on emotion', in Alberti and Sharples (eds.): 96–106.

2004. *The Philosophy of the Commentators, 200–600 AD*. London. (References to this work are given by volume number and either passage number, in the form (e.g.) "1(a)(1)", or page number(s).)

2007a. 'Modifications to Aristotle's physics of the heavens by Peripatetics and others, 100 BC to 200 AD', in Sorabji and Sharples (eds.): 575–94.

2007b. 'Peripatetics on emotion after 100 BC', in Sorabji and Sharples (eds.): 621–6.

2007c. 'Time, place and extracosmic space: Peripatetics in the first century BC and a Stoic opponent', in Sorabji and Sharples (eds.): 563–74.

Sorabji, R. and Sharples, R. W. (eds.) 2007. *Greek and Roman Philosophy 100 BC – 200 AD* (*BICS* supplement 94). London.

Striker, G. 1996. *Essays on Hellenistic Epistemology and Ethics*. Cambridge.

Szlezák, T. A. 1972. *Pseudo-Archytas* Über die Kategorien. Berlin.

Tarán, L. 1981. 'Aristotelianism in the first century BC' (review article on Moraux 1973), *Gnomon* 53: 721–50. Reprinted in L.Tarán, *Collected Papers (1962–1999)*, Leiden, 2001: 479–524.

Théry, G. 1926. *Autour du décret de 1210,* vol. II: *Alexandre d'Aphrodise* (Bibliothèque Thomiste 7). Paris.

Thesleff, H. 1961. *An Introduction to the Pythagorean Writings of the Hellenistic Period.* Åbo.

Thillet, P. (ed.) 1984. *Alexandre d'Aphrodise: Traité du Destin.* Paris.

Todd, R. B. 1976a. *Alexander of Aphrodisias on Stoic Physics.* Leiden.

   1976b. 'The four causes: Aristotle's exposition and the ancients', *JHI* 37: 319–22.

   1995. 'Peripatetic epistemology before Alexander of Aphrodisias: the case of Alexander of Damascus', *Eranos* 93: 122–8.

   (tr.) 1996. *Themistius, On Aristotle* On the Soul. London.

Trapp, M. 2007. *Philosophy in the Roman Empire.* Aldershot.

Usener, H. (ed.) 1859. *Alexandri Aphrodisiensis quae feruntur Problematorum libri 3 et 4.* Berlin.

Verbeke, G. (ed.) 1966. *Jean Philopon:* Commentaire sur le 'de Anima' d'Aristote. *Traduction de Guillaume de Moerbeke.* Louvain and Paris.

Verdenius, W. J. 1960. 'Traditional and personal elements in Aristotle's religion', *Phronesis* 5: 56–70.

Wachsmuth, C. (ed.) 1884. *Ioannis Stobaei Anthologii libri duo priores.* Berlin.

Waszink, J. H. (ed.) 1975. *Plato Latinus:* Timaeus *a Calcidio translatus commentarioque instructus.* London and Leiden.

Waitz, T. 1844–6. *Aristotelis* Organon *graece.* Leipzig.

Wedin, M. V. 1988. *Mind and Imagination in Aristotle.* New Haven, CT.

Wehrli, F. (ed.) 1967. *Die Schule des Aristoteles,* vol. II: *Aristoxenos,* 2nd edn. Basel.

   (ed.) 1969a. *Die Schule des Aristoteles,* vol. VIII: *Eudemos von Rhodos,* 2nd edn. Basel.

   (ed.) 1969b. *Die Schule des Aristoteles,* vol. X: *Hieronymos von Rhodos: Kritolaos und seine Schüler,* 2nd edn. Basel.

   (ed.) 1969c. *Die Schule des Aristoteles,* vol. V: *Straton von Lampsakos,* 2nd edn. Basel.

Westerink, L. G. (ed.) 1977. *The Greek Commentaries on Plato's Phaedo,* vol. II. Amsterdam.

White, S. A. 1990. 'Is Aristotelian happiness a good life or the best life?', *OSAPh* 8: 103–43.

   2002. 'Happiness in the Hellenistic Lyceum', *Apeiron* suppl. vol. 35: 69–93.

   2004. 'Lyco and Hieronymus on the good life', in *Lyco of Troas and Hieronymus of Rhodes,* ed. W. W. Fortenbaugh and S. A. White (*RUSCH* 12). New Brunswick, NJ: 389–409.

Wilke, C. (ed.) 1914. *Philodemi* De ira *liber.* Leipzig.

Winden, J. C. M. van (ed.) 1971. *An Early Christian Philosopher: Justin Martyr's* Dialogue with Trypho, *Chapters One to Nine.* Leiden.

Wright, L. 1973. 'The astronomy of Eudoxus: geometry or physics?', *Studies in the History and Philosophy of Science* 4: 165–72.

Wurm, K. 1973. *Substanz und Qualität: ein Beitrag zur Interpretation der Plotinischen Traktate VI.1–3*. Berlin.

Zhmud, L. 1998. 'Plato as "architect of science"', *Phronesis* 43: 211–44.

Index of sources

Where editions are cited, the first given is that from which the page and line references have been used in citing the works in question, even where use has been made of more recent editions or annotated translations (indicated by cross-references to the Bibliography) which incorporate these references; only those of the latter actually cited in this sourcebook are mentioned here – this is not a complete listing of all editions and translations of the works in question.

ADRASTUS OF APHRODISIAS (commentator on Aristotle and on Plato, first half of second century AD, see commentary on 1UV), reported by Theon of Smyrna (q.v.), *Exposition of Mathematics Useful for Reading Plato*
> 149.4–150.4 **22I**
> 181.12–182.25 **21M**
> 201.20–202.2 **21N**

AËTIUS (*c.* AD 100 (ed. H. Diels, *Dox.*); see also Stobaeus, *Selections* and the Preface, p. xvi)
> 1, prologue **5E**
> 1.7.21 **22B**
> 1.7.32 **22E**
> 1.11.4 **12B**
> 1.22.6 **19A**
> 1.29.2 **23A**
> 2.3.4 **22H**
> 4.2.6 **24G**
> 4.3.10 **24K**
> 4.8.4 **26H**
> 4.8.14 **26I**
> 4.9.11–12 **14J**
> 5.1.4 **27G**
> 5.5.2 **25D**
> 5.4.2 **25E**

ALEXANDER OF APHRODISIAS (commentator on Aristotle, *fl. c.* AD 200)
On Aristotle's Metaphysics (ed. M. Hayduck, *CAG* 1, 1891)
> 166.18–167.3 **1Aa**
On Aristotle's Meteorology (ed. M. Hayduck, *CAG* 3.2, 1899)
> 141.3–142.20 **26G**
> 142.34–143.14 **26D**
> 155.24–30 **26F**
On Aristotle's Prior Analytics (ed. M. Wallies, *CAG* 2.1, 1883)
> 125.3–31 **13I**
> 140.14–141.6 **13H**

On Aristotle's Topics (ed. M. Wallies, *CAG* 2.2, 1891)
  27.8–18 **4H**
On Fate (ed. I. Bruns, *SA* 2.2, 1892)
  1.164.3–15 **1Ab** (Sharples 1983a)
  6.168.18–171.17 **23S**
  11.178.15–28 **23H**
  25.195.8–18 **23T**
  25.196.7–12 **23U**
On Mixture (ed. I. Bruns, *SA* 2.2, 1892)
  11.226.24–30 **22G** (Todd 1976a)
On Providence (ed. H.-J. Ruland, *Die arabischen Fassungen zweier Schriften des Alexander von Aphrodisias: Über die Vorsehung und über das liberum arbitrium*, diss. Saarbrücken, 1976)
  87.5–89.12 **22U** (this treatise for the most part survives only in Arabic, Fazzo and Zonta 1998; my translation is based on the German of Ruland and the Italian of Fazzo and Zonta. For a translation of **22U** directly from Arabic into English by F. W. Zimmermann, see Sorabji 2004, vol. 11 4(a)(4))
On the Soul (ed. I. Bruns, *SA* 2.1, 1887)
  16.10–12 **24H** (Accattino and Donini 1996)
  22.7–12 **24Ab**
  24.21–3 **24Ac**
  42.11–19 **26B**
Quaestiones (ed. I. Bruns, *SA* 2.2 1892)
  1.25.40.30–41.19 **22T** (Sharples 1992)
Supplement to On the Soul (*Mantissa*) (ed. I. Bruns, *SA* 2.1, 1887) (= *On Intellect*)
  2.106.19–26 **27B** (Sharples 2004, 2008a)
  2.110.4–25 **27K**
  2.112.5–113.6 **27I**
  2.113.6–15, 16–17 **22F**
  2.113.18–24 **27J**
  5.120.9–17 **12J**
  5.120.33–121.7 **12K**
  15.145.25–30 **26C**
  17.151.3–13 **17C**
  17.151.18–27 **17D**
  17.151.30–152.10 **17E**
  17.152.27–153.8 **17F**
  17.153.20–7 **17F**
  25.185.8–186.31 **23V**
reported by Philoponus (q.v.), *On Aristotle's* On the Soul 3
  15.65–9 (Verbeke) **27A**
reported by Simplicius, *On Aristotle's* On the Heaven (q.v.)
  285.32–286.6 **21I**
  430.27–36 **1Y**

AMMONIUS (Neoplatonist commentator on Aristotle, AD 435/445–517/526)
On Aristotle's Categories (ed. A. Busse, *CAG* 4.4, 1895)
  13.20–5 **8C**
On Aristotle's On Interpretation (ed. A. Busse, *CAG* 4.5, 1897)
  5.24–6.6 **11A**
On Aristotle's Prior Analytics (ed. A. Busse, *CAG* 4.6, 1899)
  31.11–15 **13E**

SOPHRONIOS (*c.* AD 560–638)
Encomium of Saints Cyrus and John
   PG LXXXVII/3.3622D **1Q**

SOSIGENES (Peripatetic philosopher, second half of second century AD)
reported by Dexippus, *On Aristotle's* Categories (q.v.)
   6.27–9.14 **8G**
reported by Simplicius, *On Aristotle's* On the Heaven (q.v.)
   504.17–506.3 **21K**

(JOHN) STOBAEUS (anthologist, early fifth century AD; see also Aëtius, and the Preface, pp. x, xvi)
Selections (ed. Wachsmuth 1884 and Hense 1894)
   1.1.29b, 35.5–6 **22B**
   1.8.40b, 103.7–8 **19A**
   1.13.1b, 138.9–12 **12B**
   1.49.1b, 320.5–8 **24K**
   1.50.3, 473.1–3 **26H**
   1.50.16, 474.22–3 **26I**
   1.50.28–9, 476.23–7 **14J**
   2.7.1, 38.18–24 **16U**
   2.7.3b, 46.10–17 **18I**
   2.7.3d, 48.6–11 **18V**
   2.7.13, 116.19–152.5 **15A**
   3.1.106, 56.13–57.6 **16I**
   4.39.28, 918.15–919.6 **15B**

STRABO (*c.* 64 BC – after AD 21)
Geography (ed. Radt 2002–. References of the form '608.28-609.22' are to Casaubon's pages
      and Radt's line-numbering, which is based on these; the actual pages in Radt's edition are
      given in brackets)
   13.1.54, 608.28–609.22 (vol. III 602–4) **2A**
   14.2.19, 658.1–4 (vol. IV 70) **1G**
   14.5.4, 670.25–9 (vol. IV 102–4) **1I**
   16.2.24, 757.27–9 (vol. IV 330) **1N**
   17.1.5, 790.22–8 (vol. IV 420) **1H**

SUDA (encyclopaedia, end of tenth century AD) (ed. A. Adler, *Suidae Lexicon*, Leipzig, 1928–38) s.v.
      Alexander of Aegae
   (A 1128) **1S**

SYRIANUS (Neoplatonist commentator on Aristotle and rhetorician, first half of fifth century AD)
On Aristotle's Metaphysics (ed. W. Kroll, *CAG* 6.1, 1902)
   106.5–7 **12R**

TERTULLIAN (Christian apologist, *c.* AD 160 – *c.* AD 240)
On the Soul (ed. J. H. Waszink, Amsterdam, 1947)
   5.2 **24B**

THEMISTIUS (philosopher and rhetorician, *c.* AD 317 – *c.* AD 388)
On Aristotle's On the Soul (ed. R. Heinze, *CAG* 5.3, 1899)
   32.22–31 **24R** (Todd 1996)
On Aristotle's Physics (ed. H. Schenkl, *CAG* 5.2, 1900)
   26.20–4 **12O**
   160.22–8 **19E**
   163.1–7 **19F**

Index of passages cited

Index of personal names (ancient)

General index

Academy, Academics 36, 38–9, 106, 179
  Old Academy 106, 150, 159, 209
action, appropriate (*kathēkon*) 14, 128; *see also*
    function, proper
  correct (*katorthōma*) 128
  voluntary and involuntary 212–13
actuality 32–4, 74, 81, 121, 151–2, 172, 237, 266,
    269, 271
  see also potentiality
affinity (*oikeiotēs*) 113, 222
aither *see* elements
anger 137–8, 144
Anscombe, Elizabeth 88
appetition 151–2
appropriation (*oikeiōsis*) 112, 140, 150–4,
avoidance *see* choice

Barnes, Jonathan 28–30, 99, 106
body 32
  moved by soul 184, 189, 244–5
  organikon 237, 246
  simple 79, 181, 183; *see also* elements
  see also soul

categories 34, 47–69 *passim*, 79
causes 52, 76, 202, 211, 216, 219, 229
  no infinite number of 18
  use of statue example to illustrate 84–5
  see also principles
chance 209, 211, 222
choice 212–15, 230
  and avoidance 113–19, 127
  objects of 121–2, 164–5
colour 257–8
commentaries 3, 44
contingency 231
criterion of truth 31, 101–7 *passim*
Cynics 224

deliberation 212–15, 230
determinism 230, 232

differentia 78
divination 221–3, 267–8, 272–3
  see also prophecy

elements 32, 176, 189, 235–6
  fifth element 3, 18, 32, 180–1, 189–91, 197–8,
    207, 235–6, 245
  movements and natural place of 182–3,
    189–91, 200
  see also body, simple
emotions 134–49 *passim*
end 12, 32, 107, 119–21, 122, 151–3, 157–8, 162
  see also goal of life
entelekheia 235, 237, 238, 244, 245,
    246–7
  see also actuality
Epicureans 101, 105, 107, 207,
    208, 224
evil 160–1, 163, 165
  see also good
excellence 16, 42, 114, 118
  see also virtue

fate 177, 204, 209, 216, 223
  and nature 217–9, 221, 231, 233
  co-fated events 227
  exceptions admitted by 231–2
  no position by Aristotle on 229, 231
female anatomy 256
figures, syllogistic *see* syllogism
form 18
  and matter 74–89 *passim*, 239, 266; discrepancy
    between *Categories* and *Metaphysics* 86; in
    reproduction 251, 253–6
  distinction from Platonic Forms 83–4
  immanent, enmattered 83
  see also soul
Forms (Platonic) 82, 88–9, 105
  separation of 83
friendship 126–7
function, proper 112–13

307